MARGIN

Jar

Restoring
Emotional,
Physical,
Financial,
and Time
Reserves to
Overloaded
Lives

MARGIN

The

OVERLOAD
SYNDROME

Learning to Live Within Your Limits

RICHARD A.
SWENSON, M.D.

NAVPRESS

Bringing Truth to Life
P.O. Box 35001, Colorado Springs, Colorado 80935

The Navigators is an international Christian organization. Our mission is to reach, disciple, and equip people to know Christ and to make Him known through successive generations. We envision multitudes of diverse people in the United States and every other nation who have a passionate love for Christ, live a lifestyle of sharing Christ's love, and multiply spiritual laborers among those without Christ.

NavPress is the publishing ministry of The Navigators. NavPress publications help believers learn biblical truth and apply what they learn to their lives and ministries. Our mission is to stimulate spiritual formation among our readers.

© 2002 by Richard A. Swenson
All rights reserved. No part of this publication may be reproduced in any form without written permission from NavPress, P.O. Box 35001, Colorado Springs, CO 80935.
www.navpress.com
ISBN 1-57683-329-1

Some of the anecdotal illustrations in this book are true to life and are included with the permission of the persons involved. All other illustrations are composites of real situations, and any resemblance to people living or dead is coincidental.

Margin: Unless otherwise identified, all Scripture quotations in this publication are taken from the *HOLY BIBLE: NEW INTERNATIONAL VERSION*® (NIV®). Copyright © 1973, 1978, 1984 by International Bible Society. Used by permission of Zondervan Publishing House. All rights reserved. Other versions include: the *New American Standard Bible* (NASB), © The Lockman Foundation 1960, 1962, 1963, 1968, 1971, 1972, 1973, 1975, 1977; *The New Testament in Modern English* (PH), J. B. Phillips Translator, © J. B. Phillips 1958, 1960, 1972, used by permission of Macmillan Publishing Company; and the *New King James Version* (NKJV). Copyright © 1982 by Thomas Nelson, Inc. Used by permission. All rights reserved.

The Overload Syndrome: Unless otherwise identified, all Scripture quotations in this publication are taken from the *HOLY BIBLE: NEW INTERNATIONAL VERSION*® (NIV®). Copyright © 1973, 1978, 1984 by International Bible Society. Used by permission of Zondervan Publishing House. All rights reserved. Other versions include: the *New American Standard Bible* (NASB), © The Lockman Foundation 1960, 1962, 1963, 1968, 1971, 1972, 1973, 1975, 1977; and the *King James Version* (KJV).

Printed in the United States of America

1 2 3 4 5 6 7 8 9 10 / 05 04 03 02

FOR A FREE CATALOG OF
NAVPRESS BOOKS & BIBLE STUDIES,
CALL 1-800-366-7788 (USA)
OR 1-416-499-4615 (CANADA)

Contents

For Linda

✦

It's hard to imagine this book—or life—
without your presence and love.

List of Figures and Graphs

Acknowledgments

This book was ten years in the making, which means that a number of deserving people have waited a long time for their official acknowledgment.

Bill Tomfohr, perhaps more than any other, kept the work alive in the early years. For preliminary ideas about the theme of margin, credit goes to Ralph Suechting. I wish to thank those who read portions of the book during the formative process for their comments and criticisms: Bill Thedinga, Walter Schultz, Dan Johnson, Hector Cruz, Mike Simpson, and Jim Eggert.

Many contributed in various other ways, including practical and sensitive expressions of encouragement: Everett and Genevieve Wilson, Ruth Swenson, Caroline Miller, Jerry and Marcie Borgie, Craig and Linda Wilson, Aggie Wagner, Donna Knipfer, Chuck and Becky Folkestad, Dave and Judy Hatch, Hazel Bent, Betty Cruz, Gail Thedinga, Mary Schultz, and Michael Bailey. In addition, I remain grateful to family and friends around the world who have demonstrated their sustained and prayerful interest in this project.

I owe a great debt of gratitude to Don Simpson, whose counsel was always as accurate as it was gracious. As editor, Steve Webb was both an enthusiastic supporter of the author and a faithful advocate for the reader. Knollwood Lodge was initially timely and later essential for allowing special arrangements to write in that beautiful, secluded winter retreat.

My wife, Linda, has been encourager and critic, copy editor and typist, reader and researcher—in short, collaborator throughout the entire decade. This work would have been abandoned long ago without her help. Our two sons, Adam and Matt, have been more than patient, but are nevertheless pleased at the prospect of having their parents returned to them.

My margin has been devoted to writing for a very long time. It will be an uncommon joy to devote it once again to my family.

Marginless is red ink; margin is black ink.
Marginless is hurry; margin is calm.
Marginless is anxiety; margin is security.
Marginless is culture; margin is counterculture.
Marginless is reality; margin is remedy.
Marginless is the disease of the 1990s.
Margin is its cure.

PIECES OF BROKEN HUMANITY

It was my lunch hour on a beautiful autumn day, but I did not mind. A bloody towel clutched over a bloody face revealed the need.

At seventy-six, John was slim, fit, and active. Following retirement and a heart attack, he determined to take care of himself and have fun at the same time. It was Wisconsin in the summer and Florida in the winter, but mostly it was golf every day.

As his wife was otherwise occupied, John challenged Glen to eighteen holes. Approaching the first hole, John drove his ball down the middle of the fairway and then moved to the side. Glen prepared his ball, lifted the club, and swung vigorously. The ball, however, came off the toe of the club, angling hard to the right. At a speed exceeding one hundred miles per hour, it struck John in the left eye. Blood instantly came gushing out as his eyeball dropped into his hand.

By the time they arrived at the clinic, Glen was still as white as a sheet. The injured John, however, was obviously enjoying himself—even though covered with blood.

"I guess Glen never knew I had an artificial eye," he twinkled. "I popped it out to make sure it wasn't broken. I didn't really mean to scare him like that."

Rarely a day goes by that I don't pick up some pieces of broken humanity and attempt to put them back together again. In John's case, the wounds turned out to be humorous, and his lacerated eyebrow was easily sutured. Unfortunately, not all my patients have stories that are humorous. And not all "broken pieces" are so easily repaired.

Some people come in for broken legs; others, broken hearts. Some have irritable colons; others, irritable spouses. Some have bleeding ulcers; others, bleeding emotions. And compounding these wounds, many patients show signs of a new disease: marginless living.

How often do I see the effects of marginless living? About every

ONE

Marginless Living

T he conditions of modern-day living devour margin. If you are homeless, we direct you to a shelter. If you are penniless, we offer you food stamps. If you are breathless, we connect the oxygen. But if you are marginless, we give you yet one more thing to do.

Marginless is being thirty minutes late to the doctor's office because you were twenty minutes late getting out of the hairdresser's because you were ten minutes late dropping the children off at school because the car ran out of gas two blocks from the gas station—and you forgot your purse.

Margin, on the other hand, is having breath left at the top of the staircase, money left at the end of the month, and sanity left at the end of adolescence.

Marginless is the baby crying and the phone ringing at the same time; margin is Grandma taking the baby for the afternoon.

Marginless is being asked to carry a load five pounds heavier than you can lift; margin is a friend to carry half the burden.

Marginless is not having time to finish the book you're reading on stress; margin is having the time to read it twice.

Marginless is fatigue; margin is energy.

been hard," they say. "People have always been stressed. It is simply part of living. There has always been change to cope with. There have always been economic problems, and people have always battled depression. It is the nature of life to have its ups and downs—so why all the fuss?"

I'm not the one who's making the fuss; I'm only writing about it. I'm only being honest about what I see all around me. I sit in my examining room and listen. Then I report what I hear. Something is wrong. People are tired and frazzled. People are anxious and depressed. People don't have the time to heal anymore. There is a psychic instability in our day that prevents peace from implanting itself very firmly in the human spirit. And despite the skeptics, this instability is not the same old nemesis recast in a modern role. What we have here is a brand-new disease.

To be sure, the pains of the past were often horrible beyond description. To have your wife die in childbirth, your children crippled with polio, your cattle ravaged by tuberculosis, and your crops leveled by locusts is not the common definition of the good life. But those were the pains of the past, and most of them are gone. Unfortunately—and unexpectedly—the pains of progress are now here to take their place. Prominent among them is the disease of marginless living.

THE FOCUSING VALUE OF PAIN

No one likes pain. We all want to get rid of it as soon as possible, in any way possible. But physical pains are usually there for a reason, to tell us something is wrong and needs to be fixed. Emotional, relational, and societal pains, too, are often indicators that all is not well. As such, they serve a valuable purpose. They help us focus.

Modern-day living, however, opposes focusing. Surrounded by frenzy and interruptions, we have no time for anything but vertigo. So our pain, it turns out, is actually an ally of sorts. In the hurt is a help. Pain first gets our attention—as it does so well—and then moves us in the opposite direction of the danger.

If you were my patient, you would come to me already focused on your pain. You would want me to explain it and would hope I could make it go away. My responsibility would be to listen to your symptoms, diagnose your problem, offer a prescription, and encourage you in the direction of health. And because drawing diagrams often helps us to understand, I might write it all on a prescription pad for you to refer to and remember. It would look something like this:

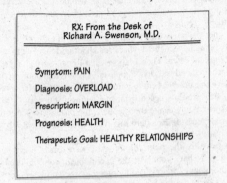

RX: From the Desk of
Richard A. Swenson, M.D.

Symptom: PAIN

Diagnosis: OVERLOAD

Prescription: MARGIN

Prognosis: HEALTH

Therapeutic Goal: HEALTHY RELATIONSHIPS

IS THERE A CURE?

If we focus and work to understand, is this painful disease of margin-less living curable? Is health possible? Of course it is. But the kind of health I speak of will seldom be found in "progress" or "success." For that reason, I'm not sure how many are willing to take the cure. But at least we all deserve a chance to understand the disease.

PART ONE

THE PROBLEM: PAIN

The Pain of Progress

Erick Ostrom was born in Sweden in 1894 and came to the United States in 1912 at the age of eighteen. No one is quite sure why he came, for Grandpa never wanted to talk about it. Not knowing the language and having only a third-grade education, he sometimes slept in theaters while going from job to job. A few years later he married Anna, whose love and gentleness buffered but could not prevent the hardness of life. The Ostroms had six children, losing two of them in infancy—the causes of their deaths unknown. Grandpa would tell of transporting one of the dead infants in a blizzard to the neighboring town, burying her there in the frozen ground.

During the Great Depression, Grandpa developed tuberculosis. He was in and out of the sanitarium for the next eleven years, had one of his lungs removed, and was never again to reach one hundred pounds. The doctors told him he probably contracted the disease from the fumes in the steel mills. To make ends meet, the children began working while Anna cleaned houses and took in washing. After his release, the family tried farming, but the cows got sick and Grandpa got sicker.

Although he lived to the remarkable age of eighty-four, life was always hard for Grandpa. It never did get easy. Neither did he expect that it would, or should.

If my grandfather could have asked for whatever he wanted to make his life easier and more fulfilling during those difficult years, he would have requested health for himself and his family, and that his babies would not die from unnamed diseases. He would have wished for education, a warm home in the winter, and a reliable supply of safe and healthy food. He might have requested a good team of horses, good seed, and fertilizer. Perhaps he would have wished to visit his family in Sweden.

All of these advantages have been granted in America today. Yet the formula for happiness has proven to be more elusive than the simple bestowing of these benefits. Somewhere the equation has broken down. Food plus health plus warmth plus education plus affluence have not quite equaled Utopia. We live with unprecedented wealth and all it brings. We have leisure, entertainment, convenience, and comfort. We have insulated ourselves from the unpredictable ravages of nature. Yet stress, frustration, and oftentimes even despair unexpectedly accompany our unrivaled prosperity.

PROGRESS AND PANDEMONIUM

While visiting our family recently, an eleven-year-old friend from a large city announced, "There's an epidemic going on down there. I think it's pandemonium."

We live in a troubled age. We have more questions than answers, more problems than solutions. Few know where we are headed, but universally acknowledge that we are careening along at breakneck speed.

How can this be? Aren't we advancing, improving, evolving? Aren't technological development and social learning bringing us an ever better world? That progress might be in trouble today is unexpected news, for we always assumed it could do the job. Never did we suspect that pandemonium and progress would one day walk on stage together, or that pain and progress would one day join forces against us.

People everywhere are in anguish, and progress does not seem to care. It is time to reexamine our assumptions.

ONWARD AND UPWARD

Exactly what is progress? Simply stated, progress means proceeding to a higher stage of development. *"The idea of progress holds that mankind has advanced in the past . . . is now advancing, and will continue to advance through the foreseeable future,"* explains historian Robert Nisbet. "From at least the early nineteenth century until a few decades ago, belief in the progress of mankind, with Western civilization in the vanguard, was virtually a universal religion on both sides of the Atlantic."[1] Progress was automatic, the inevitable function of chronology. Thus, saying we had lived from 1950 to 1970 was synonymous with saying we had *progressed* two decades. The flow of progress was assumed to be inherently positive.

Progress is so natural and axiomatic an idea that twentieth-century Westerners can't conceive of life without it. The modern mind has been so reared under its assumptions that devising alternative scenarios seems impossible. If not progress, then what? Regress? Who in their right mind would advocate regress? Even the connotations of these words are laden with bias. Progression is forward; regression is backward. Enlightenment versus darkness. Perfection versus primitivism.

Most of us, no doubt, trust the idea of progress more than we realize. It is the train we all boarded for the ride to the good life. *"We have faith in progress,"* observes philosopher Nicholas Wolterstorff. "Until recently, the general public . . . regarded modernization as a *good* thing, typically giving it the honorific title 'development.' Development was touted as the cure to a multitude of human miseries."[2]

Is there a disease? We will soon have a remedy. Is there poverty? We have enough wealth to go around, and a social program or two will solve the problem of the poor. Is there an energy shortage? We will find new technologies to harness the power of the nucleus and to capture the sun. Is there famine? We will use fertilizers and hybrid seeds to conquer hunger. In our most idolatrous moments, we actually began to assume that the solution to any problem could be confidently entrusted to progress. Thanks to its blessings, we came to perceive the future as a safer place to live.

FAILED FAITH

For a while, it appeared progress was going to lead us to the mountaintop, and we were euphoric in anticipation. One after another, progress paraded before us its spectacular successes, prominent among which were an incredible array of technical achievements that test the limits of imagination. We can now transplant both the heart and lungs and get you out of the hospital in six days. We have robots that work, pop machines that talk, and trains that hover. From atom smashers to earth movers to "smart" bombs, it is an amazing age. "The broad populace has naively come to believe," explains religion professor David Hopper, "that technological novelty is identical with progress."[3]

Then, almost without warning, failures began to take their place on stage alongside the successes—first a few, then more, and now many. When you ignore them, they intensify. When you try to explain them away, they double. As a result, faced with a torrent of disconcerting evidence, many people once loyal to progress are defecting. Formerly uncontested, the tenets of progress are now openly challenged. "Everything now suggests, however," writes Nisbet, "that Western faith in the dogma of progress is waning rapidly in all levels and spheres in this final part of the twentieth century."[4]

Our enthusiasm for both progress and the future has moderated. For some, it has disappeared. "How does it happen that serious people continue to believe in progress," asks historian Christopher Lasch, "in the face of massive evidence that might have been expected to refute the idea of progress once and for all?"[5]

Polls reveal many Americans no longer believe their children will have a better life than they did. We are not sure whether progress is a cause for celebration or a reason to run and hide. Many are not quite sure they want to enter the future linked hand in hand with it. When we discovered an unexpected pain so often accompanying each new development, our hope for the promise of tomorrow understandably waned.

After all, we did not have acid in our lakes or holes in our ozone layer until progress gave them to us. Margin was as abundant as prairie grass until progress took them both away.

RUINOUS IMPROVEMENTS

It is not my intention to denigrate the value of progress's achievements. We have all benefited greatly. As a physician, I understand the tremendous advantages of immunizations, antibiotics, and anesthesia. We all marvel at the power of communications and the speed of transportation. The print media has vastly increased access to learning. Wealth has permitted opportunities far beyond the imagining of our great-grandparents.

The United States in particular has been a prodigy from the womb of progress. Our technology is celebrated, our medicine awe-inspiring, our universities prestigious, and our research of consistent Nobel-Prize quality. Knowledge of our language is desired the world over. In many ways the Church is large, wealthy, and strong. Our freedoms set a standard for other nations to compare themselves to.

Yet as visible as these achievements have been, our faults demand a glaring prominence of their own. If we lead the world in successes, we also lead in far too many failures. Through much of the last decade, we had the developed world's highest rates of divorce, teenage pregnancy, illicit drug abuse, crime, homicides, AIDS, litigation, functional illiteracy, national debt, and foreign debt. We even make more garbage than anyone else.

If progress is so wonderful, why are we plagued, as Lasch accuses, by such "a baffled sense of drift"? Why do we drink and drug to forget our problems? Why are we divorcing and suing at such rates? Why are people killing themselves—and others—in such numbers?

Forty years ago our nation's schoolchildren were being disciplined for talking, chewing gum, making noise, and running in the halls. Today, the biggest discipline problems are rape, robbery, assault, vandalism, and drug abuse. Is this then what we might call forty years of progress? Over those forty years we have had more education, more wealth, more science and technology, more medical care, more media and communications—in short, more of everything. Does this mean we have "proceeded to a higher stage of development"?

Eighty years ago we had no national debt. Today, we have a multitrillion-dollar debt that keeps running away from us like an escaping convict.

One hundred years ago we had fresh air and clean lakes. Today, much of our atmosphere is hazardous and our water polluted.

Two hundred years ago we had lush forests and thick prairies. Today, our forests are threatened by acid rain, and our prairies are being flushed down the Mississippi.

CRISIS TO CRISIS

With the aid of progress, perils now encircle us. No matter which direction we turn, yet another crisis stares us in the face. Not only has progress been unable to solve these crises, it has not even been able to slow them. Thus, as British economist E. F. Schumacher observed, the modern world finds itself "tumbling from crisis to crisis."

We are immersed in a crime and prison crisis; a drug-abuse crisis; a national-debt and international-trade-deficit crisis; a savings-and-loan and banking crisis; a health-care system and Medicare crisis; a sexually-transmitted-disease crisis, including AIDS; an adolescent-suicide crisis; a liability-and-litigation crisis; an ethics crisis at every level of personal and public life; and the inexorably deepening environmental crisis. Our families are relentlessly torn apart by divorce, abuse, incest, and teenage pregnancies. Our educational system remains woefully deficient. Inner cities are war zones. Breakdown on a large scale is now within our reach.

"Each day we awake to a world that appears more confused and disordered than the one we left the night before," complains social critic Jeremy Rifkin. "Every time we think we've found a way out of a crisis, something backfires. The powers that be continue to address the problems at hand with solutions that create even greater problems than the ones they were meant to solve."[6]

All of this is not to say, of course, that crises are a new arrival, unique only to modern-day America. Still, one would have expected progress to bring us fewer rather than more.

FOR THE RECORD

Thirty years ago, the record of progress was still relatively intact. Of course, there were the expected problems and setbacks, but gains and the promise of prosperity always offset them.

Then came the 1970s. Apocalyptic talk flowed heavily, as energy and OPEC threats distressed us and economic news was glum. Ecological degradation stuck a pin in our global eye, while fear of nuclear annihilation chilled the air. Those were days custom-made for somber prophets. Their warning bells alerted the world, touching off a prognostication free-for-all that persists to the present.

Leading the charge was *The Limits to Growth* by Dennis Meadows and fellow researchers. This first report of the Club of Rome used world-system computer models developed at Massachusetts Institute of Technology to examine the question of exponential growth in a finite system. "If the present growth trends in world population, industrialization, pollution, food production, and resource depletion continue unchanged, the limits to growth on this planet will be reached sometime within the next one hundred years," they concluded. "The most probable result will be a rather sudden and uncontrollable decline in both population and industrial capacity."[7]

Millions of copies were sold in over thirty languages, and the book sparked an international debate. Though the Meadows team was praised for the scope of their innovative work, their methodology was criticized for incomplete data, inaccuracies of mathematical models, missing economic variables, and failure to account for regional differences. Many of their conclusions were later revised or retracted. Nevertheless, the ground was irreversibly broken by a landmark study. The fight was on.

Two years later, the Club of Rome struck again: "Suddenly—virtually overnight when measured on a historical scale—mankind finds itself confronted by a multitude of unprecedented crises," warned systems researcher Mihajlo Mesarovic and engineering professor Eduard Pestel in *Mankind at the Turning Point*. This second report of the Club of Rome used revised computer models to conclude that "mankind's options for avoiding catastrophe are decreasing, while delays in implementing the options are, quite literally, deadly."[8]

Economics professor Robert L. Heilbroner contributed a provocative analysis of our future in his widely discussed *An Inquiry into the Human Prospect*: "The outlook for man, I believe, is painful, difficult, perhaps desperate, and the hope that can be held out for his future prospect seems to be very slim indeed. . . . The answer to whether we can conceive of the future other than as a continuation of the darkness, cruelty, and disorder of the past seems to me to be no; and to the question of whether worse impends, yes."[9]

For the most part, progress did not fare well in the seventies. True, there were optimistic predictions coming from such heavyweights as Harvard's Daniel Bell (chairman of the Commission on the Year 2000; a "moderate optimist") and Herman Kahn (founder of the Hudson Institute; an "enthusiastic technological optimist"). But even these respected futurists wavered in subsequent years.

The 1980s seemed to bring respite. Sustained economic prosperity throughout the Western world alleviated some of our problems and masked many more. Faith in our cleverness at finding solutions was reinforced by this financial balm. Yet somehow the problems kept building, even if now they had been pushed off center stage: two problems and one solution, two more problems and one more solution. Crime, drugs, pollution, AIDS, debt—prosperity, it turned out, was more placebo than penicillin.

The prophets, for the most part, softened their rhetoric. Some took a different tack, what I call the transitionist approach: Yes, life is traumatic, but these are only birth pains. The squeeze through society's pelvis is unexpectedly wrenching, but a fresh new life will be awaiting us in the natal world. According to this scenario, new trends and power shifts will be enormously disruptive but must be tolerated. The information age is here, like it or not. Decentralization and demassification will result in a wildly pluralistic society, so we might as well begin to appreciate the value of pluralism. And if all goes well, cooperation of the human community will replace conflict.

This, of course, is a mixture of futurology and crossing one's fingers. In *The Third Wave*, Alvin Toffler placed his considerable influence behind such a transitionist idea. The caution in his optimism, however, is evident: "Often, as Second Wave institutions crash about our heads, as crime mounts, as nuclear families fracture, as once reliable bureaucracies sputter and malfunction, as health delivery systems crack and industrial economies wobble dangerously, we see only the decay and breakdown around us. Yet social decay is the compost bed of the new civilization."[10] "One of the most important things we can give to our kids," Toffler advises parents in a later interview, "is the sense that they live in a world being born, not a world dying."[11]

John Naisbitt reinforced the transitionist theory in his megapopular *Megatrends*: "We are living in the *time of the parenthesis*, the time between eras. It is as though we have bracketed off the present from both the past and the future, for we are neither here nor there." Naisbitt goes on to argue that this traumatic transformation zone "is a great and yeasty time, filled with opportunity" if one can only leverage it correctly. He concludes with this exclamatory: "What a fantastic time to be alive!"[12] If you enjoy convulsions.

THE NINETIES: OPPORTUNITY VERSUS ANGST

These prognostications, however abbreviated, give some flavor of the debate that has carried us into our current decade. Hundreds of additional prophetic opinions have been generated by the remarkable circumstances of the latter twentieth century, and indeed, we are not starving for opinions. As we close in on the end of a millennium, there is much excitement, not a little anxiety, and certainly a lot of press. It makes for fascinating reading and sleepless nights. Yet when all the data is analyzed, it becomes apparent that our crystal ball remains filled with fog. No one knows for sure what will happen. Will we collapse? Will we thrive? Will we transition? One fact, however, is certain: Something historical is happening in our lifetime.

Given that modernity has become such a paroxysm, for us to have survived as long as we have is, in itself, an accomplishment. Now, where are the planners who will lead us into the unknown? Which prophet should we listen to? There are many, but their words argue among themselves. As the forecasts fly, they collide. What for one futurist is an opportunity, for another is angst. For every up, there's a down; for every levo, a dextro.

TOO MUCH PAIN

My advice is to stay away from the futurists who predict destruction and then recommend it, too. They describe the future but cannot bring themselves to judge it. Instead, whatever seems inevitable they endorse. The rest of their text is spent telling us why we must conform.

Such value-devoid passivity is an approach I would not recommend. There are too many dangers. There have been too many failures. There has been far too much pain.

Analyzing progress and social trends from the macroscopic view, as we have done thus far, lends a valuable perspective. But we do not see pain as clearly from this distance as we do when it sits in front of us. Pain comes alive when it talks—even more so when it cries. My initial observations about progress, pain, and margin came not from the distance of the macroscope but instead from the closeness of my examining table. One patient at a time, one story at a time. I worry about the deteriorating statistics, but numbers don't feel pain. It is the face I see behind each statistic that motivates me to write.

These patients are depressed, stressed, and exhausted. Some are desperate. Their jobs are insecure. Their farms have been repossessed. They are over their heads in debt. Their marriages are in trouble. Their sons are using drugs, and their daughters are getting pregnant.

These patients don't know what to do or where to turn. They have no social supports, no roots, no community. Their stomachs won't stop burning. They can't sleep at night. They think about drastic solutions. The public blames the medical profession for giving too many tranquilizers and antidepressants. But what would you do? Doctors like to see healing as the result of their work. Yet today we often must be content with far less. There are so many things wrong with - people's lives that even our best is only a stopgap.

Mental torment hurts. Stress hurts. Overload hurts. Crime and violence hurt. Debt hurts. Divorce hurts. Poor parenting hurts. Abuse hurts. Sexual diseases hurt. Alcoholism hurts. Drug addiction hurts. Abortion hurts. And when you add up all the hurts, we hurt more than we used to.

WHO IS AT FAULT?

The promise of progress has soured into epidemic personal, relational, and environmental pain. I have spent the last ten years of my life striving to understand what went wrong and why. A full explanation is beyond the scope of this book, but I do want to touch on four points germane to our discussion.

Progress Sabotages Margin

There can be little doubt that the ubiquitous contemporary absence of margin is directly linked to the march of progress. Those cultures with the most progress are the same as those with the least margin. If you were wondering why there is a chapter on progress in a book on margin, this is the reason. Margin has been stolen away, and progress was the thief. If we want margin back, we will first have to do something about progress.

We *must* have some room to breathe. We need freedom to think and permission to heal. Our relationships are being starved to death by velocity. No one has the time to listen, let alone love. Our children lay wounded on the ground, run over by our high-speed good intentions. Is God now proexhaustion? Doesn't He lead people beside the still waters anymore?

"Something has been stolen from us that we can't quite name," accuses Norman Mailer.[13] Who plundered those wide-open spaces of the past, and how can we get them back? There are no fallow lands for our emotions to lie down and rest in. We miss them more than we suspect.

Certainly one cannot blame all the pains of the world on lack of margin. But it is fair to say that the lack of margin is a much greater component of our pain than most realize.

nearly every human flaw. We have put armaments in the hands of our hostility, litigation in the hands of our cynicism, affluence in the hands of our greed, the media in the hands of our decadence, advertisements in the hands of our discontent, pornography in the hands of our lust, and education in the hands of our pride. These have not been stabilizing developments. Trying to solve man's problems by giving him more power is like trying to tame the wolf by letting it play with the lamb.

REGAINING CONTROL

Should we jettison progress and start over? That would not be wise. We do not really wish to abandon its many benefits. But neither do we any longer wish to endure its many complications. "As the twentieth century draws to a close," summarizes Lasch, "we find it more and more difficult to mount a compelling defense of the idea of progress; but we find it equally difficult to imagine life without it."[16]

Is there perhaps another option available to us? Can we put progress on probation while we work out its many problems? Two actions would be required of us for this approach to succeed: First, we must regain control of progress; and second, we must redirect it.

To control progress will not be easy. If we decide to put on the brakes, which pedal do we push? If we want to call "foul," which referee should we approach? To what authority does progress submit? The answer is: None. There are no brakes, no referees, no authorities. As one social critic complains, "Progress itself goes on progressing; we can no longer stop it or turn it around."[17]

After gaining an autonomous strength, progress has built up a good head of steam; it does not depend on us to push it along. The trouble is, it no longer *responds* to us either. "The very progress which we first applauded has now become a problem," observes economist Bob Goudzwaard. "The production system, initially a willing servant laboring to end our misery, seems to have taken charge."[18] Has the servant become greater than the master?

Progress calls the shots. When it wrestles, it wins. If progress and pain are linked, well, a little pain never hurt anyone. If progress and margin are enemies, well, what is margin? So what if we are all stressed? So what if the divorce rate is 50 percent? So what if my backyard is polluted?

We are addicted, and progress knows it. We now do *its* bidding. Before we can subjugate progress, we must first break the addiction. Contentment and simplicity, as described in part 3 of this book, will help. Abiding by scriptural teaching concerning money, possessions, education, and priorities will help immensely.

As we subjugate progress, we make it subservient to our greater goals and needs, especially relationships. We once again practice eco-nomics "as if people mattered." We once again agree that things do not own us and are not even very important. We once again assert that jobs are only jobs, that cars are only organized piles of metal, that houses will one day fall down—but that people are important beyond descrip-tion. We once again assert that love stands supreme above *all* other forces, even to the ends of the universe and beyond.

If, however, we fail in our attempts to break the addiction and to subjugate progress, we had better put on our crash helmets and brace ourselves. The train continues gaining speed, and noone is at the con-trols. Progress is leading us to a threshold, but when asked, will not tell us which threshold we near. As sociologist Robert Bellah and col-leagues have pointed out; "Progress, modernity's master idea, seems less compelling when it appears that it may be progress into the abyss."[19]

A MATTER OF (RE)DIRECTION

I am not abandoning all faith in progress. I am not for regress. But I am for redirection. The abyss is not my favored destination.

If you are traveling from Chicago to New York and instead find yourself in Houston, the sensible thing to do is to stop the car, consult the map, and turn in the right direction. In the same way, if we have traveled down the road of progress and now find ourselves in a situa-tion where relational, emotional, and spiritual pain are pandemic, where stress and overload rule our daily schedules, and where margin as a component of living has virtually disappeared, we do not need to apologize for stopping and redirecting ourselves.

In turning deliberately onto the broad road of wealth, education, and material possessions, we have left behind the better way, covered by the dust of our hurry. If we had followed the signposts of that narrower road by acting justly, loving mercy, and walking humbly with our God, we wouldn't now have the anguish we find ourselves buried under.[20]

Micah 6:8

HOLD THE TRAIN

Perhaps we should not go any further until we have accomplished this redirection and defined progress in more wholesome terms. Perhaps we ought to defer the future for a while until we have developed a satisfactorily integrated model to guide our journey. Under the new understanding of accounting we would not call it progress if we gained in wealth but lost in relationship; we would not call it beneficial if we improved in estate but injured the psyche; and we would not call it profitable if we achieved a promotion but lost spiritual integrity.

Until we find ways to guard our mental and spiritual health as well as our "social ecology" (that is, our interrelational environment), we will only compound our troubles and further destabilize our future. As Bellah has warned: "Unless we begin to repair the damage to our social ecology, we will destroy ourselves long before natural ecological disaster has time to be realized."[2] Only when progress begins to show discipline and restraint, as well as a respect for the inward and transcendent needs of human beings—including our need for margin—will we again be able to trust it.

RIGHT RELATIONSHIPS

Progress's biggest failure has been its inability to nurture and protect right relationships. If progress had helped here, I would have no quarrel with it. But it didn't help. So we must either teach it to use new tools or put it on the sideline.

As we have already seen, progress builds by using the tools of economics, education, and technology. But what are the tools of the relational life? Are they not the social (my relationship to others), the emotional (my relationship to myself), and the spiritual (my relationship to God)? None of the tools of progress has helped build the relational foundation our society requires.

Margin knows how to nurture relationship. In fact, margin exists for relationship. Progress, on the other hand, has little to say about the relational life. Even our language gives us away. When we talk of progress, we do not mean social, emotional, and spiritual advancement. Instead, the word is reserved in our common usage to mean material/physical and cognitive/educational gains.

In analyzing our age, commentator after commentator will demonstrate how much better-off we are. Yet, invariably, they are talking about money, energy, transportation, housing, communications, technology, and education. People, however, have relational needs that go much deeper. And while all the focus was on the material and cognitive, our relational environments suffered from neglect.

FIVE ENVIRONMENTS

MOST OF OUR *PROGRESS*:
1. Physical environment (wealth, technology, health—the material world)
2. Cognitive environment (knowledge, information, education—the intellectual world)

MOST OF OUR PAIN:
3. Social environment (family, friends, neighbors, church—the societal world)
4. Emotional environment (feelings, attitudes—the psychological world)
5. Spiritual environment (the eternal and transcendent—God)

While the *progress* we boast of is found within the material and cognitive environments, most of the *pain* we suffer is found within the social, emotional, and spiritual. The material and cognitive environments are unquestionably important. They also have an advantage in that they are more visible and thus more highly pursued. Scripture teaches us, however, that the social, emotional, and spiritual environments are more important. *A crucial task for our society today is to reverse the order of emphasis and visibility of these environments.*

How might we know that the relational environments are where God would have us concentrate? Simply put, these are the same areas Christ spent His time developing and where His teaching is focused.

Where do you think God would have us search for answers regarding drugs, crime, divorce, suicide, depression, teenage pregnancies, sexually transmitted diseases, and litigation? In the material and cognitive realms, or in the relational ones? Our society tries in vain to remedy these problems using the popular notions of progress—appropriating more money (that is, material/physical answers) and setting up more classes (that is, cognitive/educational answers). But insufficient funds and lack of education are not the problems. The problem is lack of love.

With the establishment of a proper emphasis, all appropriate needs will be met. Should we fail in this task, however, progress will only bring us increasing pain. Our wallets will get fatter, our houses bigger, our cars faster, and our brains smarter. Yet when we neglect the most important priorities, our final reward will fittingly be all the unhappiness money can buy.

MEASURING PROGRESS

Progress—tempting, willful, arrogant, divisive, unruly, godlike—what shall we do with you? We have trusted your guidance and followed your lead. In many ways, you've tried to build a successful world. But you have been getting us into trouble of late. We need to stop doing the things that get us into trouble and start doing better things.

"The whole point," contends Schumacher, "is to determine what constitutes progress."[22] What *should* constitute progress? Suspending our "chronological arrogance," let's stay with the British and back up to the days before progress had much momentum. Two centuries ago, an eloquent statesman stood before England and battled tirelessly—and successfully—the evils of slavery. William Wilberforce served in Parliament for forty-five years, universally honored for his integrity.

In his influential writings, Wilberforce makes several references to the importance of progress. Yet it is not progress in wealth, education, and power that he speaks of, but instead, progress in virtue. This, he suggests, could be measured by "the fear and love of God and of Christ; love, kindness, and meekness toward our fellow men; indifference to the possessions and events of this life compared with our concern about eternity; self-denial and humility."[23] It does not sound much like our current definition of progress, but it *does* sound hopeful.

Discerning Christians have long known that God is not impressed with our wealth, education, or power.[24] Nevertheless, we have labored willingly in those fields. What if, instead, we were to begin measuring our progress not by our wealth but by our virtue; not by our education but by our humility; and not by our power but by our meekness?

Graduate degrees and GNPs will never usher in the Kingdom—only love can do that. And love brings us back to Wilberforce: "Above all, measure your progress by your experience of the love of God and its exercise before men."[25]

THREE

The Pain of Problems

A few years ago, I attended a late-night delivery by a very young-looking twenty-two-year-old mother. As I was the faculty member "on call" and was simply assisting the resident with the case, I had not met the family before.

This was Brenda's first baby. She was acting bravely despite her obvious discomfort. An occasional cry escaped as the contraction peaked. Then she would close her eyes in exhaustion and await the next wave of pain.

The nurse who both coached and comforted Brenda would occasionally glance over to the window ledge where the husband sat watching television. Brenda had a long second stage of labor, and we were in the room for over two hours. But I never heard him utter a sound.

The resident and nurse were doing most of the work with the patient, so I just stood back and watched. Then I leaned against the wall and watched. Then I sat down and watched. I was tired. But despite my tiredness, I was also fascinated by the increasingly bizarre social event that was unfolding in the room.

It was around midnight. Brenda's labor happened to coincide with the end of one slasher-type movie and the beginning of another. The final hour of the first movie was filled with violence. I counted at least ten different extended sequences of knifings, bloody machine gun fights, and exploding cars and boats.

The nurse and I looked at each other and rolled our eyes in disgust. Should I use my authority to demand that the set be turned off? I thought about it for a while and then decided the husband might pull out his own submachine gun and blow me away. Anyway, the first movie was mercifully wrapping up, body bags all over the place.

By this time, the baby's head was crowning. Brenda was still fairly well controlled, but her cries were getting louder and lasting longer. Another ten minutes, I figured.

Still no response from the husband, who was settling in for the beginning of the next movie. On the television screen, a mother, father, and small child were strolling down a big-city street when they stopped to watch a clown act. Suddenly, one of the clowns grabbed the little boy by the hand and took off running across the street. With the boy yelling "Daddy, Daddy!" the clown leaped into the back of a waiting van, the father in pursuit. Just as the vehicle started to pull away, the father tore open the back door. The clown inside shot the father pointblank in the face. Blood was everywhere.

Just then—*exactly* then—Brenda screamed and the baby was born.

Go back inside, little one, I thought. *You really don't know what kind of world awaits you.*

DIFFERENT GAME, DIFFERENT RULES, DIFFERENT STAGE

As this baby will surely grow up to discover, we live in a problem-laden world. If these problems would stay in one place, perhaps we'd have a better chance at solving them. But progress has given them wings. And with the advantage of speed, problems are harder to hit than a swooping bat at midnight.

Not only have problems picked up speed, but so has history itself. The flow of history is now the flood of history. The "throughput" of change, information, and people has accelerated explosively. Despite our best attempts to manage the sweep of events, history has escaped. Now we count ourselves fortunate if we are even able to track it, let alone predict it, interpret it, or manage it.

In the past, as we have already noted, progress implied upward and onward, and we developed a linear, ascending way of thinking.

Somewhere in the last few decades, however, we took a quantum leap off the straight line. The astounding acceleration of change and the increasing complexity and interrelatedness of issues have time-warped us into a new era. "If failure to grasp this fact impairs one's ability to understand the present," observes Alvin Toffler, "it also leads otherwise intelligent men into total stupidity when they talk about the future. It encourages them to think in simple-minded straight lines."[1]

Despite uninformed claims to the contrary, we live in an unprecedented day with unprecedented problems. We have been disarticulated from our own past and do not yet know how to deal with the present, let alone the future. Having been selected to live out this great drama, we are playing a different game by different rules on a different stage than any other people in the history of the world.

SKEPTICS AND STOICS

That we live in an unprecedented era with unprecedented problems would seem to be self-evident, yet I have difficulty convincing people of this. When I explain the concept, nine out of ten do not have the slightest idea what I am talking about.

Many of these people can be characterized as *skeptics*. Attempting to understand the reason for their skepticism, I finally realized that most in our modern age are simply not trend-perceptive. The vast majority see only the little bits and pieces around them that reach back to last week and forward to tomorrow. From this vantage point, skeptics insist our situation is not unprecedented because "there is nothing new under the sun."

The *stoics* also disbelieve. They especially disdain the whining and sniveling of the weak who complain incessantly about life's problems. When you discuss the unprecedented difficulties of the age with them, a challenge invariably results: "I don't believe life is any different now. Sure, that little newborn baby might have a difficult life—but people have always had problems and always will. If you went back to the 'good old days,' you couldn't stand it for a week. You'd come flying back to the 'troubled' twentieth century in a flash!"

THE GOLDEN FRAME OF NOSTALGIA

Too often the discussion of contemporary problems ends up being detoured by this same debate about the past. People assume that expressing concerns about today's world implies a preference for yesterday's world. But this is a detour I don't wish to make.

<u>Comparisons with the past are risky.</u> Our tendency is to select what we wish to remember and conveniently forget the rest. "Christians in particular are prone to abbreviate the historical record, pruning from the past that which is messy," explains Notre Dame historian Nathan Hatch. "By a subtle and often unconscious process we pick out of the historical tapestry only those strands which reinforce our own points of view."[2] Or, as Jackie Gleason quipped, "The past remembers better than it lived." So when I say that our age is difficult and our problems are unprecedented, it does not mean I am pining for a romanticized past. It only means that our age is difficult and our problems are unprecedented.

In fairness to the skeptics and stoics, I will concede that comparisons between times present and times past do reveal several similarities:

- ▶ We have problems, and our ancestors had problems.
- ▶ Our problems are painful, and our ancestors' problems were painful.
- ▶ We have some advantages in our lifestyle, and our ancestors had some advantages in their lifestyle.

All of this is true—so far as it goes. But where we differ radically from our ancestors and indeed, even from our own recent past, is that <u>suddenly, almost overnight, an entire new wave of social, technological, and economic experience has descended upon us.</u> It is as if history sneezed, and we have been thrown into a different trajectory.

The list in figure 3.1 illustrates how, in a very pervasive sense, our day is unique. Many readers will scan the list and think, "There is nothing very special about these issues." But this is only true for those who are not trend-perceptive, who think in terms of three weeks instead of three decades.

Figure 3.1—Unprecedented . . .
a partial list

Speed of travel	Power of computers
Information age	Litigation levels
Collapse of information float	Specialization
Speed of communication	Number of scientists/researchers
Technological advances	Energy utilization and dependence

Shrinking world
Tightly coupled world system
National indebtedness
International indebtedness
Corporate indebtedness
Personal indebtedness
Pervasiveness of pollution
Vulnerability to terrorism
Overpopulated prisons
AIDS
Aging populace
Prevalence of divorce
Disappearance of traditions

Nuclear waste-disposal problems
Destructive power of weaponry
Electronic money
Mobility
Complexity
Media pervasiveness and power
Population congestion
Traffic congestion, land and air
Availability of illicit drugs
Abortion
Disintegration of extended family
Changing role of women
Daycare for children

Each item listed has played a significant role in making our era different from all those that preceded it. And when we factor in the interrelatedness of issues, the dimensions involved, and the speed of change, then unprecedented becomes too mild a word.

To help us understand it better, let's explore how the claim "unprecedented" is both a statement of history and, importantly, a statement of mathematics.

LESSONS OF HISTORY

History is a valuable teacher. Yet when I maintain that we live in an unprecedented era, it implies that the lessons of history will only be marginally successful in framing our questions and suggesting our remedies. Having navigated ourselves off the map, we do not know what is around the next bend. Furthermore, we cannot depend on the lessons of history to tell us, for history, too, has never been here before.

"One of the reasons we have not been as good at understanding change as we might have been," explains futurist Harry Clay Blaney III, "is that we are taught about a past world as if it were still existing; we are preparing ourselves for a world we no longer face. Even now our schools teach about the world of past decades and largely ignore the present let alone the future."[3]

I am certainly not intending to deprecate the tremendous value of a historical perspective. I am aware that to disqualify history, even partially, is at best presumptuous and at worst idiotic. We should all be warned, however, that at this particular juncture, an analysis of the past could be more misleading than revealing when it comes to understanding the uniqueness of our day and the dangers of tomorrow.

Many historians will get their hackles up, and I cannot say I blame them. It is a wild idea. However, it is born of an analysis, not of straight lines or cyclical theory, but of mathematical exponentiality.

THE EXPONENTIAL CURVE

One major reason our problems today are unprecedented is because the mathematics are different. Many of the linear lines that in the past described our lives well have now disappeared. Replacing them are lines that slope upward exponentially.

Figure 3.2

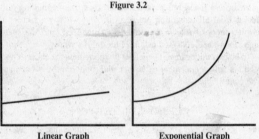

Linear Graph
(Describes much of the past.)

Exponential Graph
(Describes much of the present.)

These figures help us to understand what is happening in our society in a *quantitative* way. The linear graph on the left represents how most of life used to unfold. In contrast, an increasing amount of today's experience is better described, even if approximately, by the exponential curve on the right.

Because there is little in our day-to-day lives that changes exponentially, we tend to think and plan with a linear mind-set. The sun rises and the sun sets. Twenty-four hours is still only twenty-four hours. Week after week, everything seems about the same.

Meanwhile, largely unnoticed by us, history has shifted to fast forward. If linear still best describes our personal lives, exponential now best describes much of historical change. The significance of this is incalculable, yet the typical American, not knowing how to think in exponential terms, consistently underestimates it.

To illustrate how rapidly exponential numbers accumulate and why they are so hard for us to envision, long-range forecaster J. Scott Armstrong gave a graduate class of twenty business students the following puzzle: If you folded a piece of paper in half forty times, how thick would the result be? The answers given were as follows:

Answer	Number of Students
Less than one foot	13
Greater than one foot, up to one mile	5
Greater than one mile, up to 2000 miles	2
Greater than 2000 miles	0

The correct answer is that the paper would be thick enough to reach from here to the moon![4] Such an answer is more than unexpected—to most of us, it is incomprehensible. This is why it is so hard to appreciate the radical quantitative dimensions of contemporary change. Yet unexpected or not, incomprehensible or not, changes that—at least for a time—follow an exponentially increasing curve are what we must often now contend with.

The appendix contains many graphs demonstrating such exponential change. This compilation of graphs is diverse—from population to prisoners, from advertising to air travel, from divorce to debt. Even a glance will provide abundant evidence that the circumstances of our age are different from anything previously encountered. Once we grasp this quantitative uniqueness, we will be in a much better position to understand what is happening in the world around us.

LIMITS

Because so much in life has now shifted to exponential terms, the issue of limits has suddenly become an important one. We coast along for decades on the slow-growth portion of the exponential curve without encountering significant limit problems. Then, suddenly, we hit our head on the ceiling.

Previously, there was abundant margin in the world system, and we did not have to worry about limits. We could grow, expand, and waste as much as we wanted without worry. This is no longer the case. We have met or exceeded limits in scores of areas, but we do not know how to pull back. How do you slow a careening world when the throttle is stuck wide-open?

All things have limits—people, governments, buildings, bridges, brains, and organizations. Even more subjective things such as friendships, creativity, or adaptability have limits. If we are well within boundaries, we can be expansive and growth-oriented. When approaching a limit, however, the rules change.

If a car goes twenty miles per hour, there will be few problems. If, however, that car goes two hundred miles per hour, all kinds of dangers arise. Cars have limits.

In a similar way, progress has limits. Some limits are external (for example, environmental, material, economic) while others are internal (for example, psychological, social, spiritual). Since we are impinging on many of these limits, much of our life experience is now traveling through uncharted territory. And because margin is closely related to the issue of limits, most of it has disappeared.

EXPONENTIALITY AND PROBLEMS

Up to this point I have not necessarily implied that exponentiality is a negative phenomenon. Just because something changes exponentially does not mean the development is automatically painful. In fact, such rapid changes can be positive (as in the accumulation of interest on your bank account), mixed (as in the rapidly increasing numbers of elderly), or negative (as in the astounding rise in health-care costs). This "negative" category is what should concern us. For when we apply the principles of exponential growth to our *problems*, we find ourselves quickly mired in deep trouble. Crisis points are reached almost overnight.

When we realize that exponentiality approximates the growth pattern of such problems as national debt, health-care costs, complexity, the prison population, births to unmarried women, the number of divorces, litigation rates, bank failures, and bankruptcies, then it becomes clear that we are in trouble. (Again, see the appendix.) And it is trouble of a dimension foreign to human experience. Maybe we can solve the problems, maybe we can survive, maybe we can even thrive. But the simple truth is—no one knows.

THE S-CURVE

Obviously, the mathematics of human experience can't actually go to infinity. All things stop before that, even explosions. For example, if previous exponential curves for projecting human longevity and vehicular speed had continued, by the year 2000 humans would be able to live forever and travel at the speed of light.[5]

When most exponential slopes approach the impossible, they begin to level off again. This often results in a slope called the logistic curve, or the "S-curve." (The pure exponential curve, in contrast, is called the "J-curve.") The point at which the exponential curve begins sloping into the S-curve is called the turning point. Predicting where this turning point will occur is important but difficult. If it comes early we will be okay. But if it comes late, acceleration alone will cause widespread breakdown in many of our social systems.

Figure 3.3

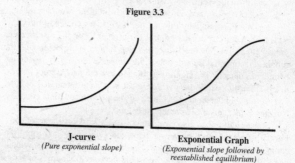

J-curve
(Pure exponential slope)

Exponential Graph
*(Exponential slope followed by
reestablished equilibrium)*

Realizing that the S-curve lies ahead gives us some respite from our anxiety. And this respite is valid. But we should not be complacent. That we have leaped off the linear and onto the exponential is a very significant phenomenon, a historical disruption. A disruption of this magnitude makes it an exciting day in which to live—in a frightening sort of way.

ISOLATE OR INTEGRATE?

There are two ways (at least) to address our many problems. The first way is to *isolate* each one, treating each as a single independent entity. If we were to apply this strategy to our long list, each individual problem would no doubt be solvable. Dealing with one problem at a time is not a bad strategy with which to approach life, particularly a very complex life.

The analytical, reductionistic strategy is, in many instances, the correct approach. We dissect and analyze, and once we can wrap a plan around the difficulty, we go for it.

The second approach, to *integrate* them all together, is an entirely different proposition. Here we use a wide-angle lens instead of a microscope. Stepping back, back, back . . . until the integrated picture comes into view, we learn some things we did not suspect when studying only isolated problems. Seeing everything together and connected gives us a more accurate assessment of the immensity that confronts us. It is this perspective that is so troubling about our modern-day situation.

This sort of integration, though essential, is seldom done because it is very difficult. Yet if we wish to accurately understand the uniqueness of both our day and our problems, it is an effort we must make.

Let me illustrate why this is true. If a patient comes to the clinic with diabetes, I can usually control the problem. But if I discover this same patient also has heart disease, renal failure, and pneumonia, the prognosis is much different, that is, much worse. So simply saying the patient has diabetes is a significant thing to say, but we have not learned much about the whole patient. We must know the integrated picture, and we must understand the context of the disease. In some contexts, diabetes is manageable. In others, it is fatal.

Space shuttles can also have fatal diseases. Possibly the most complicated piece of machinery ever built, the *Challenger* had a million components when first assembled. Had we examined each individual piece of technology separately, we would have seen hundreds of thousands of flawlessly constructed and assembled parts. A marvel of human engineering. And yet it blew up. Therefore it was not a marvel—it was a disaster. The disaster, however, is only understood when the faulty O-rings are factored in with the other 99.9999 percent of perfectly functioning parts. The disaster, in other words, becomes apparent only when the analysis integrates all the technology together to discover how one flaw doomed the entire project in a tragic fireball.

One cannot even begin to assess how future forces will interact without factoring in each piece of important data. Futurists and forecasters understand the significance of integration. "The integrative thrust of futures studies constitutes, in fact, one of their most distinctive characteristics," explains international studies professor Barry Hughes. "And they are *integrative*, not just encompassing. 'Systems thinking,' popularly defined in the expression 'everything is connected to everything else,' has characterized most futures work."[6]

Yet, for the most part, integration is absent from the contemporary American landscape. Scientists, physicians, educators, analysts—all perhaps would adhere to integration in principle but practice its opposite. Information overload causes us to burrow ever deeper into specialization, subspecialization, and then supersubspecialization, thus effectively burying ourselves with our own problem. This is not to say that specialized analysis cannot yield useful information. But reducing all of life into ever smaller particles is taking us in the wrong direction. "What has failed at every level—from the society of nations to the national society to the local community to the family—is integration," observe the authors of *Habits of the Heart*. "When the world comes to us in pieces, in fragments, lacking any overall pattern, it is hard to see how it might be transformed."[7]

STEAMROLLED BY HISTORY

When we finally do open our eyes to the totality of what confronts us, it is frightening. It hurts, like looking at the sun. There is too much to take in. How do you talk about something this big other than in generalizations? Forced by dimension alone, back we go to debating just one problem, one detail, one statistic. Yet we must resist returning to the one-at-a-time strategy. We could, for example, be drawn back to discussing how acid rain might be decreased with more widespread use of flue-gas desulfurization scrubbers. And that might be a valuable discussion in one context. But it would also be like arguing over who's going to kill the cockroach in stateroom 219 as the *Titanic* nears its iceberg.

Even if we do not have the courage or vision to understand life in an integrated way, *life* happens to us integrated. Whether we like it or not, history will steamroll us with the whole, not with particles.

A MORNING IN THE OFFICE

Now, let's apply what we have learned about integration and see how it changes our perceptions. Come with me to the office. Look over my shoulder and see what pain looks like. Not the headache or bruised-knee kind of pain, but the kind of pain that swallows up human beings.

In medicine, there are two ways you can get through the day. One is to see each patient as an isolated problem and do all you can before the fifteen minutes are up. Then you move on to the next patient. This, in fact, is the way physicians usually work.

The other mode is the integrative approach, and it is much more time-consuming. But if you are serious about understanding the patient's pain, integration is essential. You back up and try to see the whole. You try to see the patient in the context of the patient's past and probable future. You look at the mental status, lifestyle, and health habits. You look at the family, the social-support network, and even the society.

Taking that approach on this Monday morning, see if you don't agree: something here disturbs.

Monday, 9:30 a.m.—Room 7
JACKIE: Postpartum Exam

Jackie is in for her six-week postpartum check. A twenty-one-year-old single mother of three, she left her husband at age sixteen but has not yet divorced him, despite living with another man since then.

Her current boyfriend uses marijuana regularly.

Monday, 10:00 a.m.—Room 8
SONYA: Birth-Control Pills

A twenty-eight-year-old divorcée with four children, Sonya is requesting birth-control pills even though she doesn't have a sexual partner. There is a medical history of gonorrhea and pubic lice. She hasn't menstruated for twelve months since stabbing herself in the abdomen during an unsuccessful suicide attempt.

Monday, 10:15 a.m.—Room 9
CINDI: Prenatal Care

Cindi is a twenty-year-old unwed woman about to deliver her first baby. Herpes, chlamydia, and pelvic inflammatory disease have complicated the pregnancy.

Monday, 10:30 a.m.—Room 10
GWEN: Broken Arm

Gwen needs an X-ray. After she reported her boyfriend to the police for pushing drugs, he beat her up. While trying to run away, she fell and broke her arm. Gwen is now twenty-one. When she was only three, her mother died of an overdose of heroin. Her father was later shot to death by his girlfriend.

If, on this particular morning in May, I were to use the "assembly line" approach, nothing remarkable would have struck me. My first four patients consisted of a postpartum exam, contraceptive counseling, a prenatal visit, and a broken arm.

But I stepped back and opened my eyes a little further. Then my morning looked different. Using the lens of integration, these same four young women carried as baggage the painful problems of teenage pregnancies, unwed mothers, single parents, divorce, domestic violence, homicide, suicide attempts, unemployment, lack of education, drug overdoses, welfare, depression, cohabitation, illicit drug abuse, sexually transmitted diseases, and pelvic inflammatory disease.

Yes, it is a satisfying feeling to know that you have alleviated the pain burden of the world just a little bit. But it would be even more satisfying to know that the world you were working on was progressing in a better direction.

CONTEMPORARY ACCOUNTING

Perhaps you are still not convinced. "After all," you argue, "we have so many *benefits* to living in our modern day. Surely we can learn to live with these problems. If we counted up all the good and measured it against all the bad, we would *still* come out ahead. Besides, aren't we supposed to focus more on the positive things and not spend all of our time worrying about the negatives?"

Yes, of course we should always be grateful for the benefits. Yet problems are real, and they must be dealt with. Christ certainly lived a life of grace and gratitude—but He also dealt with problems head on.

There is an exceptionally dangerous trap here if we are not careful. It lies in the accounting method commonly used to calculate positives versus negatives. If, in analyzing this labyrinthine snarl we call the twentieth century, we were to use standard accounting methods, we would add up the credits and subtract the debits. A positive net balance indicates that a gain has been realized. Unfortunately, this summation method applied to contemporary conditions is misleading. Modernity is not cooperating with the accountant.

If we listed all the positives, we would have a very long list. There can be no question that we enjoy many advantages over previous generations. The trouble is revealed, however, when we begin to tabulate the negatives. Here we find a daunting list of problems that threatens the viability of our entire society. *If the negatives are sufficiently dangerous, they cannot be offset by the positives, no matter how beneficial the positives are.* You cannot simply subtract the negatives from the positives and look at the sum. The negatives must be accounted on their own.

To illustrate this principle, suppose we have a train with 500 cars bound for an impoverished Third-World village. Four hundred of these cars are loaded with all the bounty science has to offer: medicines, microscopes, computers, automobiles, televisions, telephones, libraries, food, and recreational equipment. An additional fifty cars are filled with tons and tons of gold. The remaining fifty cars, scattered throughout the length of the train, contain deadly viruses, pollutants, poisonous gases, heroin, cocaine, and nuclear weapons poised to explode should they be jostled inadvertently.

Now, what shall we say about this train? Is it a "good" train or a "bad" train? It has 450 "good" cars compared to only fifty "bad" cars. Will it bring blessing to the impoverished village it is headed for, or will it bring pain and disaster? Do we recommend it or condemn it?

Progress and the train have much in common. Progress, like the train, brings us many benefits but, at the same time, many problems. For progress to be simultaneously profitable and painful is annoying. Nevertheless, this coexistence of positives and negatives is exactly where we find ourselves. The positives bless, but the negatives can kill. The *Challenger*'s positives outnumbered its negatives a million to one. Yet in seventy-three seconds, it was gone.

CRITICAL MASS

A serious question now presents itself: Is there a critical mass of problems beyond which a society—or, for that matter, an individual—will be destroyed no matter how wonderful the benefits it enjoys? If so, what is that critical mass? Are we approaching it? Have we reached it?

The first question I have already answered. Yes, there is a critical mass, for *if the negatives are sufficiently dangerous, they cannot be offset by the positives no matter how beneficial the positives are.*

What is that critical mass? Undetermined.

Are we approaching it? Without question.

Have we reached it? Possibly.

It is true that humankind has always had problems and always will. It is not true, however, that yesterday's problems and today's problems are automatically the same. To assert that all problems have equal weight is not only foolish but dangerous. No one has ever stood where we stand, nor has anyone ever faced what we face. We live in a paroxysm, and it is still uncertain as to whether it is a paroxysm we can survive.

When we integrate our criminal activity, urban war zones, street gangs, drug addiction, skyrocketing prison population, national debt, foreign trade deficit, corporate and consumer debt, savings and loan and banking crises, record closing of hospitals, soaring costs of health care and college education, deteriorating education, sexually transmitted diseases, hundreds of thousands of AIDS cases, alcoholism, family breakdown, divorce, teenage pregnancy, single parenting, child abuse, collapse of our child-protection system, increasing stress, complexity, overload, anxiety, depression, suicide, pollution, litigation, crumbling infrastructure, "death-oriented hopelessness" of the contemporary arts, and the vanishing of both tradition and community, we find that the specifics, the dimensions, and the threat are all very different today than ever before.

"As I've come to feel a deep sense of urgency about the Future Forces at work today, I've decided to do all I can to communicate to you the pressing need for action," writes Princeton pollster George Gallup, Jr. "If swift, forceful steps aren't taken to defuse the political and social time bombs facing us, we may well find ourselves on a track that could lead to the destruction of civilization as we know it."[8]

Many of the problems we have today are not new. "What is new," continues Gallup, "is the intensity with which they demand our attention." He concludes his book *Forecast 2000* with a warning shared by many futurists: "I'm sufficiently convinced that our society is heading in a dangerous direction that I feel compelled to sound a note of extreme urgency."[9]

SOME IMPLICATIONS

In my efforts to show how our contemporary problems are without precedent, I have escorted you through what is perhaps uncharted territory, land mined with concepts such as exponentiality, S-curves, integration, and accounting methods. In simplified terms, what are some implications of this discussion?

Margin—Our margin is negatively influenced by both the number and size of our problems. The *more* problems we have, the *less* margin we have. And the *larger* our problems become, the *smaller* our margin becomes.

Humility—Our problems are so unprecedented that we must never be complacent or self-assured concerning our ability to solve them. Just because we have solved our problems in the past says nothing about our ability to solve them now. We have never had problems like these before.

Quick catastrophes—Because the math is so different, problems can go from small to immense almost overnight. Indeed, many have—as, for example, the savings and loan fiasco. And, historically speaking, the disappearance of our margin happened in the blink of an eye.

Vigilance—Having learned about exponentiality, we now understand that our problems are growing much faster than we had previously believed. Having learned about integration, we now understand that our problems are far more interconnected than we perhaps thought. And having learned about contemporary accounting, we now understand that the danger of our problems can't always be offset by the many positives we enjoy.

It is a day for vigilance. If something historic is happening, the Church should not be the last to know.

The power of evil—When exponential growth is applied to money, power, speed, communications, and technology, society might be benefited—but so is evil. Evil today has more power at its disposal than ever before.

My greatest worry about our prospects for the future stems from a full awareness of the following linkage: (1) Mankind is fallen and capable of limitless acts of evil, and (2) progress exponentially increases the power available for the purposes of evil.

Think about it.

Relational collapse—A frightful consequence of the dramatic changes of the last few decades is how rapidly and thoroughly the relational life has come unglued. It has amounted to not only a social revolution but also an unprecedented social catastrophe. And yet it has been largely ignored by many futurists. The common focus of most long-range forecasting is the economy, resources, energy, pollution, population, education, and technology. But what about relationships? Neglecting to factor in the state of the relational life is surely incomplete integration. Our society could easily succumb to internal dissonance long before the external threats become fatal.

Nearly all indices of the scripturally prescribed relational life have suffered major setbacks over the last three decades. Marriage — worse; parenting — worse; the extended family — worse; the sense of community — worse; social-support systems — worse; church commitment — worse; church unity — worse; and one-anothering in the church — worse. And it happened seemingly overnight. Little wonder our pains are so acute.

THE DISAPPEARANCE OF MARGIN

Whatever happened to margin? It was steamrolled by history. Let's go back and see how this happened.

First, we start with margin. As noted, progress is the enemy of margin, and they have competed from the start. While margin can usually be counted upon to stay in one place, progress is always on the move — otherwise it would not be progress. After a time, progress turned over the speed controls to exponentiality, and we shifted into overdrive. Limits were hit with frightening suddenness. The speed and complexity of these developments were unprecedented, causing widespread confusion and pain.

Margin, the space that once existed between ourselves and our limits, was an early casualty. When you reach the limits of your resources or abilities, you have no margin left. So as history and progress picked up speed, we hit limit after limit. Slowly, margin began to disappear. Then when exponentiality took over the controls, margin vaporized.

Now that we have exceeded so many of our limits — personal, emotional, relational, physical, financial — we have no margin at all. Yet because we don't even know what margin is, we don't realize it is gone. We know that something is not right, but we can't solve the puzzle beyond that. Our pain is palpable, but our assailant remains unnamed.

Much of this pain is in our relational life: to self, to others, to God. We *miss* margin in many areas. But we *require* it in our relationships. We need to get it back.

When we have no margin and our limits have been exceeded; when we are besieged by pain, stress, and overload; when our relational life is ailing; when it seems the flood of events is beyond our control; then problems take on a different dimension. One at a time they are perhaps manageable. But they just won't stand in line. Instead, they grow from problem pile into problem mountain and then all fall on us at the same time.

NOT GLOBALONEY

After looking at our problem mountain—whether global, societal, or individual—and doing the work of integration, there are four judgments we can make: *Our problems are real* (not artifacts), *they are systemic* (not superficial), *they are serious* (not globaloney), *and they are <u>unprecedented</u>* (not a simple continuation of what we have always known).

If we are strong, we can confront our problems—even if they are real, systemic, serious, and unprecedented. If, however, we have been bled to death by stressful, marginless living, we may be defeated before we even start.

It is hard to solve the problems of the world when you can't even make it through the next day.

FOUR

The Pain of Stress

Many of the annoyances of <u>modernity</u> do not yield to quick analysis. We wouldn't exactly label them evils—more like frustrations or nuisances. They are more like heartburn than homicide. You can't really pick out a villain, yet you have a headache anyway. Sometimes you suspect there must be a computer virus hiding deep inside the center of the earth, clogging up all its gears. Maybe that's why so many things continue to backfire after all these years. It's confusing: We have all this information but still can't seem to figure out what we need to know to solve our problems.

Why does the airplane keep arriving late—wouldn't you think they'd have that worked out by now? Why can't the person using the sophisticated computer seem to clear up my magazine subscription? Why doesn't the Internal Revenue Service know the answers to its own questions? What causes people to shoot at total strangers on the freeway? Whatever happened to friendly clerks? Why does the addition of yet one more program at my local church sound like a penalty rather than an opportunity? Why is it we don't feel confident that when the world awakens tomorrow, we will all be one day closer to victory?

YET ANOTHER POLLUTANT

High levels of stress follow as naturally after progress as does exhaust after traffic. It is a byproduct of our age, yet another societal pollutant. Nearly every patient I see leads a life influenced in some way by inordinate levels of stress. Pick up any periodical at the public library — on farming, business, psychology, health, teaching, religion, sports, fashion, or family — and see if it doesn't contain an article mentioning the subject. "Death and taxes aren't the only sure things anymore," comments one such periodical. "Stress has become an inevitable part of life for most people."[1]

Four out of five Americans report a need to reduce stress in their lives. Because these painful stressors are so ubiquitous and our coping skills so poorly developed, many resort to tranquilizers. Why, in such a prosperous age, is it necessary to sedate so many?

"More and more tranquilizers, stimulants and other 'happy' pills are handed out every year, but they serve only to hide the cause of the problem," comments world-renowned surgeon Christiaan Barnard. "We have to find and remove or reduce the stress."[2] The negative aspects of stress disable not only our personal lives and the lives of our families but the workplace as well. According to the American Institute of Stress, stress-related illnesses cost the American economy $100 billion annually.

OUR RESPONSE TO CHANGE

Hans Selye, the late Canadian endocrinologist and "father" of stress research, defines stress as *"the nonspecific response of the body to any demand made upon it*."[3] This definition is contrary to the popular thinking that defines stress as an unpleasant circumstance, such as tax time or a screaming baby. Stress is *not* the circumstance, it is our *response* to the circumstance. It is not "out there" but rather *inside us.*

It makes little difference if the situation we react to is a positive one, such as buying a new home, or a negative one, such as bankruptcy. Although the ultimate consequences of frustrating stress can be very different from those of rewarding stress, nevertheless, the initial adaptive response mechanism is similar in both cases. Merely encountering the word stress should not connote a positive or a negative feeling (though it probably does). The word only describes an entirely normal psychophysiological process without which we would die.

Our bodies are constantly adapting to the environment. This adaptation is a marvelous process, more intricate than we imagine. It involves the brain and nervous system, the heart and circulatory system, the liver and spleen, the adrenal glands and immune system, and many other organs as well. An incredibly sophisticated communication network functions continuously at a low level. It is on perpetual standby alert, monitoring for sudden changes in the environment. At times of increased need the system surges, preparing us for any necessary response.

This stress system is important and, in fact, vital. When it is overactive, however, damage can result. While stress itself need not be destructive, the overstimulation of an uncontrolled stress response may be both painful and destructive.

Stress then is the name given to the normal internal physiological mechanism that adapts us to change. *Distress* is the negative, destructive aspect of this mechanism, and eustress is the positive, constructive aspect of the adaptation response. *Hyperstress* describes a condition whereby the system is stimulated too often for too long. *Stressors* are those environmental changes that set in motion the adaptation response.

EUSTRESS, DISTRESS, HYPERSTRESS

Many of us, often without realizing it, use stress to our advantage. This eustress energizes us. It is what football players call "psyching up" before a game. Eustress is what makes us especially creative before a deadline, when concentration and efficiency are so much easier. It is what a doctor uses in the middle of the night to shake off somnolence when an ambulance brings in an accident victim. Or what sleeping mothers use when they hear an infant gagging in the next room and they have to be instantly awake. This is what employers consciously induce in a work environment to make employees alert and productive—a kind of creative tension. Some people love this feeling, thrive on it, and almost become addicted to it.

When the stress response becomes negative or destructive, it is accurately called distress. This is what most of us mean when we use the word *stress*. We are really referring to the negative aspects of stress, or distress.

An excessive volume of stress is called hyperstress. The volume is important because how we deal with stress depends on how much of it we are confronted with and what type of personality we have. If the amounts are manageable, we can learn to avoid distress and possibly turn it into eustress. If, however, the amounts are at hyperstress levels, then stress reduction is more important than stress management.

Clarifying Stress Terms

STRESS: the normal internal physiological mechanism thatresponds to and adapts us to change

DISTRESS: the negative, destructive aspect of stress

EUSTRESS: the positive, constructive aspect of stress

HYPERSTRESS: a condition whereby the stress response isstimulated too often for too long

STRESSORS: those environmental changes that set in motion the stress adaptation response

NO ONE TO SLUG

When we encounter a stressor, our body reacts with a cascade of neurohormonal changes. The brain releases CRF (corticotropin releasing factor), which immediately arouses the entire central nervous system. In turn, the central nervous system triggers at least three reactions: the sympathetic nervous system releases adrenaline and other similar hormones; the pituitary gland releases multiple hormones, including ACTH (adrenocorticotropic hormone), which causes the adrenal glands to put out the hormone cortisol; and the brain releases natural painkillers such as endorphins. As a result of this rapid deployment, we are instantly more alert, have more oxygen and sugar available, and shunt more blood to the brain and muscles. Such a reaction is called the "fight or flight" phenomenon. It perhaps served humankind well for most of our history, but today, notes cardiologist and stress expert Robert Eliot, "Nature's plan is seldom appropriate, for there is no one to slug and there is no place to run."

Dr. Selye classifies the stress response or General Adaptation Syndrome as having three phases: the Alarm Stage, the Resistance Stage, and the Exhaustion Stage. The Alarm Stage is the "fight or flight" phenomenon noted above. Following the Alarm Stage comes the Resistance Stage, a period of vigilance and resistance. Such vigilance cannot be sustained for long, however, and the Exhaustion Stage follows.

Once we understand this sequence, the implications may begin to clarify some of our own behavior patterns. If we trigger the response too frequently, we will be in states of alarm or resistance too often. This overdosing on our own adrenaline has potentially serious adverse consequences.

If the stress reaction is resolved in a way that results in success, no apparent damage is noticed. If, however, the result is failure or frustration, multiple pathologies may ensue: tissue aging occurs at the cellular level; the immune system may malfunction, leading to infection or cancer; cardiovascular catastrophies, such as stroke, heart attack, or arrhythmias, may occur. We feel the pain, and the pain is real. "Each period of stress, especially if it results from frustrating, unsuccessful struggles, leaves some irreversible chemical scars which accumulate to constitute the signs of tissue aging," explains Selye.[4]

Selye's research appears to indicate that humans have only a limited supply of deep adaptive energy. Most of the energy expended in the stress response can be recovered through rest. But a certain amount of this energy resource may be irretrievably lost. For this reason, it is important to reserve this adaptive energy for those occasions where the issues are significant and not to squander it on trivial conflicts.[5]

Let me illustrate further. At the risk of being overly simplistic, perhaps we can make a comparison between stress and driving an automobile. Every time we enter into a stress response, we are taking our car for a ride. When the gas tank runs out, we can always fill it up again (replenishing our supply of superficial adaptive energy). Yet each trip also puts wear and tear on the vehicle that is irreversible (depleting our supply of deep adaptive energy). This is not a reason to never drive. But it is a caution to beware what kind of trips we take.

IS IT WORSE TODAY?

Stress has been called a national epidemic. Is it a modern disease? Haven't people always had stresses? The answer to both questions is yes. Humankind has always had problems, and many of them were caused by stress or resulted in distress. Yet our current stress plague differs both quantitatively and qualitatively from the experience of our ancestors. Conditions of our modern age tend to overstimulate our stress-response system more than in previous times, and many of the issues are too complex for successful resolution.

"But look at the statistics," you protest. "Infant mortality is down and life expectancy is up. We have one of the highest standards of living in the world. The elderly have Social Security and Medicare, while the poor have food stamps and Medicaid." Yes, and we all have stress. It is woven as tightly into the fabric of modern life as is television.

No one in the history of humankind has ever had to live with the stressors we have acting upon us today. They are unprecedented. The human spirit is called upon to withstand pressures that have never before been encountered.

Our stress levels are unprecedented for many reasons. Some have already been discussed in the previous chapters, and more will be discussed throughout the book. Exponential change is one stressor we dare not underestimate. Universal indebtedness is a relatively new stressful phenomenon. Hurry and noise contribute their share to our stress load. Complexity and overload remain hidden to most people's understanding but are crushing stressors. Both parents working stresses the parents, the family unit, and the children. Child-development experts repeatedly warn that children are pressed to grow up too soon.

Child psychologist David Elkind believes there are at least three contemporary sources of stress that mark our age as a difficult one. First, due to the alarming increase in violence and crime, we are more *afraid*. Second, due to rapidly changing job markets, technology, and economic factors, we are more professionally *insecure*. Finally, due to widespread separation and divorce, we are more *alone*.[6]

Such "aloneness" is a more important factor in stress disease than most realize. Social supports have been bowled over by progress. Although affirming relationships are probably the single best protector against stress-induced damage, we live in an impersonal world. *Study after study* confirms that a healthy marriage, family, or community support structure yields better health and increased longevity—a kind of buffering system against the pain of distress.

One of the largest surveys followed five thousand residents of Alameda County, California, for nine years. The conclusion? After correcting for all other variables: "Those who were unmarried, had few friends or relatives and shunned community organizations were more than twice as likely to die during that time than people who had these social relationships."[7]

Understanding the linkage between supports and stress helps us to define a contemporary trend: Over the last several decades, stresses, expectations, and pressures have increased, while social and emotional support systems have decreased. It is little wonder, then, that stress disorders are experienced in nearly every household.

PHYSICAL STRESS, MENTAL STRESS

An additional contribution to our stress problem is revealed by examining the difference between physical and mental pressures. Our bodies distinguish between stressors that are mental in nature and those that are physical. Physical hard work, for example, is not really a stressor at all, as long as one has some control over it. One can work twelve hours a day, six days a week for an entire life at hard physical labor and suffer no ill effects—as long as the person has decision-control over the work schedule. As a matter of fact, such hard physical labor would almost certainly have salutary health benefits. But if the strain is mental and a person is constantly being frustrated and thwarted, the negative health effects can be catastrophic.

"Even the greatest experts in the field do not know why the stress of frustration is so much more likely than that of excessive muscular work to produce disease (peptic ulcers, migraine, high blood pressure, or even a simple 'pain in the neck')," admits Dr. Selye. "In fact, physical exercise can even relax and help us withstand mental frustration. . . . Certain emotional factors, such as frustration, are particularly likely to turn stress into distress, whereas in most instances, physical exercise has an opposite effect."[8]

In one study, a patient was first given a cardiac treadmill exam. Despite vigorous physical exercise, the patient's cardiovascular status remained normal throughout. He then was asked to subtract seven from 777 serially for three-and-one-half minutes. His blood pressure went up forty points. Similar results have been achieved in other studies. Certain biochemical stress parameters, such as plasma cortisol levels, are more affected by psychological stressors than by physical stressors. Chronic uncertainty, sustained levels of increased vigilance, or struggling with a mental task are more stressful than chopping wood.

"The widespread substitution of mental strain for physical strain is no advantage from our point of view," maintained E. F. Schumacher. "Proper physical work, even if strenuous, does not absorb a great deal of the power of attention, but mental work does; so that there is no attention left over for the spiritual things that really matter. It is obviously much easier for a hard-working peasant to keep his mind attuned to the divine than for a strained office worker."[9]

SPICE OF LIFE, KISS OF DEATH

Individuals differ significantly regarding how much stress is desirable or what types of events are stressful. What strains some does not bother others. I, for example, do not mind waiting in lines but do not enjoy going to formal parties. Another person might react the opposite—despising lines but loving parties. A stressor that for one might be pleasure, for another might be pain. For one, the spice of life; for another, the kiss of death.

Some people desire a low level of stress to feel comfortable. Our modern pace was not particularly designed with them in mind. Others seek a high, almost frenzied level of stress and seem to thrive on it. Different stressors, different personalities, different results. Let's look at some of these.

Type A

The type A personality, usually male, is commonly characterized as "driven." Their most common traits are a sense of time urgency and free-floating hostility. Type As have a drive to control others, an aggressiveness and competitiveness characterized by a need to win, and a tendency toward self-destruction. They think multiple thoughts and do multiple actions at the same time. Margin is not a priority to preserve but a gap to be filled.

These hardworking, time-pressured individuals are more prone to cardiovascular disease. (Of the thirty-one traits identified, hostility is the most pathogenic.)[10] Their carburetors are set on high, and they surge into overdrive at the slightest provocation. One physician describes "a distinct profile of the vigilant male beset with internal fury and living in a state of relentless, joyless striving."[11]

Most people find a vacation relaxing, but type As often do not. Relaxing is one of the most stressful things on their agenda, which is why they seldom do it. Progress and type As feed on each other. They are very productive people and usually the leaders of companies, programs, or institutions. They live on a high level of stress, however, and have significant health problems because of it.

The Extrovert or Introvert

The introvert is a personality type vulnerable to the stresses of the crowd. Introverts like to be alone. They appreciate quiet, solitude, and time to think and feel in their own internal world. They generally do not like having a large number of social interactions, going to parties, or meeting new people.

The majority of Americans (by a three-to-one margin), however, are extroverts, and extroverts are energized by such social exchange. Extroverts usually don't understand introverts and try to push them into situations where they simply don't wish to be.

The Depressed or Anxious

Another group of people in a special stress category are those who have generalized depression or anxiety. According to psychologist Judy Eidelson and psychiatrist David Burns, "depression is the certainty that things are horrible and hopeless; anxiety is the belief that at any moment things *will become* horrible and hopeless."[12] Whether depressed, anxious, or both, these people feel pressure from stressors that are inflated or sometimes not even there at all.

Some, for example, are always stressed when they ride in a car. They have never been in an accident but are fearful that today will be the day. Every car they pass along the route, therefore, becomes a stressor. These anxious and/or depressed people will be burdened much of their lives simply because they perceive stressors as more of a threat than they really are. One important lesson emerges from such an illustration: Often our *perception* of the stressor damages us more than the stressor itself.

The Elderly

Some evidence indicates that mental stressors induce more tension in the elderly than in the young. Performing serial seven subtraction is only mildly stressful for those in their twenties. Many elderly, however, are hyperresponsive to such stimuli and become agitated in performing the task.

Children

Pediatricians, child psychologists, and developmental experts all believe that our current age is more stressful for children. According to one Harris poll, three of every four adults agree. Social change is too rapid, competition is too stiff, and expectations have risen too high. Added to the host of already oppressive burdens are children's insecurities about family stability. Children have a great stake in whether their parents stay together or not, but virtually no control over the issue.

CONTEMPORARY STRESSORS

Life is full of the daily *minor struggles*: ringing telephones, fighting children, traffic jams, and overdue bills. These chip away at our lightheartedness and erode our joy. Then there are the *major struggles*, such as the infirmities of aging, the loss of a job, or the divorce of your closest friends. These stressors don't chip, they detonate. We reel under the impact, and the pain is often palpable.

Our lives are riddled with stressors that intersect and cross-connect in a hundred different ways. It is often hard to separate them, to discern patterns. We feel ourselves being hit but cannot pin down the enemy. Yet identifying the stressors is an important task. Without correct isolation of the culprit, we will be ill-equipped to defend ourselves.

Our stress diet selects from a diverse menu. The following are some of the most prominent items.

Change—Do not underestimate it. We pay a price for each change we must adapt to. The Life Change Index is one scale that quantifies change and assigns a corresponding health risk: The greater the change, the higher the risk. Yet how to control the pace of change has so far eluded us.

Mobility—Mobility is a subset of change. People move, for the most part, because of perceived advantages. Each move, however, entails an adaptation to the new environment (which is stressful) plus a severing of old ties (oftentimes even more stressful).

Expectations—Modernity has increased our expectations but has not permitted a commensurate ability to meet them. Frustration results. This might occur in athletic skill, academic performance, physical attractiveness, occupational prestige, family functioning, or fulfillment of "the good life."

Time pressure—The clock dominates our schedule as never before in history. We have more activities to arrive at and more deadlines to meet. Most of us are all too familiar with the feeling of panic as an appointed hour nears with work yet undone.

We are ruled not by the week or day but by the minute. Margin would like to help free us from the reign of the clock but so far has had little cooperation from us.

Work — For many, distress and work are the same word. There is, for example, the Boston obstetrician who left his practice and opened a laundromat instead. Or the commercial airline pilot who, after waiting in line to take off, taxied back to the terminal, walked off the plane, and quit. Or the advertising salesman who shouted so loudly at his boss that he punctured a lung.

We change jobs more frequently, and we rotate more shifts. We have more deadlines yet less control. "The pressured job pace has caused thousands of males to 'outrun their hearts,'" comments sociologist Jon Johnston.[13]

Control — Stress can be successfully managed if we have control over what is happening. If the situation is beyond our influence, however, frustration leads to psychic or physical damage.

Fear — Some researchers believe fear to be the root cause of all stress reaction. We have many reasons for our insecurities: pressured deadlines, fragile job futures, economic vulnerability, loss of control, conditional relationships, overloaded lives.

Relationships — The intact, supportive relationships we all require for healthy living have dissipated under the tutelage of progress. The family has been systematically dismantled, and at the same time, long-term friendships are increasingly rare. Too often, "negative people" appear, unbidden, to take their place. "Negative people are the worst energy drains of all because they take away your enthusiasm, shoot down your ideas, chip away at your self-confidence and leave you feeling weak and drained," notes wellness expert Dr. Ann Tyndall.[14]

Competition — Our modern world is an overly competitive place in which to live and work. When we couple a win-lose format with a pyramidal system, the winner gloats while the multitude of losers try to deal with the stress of not measuring up.

Overload — Overloading is a widespread stressor as yet invisible to most. The entity of concern is not what we are overloaded with, but overload itself. More on this in the next chapter.

Illness and death — As we live to increasingly older ages, we are susceptible to more illness. These are often chronic diseases, causing disability and pain while straining financial resources. Many fear being old and sickly more than they fear death — not only for their own sake but also for the sake of their families.

The death of a family member is another profound stressor. Studies of the surviving spouse have consistently revealed prolonged depression of not only the emotions but also the immune system. In days past, sickness and death were often accepted as "the will of God" and as such directed us to His comfort. Today, our expectations point us in other directions, and profound stress often results.

Frustration, anger—Perhaps the greatest emotional stressors are frustration and anger. These block our ability to use stress in a positive manner and virtually assure painful and destructive results at some level. It is therefore wise to scout society's landscape for their presence.

While it is important to identify these stressors for the purposes of understanding, it is equally important to reintegrate them into life and then analyze the effect of combined stressors. The whole is greater than the sum of the parts. We might be able to adapt successfully to one or two assaults on our internal response mechanism. When six or eight major stressors compound the challenge, however, our chances of success are diminished. Yet multiple stressors all at once are what our culture throws at us. Little wonder we see dysfunction all around.

CHARRED BACON

Stressors not successfully handled can have serious consequences, with effects persisting long after the stressor has ceased to act. Such symptoms often result in a visit to the doctor's office.

The effects of stress disorders are noticed in three spheres: psychological, physical, and behavioral. Burnout is a pervasive disturbance in all three areas.

Psychological Symptoms

Most people are aware of the link between stress and our emotional response. The other secondary physical and behavioral effects are somewhat more obscure and need to be taught, but the emotional/psychological effects are self-evident. The psyche, it seems, is the point of entry for the stress virus, with symptoms including:

- Depression, withdrawal
- Mental fatigue
- Chronic anxiety
- Feeling that things are slipping out of control

- Negative thinking
- Difficulty making decisions
- Exaggerated worrying
- Paranoia
- Impatience
- Forgetfulness
- Apathy
- Confusion
- Anger and hostility

Physical Symptoms

Our response to stressors takes place not only at the thought level but also at the organ and even the cellular level. "The brain writes prescriptions for the body," explains Dr. Eliot. Driven by the alerted nervous system and a host of biochemical messengers, our body is charged for the assault but has no foe to fight. Symptoms we might experience include:

- Stimulation of the cardiovascular system—rapid pulse, palpitations, increased blood pressure, chest pain, arrhythmias (can be fatal)
- Gastrointestinal overactivity—hyperacidity, ulcers, irritable bowel, diarrhea
- Tightening of the muscles—especially of the head and neck or low back
- Headaches
- Weight changes—food used as a tranquilizer
- Increase in infections and cancer—compromised immune system
- Rashes, itching
- Insomnia
- Unexplained fatigue
- Shortness of breath
- Perspiration or cold, clammy hands
- Nervous tics, tremors
- Teeth and jaw-clenching

Behavioral Symptoms

What our mind and body experience, our behaviors often express. If, for example, we are psychologically depressed and physically exhausted, we will begin to act in a manner consistent with these symptoms. These behaviors include:

- Irritation with friends, colleagues
- Bossiness
- Outbursts of temper
- Withdrawal, detachment
- Change in sleep pattern
- Change in eating pattern
- Change in sexual drive
- Accident proneness
- Reckless driving
- Inappropriate laughing
- Reversals in usual behavior
- Compulsive shopping
- Increased use of tranquilizers, alcohol, cigarettes

Burnout

Next time you fry bacon, leave one strip in the pan for an extra fifteen minutes. Then pick it up and look it over. This shriveled, charred, stiffened strip is analogous to what a person experiences in burnout. Some of the symptoms and attitudes of burnout include:

- Exhaustion
- Depression
- Irritability, hostility
- Paranoia, suspiciousness
- Withdrawal, noninvolvement
- Multiple psychosomatic illnesses
- "I can't stand this any more."
- "I dread going to work."
- "I'd rather be alone."
- "I don't care."
- *"I hate it!"*

STRESS REDUCTION, STRESS MANAGEMENT

Avoiding all stress is not an alternative to our overloaded condition. Those who have *no* stress in their lives—no novelty, no challenge, no change—are as miserable as those who have too much. "The majority equally dislike a lack of stress and an excess of it," points out Selye. "Hence each of us must carefully analyze himself and try to find the particular stress level at which he feels most comfortable, whatever occupation he selects. Those who do not succeed in this analysis will either suffer the distress of having nothing worthwhile to do or of being constantly overtaxed by excessive activity."15

There are two broad recommendations for the overly stressed:

❯ Stress reduction—decrease your stress load.
❯ Stress management—learn how to control your stress response.

Although most books dwell on stress management, I strongly feel both approaches are important. Margin can assist with either approach but is much more closely related to reduction.

Stress reduction often requires courage. It may mean rearranging life: getting a different job, living with less income, establishing boundaries (saying no), creating some margin. Once you have identified the stress dynamics in your life, it is important to remedy the destruction, even though at times the remedy might require radical change.

Stress management is accomplished by realizing we do have some control in our response to stressors. We can learn how to relax in the midst of strife, to slow our heart rate, to talk to ourselves positively, to behave rationally. It is not always easy, but it is possible.

Below are suggestions for decompressing stress-filled lives. These are not dreamed-up platitudes but the recommendations of researchers and experts in the field.

❯ Practice gratitude.
❯ Generate goodwill.
❯ Do volunteer work.
❯ Set realistic expectations.
❯ Laugh ("inner jogging").
❯ Play.
❯ Meditate.
❯ Pray.
❯ Accept what cannot be changed.
❯ Avoid frustration.
❯ Exercise ("sweat to forget").

❱ Learn to relax ("behavioral aspirin").
❱ Put more control in your life.
❱ Reconcile conflict in personal relationships (confession/
   forgiveness).
❱ Above all, avoid anger and the desire for revenge.

A DOSE OF MARGIN

Some in our midst (usually our leaders) quickly grow impatient with
all this stress talk and would instead challenge the weak to quit all the
whining and get with the program. They love stress and seem to thrive
on marginless living. The driven live on the edge and wouldn't have
it any other way. They eat, breathe, and sleep adrenaline. Productivity
is the goal, not living. Margin is a hole to be plugged as quickly as
possible.

   Yet even these racehorses have their limits, as they will eventually
learn. And when they do, I hope they will not underestimate the stress-
reducing value of taking a dose of margin against the pain.

FIVE

The Pain of Overload

"It hurts," said David Tate.

As a mere 180-pound member of the Chicago Bears' defensive secondary, one would think he was discussing taking a hit on the playing field. Instead, the pain comes from being "splashed" in the 1990 Bears' "Locker Room Wars."

The Bears' huge defensive linemen and the smaller defensive backs have a good-natured but weighty battle of intimidation going on. Following an exchange of verbal assaults, the big guys start moving, trying to circle and isolate one of the "Brat Pack." On most occasions, the smaller, faster defensive backs are able to strike and quickly escape. But if captured, they pay a huge price. Tate was dropped to the ground and the 320-pound William "Refrigerator" Perry collapsed on top of him. Then 270-pound Richard Dent, 275-pound Dan Hampton, and 270-pound Steve McMichael jumped on top—1,135 pounds of pain.

"I don't think they know how heavy they are," said Tate. "Once you've gotten splashed, you avoid it at all costs—even if it means backing down."[1] "Splashing" is perhaps the consummate picture of overload.

73

Overloading is a painful occurrence. Yet, in one form or another, it happens daily to nearly every one of us.

A MATTER OF THRESHOLDS

The spontaneous tendency of our culture is to inexorably add detail to our lives: one more option, one more problem, one more commitment, one more expectation, one more purchase, one more debt, one more change, one more job, one more decision. We must now deal with more "things per person" than at any other time in history. Yet one can comfortably handle only so many details in his or her life. *Exceeding this threshold will result in disorganization or frustration*. It is important to note here that the problem is not in the "details." The problem is in the "exceeding." This is called overloading.

Overloading occurs whenever the requirements upon us exceed that which we are able to bear. For example, camels are able to carry great loads. If, however, a mere straw is placed on a camel maximally loaded down, its back will be broken. The back is not broken by the proverbial straw. It is broken by overload.

Breathing and hyperventilation serve as another example. Necessary to sustain life, breathing is obviously good for us. If, however, we start breathing thirty times a minute instead of sixteen, we hyperventilate and become sick. Air and breathing are not the villains here. Too much, however, causes overloading. A threshold is exceeded.

THE LAW OF LIMITS

As we have already discussed, all systems have limits. Human beings are systems, and as such have physical, performance, emotional, and mental limits. To understand the concept of overloading, it is helpful to understand the law of limits, for overloading is a phenomenon of limits. "Researchers," according to sociologist Alvin Toffler, "strongly agree on two basic principles: first, that man has limited capacity; and second, that overloading the system leads to serious breakdown of performance."[2]

Physical Limits are easiest to recognize. A room of a given size can hold only so much furniture. We might comfortably put ten pieces of furniture in the room and possibly even thirty. But we would not try to put one thousand tables and chairs in a room too small to hold them.

This would overload the room in a visibly foolish way.

To cite another example, engineers study stress loads when designing bridges, and we often see "Load Limit Ahead" signs as we approach such a bridge. A forty-ton truck would not attempt to cross a bridge limited to twenty-ton vehicles. Because such physical limits are visible and measurable, humans do not commonly overload in these areas. Few attempt to swim the Pacific Ocean or to climb the stairs of the Sears Tower.

Performance limits are related to physical limits but also introduce the factor of will. The endpoint is not as objectively defined, and we often are not quite as willing to accept the fact that there are limits. This is where stress fractures come from—people want to push themselves just beyond the limit of breakdown.

Figure 5.1 - Human Function Curve

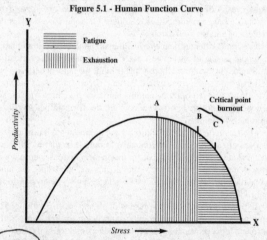

Sleep might serve as another example. We all need sleep. But how much? Those who regard the need for sleep as a sign of weakness might try to push the limit and see how few hours they can get along on. Four hours a night? Three? Yes, you can sleep three hours a night, but you are impinging on a limit, and there will be painful consequences.

The human function curve (figure 5.1) illustrates the principle well.[3] Our performance increases with increasing demand and increasing effort—but only up to a point. Once we reach our limit, fatigue sets in, followed quickly by exhaustion and collapse.

Emotional limits are even more vague. How much straining can the psyche withstand before being overloaded? Physically, most of us could carry a one-hundred-pound person on our back. But we could not carry ten. We would not even try. Our refusal would not be viewed as a statement against carrying people but rather as a statement about physical limits, about overload and pain.

What is clear to us in the context of physical limits is less clear regarding emotional limits. To extend the analogy of carrying people into the emotional context, you might be able to emotionally "carry" one person. But what about five? ten? one hundred? Where should we draw the line? What boundaries should we establish? One of the most serious causes of emotional and spiritual struggles experienced by Christians today, according to psychologist Dr. John Townsend, is the "problem of unclear boundaries."[4]

The limits of emotional overloading are hard to define, and helping people is one of the easiest places where emotional overload is manifested. "In a culture where whirl is king, we must understand our emotional limits," asserts Richard Foster. "Ulcers, migraines, nervous tension, and a dozen other symptoms mark our psychic overload. We are concerned not to live beyond our means financially; why do it emotionally?"[5]

Mental limits are as difficult to define as emotional limits, but the existence of such limits is indisputable. "Could it be that by information overload and complexity, or by mechanical actions whose speed outpaces human response time, technologies are 'stretching the mind beyond the end of its tether'?" asks science policy analyst Edward Wenk, Jr.[6]

Information overload soon results in mental short-circuiting. The memory banks are full, and the mind shuts down for a rest. Air-traffic controllers are a prime example of too much mental stress too fast, and burnout on this job is routine. "Man has committed himself so deeply to constructing ever larger and more complex artificial systems," explains Aurelio Peccei, founder of the Club of Rome, "that it has become difficult for him to control them." Peccei continues by emphasizing, "No one can say with certainty; but psychic and social damage . . . warn us that inner limits have perhaps been surpassed, that our minds and our nervous systems cannot take much more overloading."[7]

"I CAN DO ALL THINGS . . ."?

In running and swimming, we continue to break old records nearly every year. Runners keep running faster, and swimmers keep swimming faster. But there must be an end to this, true? We cannot run the mile in one second. Neither will it ever be possible for anyone to run it in one minute. There is a built-in physiological limit beyond which records will rarely be broken.

So it is in life. We are not infinite. The day does not have more than twenty-four hours. We do not have an inexhaustible source of human energy. We cannot keep running on empty. Limits are real, and despite what some stoics might think, limits are not even an enemy. Overloading is the enemy.

Some will respond: "I can do all things through Christ who strengthens me."[8] Can you? Can you fly? Can you go six months without eating? Neither can you live a healthy life chronically overloaded. God did not intend this verse to represent a negation of life-balance. Jesus did not heal all, He did not minister to all, He did not visit all, and He did not teach all. He did not work twenty-hour ministry days.

It is God the Creator who made limits, and it is the same God who placed them within us for our protection. We exceed them at our peril.

LIMITS AND THE SATURATION POINT

Often we do not feel overload sneaking up on us. We instead feel energized by the rapidity of events and the challenge of our full days. Then one day we find it difficult to get out of bed. Life has become a weight. Perhaps it is in our parenting that we feel exhausted. Perhaps it is that second job we took to pay for the new car. Or perhaps we can't bear to hear of yet one more people problem.

What happened to change our enthusiasm to pain, and why did the change come upon us so unexpectedly? Not all threshold limits are appreciated as we near them, and it is only in exceeding them that we suddenly feel the breakdown.

According to electronic systems expert Roberto Vacca, the development of many modern systems exhibits, "the character of continuous and exponential growth, and their variation obeys a well-known mathematical law, the law of the phenomenon of growth in the presence of limiting factors. At first the effect of these limiting factors is hardly noticeable, but there comes a time when they begin to predominate and to produce the phenomenon known as 'saturation.' . . . Often the effect of the limiting factors is not felt gradually: it may be felt all of a sudden."[9]

Returning to the high school chemistry lab may help us better understand the principle of saturation. Let's begin with a flask of hot water. Next, let's dissolve as much of a chemical salt into the hot water as we possibly can. Spoonful after spoonful disappears easily into solution. Then, perhaps with the fiftieth spoonful, all of a sudden no more dissolves. Instead, the added salt just sinks to the bottom of the flask. At the "saturation point," the water was unable to make any more salt go into solution. The tenth spoonful dissolved nicely, as did the twentieth, as did the forty-ninth. Then, bump, we hit a limit.

Next, let's take the experiment one step further. Add a little more hot water to the flask until all the salt is completely dissolved. Now let it cool. As we cool the salt water down, the solution finds itself in a dilemma. Cold water can't hold as much dissolved salt in solution as hot water can. But neither can the salt find a way to precipitate out. The cold water is stuck, holding more dissolved salt than it is supposed to be able to. It is "supersaturated."

A very interesting thing happens if we introduce a salt crystal into this supersaturated solution. Suddenly, all kinds of crystals precipitate out. The solution knew it was overloaded, and the added salt crystal allowed it the opportunity to dump its overload.

Now let's apply these principles to our own experience. We keep adding more and more to our lives—details, activities, decisions, debt, etc. At first, they all "dissolve" into the flow. But then we reach a limit and nothing more seems to dissolve. We are "saturated."

Some, however, won't accept saturation. In order to force more in they turn up the heat. By working harder, talking quicker, and running faster they are able to dissolve a little more. But when they slow down again, they find themselves "supersaturated."

When our lives are saturated, we dare not take on anymore. Have you ever been there? And when our lives are *super*saturated, we dare not stop to even think about it. Otherwise one piece of well-timed salt falling into the wound might cause us to precipitate out all over the place.

Most of us can identify with one of these two conditions: saturated or supersaturated. We have dissolved as much into our lives as they can possibly hold—and, in some instances, even more than they can hold.

At first we didn't realize this was happening because each new thing seemed to dissolve so nicely. But then we came to the fiftieth spoonful—and bump—we hit our limit.

It is similar to the straw that broke the camel's back. The camel was doing fine until. . . . Most times we seem to be bearing up fine under the heavy load, but then something snaps. When you feel such a snap, understand it for what it is. Don't blame your work, your friends, or your children. Blame overload.

EVERYWHERE AND INESCAPABLE

While working at a hospital in central India I observed that poverty was omnipresent and inescapable. The poor were at the train station, alongside the road, and on every city street. Even the wealthiest people could not isolate themselves from the presence of poverty.

Overload in the United States is similar to poverty in India. It is everywhere and it is inescapable. Everyone I know suffers from overload in at least some form. For one person it might be traffic overload, for another change overload, and for a third it might be expectation overload. For most of us, it is a combination of multiple overloads, configured according to the context of our individual lives. Wherever we go, the syndrome has gone before us. It is not chosen. It is simply a part of living, compliments of progress.

THE VARIED WAYS WE HURT

Despite its universality, the syndrome manifests itself differently in each person. Everyone is overloaded, but the degrees vary. Also, each person has a different tolerance. The threshold point where breakdown begins to occur varies from person to person. But I have not yet met a person who could tolerate ever-escalating overload without eventually feeling its painful weight. We are all camels awaiting the straw.

If the overloaded seek professional help, what kinds of manifestations of the disorder might the counselors discover? Some victims of overload experience *anxiety*. The load is simply too much to manage, and tranquilizers are a hoped-for solution. If the load is not lightened soon, however, *breakdown* can occur. "When our bodies and feelings can't cope any longer with the demands made upon them, when the overload becomes too great, their only course of action is to shut everything down," explains Robert Banks. "For many people, physical or nervous breakdown is the only way out of the impasse."[10]

Others manifest *hostility*, blaming their overload on those around them. The nightly news details the results: shootings on the freeway due to traffic overload; rudeness in big cities blamed on people overload; brawls in the NBA because of competition overload.

Some personality types lapse into *depression* when overloaded. They might feel hostile, but the hostility is directed inward. Having failed their own expectations and the expectations of others, they withdraw into a fog of gloom.

Many develop *resentment*, often toward their jobs. I love medicine, but the one thing that takes away the love faster than anything else is overloading. Then work becomes an enemy. A physician friend was recently lamenting his continual twelve-hour days. "No, your ulcer isn't bleeding," he moaned silently while listening to the patient describe his stomach pain. "It can't be. It just can't be!"

EASILY MISDIAGNOSED

Because the overload syndrome expresses itself differently in different people, we must be careful with our judgments. Misdiagnosis is common. As a matter of fact, I would say that misdiagnosis is the rule. The overload syndrome is often inaccurately labeled weakness, apathy, or lack of commitment.

For example, I recently read an article very critical of the phrase, "I'm too busy." The author, a nationally known spiritual leader (whom, incidentally, I greatly respect), was quite upset at hearing this excuse so frequently. Saying you're too busy is the perfect cover, he wrote, because the pretense of busyness is very difficult to counter. After all, how can someone tell you, "No, you *aren't* too busy. You're just using that as an excuse"? The excuse of busyness, he concluded, should be recognized for what it is — the problem of not caring enough.

There is obvious frustration in these accusations. But in many cases his clinical opinion will have missed the diagnosis. The problem is indeed busyness, not apathy. The problem is overload. It is real, and it is here to stay. Let's blame it, not each other.

Each of us needs to seek his or her own level of involvement and not let the standard be mandated by the often exorbitant expectations of others. Some around us who are much more involved than we are may not understand why we choose to hold back. Others might be much less involved than we are—we assume they don't care. We must understand that everyone has a different tolerance for overload and a different threshold level when breakdown begins to occur. It is important for us to set people free to seek their own level.

When given this freedom, some unfortunately will still use the overload principle as an excuse for laziness. Here we return to the accusations of apathy leveled by the frustrated leader. This will inevitably happen. Exploitation will occur by some who claim to be overloaded but instead are simply undisciplined. In this case I may wish to employ a large measure of grace as I talk to them about their level of involvement. But as soon as I condemn them, judge them, or try to control them, I violate who they are before God. Making them accountable to Him does not mean that they must then do as I wish them to do, to live their lives as I think their lives should be lived. My own spiritual walk in the midst of my own overload is enough of a burden to keep me fully occupied.

In my experience, the greater problem in our society, including the Christian community, is not the lack of accountability but the desire to control other people's lives. It is better to not judge the sluggard than it is to mistakenly judge the already overloaded. When people are overloaded, the last thing they need is the additional burden of our reproof. So if we err, at least let us err on the side of grace.

UNPRECEDENTED

Hasn't overload always been with us? No.

An important thesis of this book is that we live in an unprecedented age. Our modern day is not only qualitatively different from any other but also quantitatively different. Future history books will need to use a different vocabulary to describe contemporary phenomena, and prominent among these words will be "exponential," "limits," "thresholds," and "overload."

Overload is a matter of mathematics, and as already shown in chapter 3, today's math computes differently. If in 1960 you dumped one tablespoon of gasoline on my front yard, chances are I would not be upset. I probably would not have even noticed the spot. If you returned every year and doubled your dumping, by 1968 the tablespoon would have grown to a gallon. At that point I would be asking you questions. When you showed up in 1990 with a tank truck and dumped four million gallons, I would probably have become hostile.

This example once again illustrates the dramatic principle of exponentiality. Under the power of exponential influence, matters erupt—they explode. But let's look at this same illustration taken linearly. If the amount of gasoline was only increased by one tablespoon per year instead of doubled, then by 1990 the amount dumped would only be two cups. I would still have a lawn, and we would probably still be friends.

Life, change, history—all are unfolding exponentially. We are not dealing with two cups but rather with four million gallons. Threshold limits are being reached with frightening suddenness. Overload is happening overnight.

Many people, however, are trapped in a linear paradigm, a mindset that can only see straight ahead. While they understand our qualitative changes, they have failed to comprehend the quantitative nature of "future shock." As long as this is the case, the reasons for our contemporary problems will remain invisible to them.

INVISIBLE KILLERS

Ignaz Philipp Semmelweiss, a nineteenth-century surgeon, is one of my heroes. Many of his obstetrical patients in Vienna were dying of postpartum infections, and Semmelweiss was not only puzzled but deeply disturbed. Finally an observation struck him. The mothers who developed the fever and died were the same ones being examined by physicians just returning from performing autopsies on recently deceased victims. It appeared something was being carried from the morgue to the postpartum ward and was killing patients. He had all the doctors under his authority begin washing their hands in a solution of chlorinated lime after performing autopsies. The infections stopped.

What an exciting discovery! The beginnings of a secret had been unlocked, and lives were saved. Semmelweiss told his other colleagues and suggested they also wash their hands following autopsies.

The response was brutal. How could physicians' hands carry invisible agents of death? Semmelweiss was scorned and rejected, and he ended his days prematurely in an insane asylum. Meanwhile, mothers continued to die. Shortly thereafter, Pasteur and Lister proved the existence and contagiousness of microbes, and only then was the Austrian surgeon vindicated.

Overload, limits, exponentiality—these too are invisible killers. I see the carnage in my friends, in my community, in my church, in my work, and, yes, in my own life. I see the damage in our nation and in the world. Yet we have no shortage of scorners who say, "Life is no different. We have always had troubles." Trapped in a paradigm that wears blinders, we continue to strain under the load. Finally, inevitably, someday we will understand. But in the meantime, what needless pain we bear.

SPECIFICS OF THE SYNDROME

The following are abbreviated discussions of the overload syndrome in its varied manifestations. Perhaps some of the distresses in your life will be clarified as you read. Yet as relevant as the specifics are, the overarching theme of this chapter focuses not on those specifics but on the parent pain: overload.

Activity overload—Booked up weeks in advance, we are a busy people. In an attempt to squeeze more things in, we try to do two or three at the same time. Activity overload takes away the pleasure of anticipation and the delight of reminiscence.

Change overload—"Nothing defines our age more than the furious and relentless increase in the rate of change," summarizes historian Arthur M. Schlesinger, Jr.[11] For millennia upon millennia, change was slow, controlled, assessable; now it convulses at warp speed.

Choice overload—In 1978, there were 11,767 items in the average supermarket; today the number is 24,531—including the 186 different choices of breakfast cereal we found in our local grocery store. Purchase a satellite dish and choose from 1,500 movies every month. But realize, warns Toffler, "We are, in fact, racing toward 'overchoice.'"[12]

Commitment overload—Most of us have more commitments than time. "Some people can't say no," observes Dr. J. Grant Howard. "They take on too many relationships and too many responsibilities. They enroll in too many courses, hold down too many jobs, volunteer for too many tasks, make too many appointments, serve on too many committees, have too many friends. They are trying to be all things to all men all at once all by themselves."[13]

Competition overload—Few things have been as consistently emphasized in the "American dream" as the virtues of competition. Though its effects are widely evident in business, in academia, and in politics, this mania is perhaps best illustrated in athletics. One boy had a wrestling record of 30-1 and won the state tournament. In the first grade.

Debt overload—Currently every sector of society is awash in red ink. Concerning our national debt, "We're institutionally incapable of saying 'No,'" complains Senator Alan Simpson. In our foreign trade deficit, we are now the world's largest debtor nation. Corporate and personal consumer debt levels are functioning more like anchors than catalysts.

Decision overload—Every year we have more decisions to make and less time to make them. The small decisions don't cost us much but are objectionable by virtue of sheer numbers: Which soda? Which pizza toppings? Mint toothpaste or tartar control gel?

Along with these trivial decisions have come a myriad of relatively new choices that are not at all easy: whether or not to have children and how many; whether to move or change jobs; whether both spouses should work outside the home; whether to put Grandma into the nursing home. Trivial or tough, having too many decisions to make in too short a time is vintage overload.

Education overload—Each decade the educational level of the general populace rises. While agreeing that education is important, I must ask the heretical question: How much education is enough? Information proliferates far faster than our ability to assimilate it. So, although we study more and more, we are always falling farther behind.

Expectation overload—Expectation overload is one of the most difficult to control—and one of the most dangerous. Nevertheless, a clear result of our affluent communications age is the steady rising of expectations. "Your world should know no boundaries," advertises one investment firm. "If you can dream it, you can do it. Now there's no limit to your ability," claims an insurance company.

Fatigue overload—We are a tired society. Even our leisure is often exhausting. With generator indicators continuously pointing to "discharge," it is little wonder our batteries are drained. Our weary, withered state is not God's plan. Fatigue overload attacks our emotions, leaving us self-protective; it attacks our bodies, leaving us weak; and it attacks our relationships, leaving us isolated. That we are fatigued is not the fault of activities or friends—it is the fault of overload.

Hurry overload—Haste is a modern ailment. It also is fashionably

American. Our lives are nonstop, lived at a breathless pace. We walk fast, talk fast, eat fast, and then excuse ourselves by saying, "I must run." Time urgency is a national emblem. "Hastiness and superficiality— these are the psychic diseases of the twentieth century," accuses Aleksandr Solzhenitsyn.[14] But, as the Finnish proverb teaches, God did not create hurry.

Information overload—A single edition of the *New York Times* contains more information than a seventeenth-century Britisher would encounter in a lifetime. In the field of health, I would have to read 250 articles every day to stay current. If you add the 30,000 scientific journals in the world to the 22 million books in the Library of Congress, it is little wonder one observer advised, "'Print control' is probably more urgent than birth control."[15]

Media overload—Ninety-eight percent of American homes have television, with the average family having two sets turned on seven hours a day. We buy more books per capita than ever before and can choose from forty-five thousand new titles every year. Seventeen hundred daily newspapers keep us informed. But how does one read a three-and-one-half-inch thick Sunday paper?

Ministry overload—"Christians will run you into the ground," someone once commented. Seeing the great number of needs, pastors and laypeople often place unbearable demands upon themselves—and others. "I think churches may tear a family apart by overloading and overburdening," observes one family-ministry pastor.[16]

Pastors, too, are at risk: "Many ministers today are headed toward the mental, physical, and spiritual salvage yard because they expect too much of themselves," says one physician who counsels pastors. "And most do not have a clear idea of the forces driving them to that tragic end."[17]

Noise overload—Noise "is perhaps the most pervasive and insidious pollution in our industrial world," declares Theodore Berland, author of *The Fight for Quiet*.[18] "Fifty percent of the U.S. population is exposed every day to noise that interferes with speech or sleep," according to Rutgers University's Noise Technical Assistance Center.[19]

People overload—"I would rather sit on a pumpkin and have it all to myself, than be crowded on a velvet cushion," confessed Thoreau. Personally, as a fellow introvert, I agree with him. But such is not the world we live in. God has given us people to love and appreciate. Many people. *Billions* of people. Now every time the world turns, two hundred fifty thousand more people are added. Each of us is exposed to a greater number of people than ever before. Socialization and community are wonderful. Unfortunately, such crowding often leads to depersonalization, rudeness, and violence.

Pollution overload—Billions of tons of sulfur dioxide, nitrogen oxide, carbon monoxide, smog, smoke, ozone, soot, dusts, carbon dioxide, pesticides, fertilizers, lead, PCBs, asbestos, and thousands of assorted chemicals all complicate our air, soil, and water. A little pollution will not hurt us, as the earth, like its Creator, is willing to forgive. Pollution overload is another matter.

Possession overload—We have more "things per person" than any other nation in history. Closets are full, storage space is used up, and cars can't fit into garages. Having first imprisoned us with debt, possessions then take over our houses and occupy our time. This begins to sound like an invasion. Everything I own owns me. Why would I want more?

Problem overload—The process of evolving civilization has not succeeded in diminishing our problem load. As we have already seen, we solve one problem only to create another one—or two or three. A problem pile can be worked on. But overloading has turned the pile into a mountain.

Technology overload—It has been estimated that the average person must learn to operate twenty thousand pieces of equipment. Some elicit our gratitude, others our exasperation. Engineer Donald A. Norman criticizes gadgets which are "infuriating by design": "'You would need an engineering degree from MIT to work this,' someone once told me, shaking his head in puzzlement over his brand-new digital watch. Well, I have an engineering degree from MIT. Give me a few hours and I can figure out the watch. But why should it take hours?"[20]

Traffic overload—Roadways are called "clogways," our national flower has become the cloverleaf, and rush hour is neither rush nor an hour. Cars are multiplying twice as fast as people. Americans drive nearly two trillion miles a year. The word *travel* comes originally from travail, and we are rediscovering its true meaning.

Waste overload—"Without further action, New Jersey could actually choke on its own garbage," proclaimed Governor Thomas Kean in 1987. The nation's fourteen thousand landfills are rapidly filling up. It seems most people again assume that the world is flat and that we can dispose of our waste by pushing it over the edge.

Small amounts we could bury in the backyard. But garbage piled this high can't be dumped anywhere without interfering with flight patterns.

Work overload—Work is God-ordained. Work overload, however, was not part of the original plan. Yet every morning millions of Americans head drudgingly to an exhausting work schedule that leaves them stressed and worn-out. Because there are more things to buy at higher prices, people work longer. Yet somehow they manage to get deeper into debt. Now Mom and Dad both work outside the home. Total family work-hours often exceed eighty a week, and we find yet another family "over-working and under-relating."[21]

WHY DO WE DO IT?

If overloading causes such widespread social and personal dysfunction, why do we do it?

One reason we so casually overload is lack of understanding. Because it is a relatively new phenomenon, we don't see it even when it has us by the throat.

Second, some accept overload uncritically because of conscientiousness. "It is our duty to do all that we can," they reason. But how does one define "all that we can"? A line must be drawn this side of overload if we are to stay healthy. Drawing such a line causes the overly conscientious to feel guilt. I appreciate those who have this sense of duty. Nevertheless, chronic overloading is not God's will. It is okay to draw a line.

Yet a third dynamic that inflicts overload on many unwilling victims is "follow the leader." Our economy and our society are run by the driven. They climb to positions of power by force and then demand the same overcommitment from those under them. That our leaders should require of us an honest hard day's work is not disputed. But when they require overloading that destroys the worker, then they have exceeded the moral mandate for leadership.

In all that precedes, I *am not* suggesting that we should strive to have a pain-free, stress-free life. The Christian walk will always be full of problems and work. Many times we must be prepared to suffer willingly. What I *am* suggesting, however, is that given the ubiquity of overload, we need to choose carefully *where* our involvement should come. We must not allow ourselves to be hammered by distress in the many areas of life that have absolutely no *transcendent importance*. It is not the will of the Father for us to be so battered by the torment of our age. There must be a different way—a way that reserves our strength for higher battles. And indeed there is.

SETTING LIMITS

To date, people do not operate on the principle of overloading. Instead, they operate on the basis of "one more thing won't hurt." Yet this is only true if it is true. Once we are maximally loaded down, adding one more thing will hurt. The pain of overload is real pain.

Chronic overloading also has a negative effect on our spiritual lives. We have less time for prayer and meditation, less energy for service, and less interest in relationship.

If we don't move to establish effective priorities, overloading will continue to fill up our schedules and keep us captive. We must learn the art of setting limits. We must learn to accept the finality and nonnegotiability of the twenty-four-hour day. We must learn not to overdraw on our account of emotional energy. And we must learn to respect such limits in others.

Margin can teach us these things. Margin can restore to us that which has been taken away. It is an idea whose time has come.

PART TWO

THE PROBLEM: MARGIN

Margin

Despite its timeliness, few people are aware of the concept of margin. Not that the concept is inconsequential. Indeed, it is compellingly important. Nor is the concept difficult to understand. Quite the opposite, it is elementary. Rather, the reason margin has not become a household word is simply because it has not yet been properly introduced.

It is now time. For if today margin is useful, tomorrow it will be urgent. If today it is valuable, tomorrow it will be essential.

Although some people seem capable of thriving without margin, most of us find it a prerequisite for well-being. Margin grants freedom and permits rest. It nourishes both relationship and service. Spiritually, it allows availability for the purposes of God. From a medical point of view, it is health-enhancing. It is a welcome addition to our health formulary: Add a dose of margin and see if life doesn't come alive once again.

THE OPPOSITE OF OVERLOAD

Margin is the amount allowed beyond that which is needed. It is something held in reserve for contingencies or unanticipated situations.

Margin is the gap between rest and exhaustion, the space between breathing freely and suffocating. *It is the leeway we once had between ourselves and our limits*.

Margin is the opposite of overload. If we are overloaded we have no margin, or we have negative margin. If, however, we are careful to avoid overloading, margin reappears. Most people are not quite sure when they pass from margin to overload. Threshold points are not easily measurable and are also different for different people in different circumstances. We don't want to be underachievers (Heaven forbid!), so we fill our schedules uncritically. Options are as attractive as they are numerous, and we overbook.

If we were equipped with a flashing light to indicate "100 percent full," we could better gauge our capacities. But we don't have such an indicator light, and we don't know when we have overextended until we feel the pain. As a result, many people commit to a 120-percent life and wonder why the burden feels so heavy. It is rare to see a life prescheduled to only 80 percent, leaving a margin for responding to the unexpected that God sends our way.

POWER MINUS LOAD

One reason margin is easy to define is because the math involved is straightforward:

Power – Load = Margin

   Power is made up of factors such as skills, time, emotional strength, physical strength, spiritual vitality, finances, social supports, and education.

   Load combines internal factors (such as personal expectations and emotional disabilities) and external factors (such as work, relational problems and responsibilities, financial obligations, and civic involvement).[1]

When our load is greater than our power, we enter into negative margin status, that is, we are overloaded. Endured long-term, this is not a healthy state. Severe negative margin for an extended period of time is another name for burnout.

When our power is greater than the load, however, we have margin. Even a cursory examination of this formula reveals that to increase or the octogenarian being force-fed in the nursing home? By what economic and cognitive parameters do we measure their "progress"?

In our enthusiasm to improve material and cognitive performance, we neglected to respect the other more complex and less objective parameters along the way. The social, emotional, and spiritual contributions to our well-being were, and continue to be, overlooked and underestimated. Not only are they more difficult to measure, but we apparently believed they would simply "improve" along with everything else. Or else, in our rush for the future, we didn't care.

So when the family began to crumble, we did not know what to think of it. When mobility began to tear apart community, we took little notice. When psychological stress and pain appeared on nearly every doorstep, we attempted to invalidate it. Our paradigm does not know how to accommodate this type of data. If you are better off, then how can you be worse off? Since you have progressed, you cannot feel sick. As long as the stock market is up and houses are bigger, you must be doing well—even if you're not.

"All that 'endless progress' turned out to be an insane, ill-considered, furious dash into a blind alley," accuses Nobelist Aleksandr Solzhenitsyn.[15] Until we can find a way to integrate the social, emotional, and spiritual into our notion of progress, we are destined to race into one blind alley after another.

Did progress betray us? Not really. We should never have expected material and cognitive well-being to carry us very far. We should have known from the start there was more to life than that. Until we understand what progress is and isn't (that is, should be and can never be), we will remain trapped in a paradigm that is not taking us where we need to be going.

OUR SHARE OF THE BLAME

To lay all the blame for our considerable woes on progress is neither accurate nor fair. Humans are also culpable. Progress is only guilty of what it is guilty of; the rest of the blame belongs to us. If progress gave us the gun, we pulled the trigger. If progress gave us wealth, we contributed avarice. It was progress that showed us the atom, but we who dropped the bomb. Are we really building a better world—or simply nourishing evil?

By putting progress in the hands of our fallenness, we have magnified

Progress Leads to Stress

The automatic development of a society under the tutelage of progress leads to stress, overload, and complexity. This is closely related to the point made above, but distinct enough and important enough to warrant separate mention. I will explain more in the chapters that follow. For now, suffice it to say that progress, as currently defined and practiced in American culture, flows strongly in the direction of increased pressure on the individual and on the system.

Progress Has Unanticipated Consequences

We do not know what we do not know, and we cannot foresee the unforeseen. We can never fully anticipate the future—it will always hold surprises. Progress has been victimized by this improvidence and, at times, devastated by it. For example, we did not know acid rain would result from burning fossil fuels. We did not know mobility would disrupt family and community stability. We did not know inner-city housing projects would turn into ghetto war zones. We did not know thalidomide would deform babies. We did not invent suburbs to throw our traffic patterns into chaos.

"Many of the crises of the present have *positive* origins," explain scientists Mesarovic and Pestel in *Mankind at the Turning Point*. "They are consequences of actions that were, at their genesis, stimulated by man's best intentions."[14] Best intentions, however, do not guarantee problem-free outcomes. And because unanticipated consequences are so common and so vexatious, we can never fully trust even the brightest sounding intentions.

Progress Has Been Based on Faulty Premises

In its specifics, the definition of progress varies from culture to culture and from age to age. Within contemporary American society, however, our notion of progress was first defined and later dominated by money, technology, and education. Each of these areas is of value, but none of them cares much about our transcendent needs. That indifference constitutes a fatal flaw.

Americans have a widespread perception that inextricably associates our overall well-being with our material and cognitive status. This, in fact, is how we measure progress. If we earn a Ph.D., get a raise, and buy a new house, we are "better-off." But what about the depressed schoolteacher, the recently divorced executive, the suicidal adolescent, margin one need simply increase power or decrease load — or both.

Given that the formula is simple and the consequences of living without margin are painful, why is the concept not universally understood? The answer reveals a principle: not all societal pathogens are equally opaque. Or, in other words, the causes of some pains are more readily apparent than others.

THE SEMIVISIBLE

If starving, we need not be told that food is what we lack. If thirsty, we need not be told that water is what we desire. If sleep-deprived, we need not be told that sleep is what we yearn for. If exhausted from a thirty-mile walk, we need not be told that rest is what our body craves. If bankrupt, we need not be told that money is what we require.

Why, then, when we so desperately need margin in our lives, is it necessary to *explain* our need for it? Why don't we understand it by instinct?

In answering this question, it is helpful to note that some burdens and pains in life are visible while others are not. "Visible" means that they can be perceived with one of the five senses or they can be quantified, measured, or weighed. For example, if you smash your finger with a hammer, you do not have to guess about what hurts or why. Physical pains are obvious and visible. In much the same way, financial pains are usually visible. If the credit-card statement reveals a three-thousand-dollar debt, the source of your distress is not obscure.

Other pains, however, cannot be perceived by the senses in quite the same way; neither can they be weighed, measured, or quantified. They are invisible or, perhaps more accurately, semivisible. Emotional, psychological, social, relational, and spiritual pains often fit this description. The pain is real, to be sure. But the details of cause and effect are hard to sort out. It often requires months of introspection or counseling to clarify wounds in these areas.

In this same way, margin is semivisible. Living without it does not cause a sensory pain, but instead a deep-seated subjective ache. Because the ache and heaviness are only semivisible, the pain of marginless living is hard for us to talk about. We feel guilty and weak if we complain. We feel vulnerable to the slings and arrows of the contemptuously stoical. It is hard to justify our inner pains when we don't even know who the enemy is. How do we talk about our anguish when we don't have a vocabulary to use?

Living without margin has, to date, been unseen and unexplained—but not unfelt. Yet it is not buried so deeply that we must send the philosophers out to find it. Instead, it is common and universal enough that even a simple family doctor can explain the concept. And once explained, the fog lifts.

Very seldom do people attempt to refute the diagnosis. Instead, most say, "So that's the problem!" It is as if a switch is tripped in their understanding. Instantly, they have hope that their burden is finally being understood.

A MATTER OF THRESHOLDS

To further illustrate how this historical process of discovery happens, let's look briefly at the beginnings of stress research. Stress is similar to margin; both are threshold phenomena (a certain overloading limit must be reached before the consequences are felt) and both are semivisible (the causes are not readily apparent). Understanding how the awareness of stress was brought to light will help us to understand how this same process is now happening to margin.

Our great-grandparents did not go around complaining about how "stressed" they were. As a matter of fact, no one talked about stress until at least the 1950s. As noted in chapter 4, it was not until then that the concept was discovered and published by Dr. Selye. Now, however, every American knows about stress. People throw around the term as if it has always been a given, as if our widespread use of therapeutic language (now taken for granted) dated back to the crossing of the *Mayflower*. Most of us still do not know how to quantify stress—it is semivisible. But no one tries to refute it any more.

Stress is a threshold phenomenon. Until a certain level of change and adaptational demand was reached, no one was aware of it. Once that threshold was exceeded, however, stress was explained, understood, applied, and then canonized.

Margin is also a threshold phenomenon. It is so simple a concept that one wonders why we didn't see it before. But it did not appear on our pain agenda until a certain threshold was reached, namely, until progress overburdened us to such a degree that margin disappeared. At that point, the problem evolved rapidly from latency to anguish.

It is not that we need margin today but never had need of it before.

We have *always* had need of it. It is as basic a necessity as rest. It's just that the threshold had never been reached before, allowing us to discover our need.

Margin is simply an idea whose time has come—nothing more and nothing less. It is simple, fundamental, and easily accessible. And it is a friend whose company we would be wise to cultivate.

MARGIN: YESTERYEAR'S CHARM?

Margin was an unrecognized possession of the peoples of the past. Throughout most of the history of the world, margin existed in the lives of individuals as well as societies. There were no televisions to watch or phones to answer. There were no cars, and travel was seldom undertaken. Daily newspapers were unknown. The media could not broadcast the cluster of events taking place in town. Churches and communities did not offer twenty simultaneous programs. With no electricity to extend daylight, few suffered sleep deprivation. Time urgency, daily planners, and to-do lists had not yet been adopted by the masses.

Instead, by default rather than choice, people lived slower, more deliberate lives. They had time to help a neighbor. Their church and social activities more often drew them together than pulled them apart. The past might have been poor and deprived in many respects, but its people had margin.

Perhaps this is a key to understanding why the past often holds such charm. Surely we overrate its positives and, at the same time, overlook the hardships. Yet, one suspects there must be at least some substance to our widespread nostalgia. Those who dismiss the feelings of fondness we have for the past with a haughty sweep of the hand are not being careful enough.

It is intriguing to postulate that margin might be the unsuspected link. Without even knowing exactly what it is that we miss, we miss margin. As progress arrives, margin dissipates. Progress devours margin, and we yearn to have it back.

THE THIRD WORLD'S REMAINING TREASURE

To corroborate this hypothesis, we might compare life as it was lived in our past and the lifestyle we observe in developing countries today.

Conditions in Third-World countries are sad in many respects and sometimes even heart-rending. But after working in several of these countries, I am struck by the recurring impression that the people have margin. They sit and talk, they watch children play, they walk without hurry, and they sleep full nights.

Talk to those who have spent time in the Third World and see what they report. True, life there is often frustrating—and sometimes completely exasperating. Many of the modern conveniences are distressingly absent. But the slower pace is consistently commented upon, and almost always with affection.

Good friends of ours recently returned to the States after doing medical work in Mali, West Africa. They don't miss the sand and the heat. They don't miss the scorpions and the insects. They don't miss hepatitis and malaria. But they *do* miss Mali. Why? They miss their friends, both Malian and Western, and they miss the work there. But they also miss their margin. Take, for example, the evening ritual. Following dinner, the family retired to the courtyard of their home. There Mom pitched, Dad fielded, and the boys ran the bases. When this family returned to the States, their margin vanished about ten milliseconds after the plane touched down. And with it their evening courtyard baseball game.

Do you think they miss it?

Another friend from West Africa recently visited her ailing grandmother in the States. After the return flight to Burkina Faso, she wrote, "I loved going back to Georgia but was really struck by the fast pace that was everywhere. America is years ahead on progress but also on stress. The lifestyle here is slow and relaxing."

Do you think she missed it?

From across the continent comes a similar story: "I think back to the nine years our family enjoyed on the lower slopes of the Kilimanjaro in East Africa. There, while our work was sometimes tense, the pace surely resembled more a walk than a run. There were plenty of green trees to sit under and a conscience that allowed us to sit down under them," comments former missionary Mildred Tengbom. "We weren't constantly being told that our value depended on how 'active' or 'involved' we were."[2]

Now back in the States, do you think they miss it?

Africa, it seems, is wealthy in margin. More evidence comes from a surgeon who spent one year there.

All things considered I would have to say that it was much healthier for me living overseas. There are stresses, of course, but of a much different type and magnitude. . . .

   Although I do not consider myself a "workaholic," I do find it difficult to control the time I spend in my practice. Still, I thought I was reasonably happy until I found out how beneficial a "sabbatical" in Africa can be. . . . I wasn't exactly loafing, since I did nearly five hundred operations in that year, but I still had large amounts of free time to read, rest and play. . . .

   In the absence of television, telephones and shopping centers, the inner life gets some long-needed attention. . . . I often had time for a midday nap, to eat almost all meals with my family, and to enjoy having evenings and weekends relatively free as well. With a swimming hole nearby, complete with vine swing, and surrounded by a gorgeous tropical rain forest, we could always find fun things to do. . . . We played table games, assembled puzzles together, read nearly thirty books aloud, and did creative things such as handcrafts and art. . . . The leisure time also afforded the opportunity to meditate, listen to God more, and reflect on priorities and the direction my life should take.[3]

Do you think he misses it?

ISLAND LIVING

Several years ago, after the American intervention of 1983, our family went to the small Grenadian island of Carriacou to help Project Hope and the U.S. Agency for International Development bring medical care to its seven thousand people. One observer characterized the sleepy life on Carriacou and its capital city Hillsborough as follows: "Very little happens on Carriacou, and what does happen, happens slowly. Hillsborough bustles on Monday, when produce arrives, and on Saturday, mail day. Otherwise, this little town just gazes out to sea."

   The clinics were often full, but expectations were low, paperwork was humorously minimal, and complexity was nonexistent. We could perform no laboratory tests, order no X-rays or EKGs, and do no surgery. Yet, surprisingly, as the Carriacouans often observed: "Nothing works, but everything works out."

Although our stay there was relatively brief, as a family it was one of the most memorable experiences of our lives. We got up together, ate all our meals together, and often went swimming together. We captured tarantulas together and had crab races on our living room floor together. Perhaps most notably, it was the only time in our parenting when both Linda and I were able to tuck in and pray with our boys every night we were there.

Do you think we miss it?

In a *Journal of the American Medical Association* editorial, one physician fantasized about having the ability to prescribe such an island experience for his many frazzled patients:

> I have a fantasy about a deserted island. This island is temperate, is well provisioned with water, fruits, and vegetables, and perhaps has good fishing. A safe place but no communications, no people, maybe a dog or a goat, and no way off save by a visiting ship once a twelvemonth. . . .
>
> I can write the prescription, which reads:
>
> Rx:One deserted island
>   One year
> Sig:As directed
>   No refills
>
> Such a prescription could be life-giving, even lifesaving. A kind of Statue of Liberty for the weak, tired, and dizzy, for the yearning souls eager to be cocooned lest they break or dissolve, for those certain that life cannot be lived absent pills, lotions, potions, or salves.[4]

Margin as medicine. A prescription against the pain.

There are few claims the Third World can make of superiority in lifestyle to ours. Having margin, however, is one of them.

IMPORTATION CUSTOMS AND DUTY

To be sure, Third-World living does not assure margin. Missionaries, for example, are sometimes the most exhausted people you would ever want to meet. Rather than constituting evidence against the theory of margin, however, their experience only proves its validity and importance.

Oftentimes the reason these strong and highly motivated people wither under the immense load is not because the developing culture killed their altruism, but rather because they became victims of well-intended twentieth-century self-destruction. Sometimes we take our marginless living with us. When you combine missionary conscientiousness with imported Americanized schedules, and home-office expectations with Third-World need, climate, and disease, burnout is an ever-present risk.

The nationals down the street aren't plagued by the same dangerous busyness we see in some missionaries. It only occurs in the lives of those who have been culturally caught up in the idea that to honor God they have to be "all things to all men all at once all by themselves," to revisit Grant Howard's phrase. A national would never try to administer three different programs in three different locations on three different days in three different languages using three different pieces of technology that break down on three different voltages. (By the way, neither did the missionaries of fifty years ago.)

Nobody can keep running on empty. Let's stay busy to be sure. But together let's also develop the necessary theological underpinnings for margin that will allow us to accept its importance without guilt. For just as we need to eat and sleep, so we also need to breathe.

AVAILABILITY

Avid supporters of progress would probably be quite upset at any suggestion that Third-World cultures have some superior claims to ours. I can hear the rebuttal forming: "What an incredibly regressive idea! If you want to sit on a log all day and watch your children die of disease and your society penalized by ignorance, then go ahead. I'll stick with progress."

But to defend progress and its absence of margin is to presume that all that is good in life and all that God wants us to accomplish is possible only in a booked-up, highly efficient, often exhausted way of life. I do not believe this is true. His asking us to walk the second mile, to carry others' burdens, to witness to the Truth at any opportunity, and to teach our children when we sit, walk, lie, and stand all presuppose we have margin and that we make it available for His purposes. *Obedience to these commands is often not schedulable.*

Actually, margin is not a spiritual necessity. But availability is. God expects us to be available for the needs of others. And without margin, each of us would have great difficulty guaranteeing availability. Instead, when God calls, He gets the busy signal.

EFFECTS OF NO MARGIN

What would you think if this page had no margins? What would be your opinion of the publishers if they tried to cram the print top to bottom and side to side so that every blank space was filled up? The result would be aesthetically displeasing, hard to comprehend, and probably even chaotic. Like some of our lives.

Yet even if we agree that margin is a good idea, for most of us it seems an unaffordable luxury. We don't really desire to be overdrawn on our personal reserves. It's just that we can't seem to keep it from happening. Overbooking overpowers. There is so much to do and so much to buy. Troublingly, each succeeding year the problem only gets worse.

The effects of no margin are familiar to us all: people who are harried, more concerned with personal sanity than with service to the needs of others; people who have no financial margin, painfully uninterested in hearing of yet another "opportunity" to give. Such people are no longer concerned with building a better world. Instead, they simply want to survive another day. Such people are no longer motivated to meet the needs of others. Instead, they simply want to escape their suffocating schedules. Overworked and overwhelmed victims occupy our no-margined world.

Despite these obvious drawbacks to living without margin, our age consistently deprives us of it. We work hard to gain a foothold of freedom but are quickly pushed back into the quicksand. Overload just happens. Margin, in contrast, requires great effort. Positive margin status is what we call in science an "unstable state," one which spontaneously decays. Margin flows toward overload, but overload does not revert to margin unless forced.

Progress has had many overpriced ideas, but trading us burnout for margin was one of its most uncharitable.

FOUR MARGINS

To be healthy, we require margin in at least four areas: emotional energy, physical energy, time, and finances. Conditions of modern living, however, have drained these margins rather than sustaining them. In emotional energy, seldom have we been so stressed, so alone, and so exhausted in spirit. In physical energy, we are overfed, underactive, and sleep-deprived. In time, our clock-dominated nanosecond culture leaves us wheezing and worn out. And in finances, universal indebtedness makes our societal landscape look like a fiscal Gettysburg.

An easy way to test if you have margin in one of these areas is to increase the demands on the system 10 or 20 percent. Then see what happens. If you thrive, you had sufficient margin. If you wilt, you didn't.

Let's take, for example, medical residency programs. These programs are so overloaded and tightly coupled that if we introduce added demands, the systems have no way of compensating. If, for example, influenza season hits and the patient load suddenly surges (which, by the way, is happening even as I write), there is no margin to put these patients in. Or, if residents become too ill to take call, other already-exhausted eighty-hour-a-week residents cannot take their place. Thus, you see residents with 102 degree fevers working twenty-four-hour shifts (which, by the way, happened last week). I used to do it, too, until I developed a better understanding of health.

GROWN ACCUSTOMED TO ITS PACE

My decision to be involved in medicine only half-time was not an easy one. I practiced in a wonderful community with an exceptional and compassionate group of medical colleagues and at a pleasant new hospital. My patients respected my judgments and appreciated my care. I traveled around the country attending medical meetings: Boston, Orlando, Phoenix. My income was more than comfortable. I had everything a person could desire: a loving family, a prestigious profession, grateful patients, and a life free from need or want. About the only thing I didn't have was margin.

The decision required two years of agonizing internal deliberations and, in the end, was a strongly countercultural thing to do. Yet, when coupled with other lifestyle choices, that decision has given me the margin I have been writing about. Also, Linda has not worked outside the home since our first child was born. Though we have both spent thousands of hours working on writing projects, it could nevertheless be said that our husband-wife unit works one-fourth as much outside the home as the average marital unit in the United States. Despite this level of freedom and availability, our margin is consistently used up. At the end of a tiring week, we fall into bed and sigh, "How do people manage who have no margin?"

I lived at least sixteen years without margin: college, medical school, residency, and practice. And, since the decision to cut back my involvement in medicine, I have lived ten years with it. I can say with certainty that if margin were taken away from me now, I would beg shamelessly to get it back.

SEVEN

Margin in Emotional Energy

Of the four margins—emotional energy, physical energy, time, and finances—margin in emotional energy is paramount. When we are emotionally resilient, we can confront our problems with a sense of hope and power. When our psychic reserves are depleted, however, we are seriously weakened. Emotional overload saps our strength, paralyzes our resolve, and maximizes our vulnerability, leaving the door open for even further margin erosion.

DEADLINES AND DEAD FRIENDS

Harold was in charge of organizing and teaching continuing education topics for a well-known pharmaceutical firm. He was an excellent communicator. Unfortunately, he was an even better procrastinator. Five months before each conference meeting was scheduled, Harold's employer required a detailed report of time, events, and speakers, as well as full-text handouts for the topics to be covered. All of this information was then sent to the participants.

As someone who has organized medical education conferences, I sympathized with the complexity of Harold's job. Both foresight and organization are required. Nevertheless, the demands didn't sound all that unreasonable to me.

Harold felt differently. His boss insisted that the reports be submitted on time — not one day late. Harold, however, never did anything on time. Consequently, three weeks before the approaching deadline, his collapse would begin in earnest. Telephones were ringing, printers had questions, secretaries wondered about registration information, computers were spewing out piles of only partially relevant information, and his most important notes were hiding somewhere under a mountain of paper. Harold slept little and argued much. His palms would sweat, but his mouth was dry. He lived on antacids.

Convinced his boss was out to get him, Harold complained, "You can't talk to that man! I hate my work when it gets like this. I don't even like getting up in the morning, let alone going to the office." Nor did it help that he was having trouble in his marriage or that his two teenage daughters were increasingly disrespectful.

"Could you please give me something to calm me down?" he asked. "Maybe something to help me sleep? I just can't go on like this."

After our visit, I drew some laboratory tests and sent him off to the pharmacy. Later, I called to check how things were going. "Aside from a mildly elevated cholesterol," I said, "your tests all look fine. How are you doing?"

"Much better, Doc. I'm sleeping better now that the deadline has passed. I *almost* got everything in on time. I'm definitely not as anxious as I was, and I don't feel as depressed."

"How is it going at home?" I inquired.

"Better there, too," he said. "Well, that's not exactly true. My daughter's boyfriend shot and killed himself three days ago. So we've had a lot of things to work through. It's been tough on her."

WOUNDS OF THE SPIRIT

When Harold comes in to talk, I hurt with him. I wish I could do more. But there are no quick fixes. His anguish causes me to look progress in the eye and ask, "What is going on here?" Why do so many workers have so much stress? Why do so many marriages have so little vitality? Why do so many adolescents take their own lives? Aren't these fair questions to ask of progress?

Despite the importance of emotional margin, our contemporary level of emotional stamina is not high. Those who predicted the human race would evolve out of emotional problems were mistaken. Such troubles, far from being rarities, rage throughout our society. I am constantly impressed with how drained we seem to be. Broken relationships, financial insecurities, and overburdened schedules rip through us like a chain saw. The wounds we care for in medicine today are more often wounds of the spirit than wounds of the soma.

What happens when our emotional energy reserves are chronically depleted? "If we string ourselves out, expending 100 percent of our time and energy, there is no way in which we can adjust to the unexpected emergency," concludes Pastor Louis H. Evans, Jr. "We become defensive about our expended energies because there isn't anything left to give. Having nothing in reserve, we tune out the need."[1] Stuck in survival mode, there never seems to be enough strength for service.

EMOTIONAL SKIN

Skin is a wondrous organ, and as a matter of fact, is the largest organ of the human body. It keeps out bacteria, chemicals, and the sun's rays. As importantly, it keeps out water. If we jump into a swimming pool or soak in the tub, water is not allowed to penetrate the skin and enter the body.

Simultaneously, the skin has the job of keeping our own body fluids in. Humans are 60 percent water, and if the skin did not do its job correctly, in no time at all we would be puddles on the floor.

This fascinating organ, however, does not forbid *all* exchanges between our inside and outside environments. In fact, if it did we would die. There are times when the skin must allow exchange, usually in the form of water, salts, and heat, to help us equilibrate our temperature.

Some people are referred to as "thick skinned." This does not literally mean that they have hyperkeratosis, but instead that not much penetrates through to their feelings. Not much is allowed to seep in, and not much is allowed to leak out.

Most of us, however, have an emotional skin that permits an exchange with our environment. Of course we want to feel! But not too much. And not too little. Our emotional skin must allow feelings; it must not allow the excessive depletion of our emotional reserves, however.

A QUANTUM OF EMOTIONAL ENERGY

Each morning we rise to meet the day with a certain measure of emotional energy, a quantum of stamina. For some, this energy reservoir is huge, while for others it is nearly drained empty. Some are buoyant and resilient, filled with a zest and vitality that never seems to change. Others have had their emotional chins on the ground for most of their lives and can't remember what it feels like to smile.

This quantum of emotional energy is not fixed but instead is in constant flux with the environment. We are always losing energy into the environment and receiving energy back again. Sometimes the reservoir is being drained, as when we are sad or angry. Other times the reservoir is being filled, perhaps by expressions of encouragement or activities successfully completed.

No matter how large or small the quantum of emotional energy is at the start of the day, and no matter how fast or slow it is exchanging with the environment, one thing is certain: _The amount within us is finite_. No one has an infinite capacity for emotional discharge. When our reserves are depleted, they are depleted. If we make further withdrawals, we will enter debit status. With our margin exhausted, pain will be felt, sometimes—often in our culture—at dangerous levels.

It is important to understand our emotional reserves. It is important to understand how much we have at the beginning of each day and which influences drain our emotions dry or recharge our batteries. It is important to learn what our limits are, and not to make further withdrawals if we are already maximally depleted. And it is important to respect these limits in others.

We often have trouble accepting the idea of rationing our emotional energy. It is simply too difficult to quantify feelings. We feel ashamed admitting that our spirit is exhausted and collapsing within us. But our hesitancy in no way constitutes proof that such limits are only a convenient fiction for the weak and the lazy. Instead, our hesitancy is an obstacle to overcome. Margin gives us permission.

LIKE WEEDS IN A GARDEN

One would have hoped that the process of progress would have been kind to our emotional life, making it ever easier to replenish our reserves. It might have seemed reasonable to speculate that as our society improved in the areas of education, affluence, and entertainment, we would see a commensurate improvement in overall emotional well-being. Yet such has not been the case. These advancements have not resulted in unburdened emotions and liberated psyches. But why not? Our babies seldom die anymore, and famine is virtually unknown to us. We have telephones when we get lonely, air conditioners when we get hot, aspirin when we have a toothache, and television when we get bored. Why then do so many remain so emotionally drained?

I am not suggesting that emotional turmoil and emptiness is an invention of the late twentieth century, for this type of pain has been with us since the beginning of humankind. Yet as our survival needs were secured by civilizational improvements, might we not have expected that emotional disorders would increasingly disappear? Anxiety, depression, suicide and suicide gesturing, personality disorders, obsessive behaviors, eating disorders, panic attacks, alcohol and other drug abuse, phobias, psychoses—these are not diagnoses on the verge of extinction. Instead, these maladies seem to thrive in our society like weeds in a garden. And they all drain us dry emotionally.

Is it possible we are "living in a deteriorating 'psychic environment'"? Over the last decade, the number of therapists has risen tenfold. We have more mental health workers in the United States than police. The mental health beds are the only ones in our troubled health-care system that are filled all the time. Spending for mental health is escalating more rapidly than all other health categories, increasing 100 percent in the last five years. A study by the National Institute of Mental Health revealed that nearly one-third of all Americans have experienced at least one psychiatric illness during their lifetime. It has been estimated that 40 percent of us will be in psychotherapy at some point. Another study by the Institute reported that in just six years psychiatric hospitalizations for adolescents tripled. Twenty-seven percent of high school students "reported that they had thought seriously about attempting suicide," according to a 1991 Center for Disease Control survey of over eleven thousand students in all fifty states.[2] "If we look around us we find widespread evidence of psychological breakdown," observes Toffler. "It is as though a bomb had gone off in our communal 'psycho-sphere.'"[3]

Many of those trapped in this incredible web of psychic pain are victims, and they are to be commended for seeking help. If you develop typhoid in Bangladesh, it is not the fault of a weak constitution but instead the problem of a highly infectious environment. To seek effective treatment is the appropriate response.

ESCAPING OUR AGE

To our modern era social critics have attached labels that speak of this threatened emotional meltdown. It is not uncommon to hear entire decades characterized as the "age of anxiety," the "age of depression," the "age of melancholia," and even the "age of depressed anxiety." Over the course of a lifetime, one out of seven will experience a psychiatrically significant problem with anxiety. The use of tranquilizers has become so prevalent that for decades they have been near the top of the list of most widely prescribed drugs — at a cost of nearly one billion dollars annually. All of which prompted one observer to comment, "Millions of suburbanites seem to find that 'the good life' is only endurable under sedation."[4]

When the minor tranquilizers appeared on the scene in 1960, there was great hope. Finally, something to control anxiety and to soothe frazzled nerves! The disillusionment came when we realized that while these drugs did assist in controlling symptoms, they did not cure the underlying problems. People's pain continued, now compounded by tranquilizer addiction.

The widespread use of illicit drugs in our country is evidence that many perceive their personal lot not as a blessing to celebrate but, instead, as a burden to escape from. Why would America's fifteen million problem drinkers risk their bodies, their families, their jobs, and their future for a few hours of drunken stupor? Is it not because they believe the world they enter through alcohol is preferable to the reality they leave behind?

AGENT BLUE

Norman was a patient in his early sixties, hospitalized the day before. I knew him fairly well, enough to say that we were friends. Yet when I entered his room and approached him with a greeting, he just sat there on the edge of his bed, face drawn, shoulders slumped, looking weakly at his hard-boiled egg.

There was no anger or even distance in his silence. I was not offended. I knew that his paralysis came from the malignant darkness of depression. After a minute or so, Norman mumbled in a barely audible voice, "Could you . . . peel my egg? I just . . . can't . . . seem . . ."

The suffering of depression is often unbearable. If you look, you can see it in the eyes: privately tortured eyes reflecting a sea of pain, always misty, ready to overflow at the slightest provocation. When I sit next to such a patient in the examination room, I ask a gently probing question and pass him or her the tissue box at the same time. As the pain surfaces, the tears spill over. It happens 100 percent of the time.

"It is almost impossible to convey to a person who has not had a depression what one is like," explains Jack Dreyfus, founder of the Dreyfus Fund.

> It's not obvious like a broken arm, or a fever, or a cough; it's beneath the surface. A depressed person suffers a type of anguish which in its own way can be as painful as anything that can happen to a human being. He has varying degrees of fear throughout the day, and a brain that permits him no rest and races with agitated and frightening thoughts. His mood is low, he has little energy, and he can hardly remember what pleasure means.[5]

Yet in medical practice, depression is a daily finding. It is not limited to a certain socioeconomic group, nor to a certain educational level. No one is immune. Like a flu virus, it strikes any age, any race, any occupation, at any time. Unemployment does heighten the risk, but even successful business executives, such as Jack Dreyfus, suffer from it. High school dropouts might have it, but so do many Harvard graduates. Nihilistic unbelievers feel its pain, but so have some of the greatest preachers in the history of the Church. An increasing number of children and adolescents are being diagnosed with it, and on the other end of the spectrum, many elderly spend their last days caught in its grip.

Researchers at the National Institute of Mental Health are attempting to identify Agent Blue, the unknown factor(s) that causes such a high rate of depression in our society. The Institute's Dr. Eliot Gershon calls the increase in depression and suicide "ominous because we haven't seen where it's going to stop." He goes on to explain that "the high rates among people born since 1940 cannot be explained by genetics or the increased reporting of depressive illnesses."[6]

A disturbing 1989 report in *The Journal of the American Medical*

Association examined several large epidemiologic studies concerning the incidence of depression. Ten studies from the United States, Sweden, Germany, New Zealand, and Canada revealed an increase in lifetime rates of depression for those born after 1940. (Interestingly, the article also reported that comparable studies in Korea, Puerto Rico, and of Mexican-Americans living in the United States revealed no such increase in rates of depression among these groups.) The authors summarized the findings as follows:

> The cohorts born since World War II have been among the healthiest physically and were raised during a period of economic prosperity in the United States and Western Europe. Nevertheless, they show high rates of alcoholism, substance abuse, depression, and suicide.... Clinically, the data suggest that physicians from all specialties can expect to see more and younger patients presenting with major depression.[7]

But where is this "dark undertow" coming from? Why, in one recent morning in the clinic, were nine of my eleven patients on antidepressants? Where is emotional resilience hiding these days?

CONTEMPORARY LEECHES

The answer lies in the fact that we have been ambushed by a load of psychic trauma unparalleled in human history. This is not to say that other people in other times haven't had it rough. Many have had it much rougher than we do. *But never before have people faced the particular constellation of factors which today are plotting together for our misery.*

We have already noted how the unprecedented pathogens of stress and overload often wage war on our emotions. Add the assault of speed, the kind whose sheer velocity precludes adaptation to change. Compound the situation by fracturing families, dissipating any sense of community, and decreasing social supports of all kinds. Separate the elderly from their extended families. Add uprootedness by factoring in mobility. Add individualism to narcissism. Alienate adolescents in the direction of R-rated movies, drugs, heavy metal music, early sexuality, and suicide. Add teenage pregnancy and single parenting to welfare dependency. Add child abuse, sexual abuse, and wife abuse to pornography. Add the crime in every city to the reports of crime on every television. Add indebtedness and bankruptcy to job insecurity and demanding bosses. Add unaffordable housing to unaffordable health care. Add traffic to noise to hurry to impossible work schedules to technology that doesn't work to ringing telephones to crying babies.

When you put it all together, there is little wonder we see anxiety and depression. Little wonder the therapists' offices are full. Loneliness, hopelessness, rejection, fear, insecurity, frustration, cynicism, hostility—these are not the things to fill one's emotional reserves with. The vampires have been busy, haven't they?

"Why is mental health such a major problem, and why is treatment so much more common and so expensive?" asks mental health expert Walter E. Afield, M.D. "There are a number of reasons: For many Americans, life is almost relentlessly stressful. The pressure to achieve, compete—even survive—takes a significant toll on emotional equilibrium. A serious erosion of traditional support systems (including extended family, neighborhoods, communities, schools, and churches) has occurred, and many people feel—and often are—alone with their problems and pressures, far from loved ones and without psychological support."[8]

And, as Dr. Afield goes on to point out, for each person suffering from a mental or emotional disorder, the lives of at least three other persons are significantly affected.

RESTORING MARGIN IN EMOTIONAL ENERGY

If we find our emotional energy gone, how can we get it back? What are the factors to emphasize in our lives that will not only protect our emotional reserves from unnecessary depletion but will replenish the supply at regular intervals? In such a hostile environment, who will be kind to our fragile psyches? Who will feed us and not swallow us?

Following are prescriptions that work; take as needed. *(14)*

Rx: 1 Cultivate Social Supports

Not only common sense but now also good science, the importance of healthy social supports is irrefutable. We do not simply *think* they work; we *know* they work. The California Department of Mental Health's "Friends Can Be Good Medicine" is not simply a slogan, it is state-of-the-art therapeutics.

Whether family and friends or community and church, the existence of intact, functioning, healthy, nurturing systems of social support are as good a resource for replenishing depleted energy reserves as can be found. Love, affection, nurturing, intimacy, connectedness, bonding, attachment, empathy, community—these are "feel good" words for a reason: because they *are* good.

If you find yourself emotionally empty, go to a caring friend. If you are bruised and bleeding, the empathetic response of another will stem the hemorrhage of emotion and begin the process of healing and filling. "There is perhaps no more effective way to relieve psychic pain than to be in contact with another human being who understands what you are going through and can communicate such understanding to you," advises psychiatrist Dr. Frederic Flach.[9]

I have found that, regarding emotional margin, there are three types of people: those that fill you, those that just sit there, and those that drain you. Unfortunately, the drainers outnumber the fillers about two to one (not a scientific number). We find ourselves in the interesting but precarious situation of being dependent on the benevolent interests of the fillers yet, at the same time, vulnerable to the malevolence of the drainers.

This is a great part of our modern dilemma. So many of us have unsatisfactory relationships and are afraid to risk intimate emotional contact. So we withdraw and "hide from love," only to find that isolation is unhealthy as well. The obvious answer is not to abandon people contact but to learn how to make our relationships mutually nourishing. As we become more active and effective in nourishing families, nourishing friendships, nourishing churches, and nourishing community, we will also discover that our own emotional health is nourished.

As an added note, we can say that not only verbal expressions of caring are important, but the physical are as well. Upon entering an exam room, I make it a practice to shake the hand of my patient or, on occasion, place my hand on his or her shoulder. This, I believe, is the beginning of my therapeutic intervention. We all *need* human contact. We all need to be hugged from time to time. Have you ever noticed how, when a child climbs onto a parent's lap and snuggles in, the entire room feels caressed by the warmth of it?

Rx: 2 Pet a Surrogate

Sometimes, because of social conventions, we are not allowed to touch one another. For those caught in a void and left with a dearth of physical closeness, I would strongly suggest considering surrogates—pets. When God wrote the inviolable law that requires living things to need one another, He included the entire animal world. And it is remarkable how closely we can approximate human-human warmth and affection by substituting human-animal contact. Pets are capable of bonding, are extremely loyal, and often exhibit deep appreciation for our affections—exactly the kind of responses needed to increase our emotional reserves.

Rx: 3   Reconcile Relationships

Broken relationships are a razor across the artery of the spirit. Stemming the hemorrhage and binding the wound should be done as quickly as possible. Yet all too often, it takes months or years. And sometimes, the bleeding never stops.

True reconciliation is one of the most powerful of all human interactions. Warring individuals who have done battle for years can erase all antagonism in a matter of minutes. This is not a matter of human psychology but rather a <u>divine gift.</u> One of the great privileges of our adoption into God's family is the access we have to this mysterious healing power of the Spirit. If you have not seen it happen, or if you have only seen it happen rarely, then yearn for it. Pray for it. Beg for it. And know that it is one of the gifts God most enjoys giving.

Although there is no formula, there are principles. It helps to bring God close—through our brokenness.[10] And it helps to accept God's grace—through our humility.[11] Perhaps you see that this gift is mostly a matter of emptiness and yielding. In our brokenness we confess, yielding our wrongs. In our humility we forgive, yielding our rights. And when confession and forgiveness are completed, our frozen winter of pain will also yield, <u>thawing under the warmth of the Son.</u>

Rx: 4   Serve One Another

"I happen to know that service is empowering," states psychiatrist and bioethicist Dr. Willard Gaylin, president of the Hastings Center. "It's great. It's terrific! Given the opportunity for training toward community and service, people love it and want it."[12]

A recent University of Michigan study followed 2,700 people for over a decade to see how their social relationships affected their health and well-being. <u>Those who performed regular volunteer work showed</u> dramatically increased life expectancy. Men not involved in such altruistic activity had two-and-one-half times the morbidity during the period studied than those who volunteered at least once a week.

"Doing nothing for others is the undoing of one's self," observed Horace Mann. "We must be purposely kind and generous, or we miss the best part of existence. The heart that goes out of itself gets large and full of joy. This is the great secret of the inner life. We do ourselves the most good doing something for others." The service can be noble and sacrificial, or it can be small and simple. Not to worry, explains Rudyard Kipling, "for the glory of the Garden glorifieth everyone."

Ten years ago, a 110-mile-per-hour windstorm blasted across our county, leveling trees, power lines, and buildings, and causing sixty million dollars in damage. Within days, people from several eastern states began quietly arriving in town, volunteers of the Mennonite Disaster Service. Some stayed as long as a month, living in university dormitories vacated for the summer. Most of them were involved in the rebuilding of barns. I don't remember what I did those weeks after the storm, but I will never forget what they did. They served. Every time I think of the disaster, I think also of the gift. Do you see the multiplying effects of this virtue?

I recently heard of a man who, while driving on the interstate highway system, pays not only his own toll but also the toll for the car to follow. In so doing, he is making deposits in at least three emotional bank accounts: his own, the teller's, and the following driver's.

My wife, Linda, is always alert to ways of serving others. Stopping at a convenience store recently for some ice cream, she happened to mention at the counter that it was for cherry pie. "Sounds great!" responded the youthful clerk. Fifteen minutes later, Linda brought him a huge piece of fresh cherry pie à la mode. That evening, alone in the store, he was nourished by service. A simple thing; a magnificent obsession.

And the gift goes on . . .

Rx: 5 Rest

Be with people and serve them. But be sure to get away from them occasionally.

Escape. Relax. Sleep in. Take a nap. Unplug the phone. Enjoy a walk. Don't take your beeper.

Try setting aside time every day for some quiet and for rest—perhaps fifteen or thirty minutes. Or set aside some time every week, as the

Northwestern Mutual Life Insurance Company does. Every Wednesday the company practices "quiet days." The phones in the offices are turned off, and all calls are routed to a receptionist so the employees can work in quiet.

Many of us funnel all our rest needs into already jam-packed weekends and holidays. But don't fall into the trap of thinking weekends and holidays are restful. Often they are not. Sometimes they are even more draining than the week we just escaped. In one poll, although 95 percent of working mothers looked forward to weekends, 52 percent felt exhausted when the weekend was over. Holidays, especially Christmas, can turn into the same exhausting process. Weekends, Sundays, holidays, vacations—all have been modernized, and are only restful if forced to behave.

When emotionally exhausted, the first thing I do is find quiet, solitude, and a chance to do nothing. I don't feel guilty, for fallow times are just as important as productive times. I cycle quickly, and if depleted, my energy will return shortly. All I need is quiet and some time.

Rest restores.

Rx: 6 Laugh

Humor is a medicine. It tastes better than pills, it works as well, and it costs less. Why do you think children are so buoyant, so resilient, so capable of picking themselves up and going on? There are many reasons, and laughter is prominent among them.

Only a few months after birth, and the mirth has already begun. By the time babies are four months old, they are already laughing once every hour. And by the age of four years, these clowns laugh on average every four minutes![13] Try laughing every four minutes. I guarantee that something positive will happen to your emotions and that your margin will be increased.

I am not implying that life is essentially humorous—it decidedly is not. But God has given us the gift of laughter because He knew we would need it.

Rx: 7 Cry

Sometimes we laugh so hard we cry. Other times we just cry. Crying is a form of emotional diuresis. As long as it is not an indication of a deeper depression (in which case frequent weeping is a symptom that should not be ignored), crying can have salutary health benefits. According to some studies, those who cry *more often* get sick *less often*. A good cry usually lasts six or seven minutes and releases a burdensome load of emotional pollution.[14]

Laughter lifts; crying cleanses. Both are partners in the process of emotional restoration.

Rx: 8   Create Appropriate Boundaries

The need to establish boundaries that allow us to say no is a mathematical necessity. With far too many demands and expectations upon us, we could not possibly fulfill them all, even should we desire to do so. Yet it is not easy saying no. With some, every time the word exits their mouths they have a crisis of guilt. The alternative, however, is acquiescing to the demand. Then, instead of a crisis of guilt, we have a crisis of margin depletion.

It is important to understand that most people simply are not sensitive. There is *absence of malice but presence of callous*. Other people's pain is invisible to them. Therefore, when they make demands upon us, they know not what they do.

We, then, must respond with grace, with sensitivity, yet with firmness: "I'm sorry, but I can't." To be able to say no without guilt is to be freed from one of the biggest monsters in our overburdened lives. If we decline, not out of self-serving laziness but for God-honoring balance and health, then this level of control will not only protect our emotional margin but will actually increase it.

"Boundary deficits can be deeply disabling to anyone, including Christians. People with unclear boundaries can find themselves making commitments under pressure that they would never make with a clear head. They find themselves 'caving in' to others," explains psychologist Dr. John Townsend. "We need to find maturing, caring people who will love our boundaries just as much as they love our attachment. . . . Ask yourself, 'Do the people closest to me love my *no* as much as they love my *yes*?'"[15]

If we do not learn to say no, we will never regain margin. That is a contemporary sociological axiom.

Rx: 9   Envision a Better Future

Each of us must have a transcendent vision: a hopeful, spiritually valid expectation of what the future will hold. We all must have a purpose bigger than ourselves that we can live for. We must have something we can believe in, something we can give ourselves to. We must have work, and the work must have meaning. We must have direction, and the direction must have structure. A transcendent vision with purpose, work, meaning, direction, and structure.

Unfortunately, there has been a wholesale destruction of vision, transcendent or otherwise, in modern-day living, and this destruction is seen worldwide. The only vision most live by today is the hardly transcendent television. Aimlessness is like a metaphysical black hole, swallowing up everything in sight. Perhaps the most poignant description of our existential emptiness comes from the French philosopher Jean-Paul Sartre, when he speaks of "man as a bubble of consciousness in an ocean of nothingness, bobbing around until the bubble pops."16

So here we have a clear choice, don't we? The vision and spirit of the age—which is really a vote for despair followed by death—or the vision of the revealed Word of God. "Our vision is not something we have concocted to suit ourselves," says sociologist S. D. Gaede, "but a perspective that suits the Reality that has been communicated to us. Believing this, we have no choice but to make the vision central to the life of the Christian community."17

If we believe in and work for something larger than ourselves— for our families, for the community, for the common good, and for the Kingdom—then every expenditure of emotion will have meaning, and every expenditure of emotion will be reimbursable.

Rx: 10 Offer Thanks

In everyone's life there is much to be unhappy about and much to be grateful for. Realistically acknowledging both ends of the spectrum is appropriate.

When we turn to look at our problems, we assess them and make a plan—no matter how small or grand—to work on them. This plan we formulate with our *mind* and motivate with our *will*.

Then we look in the other direction to find our obligation to gratitude. Here we may fully engage our *emotions*.

Often we send our emotions to do battle with our problems, and despair results. Then we send our will to express our gratitude, lacking any confirming passion whatsoever. *Of course*, our emotions ought to be informed about our problems; *of course*, our mind and our will ought to express gratitude. But we should send out that warrior best suited for the duty. And I think there can be little debate concerning the most appropriate assignments here.

If we can adopt such a balanced approach, we will combine a realistic and objective involvement in working on problems with a simultaneous assurance that there is much good in life. We'll recognize that the world is full of beauty, that most people are worthy of our respect and trust, and that the affairs of suffering humans are replete with acts of love, kindness, nobility, and sacrifice. And we'll remember that overseeing it all is a God who knows us well, who loves us anyway, and who is very, very good.

All people have within their grasp much to be thankful for. Gratitude fills. Discontent drains. The choice is truly ours.

Rx: 11 Grant Grace

I don't think most of us realize what a weighty emotional burden it is to judge others and to be judged in return. It is a form of emotional and spiritual suicide. Like chopping a hole in the bottom of your lifeboat because you don't want the other person to be rescued.

Grace, on the other hand, treats people not as they deserve but *better* than they deserve. Grace preempts accusation, freeing both parties. When we extend grace to our enemies, they receive a shockingly unexpected glimpse of the Kingdom. And, at precisely the same time that our adversary is released, we are as well.

Why would anyone wish to go around carrying a donkey on his shoulders when he could ride instead? Why would anyone wish to be harsh when he could instead be free? "If thou knewest all the Bible . . . and also the sayings of all philosophers by heart," asks Thomas à Kempis, "what should it profit thee without grace and charity?"[18]

Grace not only revives emotional margin, it lifts it to Heaven.

Rx: 12 Be Rich in Faith

"And now these three remain: *faith*, hope and love."[19]

"Seeing isn't believing. It's only seeing," once quipped George MacDonald. Faith, however, is seeing without seeing. The faith of our fathers that successfully withstood dungeon, fire, and sword is the same faith that leads us safely through contemporary dangers, toils, and snares. If it can withstand anything, then can it not withstand the problems of modernity? To be sure, when all hammers are dust, the anvil will yet endure. Even when all else fails us, year after year, faith remains.

"I believe the most vital ingredient of resilience," comments Dr. Flach in his book *Resilience*, "is faith."[20]

Rx: 13 Hold Fast Hope

"And now these three remain: faith, *hope* and love."

The world does not have a strong articulation of the concept of hope, nor does it have a credible basis for developing one. "The Encyclopedia Britannica has columns on love and faith, but not a single word about hope," observed the late psychiatrist Dr. Karl Menninger.[21] Despite this conspicuous textual absence, explains Harvard psychiatrist Dr. Armand Nicholi, "Psychiatrists have long suspected that hope fosters health, both physical and emotional." With the need for hope established, where in a despairing world do we find it? "When we turn to the New Testament," explains Dr. Nicholi, "we read again and again: 'Christ Jesus, our hope.'"[22]

Although acknowledging that "the optimism of inevitable progress has become tarnished," Princeton philosopher and theologian Diogenes Allen sees great cause for hope. "The kingdom of God is at hand when it becomes harder and harder to ignore or evade God's ways. Such convictions enable Christians to continue to work for the common good, to be philanthropic, even in a deteriorating situation. Because of faith in the good God intends us to have, Christian hope can survive even the disintegration of a culture."[23]

Scripture reminds us of the hope of the promise, the hope of the gospel, and the hope of salvation. The Apostle Paul writes, "And we rejoice in the hope of the glory of God. Not only so, but we also rejoice in our sufferings, because we know that suffering produces perseverance; perseverance, character; and character, hope. And hope does not disappoint us, because God has poured out his love. . . ."[24]

Rx: 14 Above All, Love

"And now these three remain: faith, hope and *love*."

To have accepted the love of God is to be armed and disarmed at the same time. No weapon is more powerful. But in using such a weapon it is the user who is broken wide-open. This is a love that cannot rightly be kept in—it is a bursting-out love. In its spilling out, it binds to others. And when it binds to others, it heals, it knits hearts, it builds community, and it brings everything "together in perfect unity."[25] "The effort to 'love thy neighbor as thyself' probably has done more good, and more to make life pleasant, than any other guideline," observes Dr. Selye, perhaps restating the obvious.[26]

Love is the only medicine I know of which, when used according to directions, heals completely yet takes one's life away. It is dangerous; it is uncontrollable; it is "self-expenditure"; and it can never be taken on any terms but its own. Yet as a healer of the emotions, it has no equal.

"But the greatest of these is love."[27]

EIGHT

Margin
in Physical Energy

When we dip into the tank for some physical energy, we all want the ladle to return with something in it. Unfortunately, for too many of us the tank dried up years ago.

A large percentage of Americans are sadly out of shape and have diminished physical energy reserves. because of poor conditioning. Others, such as mothers of newborns and those who work two jobs, are chronically sleep-deprived. Still others suffer from chronic biscuit poisoning. These three factors—poor conditioning, sleep deprivation, and obesity—constitute a physical energy desert where no margin can grow.

Lacking margin in physical energy, we feel underrested and overwhelmed. With no strength left for our own needs, let alone the needs of others, we put our tiredness to bed hoping tomorrow will be a stronger day.

THE NEW MORBIDITY

Thanks to progress, extraordinary tools are available to assist us in living healthier, longer lives. Once again, however, we unexpectedly find a dark side to it all. Gone are the old infectious foes, but replacing them are even more frustrating and, in some ways, more frightening enemies. They are variously known as "the new morbidity," "the diseases of civilization," and "the diseases of lifestyle." These ailments come as a result of our bad habits and our poor choices. The surgeon general has bemoaned "an epidemic of poor health practices."[1] The Center for Disease Control estimates that more than 50 percent of all deaths are related to lifestyle choices,[2] while Emory University's Health Policy Project explains that "64.7% of the years of life lost before age 65 result from preventable deaths."[3]

In many ways, the practice of medicine was more rewarding when patients were victimized by external tragedies than it is now when patients so often victimize themselves. As a result of this new morbidity, the heroic nature of medical practice has all but disappeared. A romanticized past envisions doctors risking their lives by working all hours to save a community from smallpox. Today, the vision has deteriorated into business-minded physicians taking care of patients with self-induced illnesses who live self-destructive lives, who expect to get well now and who threaten to sue if they don't.

Let's look at some examples of this morbid epidemic.

Stress-induced illnesses — These afflictions are the new bread and butter of medical practice. A high percentage of patients who visit a primary-care physician have stress-related ailments — headaches, hyperacidity/ulcers, irritable bowel, malaise and fatigue, insomnia, chronic-pain syndromes, anxiety, depression. Burnout in the workplace produces many physical manifestations. The eating disorders of anorexia nervosa and bulimia are prevalent and increasing.

The "worried well" — Our society has also spawned an epidemic number of the "worried well." According to Harvard psychiatrist Arthur J. Barsky, M.D., "The substantial improvements in health status have not been accompanied by improvements in the subjective feeling of healthiness and physical well-being. Instead, people now report higher rates of disability, symptoms, and general dissatisfaction with their health."[4] Such patients are anxious about their health and refuse consolation, even though they have no demonstrable disease.

Pollution-related diseases — The pathologies induced by pollution are another malady of civilization. Where you find industrialization, high energy utilization, and high population density, you will find pollution-related diseases not far behind. A majority of cancers result from environmental causes (things we smoke, eat, drink, or breathe).

The incidence of bronchospastic diseases, such as asthma, is increasing, with air pollution a major culprit. Sick-building syndrome from artificially ventilated offices causes headaches and lethargy.

Lack of sexual restraint—The diseases resulting from sexual permissiveness are seen daily. Twenty-two possible infections can be caught through a single act of intercourse, giving abundant validation to the quip "You, me, and the microbe makes three." Tens of millions of cases of sexually transmitted diseases annually are followed by cervical abnormalities and cancer, pelvic inflammatory disease, infertility, ectopic pregnancies, teenage pregnancies, abortions, and AIDS.

Illicit drug use—The scourge of drug abuse has become an equal-opportunity destroyer, affecting nearly every segment of our society. The National Institute on Drug Abuse has estimated that "during the 1960s only 5% of the U.S. population had had any experience with illicit drug use. By the early 1970s . . . this rose to 10%." By 1980, 37 percent of the population over the age of twelve had used illicit drugs.[5] As a result, through at least portions of the 1980s, the United States owned the highest per capita illicit drug use of any industrialized country.[6] It is estimated that between fifty and one hundred billion dollars annually is spent purchasing illegal drugs. What makes people feed at a poisoned trough? According to Harvard psychiatrist Dr. Armand Nicholi, "People take these drugs to alter or to escape from a less than tolerable reality, and to meet intense emotional needs."[7]

Cigarette-related disease—Tobacco kills 350,000 Americans every year, making it the leading cause of premature death in the United States. In 1915, Americans smoked 18 billion cigarettes; the number now is 575 billion. Nearly thirty years after the surgeon general announced that cigarettes can be fatal, we still have 50 million smokers. Smoking kills more people every year than do "cocaine, heroin, AIDS, traffic accidents, murder, and terrorist attacks *combined*."[8] One in six Americans dies from the effects of tobacco. Jimmy Carter convened a consultation on national health policy at Emory University's Carter Center by claiming, "If physicians listed tobacco as an underlying cause of death when appropriate, it would be apparent that tobacco kills more Americans every 18 months than were killed in all of the wars of the 20th century."[9]

Alcohol abuse—The second leading cause of premature death in the United States, with nine million alcoholics and another six million problem drinkers, alcohol abuse is implicated in half of all homicides, suicides, and automobile fatalities. The Bureau of Justice Statistics reports that drunk-driving arrests more than tripled over a recent fifteen-year period. Yet, by some estimates, only one out of two thousand drunk drivers is caught. The average age of first use for alcohol is 12.3 years. The American Academy of Pediatrics maintains that, of fourth graders, one in three believes drinking is a "big problem" in their age group.

THE PATHOLOGIES OF PROSPERITY

The prevalence of such self-destructive, lifestyle-related pathologies certainly makes medicine a secure profession. Those who predicted the human race would evolve into a communal picture of nontoxic, robust heartiness have been deeply shaken by the statistics of the last few decades. Not only are health professionals still needed, but even with the addition of fringe healers from herbalists to reflexologists, we are all still working overtime.

I will not dwell further on the above litany of sorrows other than to say that, in many ways, they are further evidence of the inability of progress to solve our deepest needs. Progress brings technology, affluence, and education, but not the kind of inner discipline necessary to maintain sound physical health.

In some ways, progress is too easy on us. It caters food in overabundance, but without regard for the requirement of restraint. It provides electricity and artificial lighting, but without regard for the requirement of sleep. And it supplies transportation and convenience, but without regard for the requirement of physical activity. As a result, we eat too much, sleep too little, and move hardly at all.

THE KEYS TO PHYSICAL MARGIN

Our bodies are, in one sense, sophisticated energy machines. If we properly care for the engine and load the appropriate fuel, our machine will operate reliably. Even when called upon to double or triple its performance, the body is capable of responding by tapping into energy reserves.

These reserves can be enhanced or depleted depending upon many factors—some external, some internal, and some eternal. It is wise for us to vigilantly do all we can to protect these reserves, for if they are drawn too low, ill results follow. We are left not only exhausted but unprotected as well.

Let's take, for example, the problem of stress. According to expert Dr. Martin Shaffer, our bodies are more vulnerable to the effects of stress when our "reserves of energy have been drawn down too low. ✳ With no reserve energy available, the body cannot resist effectively, and exhaustion sets in, often accompanied by disease. . . . This scenario suggests an important principle for stress management and control: The stronger the body's reserves, the better able the body will be to resist the ravages of stress."[10]

By what methods does Dr. Shaffer propose we build up our physical margin and strengthen our reserves? "The answer is straightforward. Maximum bodily strength and efficiency depend upon three factors: sleep, exercise, and nutrition. Only a body that is well rested, properly exercised, and correctly fed will be able to maintain its energy reserves in the face of serious stress."[11]

The keys to physical margin, then, are sleep, exercise, and nutrition. Let's check the record to see how we are doing, although I suspect you already know what we will find.

PERCHANCE TO SLEEP

A recent *Time* magazine cover bemoaned "the sleep gap." We live in "drowsy America," where factories, grocery stores, service stations, and restaurants are often open through the night. "Today new cultural and economic forces are combining to turn the U.S. into a 24-hour society," explains journalist Anastasia Toufexis.[12] Sleep disorders involve more than fifty million Americans.

Many round-the-clock cities never go to sleep. After pushing the limits to the breaking point, we push some more. Students pull "all-nighters" studying for exams; nurses check on sleeping patients and watch the monitors; taxi drivers listen to an all-night station on their radios and drive denizens of the dark around town. Mothers of young children work all day in the office and then all night in the nursery.

Shift workers, a growing percentage of the labor force, miss an extra five days of work per year solely because of fatigue, notes occupational and environmental-medicine expert Joseph LaDou, M.D. In addition, they use more caffeine, suffer more drug abuse, and take four times more sleep medication than the average American.[13] Even though sleep is not optional, "evidence is mounting that sleep deprivation has become one of the most pervasive health problems facing the U.S."[14]

BEST-SELLING ADIPOSE

Technology now exists to measure the percentage of body fat in sophisticated ways. One such machine was brought to our clinic for a conference on nutrition, and I volunteered to be tested. As they entered data into the computer, I was electronically connected and laid on a special mat. The machine calculated that I weighed twenty thousand pounds and was 99.9999 percent fat. It was funny until I felt myself jiggling when I laughed.

Obesity, or the "rounding of America," is such a ubiquitous problem that one-fourth to one-half of all adults are on a diet at any given time. The list of best sellers always has at least two or three dieting books. One in five Americans is obese (defined as 20 percent above ideal body weight)—but twice that number *think* they are. What can't be dieted off is surgically removed, at an estimated one hundred tons each year. Over the last two decades, the incidence of childhood obesity is up 54 percent in ages six through eleven and 39 percent in ages twelve through seventeen. "More die in the United States of too much food than of too little," observes John Kenneth Galbraith.[15]

EXTINCT EXERCISE

Some think the cause of our adipose problem is not that we eat too much, but we move too little. Our prosperity has allowed us to be cerebral and sedentary rather than physically robust, and lack of exercise has brought problems beyond obesity. A study from the Department of Health and Human Services revealed that 80 to 90 percent of Americans do not get enough physical exercise. Of children ages six through twelve, 40 percent of boys and 70 percent of girls can do only one pull-up.

In earlier eras, the sheer harshness of existence required a physically active, vigorous lifestyle. During Revolutionary-War days, when 90 percent of our population were farmers, physical labor was an indispensable part of daily activity. Today, however, only 2 percent of Americans earn their living off the land. Most of the rest of us left our fitness behind on the farm. Now, instead of pitching hay bales, we push pencils.

And, as we sit, we thicken.

MODELS NOT TO FOLLOW

I love medicine and am continuously aware of the privilege of my profession. I do not, however, love medicine when it takes away my margin. Yet this is precisely what medicine does for nearly all students, residents, and practitioners. Don't get me wrong. I am more than willing to put in long hours and sleepless nights when it is necessary. I have done it thousands of times. But it is no longer truly necessary. The patient and illness load, if spread out among all available physicians, does not require it any more. The system, however, has not yet caught on to that fact.

From the first day of training to the last call night before retirement, the medical system is notorious for its lack of margin. Many times I have attempted to refer patients to already-swamped doctors, only to discover that they were closer to death than the patients in their swamped waiting rooms.

The medical residents I teach are a classic example of a group of people living in continuous negative margin status. They are chronically sleep-deprived. Working from 70 to 120 hours a week, they are often physically and emotionally exhausted. These young physicians eat meals irregularly and see their families haphazardly. Yet this three-year rite of passage, which so typifies the absence of margin and violates every rule of good personal health, is defended as essential to medical education. In its defense, it does accomplish the important goal of clinical experience. But isn't there something a little perverse about teaching principles of health by violating so many of them?

My own training days are vivid in my memory. On call every third night, I would work thirty-six hours without sleep. Stumbling home the following sunset, I would begin to doze midway through supper. Finally, every third evening, I would be awake enough to recognize my wife. During my busiest week in residency, I worked 129 hours. "Having too much to do seems an integral part of the physician's life from medical school on," explains David Hilfiker, M.D. "There is always more to learn in medical school than can possibly be assimilated, more to do in internship and residency training than can possibly be done in twenty-four-hour days, more problems to take care of as a practicing physician than can reasonably be accommodated."[16]

It is only a matter of time before widespread rebellion erupts concerning the stressful, marginless lifestyle of medical practitioners, and recent medical school graduates are already demanding changes. The point is, practicing medicine does not *have* to take away margin. In the past, there was too much disease in too many patients and too few physicians. But that has now changed. Doctors continue to work sixty-hour weeks, but more out of economics and force of habit than necessity.

If the entire profession would back off a little, we could work with far less pressure, sleep in after a long night on call, not be upset when the front office asks us to see a walk-in patient with chest pain, and actually take *better* care of both our patients and ourselves. We could once again have some margin for family, service, and rest. Yet because of the profession's proud tradition of being overworked, change comes slowly.

RESTORING MARGIN IN PHYSICAL ENERGY

Virtually anyone, no matter how ravaged by insomnia, intemperance, and inactivity, can take steps to reverse self-induced bodily deterioration. The rules for restoring energy to the human body are not written out in calculus and hidden in the catacombs. On the contrary, they are a matter of public record, accessible to all.

The body can bounce back; God designed it so. But not without some cooperation from its owner. "Healing is a matter of time," understood Hippocrates, "but it is sometimes also a matter of opportunity." Let's look together at some prescriptions that might help.

Rx: 1   Take Personal Responsibility

I learned long ago that I can inform but not perform that which is needed in the lives of my patients. Until we accept personal responsibility for our own health, the road to the future will remain paved with aches and adipose.

If you are underslept, overweight, and unexercised, it is your job to change. I want to encourage you that change *is possible*. And I am more than willing to provide the needed information. But just as the body is yours, so is the responsibility.

Rx: 2   Gain Physical Margin Through Emotional Margin

In this chapter we will concentrate on the physical components of restoring energy. Never slight, however, the role that emotions play in our quest. A natural, God-ordained mutuality exists between physical and emotional well-being. We have seen how social supports, nurturing relationships, service, volunteerism, laughter, purpose, vision, gratitude, grace, faith, hope, and love are all important to emotional health. They are equally important to physical health.

I encourage seekers of physical energy to look beyond the diet and exercise books and to first seek enhanced physical vitality through enhanced emotional vitality.

Rx: 3   Change Your Habits

If you do not have margin in physical energy, you probably have habits that need changing. Poor nutrition, poor exercise patterns, and (sometimes) poor sleep hygiene are called "habit disorders." Breaking old ways and establishing new patterns are necessary.

Changing habit disorders often requires changing lifestyles. Sometimes the changes required are small. More often, however, the adjustment entails a new way of looking at and reacting to both yourself and the world around you. In making these changes, it helps to surround yourself with a subculture of people who will support the changes rather than undermine them.

THE RITES OF SLEEP

Rx: 4   Value of Sleep

Many people in contemporary society have negative attitudes toward sleep. Often these are very productive people who resent the "wasted time." They also tend to be people who need less than average sleep themselves. Unfortunately, this attitude too often forces its way into other bedrooms uninvited.

Don't get caught in a web of shame spun by other people. A good night's sleep is not an embarrassment. It is not necessary to feel guilty if you are well rested. Sleep is God's idea, not ours. He created the necessity, and "he grants sleep to those he loves."[17] The need for sleep is undeniable and should be regarded as an ally, not an enemy. To sleep soundly for a full night is a valuable restorative gift. As anyone who has read Proverbs knows, however, the sluggard is left defenseless by Scripture.

Choose to get enough rest. Determine how much sleep you need to feel your best and then determine to get it. I personally feel best with seven to eight hours of sleep, as do the vast majority of adults.

Rx: 5 Develop Healthy Sleep Patterns

Many people don't sleep well simply because they practice poor sleep habits. Develop a healthy pattern of sleep. Retire at a similar time each evening; arise at a similar time each morning. Have a quiet room and a good mattress. If you suffer from cold feet, prewarm the sheets with an electric blanket. (There is some unresolved medical controversy about sleeping under electric blankets, but there is no danger whatever in prewarming the bed.) Don't engage in disturbing conversations immediately before bedtime. Instead, begin relaxing about an hour or so before retiring. Give yourself time to unwind from the day. Don't have a big meal within two hours of bedtime. Limit the intake of caffeine in the evening and, if necessary, in the afternoon as well. If you are a clock watcher, turn the clock toward the wall.

If sleep is delayed by racing thoughts or creativity, keep a notebook or even a small tape recorder next to the bed. I have done this for years. As soon as a thought threatens my somnolence, I write it down. Then I forget it.

Rx: 6 Don't Catastrophize Insomnia

If insomnia strikes, don't panic. It happens to everybody from time to time, and one or two nights of sleeplessness do not constitute a crisis. What can become a crisis, however, is your *reaction* to the experience.

After one or two nights of sleeplessness, a pattern develops. Annoyance turns to fear, then fear turns to panic. And nothing retards sleep like panic. Trying to force yourself to sleep is the surest way of preventing somnolence. A persistent pattern of insomnia sometimes begins with exactly this reaction of desperation. "Sleep is one of the few things in life that cannot be improved upon by trying harder," explains sleep expert Dr. Peter Hauri.

If insomnia is a problem, don't stay in bed awake. Get up, sit in a comfortable chair or lie on the couch, read, write a letter, have a light snack, drink some milk, take a walk, soak in the bathtub, play relaxing music, watch television. But don't worry.

Consider turning the night into a conversation with God. Pray. Listen. Meditate. Read the Word. Begin a spiritual journal. Listen to Christian radio. And don't forget to thank Him for the special opportunity of this time together. When tiredness begins to overtake you, retire once again with gratitude for the double blessing of this night: that of fellowship and now that of sleep.

Following a night or two of sleeplessness, a common mistake is to go to bed earlier the next evening. The understandable thinking is to hope that nine hours in bed will result in at least seven hours of sleep. But this is exactly the wrong tactic. It is actually more restful to stay in bed seven hours and get six hours of sleep than to stay in bed nine hours and get seven. Go to bed later, not earlier. As the problem resolves, you can gradually resume your normal sleep schedule.

Insomnia can sometimes be a symptom of depression. Instead of poor initiation of sleep, however, the sleeplessness of depression is usually characterized by early awakening. For this condition, antidepressant medications can often be very helpful. They are not sleeping pills—although they can have a beneficial sedative side effect. They are not narcotics—although they can help greatly with chronic pain and its associated sleeplessness. And they are not addicting.

Although there are occasional indications for sleeping pills, it is not a good idea to depend on them. If you are undergoing a particularly stressful event in your life, sometimes a sleeping aid for a few days will keep sleepless exhaustion from compounding your troubles. But use them for no more than two weeks. After that time, if you try to stop taking them you will suffer rebound insomnia.

Rx: 7 Don't Oversleep

As a rule, oversleeping will make you feel worse rather than better. Extra sleeping paradoxically often causes extra tiredness. Also, headaches are more common with excess sleep.

Rx: 8 Take a Nap

Many of the world's greatest leaders were nappers. Thomas Edison is said to have catnapped up to eight times a day. John F. Kennedy napped in the White House, and Churchill took daily naps even during World War II. No doubt Jesus Himself napped.

Naps can be revitalizing. Even the Federal Aviation Administration is considering allowing the pilot to nap during long flights while the copilot takes the controls.

If you have the opportunity and need to nap, it is best to follow certain guidelines. Don't nap for more than one hour. If you do, understand that a longer nap is not necessarily more restful. The most helpful naps are in the afternoon, taking advantage of a mild drop in body temperature that induces somnolence.

A short nap in the early evening can give added stamina for the hours ahead. A longer evening nap, however, will often hinder the initiation of sleep that night.

Rx: 9 Exercise for Sounder Sleep

One of the first benefits people notice when they embark on an exercise program is sounder sleep. Healthy physical tiredness probably has no equal as a sleep-inducing sedative.

Don't, however, exercise vigorously just before going to bed. While a routine of stretching exercises or a leisurely walk can be an excellent prelude to a good night's sleep, a six-mile run is not a good idea.

THE RECIPES OF NUTRITION

Rx: 10 Decrease Intake of Fat

The typical American diet derives 37 percent of its calories from fats. This percentage should be cut to thirty or below, which means we need to eliminate two hundred to three hundred calories of fat out of our diet each day. (See figure 8.1 below.)

Figure 8.1

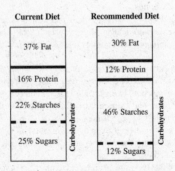

Of course, we all know we should eat less fat, but we eat it anyway. There are three main reasons for this: It tastes good, it is our habit, and we can afford to. In rebuttal: There are other things that taste good, we can change our bad habits, and we can't afford not to.

If you have three lumps of food sitting in front of you—one fat, one protein, one carbohydrate—all weighing the same amount, the lump of fat will have twice as many calories as the other lumps. So, using very simplistic math, if you want to eat a pound of food, it makes sense to eat a pound of carbohydrates or protein rather than a pound of fat with twice the calories. Pastries, donuts, ice cream, butter, hamburgers, French fries, steak, gravy—they all sound good, but they are all calorie-dense. Our margin in physical energy disappears as our waistline expands.

Good nutrition begins not in the kitchen but at the front door of the grocery store. If it isn't good for you, don't buy it. If everything looks too good, then shop only after a big meal when things don't look nearly as good. If you still can't help yourself, try shopping at a co-op that doesn't carry junk food. If that still doesn't work, send someone else.

Rx: 11 Decrease Intake of Sugars

Forty-seven percent of the typical diet is made up of carbohydrates. Of this, starches (or complex carbohydrates, such as potatoes, beans, wheat, and corn) make up 22 percent and sugars (or simple carbohydrates, such as table sugar, the fructose in fruits, and the lactose in milk) make up 25 percent. We need to change this in three ways: increase total carbohydrates as a percentage of our diet; double the percentage of starches; and cut the amount of sugar in half.

As a dominant component of the diet, refined sugar is a fairly late arrival in the Western world. Two hundred years ago we ate two pounds a year per person; now the figure is from 120 to 170 pounds a year (thirty-three to forty-seven teaspoons a day).

Actually, the use of table sugar has been declining. The real problem comes in the "invisible" or "hidden" sugar added during food processing. But food processors only sell us what we buy, and we only buy what our children beg for. Ninety-five percent of the food ads on Saturday morning television are for junk food: sugared cereals, candy, small cakes, chips, gum. It is little wonder that our schoolyards roll with obesity. "Most nutritionists agree that the worst influence on a child's eating habits is television," observes Sarah Eby.[18] Perhaps that applies to their parents as well.

Rx: 12 Replace Processed Snacks with Fruit

Fruits can be a good substitute for fats and "hidden" sugars. Oftentimes we bypass fruits thinking they are too expensive. Then we travel down the aisle and pick out cookies, chips, and candy instead.

To expose the fallacy of this expense excuse, Linda and I did some calculations based on average costs in our supermarket.

Item	Average Cost Per Pound
Cookies	$3.11
Candy	3.03
Crackers	2.80
Small Cakes	2.53
Donuts	2.49
Grapes	.99
Oranges	.89
Apples	.74
Pears	.50
Bananas	.39

The argument that fruits are more expensive just disappeared. Compared to other types of snack foods with lots of fat and refined sugar in them, fruits are a bargain. They are tasty, often sweet. They are liked by both children and adults. They are a good source of fiber. They are available year-round.

My advice is to spend less money on processed snack foods and more money on fruits. Have them available in a fruit bowl on the table as well as in the refrigerator. Have different forms — fruit juices, fruit leather, dehydrated fruits.

Give yourself permission to buy fresh fruits in abundance, and then give your family permission to consume them liberally.

Rx: 13 Balanced Diet

In recommending fruits, I certainly don't intend to slight vegetables. But when we search for a replacement for fats and sweetened snacks, fruits stand a better chance in the competition.

Indeed, balanced food groups are so universally recommended that they hardly need my endorsement. And in addition to balancing the food groups, also balance the three meals. Many people skip one or two meals, thinking they are doing themselves a favor. Instead, it's a disfavor. Studies indicate that a daily habit of all three meals, taken in moderation and without between-meal snacking, is the clear winner when it comes to healthy outcomes, whether in weight, vigor, or longevity.

Rx: 14   Avoid Overeating

Put smaller portions on the table. Use a small plate. Chew food longer. Set your fork down between every bite. Don't prepare the next bite until you have finished chewing and swallowing the one in your mouth. Consciously taste your food. Don't take seconds. Always sit down to eat. Eat at only one place in the house. Don't eat in front of the television. Don't snack. Bite your tongue.

Rx: 15   Garden or Buy Direct

There are two ways to process food: God's way and the factory way. God has our best interest at heart; the factories often don't.

The ground, taking its orders from God, fortunately doesn't process food the way factories do. And, generally speaking, the less factory processing, the better the food. Always protect the most direct connection from the Father's hand to your table. If there are too many steps in between, chances are the food has been unhealthified in proportion to the number of steps. If there is plastic around it instead of dirt, suspect that it didn't come directly from God.

Of course, just because food successfully bypasses the factory does not guarantee a healthy end product. For example, some garden fertilizers and pesticides are acceptable, while others are not. Without getting into an extensive discussion about chemicals and additives, suffice it to say that my main concern is the added salt, sugar, and calories found in factory-processed foods. Avoid them if you can.

Rx: 16   Drink a Lot of Water

The universal recommendation is six to eight glasses of water a day. For many, ice water is more palatable than tap water.

Drinking a large glass of water before sitting down for a meal can help keep you full and suppress the appetite.

Rx: 17   Use Exercise as Both Appetite and Weight Reducer

It is a myth that exercise increases appetite. In most cases, vigorous exercise diminishes appetite, sometimes even to the point of nausea. So if it works for you, sweat before you eat.

Also, if the goal is weight reduction, combine exercise with dieting. Dieting alone will result in the loss of not only fat but also lean body tissue such as muscle. On the other hand, exercise alone requires a huge amount of effort for a small amount of weight loss.

Every extra pound we gain equals 3,500 calories. Figure 8.2 demonstrates how many hours of various exercises are required to burn 3,500 calories for people weighing 100 pounds, 150 pounds, or 200 pounds. As you can see, relying on exercise alone for weight reduction will yield frustratingly meager results. The balanced and sensible approach, therefore, combines both calorie restriction and calorie incineration in a weight-reduction program.

Figure 8.2 - Burning 3,500 Calories

Number of Hours

Activity and Intensity		*100 lbs*	*150 lbs*	*200 lbs*
Walking	2 mph	29.2	19.4	14.6
Walking	4 mph	15.8	10.5	7.9
Jogging	6 mph	7.2	4.8	3.6
Running	9 mph	5.0	3.4	2.5
Cross Country Skiing	8 mph	5.6	3.7	2.8
Bicycling	13 mph	8.2	5.5	4.1
Swimming	55 yds/min	6.6	4.4	3.3
Ironing		20.1	13.4	10.1
Chopping Wood		12.0	7.9	6.0

Rx: 18   McStay at Home

There is often no comparison between the calories, fat, and sodium we consume when we prepare food at home versus dining out. For some, the difference between normal weight and obesity is the difference between eating in and eating out.

THE REGIMENS OF EXERCISE

Rx: 19   Exercise for the Heart

There are five aspects to a fitness evaluation: cardiorespiratory endurance, muscle strength, muscle endurance, flexibility, and body composition. Fitness in each of these five is recommended, but by far the most important and beneficial is cardiorespiratory endurance.

Think of your heart as a plow horse. You abuse it and abuse it and abuse it—but it never complains. And then one day in the middle of a furrow, it drops dead.

Don't abuse your heart. It is your workhorse. Every day it beats one hundred thousand times and pumps sixteen hundred gallons of blood over sixty thousand miles of vessels. Say thank you to your heart.

Buy it roses. Encourage it every chance you get.

One way you can encourage your heart is by conditioning it. Through exercise, for example, you could cut your heart rate from perhaps eighty beats a minute down to sixty. In so doing, you would save your heart thirty thousand beats a day and eleven million beats a year. As a token of its appreciation, it would send you back a gift. Try it for a few months and see what the gift is.

A specific fitness program aimed at conditioning the cardiorespiratory system focuses on the body's ability to deliver and use oxygen. *Aerobic conditioning* trains your heart, your lungs, your blood, and your blood vessels in such a way that they can deliver more oxygen faster and more efficiently to the body.

How is this accomplished? By performing thirty to forty-five minutes of *sustained* exercise — walking, jogging, swimming, bicycling, etc. — three times a week.

A common misconception people have is that they already live an active life, so why all the fuss? They are on their feet all day, up and down stairs, lifting, bending, stooping, and generally on the go continuously. They always come home tired; therefore, they assume they get plenty of exercise. It is important to recognize, however, that although this might be a busy lifestyle in one sense, it is not conditioning exercise.

Note well: Of the twenty-nine prescriptions in this chapter, this recommendation will do more to establish margin in physical energy than any of the others.

Rx: 20 Exercise for the Muscles

A second kind of exercise has to do with skeletal muscle development. Despite what many falsely believe, this is not the same as cardiorespiratory conditioning. Nevertheless, muscle conditioning is important and often neglected. While weight lifting and calisthenics do not constitute overall aerobic conditioning, they can give enhanced strength, speed, agility, and self-esteem.

There are two aspects to muscle fitness — strength and endurance. In a weight-training program, for example, lifting heavier weights with fewer repetitions increases strength, while lifting lighter weights with more repetitions increases endurance. As we age, muscle strength declines more quickly than does muscle endurance.

I do not support weight training for the vanity of it. But neither should it be forsaken simply because it is misused by bronzed bodies who flaunt it. The simple fact is, progress wrongly released us from the need to use our muscles, and if we do not use them we lose them.

Rx: 21 Exercise for Flexibility

Flexibility exercising is the least demanding in terms of wear and tear. We seldom huff, puff, or sweat. Yet it can help keep us moving and decrease our aches and pains, particularly in the back.

As we age, our flexibility becomes constricted. Watch the contortions of young children and compare them to your own creaky hinges. Undergoing a program of flexibility can help regain some of the lost range of motion with laudatory results. Our bodies much prefer wearing out to rusting out.

Rx: 22 Exercise for the Mind and Spirit

One hundred percent of people who exercise to the point of cardiorespiratory fitness will experience an increased sense of well-being. "We know that people who regularly exercise say they handle pressure better, feel more confident, happier and less depressed. . . . They even say they sleep better at night," says Jackie Kuta, University of Wisconsin exercise physiologist. "There are definite benefits for the mind, too. . . . Probably the most important thing is that it allows you to focus on something besides whatever is causing your stress."[19]

Exercise has a tranquilizing effect on the body. It helps to decompress stress and is good medicine for anxiety or depression. Along with increased energy, it grants increased alertness, increased independence, increased dignity, and increased self-esteem. "Exercise isn't just for the physically unfit. It's for the mentally unfit, too. I can recommend it for anyone who's depressed," explains aerobic expert Kenneth Cooper, M.D. "If exercise benefits the body, it can do wonders for the mind."[20]

Rx: 23 Bike or Walk

When studying in Switzerland for a year, I lived with a Swiss family. My "Swiss father," a physician-researcher for a pharmaceutical company, rode his bicycle to and from work each day, including a round trip home for lunch. My Swiss mother walked to town each morning to buy groceries for the day—bread, vegetables, meat, milk. They were not alone in these habits. As I daily made my way to the study center, the streets would be crowded with bicyclists and pedestrians.

As citizens of the most prosperous country in the world, the Swiss can afford to drive, but choose not to. Although the pattern has shifted over the years to more automobile use, I will never forget the example of health that was set for me that year.

In the United States, however, we go everywhere in our cars. Vehicles have become easy chairs on wheels. We don't even use arm strength to put down the windows. And when we arrive at our destinations, we still don't disembark. Instead, we "drive up" for our banking and "drive through" for our fast food. Now we even have drive-up churches and, of all things, I once heard of a drive-up baby clinic where you lift your child through the window to a waiting pediatrician.

Climb stairs rather than use the elevator. Park a block or two from your destination. Get off the bus or subway one stop early. *Any exercise is better than no exercise,* even if it is a walk of only ten steps.

Rx: 24 Exercise in the Morning (If You Can)
Morning exercisers seem to maintain a conditioning program better than those who choose the evening hours. One study followed exercisers for a year and discovered that 75 percent of those who worked out in the morning were able to continue their regimen. In contrast, "50 percent of those who exercised at midday and 25 percent of those who exercised in the evening" were able to maintain their programs.[21]

Rx: 25 Choose What Works for You
Try to find the kind of exercise that is most practical and enjoyable for you. "The generic drug here is exercise, and running is simply a brand," explains fitness activist George Sheehan, M.D. "It's a question of finding your brand of the drug."

Don't start playing racquetball if you hate the sport. I don't enjoy swimming and get cold every time I enter the water. So if I decided to swim as my exercise, I would be guaranteeing failure. However, I very much enjoy playing basketball with my twelve-year-old son, Matt (even though this often turns into more an exercise in futility than an exercise in conditioning, with the "guaranteed failure" coming in the score).

Rx: 26 Stick with It
You will be able to find many temptations to quit any exercise program. Prominent among them are:

Fatigue — Many complain of being too tired. But when you feel too tired to exercise is actually a good time to do it. Often, paradoxically, you will feel *less* tired after the workout than before. Several nurses at one of the hospitals where I work go to the exercise lab after a long day on the wards. Are they tired? Of course they are. But do they feel better after working out for a while? Do they have a more energized, productive, and enjoyable evening? Yes.

Have you ever noticed how you can come home fatigued, only to see the exhaustion disappear soon thereafter when doing something enjoyable? I remember one evening being very tired but needing to mow the lawn anyway (something I normally enjoy doing). After fifteen minutes, I was surprised to notice that the tiredness had disappeared. Fatigue, studies suggest, often has its source in emotional rather than muscular or cardiovascular exhaustion—although this is not to deny the validity of muscular tiredness as well.

Waning enthusiasm—Another reason for wanting to quit is diminishing enthusiasm. "Be prepared for 'going stale,' that period when you begin wondering why you ever started a training program," warns Dr. Cooper. "It happens to everyone. Just sweat it out. Go through the motions. Your enthusiasm will return."[22]

Discouragement—Yet another is the feeling that all this effort is not doing any good. What you don't realize is that it is doing good—you just can't fully sense it yet. Approach exercise as an investment. If you don't begin to receive dividends within two months, you have my permission to quit.

Rx: 27 Continue It Until the Hearse Arrives

You can't store up energy or exercise benefit for the future. If you exercise six months for cardiorespiratory fitness then stop, within two weeks the benefits will begin to disappear. Once you begin a program, plan to continue it in at least some form for the rest of your life. If that sounds like a big commitment, maybe that's because it is a big commitment. The majority of recommendations in this book for restoring margin have to do with sustainable lifestyle changes rather than "momentary compliance."

"The real battle over starting to exercise," explains Dr. Don Powell, "takes place in your mind, not in your body."[23]

Rx: 28 Be Realistic

One of my patients with advanced lung cancer came in wearing a concerned look on her face. "Doctor, I had my cholesterol tested and it is

221. Is that too high?" Her death three months later had nothing to do with cholesterol. There are enough problems to worry about without adding nonproblems to the list.

▶ Focus on the important issues. If you are forty pounds over-weight, don't worry about how much vitamin C is in a potato.

▶ Choose appropriate exercises. If you are elderly, it is probably best not to choose a running program. If you have arthritis or chronic low back pain, you may need to choose nonweightbear-ing exercises such as swimming or cycling (although a walking program is often beneficial for low back pain).

▶ If dieting, aim to lose only one to two pounds a week. Don't try to climb twenty stairs in a single bound. Slow changes are more sustainable.

▶ Be patient and persistent. "How poor are they who have no patience!" wrote William Shakespeare. "What wound did ever heal but by degrees?"

▶ Fads, scams, and frauds have a therapeutic value "as thin as the homeopathic soup that was made by boiling the shadow of a pigeon that had been starved to death," to borrow from Abraham Lincoln. Remember, *all* diets work short-term. Often the fast weight loss is water loss. John Renner, M.D., of the Consumer Health Information Research Institute, reports that there are ten thousand to fifteen thousand fad diets. If you find a new one, give him a call.

▶ Understand that this is not a definitive text on sleep, nutrition, or exercise. This chapter contains focused, practical hints that will help restore margin. Broadly applied, they can be of great help. But for more detailed information, see your physician or nutritionist.

▶ Expect to have ups and downs. Even the experts do.

▶ Set goals, but let them be reachable.

▶ Believe in yourself. I do.

Rx: 29 Give Your Body a Chance

The body is a miracle of complexity and sophistication that exceeds comprehension. Fortunately, most of it runs on automatic pilot—the heart beats, the blood circulates, the glands secrete, the enzymes cat-alyze, the electrolytes balance, the glucose metabolizes, the liver detoxifies. Even our thinking and breathing are largely automatic and involuntary; our brain and lungs function not because we tell them to but because God tells them to.

Describing the human body in detail would take an encyclopedia. Suffice it to say that God gave us an amazing gift, and all we are required to do is feed it, water it, rest it, and move it. Yet it needs to be the right food, water, rest, and movement.

If we perform our assignment well, we will find energy we never knew we had. We will work better, run better, feel better, heal better, and live better.

NINE

Margin in Time

T ed Anderson rose at 5:00 a.m. to howling winds and drifting snow. He washed, pulled on his work clothes and coat, and headed for the barn. Familiar with work he enjoys, Ted started feeding the 150 head of Angus cattle and attending to his other farm chores. By 7:00 a.m., he was back inside to have breakfast with his wife, Jae, and help get three-year-old Lottie Marie ready for the day. Quickly changing clothes, his next challenge on this frigid morning was to survive the icy roads into St. Paul. The usual one-hour commute to his systems-analyst job always takes longer when detoured through Siberia.

Meanwhile, Jae and Lottie Marie set off on an icy Wisconsin adventure of their own, braking and sliding the fifteen minutes to the veterinarian clinic where Jae is a full-time technician and animal groomer. Lottie has done well spending her first three years in the clinic. As a baby, she would sit in an infant seat or lay on a blanket. Now that she is older, she is always easily entertained. Each afternoon she takes a long nap in the back room.

After Ted returned home at 7:00 p.m., he finished the remaining chores on their eighty-acre farm. Most evenings, this was an hour or two of work.

Besides their own farm, the Andersons rent an additional eight hundred acres for open pasturing and for raising hay, corn, and oats. These crops have to be planted, cultivated, fertilized, harvested, baled, chopped, and stored. And, of course, the farm equipment—tractors, cultivators, balers—has to be cleaned, maintained, and repaired as well.

Anyone who would accept the job of vaccinating 150 head of cattle must be familiar with animals, and Jae is. She also has additional dogs, sheep, and horses of her own to care for.

Obviously, the Andersons are a hard-working young family. They love animals, farming, rural living, and challenges.

But they are marginless.

"What would happen if Lottie got sick?" I asked.

"She never has. We've been fortunate. She's been a great baby."

"Do you breed your herd?" I asked. "What happens during calving? How do you manage to monitor the births?"

"The Angus is famous for easy calving," explained Jae. "It *usually* just happens. All we do is check every day before and after work. Oftentimes we discover a calf that has already been born—or three or four. Then we take any newborns, weigh them, tag and vaccinate them, and give them back to mom. If any trouble arises, we have someone from the vet clinic come and help."

Lately, however, the system has been tested. This spring, the crops were planted late. Bad weather this fall delayed their harvest. The corn is now in storage, but wet with snow. They worry about mold.

A few months ago, some heifers were frightened out of the pasture by hunters. After the neighbors called, the chase was on. "We had to get help," explained Jae. "One person can't just run out and catch a nine-hundred-pound black heifer in the middle of the night without help." Some mischievous heifers continued to elude capture. Two were hit by cars on the road, necessitating police involvement.

Deciding to artificially inseminate one hundred cows this summer was a further strain. This type of breeding requires observing the herd closely. For several hours each morning and again each evening, the cows must be walked into a corral and watched. If any are in heat, they have to be separated out for insemination. This demand saw other chores suffer.

Since making the decision to expand their own family, Ted and Jae are planning some changes in their workload. "We are going to sell off at least half the cows and rent a smaller acreage next year,"

Jae explained. "And after the second baby is born, I will be quitting my job."

"How do you feel about that?" I inquired.

"Wonderful!" she explained through her fever and flu. "I love my job, and my boss is a good friend. But it will be wonderful to have more time at home."

TIME AND HOW WE TALK

Ted and Jae, along with millions of other Americans, live busy lives. Their industry and fortitude are in many ways reminiscent of the pioneer spirit that, centuries ago, carved a great nation out of a huge wilderness. They have work, a family, and a farm—all of which they enjoy. About the only thing they don't have is margin.

"I love a broad margin to my life," posited another farmer (of sorts), Henry David Thoreau. "Sometimes, in a summer morning, having taken my accustomed bath, I sat in my sunny doorway from sunrise till noon, rapt in a revery." Because his chronicles are so widely acclaimed, we think, *What a wonderful sentiment he expresses here.* But were our neighbor to seek this same reverie, we would criticize it as slothful. In contrast to Thoreau's love of a "broad margin," our modern view of time is to compress it and milk it for every nanosecond of productivity we can get.

To understand how a society experiences time, examine its operative vocabulary. We talk of no time, lack of time, not enough time, or being out of time. Trying to get more time, we borrow time only to incur a time debt and end up with even less time. Management in the workplace is so time-conscious that they practice time-management skills and time-compression techniques. They use a computerized timepiece to assure work efforts are time-intensive with no time lost. This sense of time urgency creates time pressure and time stress. Then, it's crisis time.

If God would allow us to delete any of these time phrases we thought destructive, which would you choose? If you had the opportunity of setting the time agenda for society, which concepts of time would you endorse and which would you renounce? Many executives and type As would vote to keep time linked with speed and productivity. A typical manager's view of margin? If you can catch it, kill it.

The rest of us, however, would strike these time phrases from our collective vocabulary as mortifying to the human spirit. Of course work time is important. But so is discretionary time, that is, margin. Some discretionary time would be used as leisure time, play time, free time, or time off. Some would be personal time, solitude time, fallow time, and time to think. We hope a good portion of it would be time together: sharing time, family time, couple time, prayer time.

Ideally, you see, our time should all be God's time, directed by Him and used for His purposes. It is not right that progress has tyrannized us so.

TIME AND TWITCHING

I have a fantasy: If a terrorist organization were to simultaneously trigger all the world's alarm clocks, stove timers, beepers, factory whistles, car horns, doorbells, dinner bells, digital-watch alarms, fuzzbusters, car phones, telephones, intensive-care alarms, smoke alarms, fire alarms, burglar alarms, civil-defense alarms, and sirens—namely, every man-made, adrenaline-shocking device that signals "Hurry!"—do you think it would be enough to bring Christ back prematurely, out of sheer pity?

Have you ever had a beeper go off in your ear when you were sleeping? It is one of the most horrifying experiences ever dreamed up by technology to ambush innocent, already-exhausted wretches. Although it has happened to me thousands of times, to date I have not even begun to approach psychic accommodation to the experience. It is fitting that a society with urgency as its emblem should have Valium as its addiction. Where are the noises that tell us to slow down? Which way to Lake Wobegon, that "quiet town, where much of the day you could stand in the middle of Main Street and not be in anyone's way"?

Columnist Bob Greene called it the "twitching of America." Futurist David M. Zach called it "hyperliving—skimming along the surface of life." The late Norman Cousins called it "a sprinting, squirting, shoving age." E. F. Schumacher called it "the forward stampede." From "fast food" to the "weekend squeeze" to the "Christmas rush," time has us in its grip.

CONFOUNDED SUNDIAL!

Long before our nanosecond culture, frustration with time urgency was apparent. Already in 200 BC, Plautus was cursing the sundial.

The gods confound the man who first found out
How to distinguish hours! Confound him, too,
Who in this place set up a sun-dial,
To cut and hack my days so wretchedly
Into small portions.[1]

Of course, time frenzy had barely begun, and were Plautus alive today he might run his chariot off a cliff. What was it like to have no notion of a second or a minute or even an hour? To never be late . . . or early. To not even know what late or early is. To never hear an alarm.

The first mechanical clocks were alarms of sorts, introduced in the Western world during the 1200s. Only a bell indicated time. In the 1300s, the dial and hour hand were added. "Here was man's declaration of independence from the sun, new proof of his mastery over himself and his surroundings," explains historian Daniel Boorstin. "Only later would it be revealed that he had accomplished this mastery by putting himself under the dominion of a machine with imperious demands all its own."[2]

By the 1600s, the minute and second hands were common. The invasion of the wristwatch began in 1865, about the same time Matthew Arnold penned his famous "The Scholar Gypsy"—a coincidence perhaps, but still one wonders.

O born in days when wits were fresh and clear,
    And life ran gaily as the sparkling Thames;
        Before this strange disease of modern life,
With its sick hurry, its divided aims,
    Its heads o'ertax'd, its palsied hearts, was rife—
        Fly hence, our contact fear!

In 1879, Thomas Alva Edison produced the first electric light. If the clock broke up the day, the light bulb broke up the night. Humanity was flushed with its presumed victory over yet another of nature's limitations. Yet all victories have their associated costs. The clock and the light—they gifted us with time, then they stole it away.

THE PREDICTION THAT TURNED OUT ALL WRONG

Thirty years ago, futurists peering into their crystal balls predicted that one of the biggest problems for coming generations would be what to do with their abundant spare time. I remember hearing this prediction often. In 1967, testimony before a Senate subcommittee claimed that by 1985 people could be working just twenty-two hours a week or twenty-seven weeks a year or could retire at age thirty-eight.[3]

Exactly when they stopped talking this way I am not sure, but they did stop. No one sits around today trying to figure out how to spend free time. On the contrary, the topic of conversation is usually how to get some.

According to a Harris Survey, the amount of leisure time enjoyed by the average American has decreased 37 percent since 1973. Over the same period, the average workweek, including commuting, has jumped from under forty-one hours to nearly forty-seven hours.[4] When you add the total hours worked by the dual-income family outside the home, the difference is even more accentuated.

Progress was billed as leisure-permitting and time-gifting. The opposite has been true. "The modern world of streamlined transportation, instantaneous communication, and time-saving technologies was supposed to free us from the dictates of the clock and provide us with increased leisure. Instead there seems never to be enough time," explains Jeremy Rifkin in *Time Wars*. "Tangential or discretionary time, once a mainstay, an amenity of life, is now a luxury."[5]

THE SPONTANEOUS FLOW OF PROGRESS

How can one explain this gap between the prediction and the reality? Instead of the workweek shrinking, it is expanding; instead of free time increasing, it is decreasing. And in spite of "time-saving" devices, we have less time.

To help us understand the answer, let us return to an axiom of progress:

> *The spontaneous flow of progress is toward increasing stress, complexity, and overload.*

Now we may add a corollary to this axiom:

> *The spontaneous flow of progress is to consume more of our time, not less . . . to consume more of our margin, not less.*

In other words, if we sit back, do nothing about it, and watch it happen, next year at this time we will have less time margin than we do right now. For every hour progress saves by organizing and technologizing our time, it consumes two more hours through the consequences, direct or indirect, of this activity. Because this fact is counterintuitive and subtle, we do not recognize it happening.

"People are submitting themselves to time-devouring technology," claims Todd Gitlin. This Berkeley sociologist is particularly concerned about the cellular phone craze creating more work rather than saving more time. "We're a nerve-racked society where people have difficulty sitting back and thinking of the purpose of what they do."[6]

"Paradoxical as it may seem, modern industrial society, in spite of an incredible proliferation of labor-saving devices, has not given people more time to devote to their all-important spiritual tasks; it has made it exceedingly difficult for anyone, except the most determined, to find any time whatever for these tasks," observes E. F. Schumacher. "In fact, I think I should not go far wrong if I asserted that the amount of genuine leisure available in a society is generally in inverse proportion to the amount of labor-saving machinery it employs."[7]

INTERRUPTIONS AND JUNK MAIL

Nearly all of us are caught scratching our heads about this mystery of having so little time in an era of so many conveniences and such vaunted efficiency. How can this be? To help bring this mystery to light, let us examine some of the uniquely contemporary ways we spend our time.

In a lifetime, the average American will

- Spend six months sitting at traffic lights waiting for them to change.
- Spend one year searching through desk clutter looking for misplaced objects.
- Spend eight months opening junk mail.
- Spend two years trying to call people who aren't in or whose line is busy.
- Spend five years waiting in lines.
- Spend three years in meetings.
- Learn how to operate twenty thousand different things, from pop machines to can openers to digital radio controls.

In addition, the average person will

▶ Commute forty-five minutes every day.
▶ Be interrupted seventy-three times every day. (The average manager is interrupted every eight minutes.)
▶ Receive six hundred advertising messages every day (television, newspapers, magazines, radio, billboards).
▶ Travel 7,700 miles every year.
▶ Watch 1,700 hours of television every year.
▶ Open six hundred pieces of mail every year.

What did we do with all our time before we had traffic lights, telephones and busy signals, televisions, interruptions, and cluttered desks? What did we do with our time before we spent it shopping for things we don't need? What did we do with our time before we used it to sort through forty-three annual pounds of junk mail? What did teenagers do with their time before they began listening to ten thousand hours of rock music between grades seven and twelve? Is it possible the time margin was used for things more inherently valuable to the Kingdom than commuter traffic, busy telephones, and junk mail? Is it possible the time was spent on things physically taxing instead of mentally frustrating? Is it possible the time margin was used for conversing, for serving, for resting, for praying?

True, we get to places faster—but we have more places to go. A net loss. We have devices to help us clean—but we have more things stuffed into more square footage to clean. A net loss. Hasn't the light bulb given us more time because now we can plan activities during the evening that were previously limited to daylight hours? Yes. The light bulb has given us more capacity to be busy, to produce, and to fill up schedules in the evening—when before all we could do was sit around the table and read or sit by the fire and read or sit with family and friends and visit until it was time for all to go to bed. A net loss.

Let's revisit the Third World. Here we find no televisions, no shopping malls, no traffic lights, no telephones, no cluttered desks, no junk mail. So what do people do with their time? It exists for them as margin. Some of their time is used for work—the physical work of growing food, which is good for the body and spirit. Some of their time is used for visiting the marketplace, which is good for community. A good portion of their time is for leisure. Time to watch the kids play or the donkeys bray. Or to talk to the neighbor. Or to sleep.

WORK AND TIME STRESS

When we think of time pressure, perhaps no thought comes as quickly to mind as the workplace. The stressors we experience there, according to business consultant Douglas LaBier, "are rooted in pure bombardment: the accumulation of too much work relative to the time we have, too many demands from our work and personal lives, and too many decisions facing us and not enough time to deliberate about them. In short, too much to deal with in a world which is too busy and . . . in which we all feel tremendous pressure to make the right decision right now."[8]

When appropriately undertaken, work is biblically required and an absolute necessity for healthy living. Many, however, are so driven by their work that they can never take a day off or enjoy a quiet walk in the woods. Whether we call them "type A," "driven," "workaholic," or "extra effort people," they have a problem with work addiction. They do not notice the lack of balance in their lives, for they are too preoccupied with leading our national charge toward production, expansion, and success.

Such a lopsided drive toward accomplishment lands work-addicted people top positions in nearly every endeavor. From this vantage point they often systematically remove from their employees the same freedoms they themselves have forsaken. It is common to see a worker wishing for some measure of breathing space, yet gasping for freedom because of the demands of an excessively controlling boss. These employers are so affixed on success that their lives—and the lives of those they control—contain little besides work.

Meanwhile, for the exhausted, frustration-filled employee, there are three assignments due at the same time—yesterday. Deadlines flood over them like the Mississippi at springtime. They are on the road; then they are transferred. Debt and taxes mount, so they work harder. Family and friends become strangers passing in the night. First, they miss Johnny's home run and Betsy's first step. Then, they miss John's wedding and Elizabeth's graduation.

Because financial margin is often nonexistent, people seek supplemental employment. Many work two jobs or extra shifts. Moonlighting is increasing. Work has invaded evenings, nights, weekends, holidays, and worship days. Stores and restaurants that once respected margin respect it no longer, often open twenty-four hours a day, 365 days a year. Such expansion pushes the issue to its limits and is hardly the way to gain more time margin.

Harvard economist Juliet Schor explains that the average American will work the equivalent of one month longer this year than twenty years ago. Not only are there more dual-earner families (nearly two-thirds of married American women are employed), but also we have record rates of overtime and moonlighting. Employed mothers now put in an average of sixty-five hours a week, when you combine domestic work with the hours of labor logged on their other jobs. "And my figures," Schor points out, "are extremely conservative."[9]

Now, however, for the first time in fifteen years, Americans are choosing leisure over work as the most important thing in their lives. Upon first reflection, many might attribute this trend to laziness and lament it as reflective of all that is wrong with our country. But I see it as a corrective reaction to time starvation.

NANOSECOND EFFICIENCY

Improving productivity in the workplace is the equivalent of body-building in the gym, and efficiency is the steroid. Bosses know that time pressure works, that it increases both productivity and efficiency. But who is to say when it has been pushed too far? How much can people take? Many video-display-terminal workers are now monitored electronically. Every keypunch is recorded, and if their quota is not met, their record is tainted and their job threatened.

Speed. Supercomputers operate at trillionths of a second. Do you know what that means? Neither do I, and I have a degree in physics. A trillionth of a second has no human reference.

Speed. Using electronic linkages, computers can make transactions so fast that the same dollars can finance seven different deals on the same day.

Speed. At international currency exchanges, traders watch their video-display screens as the constantly changing world-currency prices flash before them. If they move fast enough at the right moment, they can make hundreds of thousands of dollars in a couple of minutes. "For us, currencies have a value not for a day or an hour, but for a second," explained one trader.

Speed. In the past, it took weeks to send a letter by pony express. Then, it took days by mail. Then, hours by overnight jet. Now, it takes only seconds. "The fax has destroyed any sense of patience or grace that existed," says Hollywood publicist Josh Baron. "People are so crazy now that they call to tell you your fax line is busy."[10]

Speed and efficiency are the keys to productivity, and productivity is the key to success. But, of course, we must have quality. So we want more and more speed, more and more efficiency, more and more productivity, with better and better quality. In the end we have platinum products and dead workers.

"There is more to life," recognized Ghandi, "than increasing its speed."

TIME STRESS AND OUR FRIENDS

The marginless lifestyle and its resultant chronic time pressure are particularly devastating to our relationships: to self, to family, to others, to God. "I don't have time for relationships anymore," laments one business employee. "I got tired of calling up and apologizing— 'Sorry about dinner; I've got to work late again.'"[11]

Everyone needs personal time. Those who say they don't need time for self are probably the ones who need it the most. We all need time to let the dust settle, to evaluate how life is going, to plan for the future, to focus on that which is spiritually authentic. "Those who are caught up in the busy life have neither the time nor quiet to come to understand themselves and their goals," quotes Robert Banks. "Since the opportunity for inward attention hardly ever comes, many people have not heard from themselves for a long, long time. Those who are always 'on the run' never meet anyone any more, not even themselves."[12]

Everyone needs family time. Families have been particularly hard hit by the time famine. Nearly every study on family stress reveals time pressures to be at or near the top. Noted family researcher Dolores Curran has found that, of the top ten family stressors, four have to do with lack of time:

▶ Insufficient couple time
▶ Insufficient "me" time

▶ Insufficient family playtime
▶ Overscheduled family calendars[13]

Consider the amount of time we spend in some of these relationships. Spouse-to-spouse time averages as little as four minutes a day of meaningful conversation. Parent-to-child quality time resides in the same neighborhood: between thirty-seven seconds and five minutes a day, depending on the study. "Making an appointment is one way to relate to your child," says UCLA anthropologist Peter Hammond, "but it's pretty desiccated. You've got to hang around with your kids."[14]

There are many tempting competitors for a parent's attention today, leaving us in a quandary about how much time and emotional energy we should give to child-rearing. But human children are not capable of self-rearing; they never have been nor will they ever be. "The inevitable loser from this life in the fast lane is the little guy who is leaning against the wall with his hands in the pockets of his blue jeans," explains family psychologist Dr. James Dobson. "Crowded lives produce fatigue—and fatigue produces irritability—and irritability produces indifference—and indifference can be interpreted by the child as a lack of genuine affection and personal esteem."[15]

Everyone needs sharing time. We each must have time to give away in the nourishing of our relationships. Calendars today are so crowded, however, that there is no space to pencil in a friend. As a result, long-term friendships are vanishing and neighborhood identities are fading. "Neighbors no longer share common aspirations or values," explains one *Wall Street Journal* columnist. "Struggling just to maintain their standard of living, people don't have time for their families, let alone their neighbors."[16]

Everyone needs God time. Because He is not temporally pushy about His agenda, God is too easy to forget. He just waits . . . and waits. What does He think of "efficient" prayers? What happened to the "Be still and know that I am God" times? Societies that have the accelerator to the floor are doomed to become God-less. Speed does not yield devotion.

TIME AND THE INVENTOR OF TIME

Do you think Jesus would have carried a pocket calendar? Would He have consulted it before making commitments? Would He have bypassed the leper because His calendar said He was late for the Nazareth spring banquet?

Do you think Jesus would have worn a wristwatch? What would have been His reaction if the temple service extended past noon and alarms went off in the crowd? Would He have driven out the clock watchers along with the moneychangers? What would He have thought of the parishioner I knew who weekly timed the pastor's sermons with a stopwatch and reported the statistics on the way out of church?

Do you think Jesus would have carried a beeper? Would Martha and Mary have paged Him to come and raise Lazarus from the dead? Can you imagine Him being paged out of the Last Supper?

The clock and the Christ are not close friends. Imagine what God thinks of us now that we are so locked into schedules that we have locked ourselves out of the Sermon on the Mount—it is hardly possible to walk the second mile today without offending one's pocket calendar. We jump at the alarm of a Seiko but sleep through the call of the Almighty.

RESTORING TIME MARGIN

Progress tricked us into trusting it—then it exhausted us. But we are not helpless. The clock can be resisted. Time margin can be taken back. Let's see what steps we can take to restore sanity to our schedules.

Rx: 1   Expect the Unexpected
Nearly everything takes longer than anticipated. If you want some breathing room, increase your margin of error. For example, if you are chronically late, try adding an extra 20 percent time margin to your scheduled activities.

Rx: 2   Learn to Say No
As with emotional energy margin, saying no is not just a good idea—it is an absolute necessity. If there are one hundred good things to do and you can do only ten of them, you will have to say no ninety times.

Rx: 3   Turn Off the Television
As long as you are saying no, say it to your television set. For the average adult, this would gain more than thirty hours a week. No

other single effort will secure as much time margin as this simple, nearly impossible action.

Rx: 4   Prune the Activity Branches

"I view my life as a tree," explains Jean Fleming. The trunk is the anchor of her life, her relationship to Christ. The limbs represent those major focus areas that God has given her—family, job, ministry, and personal development. And the branches represent the ever-proliferating multitude of activities. "Even without special care, activity branches multiply. Soon the profusion of branches becomes more prominent than the trunk and limbs. When this happens, I feel trapped, frustrated, and empty. Why? Because my life is shaped and drained by activities that have lost their pertinence to Christ."[17]

Activities and commitments often have a way of self-perpetuating even when we are no longer particularly interested in them. It is much harder to stop something than it is to start it. Periodically, it is important to get the clippers and prune away.

Rx: 5   Practice Simplicity and Contentment

We all consume significant quantities of time in the buying and then maintaining of things. A life of voluntary simplicity and contentment, on the other hand, is opposed to the unnecessary proliferation of material possessions. It is free of the clutter much of society must sort through on a daily basis. With fewer possessions, we do not have as many things to take care of. With a simpler wardrobe, our choice of what to wear each morning becomes less time-consuming. With a smaller estate, there will be less debt bondage in our work schedule.

Recognize unnecessary possessions for what they are: stealers of divine time. At the beginning of every day we are given assignments that have eternal significance—to serve, to love, to obey, to pray. Instead, we squander much of this time on things that very soon will leave us forever.

Rx: 6   Separate Time from Technology

Remembering that technology is responsible for a great deal of our time famine, it is good to go on strike occasionally. Try disconnecting from clocks, watches, alarms, beepers, telephones, and faxes for a day, a weekend, or a week.

As an example, during our most recent trip to the developing world my wristwatch of twenty years gave out. Upon our return to the United States, I did not replace it. Without a watch it is true that I was handicapped in a certain way. But it also gave a very interesting sense of freedom. After a year, I finally purchased an inexpensive watch because my patients didn't quite know what to think of a doctor who had to borrow their watches to measure their pulses!

Cutting adrift technology is a good way to reassert our independence over the tyranny of the clock. Fasting from food leads to a starvation that purifies the body; fasting from technology leads to a margin that fortifies the spirit.

Rx: 7 Short-Term Flurry Versus Long-Term Vision

Americans are notoriously shortsighted. We live in a state of myopic mania that blurs the future. The horizon is never visible in the middle of a dust storm. But we must have a vision that extends beyond tomorrow. Living only from week to week is like a dot-to-dot life.

It is good to have five-year plans, even ten-year plans. For many these plans will be vague, for others specific. Our goals should be flexible to the redirecting God so often asks of us. But each of us needs a direction and a vision that can inform his or her focus.

Rx: 8 Thank God

If you have two meetings scheduled on the same evening, you obviously can attend only one. Don't overlook the possibility that this might be God's way of being kind to you.

Rx: 9 Sabotage Your Fuse Box

Have you ever noticed how a major storm freezes the clock? Time stands still as the whole world skids to a sudden halt. Once confident there is no danger to loved ones, we all begin to enjoy ourselves. The lights go out, and we rush for candles and flashlights. Then we sit and watch the sky or visit with each other or play board games. And sometimes we are tempted to pray that electricity isn't restored until a week from Tuesday.

Our family enjoys Wisconsin winters. A two-foot snowfall is a thrill, not a torment. When the world is snowed in, cars can't move, businesses can't open, and schools can't convene. A spirit of holiday reigns. Part of the reason for this is the unexpected gift of time margin.

"I'm not sure I understand it," commented Pastor Gordon

MacDonald after just such an occasion, "but I have this feeling that an increasing amount of conversational time between friends is spent on the subject of weariness, overcommitment, the perceived need to drop out. . . . Why on the one Sunday in five years when a New England snowstorm forced us to close down our church was it universally recognized by the congregation as the most wonderful Lord's day they had ever had?"[18]

Rx: 10 Get Less Done But Do the Right Things

Busyness is not a synonym for Kingdom work — it is only busyness. All activities need to be assessed as to their spiritual authenticity. Again, if we have one hundred things to do and can do only ten, how do we select from among them? We must have God-authored criteria with which to judge our activities, and we must be willing to use them. "The goal of much that is written about life management is to enable us to do more in less time. But is this necessarily a desirable goal?" asks Jean Fleming. "Perhaps we need to get *less done*, but the right things."[19]

Especially be on guard against the urgency we see in so much of life's flow. If this urgency regularly erodes either your time for relationships or your time for rest, reevaluation is appropriate.

Rx: 11 Enjoy Anticipation, Relish the Memories

Calendar congestion and time urgency have robbed us of the pleasure of anticipation. Without warning, the activity is upon us. We rush to meet it; then we rush to the next; and the next. In the same way, we lack the luxury of reminiscing. On we fly to the next activity.

For this reason, our family intentionally lingers on both of these relatively unremembered sources of delight. Fishing trips are planned at least six months in advance. Because our son Adam has spent the last two summers working in Alaska, this past winter I announced at a family meeting that we would be taking a trip there — in eighteen months. You can't imagine how much fun we have already had just thinking and planning.

When the activity is over, remember. Tell stories. Tell them again. Frame a picture. Mount a fish. Make a special effort to remember the funny happenings. With the gift of remembrance, we don't always have to do a lot. We can do a little and remember it a lot.

Remember that box full of old photos in your attic or basement? Gather your kids around and spend some evening arranging them in albums or picking out the best ones for collages. You won't believe the fun you'll have reminiscing together!

Rx: 12 Don't Rush Wisdom

In our current system, the decisive executive is rewarded. But seldom is true wisdom a product of speedy deliberation. As a matter of fact, wisdom is almost always slow. The more important the decision, the slower it should be made.

If life's pace pushes you, push back. Take as much time as you need for clearness to develop.

Rx: 13 For Type A's Only: Stand in Line

Cardiologist Dr. Meyer Friedman, one of the first to describe the type A personality, offered this practical advice to his patients: "Practice smiling. Purposely speak more slowly, stop in the middle of some sentences, hesitate for three seconds, then continue. Purposely say, 'I'm wrong' at least twice today, even if you're not sure you're wrong. Listen to at least two persons today without interrupting even once. . . . Seek out the longest line at the bank. Verbalize your affection to your spouse and children."

To the physician subset of type As (a large subset), he suggests, "Trash the extraneous. Cut out some of the committees, perhaps all. Give yourself a lunch break—out of the office. Browse in a bookstore, sit in a deserted church, go to a museum. During office hours, have your secretary schedule imaginary patients, whose names you don't know. Naturally, these patients will be no-shows. You will be able to use that time to catch up . . . or best of all, renew your spirit."[20]

Rx: 14 Create Buffer Zones

If you have a busy schedule with nonstop appointments, consider creating small buffer zones between some of the obligations, a kind of coffee break for the spirit. Even ten or fifteen minutes can allow you to catch up, make phone calls, close your eyes, pray, call your spouse, reorient your priorities, and defuse your tension.

Rx: 15 Plan for Free Time

If God were our appointment secretary, would He schedule us for every minute of every day? Well-meaning Christians might differ in their answers, but by now it must be obvious that I think the answer would be no. Many arguments could be made in defense of my answer, but perhaps the strongest is the lifestyle that Christ Himself chose. Time urgency was not only absent, it was conspicuously absent. And I doubt its absence had to do with cultural context.

Christ's teaching, His healing, His serving, and His loving were usually spontaneous. The person standing in front of Him was the opportunity He accepted. If He chose spontaneous living, isn't that a signal to us? Overloaded schedules are not the way to walk *In His Steps*.

"An exciting possibility is for individuals or families to arrange their schedules so one evening a week is free, not for church meetings, but for direct involvement in the lives of needy people," challenges Tom Sine. To such a suggestion one pastor responded: "There are three hundred active lay people in my congregation, and if they each volunteered one evening a week we could change the entire community!"[21]

Rx: 16 Be Available

This prescription is not a way to gain time margin, but instead a suggested way to use it up. Margin exists for the needs of the Kingdom, for the service of one another, for the building of community. It exists, just as we exist, for the purpose of being available to God.

"But it is possible that the most important thing God has for me on any given day is not even on my agenda," observes Pastor Bruce Larson. "Am I interruptible? Do I have time for the nonprogrammed things in my life? My response to those interruptions is the real test of my love."[22]

There are two ways we can be available. First, we can be willing to cancel our current activities at any time and go do what the Lord is bidding us to do. But, for obvious reasons, this seldom happens. It is understandable that we would continue with our task and say to the new need, "Sorry, I'm busy." That is part of why we make schedules in the first place, to organize our time.

For the very reason that we are seldom willing or able to interrupt our schedules, we ought to consider a second way of being available. The essence of this method is to acquire time margin and then offer it to the Father: "What do you want me to do with this time today? It would be a privilege to use it on behalf of the Kingdom." God's intention might be for us to use the time to pray, to meditate, to rest, to serve, to parent, to tell of the good news, or a thousand other ways of cooperating with His eternal purposes.

Being useful to God and other people is a large part of what life is meant to be. And yet "usefulness is nine-tenths availability." When others need help, they don't need it two days from now. "We must be ready to allow ourselves to be interrupted by God," explained Dietrich Bonhoeffer. "God will be constantly crossing our paths and canceling our plans by sending us people with claims and petitions. . . . It is part of the discipline of humility that we must not spare our hand where it can perform a service and that we do not assume that our schedule is our own to manage, but allow it to be arranged by God."[23]

DO YOURSELF A FAVOR

When flying from New York to San Francisco, we don't allow only three minutes to change planes in Denver. A much greater margin of error is needed. But if we make such allowances in our travels, why don't we do it in our living? Life is a journey, but it is not a race. Do yourself a favor and slow down.

It is not easy to reassert our right to time margin, but it helps when we are convinced that legitimacy exists for such a right. This legitimacy comes from the same God who exalts faithfulness over productivity, rest over speed, and availability over schedulability. It comes from the same God who invented time in the first place and reserves the right to set the rules for its use.

God never intended for time to oppress us, dictating our every move. That was progress's idea. Instead, time was simply His way of making sure "everything didn't happen all at once." We are free to use it, and if we are wise, we will use it with eternity in view.

Regaining margin in our use of time is one way of restoring freedom to overloaded lives. With time margin we can better enjoy what we are doing, we have a more wholesome anticipation of our next activity, we are more contemplative, we are more in touch with God and with each other, we have more time for service, and we actually delight in looking for the divine interruptions He sends us.

Margin in Finances

Moira was a forty-year-old overweight psychology professor from Texas. I first saw her during the second year of my residency training in Iowa, where we met over her gall bladder symptoms. Several visits later, her symptoms persisting, we decided on surgery. After a thorough history and physical, I predicted a successful operation followed by an inevitable demise. I was right. Her demise, however, had nothing to do with her physical health. Instead, she aspirated her own red ink.

Moira and her husband had no children. In substitute, they had seven cars, two boats (one that never touched water), a hot-air balloon, and a home with four thousand square feet of living space chock-full of brand-new clutter.

After bankruptcy proceedings, I happened to meet Moira downtown. "We are leaving for Texas next week," she smiled. "I was able to get a good job down there. The Lord has been good to us." I had never heard her talk about the Lord before and wondered about her theology. I also wondered if she had paid the clinic bill.

Both Moira and her husband worked. I never knew how much money they made. But however much it was, they spent more. About the closest they ever came to margin in their finances was the ledger sheet of their certified public astrologer.

THE BEST OF TIMES AND THE WORST OF TIMES

At last count, there were about 210 countries in the world. Every year, Americans spend more on trash bags than the individual gross national product of 90 of these countries. Even more astoundingly, we spend more on eating out than the individual gross national product of 200 of these nations.

Wealth. Is it the blessing of a generous God or the fast track to moral and spiritual ruin? Are we to feel guilt for the trash we put in our plastic bags or gratitude for the pizza and prime rib?

Our unprecedented affluence has brought benefits that even the most cynical ought to acknowledge. We have been able to afford education, housing, extended communications, and transportation to just about anywhere. We have health-care advancements that free us from grievous disease. Our food is plenteous. Recreational options seem limited only by the imagination. The elderly are, by and large, better-off financially than they have ever been. We even have enough to be generous benefactors, privately and governmentally, to the impoverished at home and abroad. It is clearly the best of times.

Unfortunately, however, these benefits do not constitute the whole story; luminous advancements often cast dark shadows. In the case of our economic prosperity, the shadows of debt, vulnerability, and uncertainty extend far into the future. For every positive economic indicator, there is a corresponding dismal one. We are in troubled water on nearly every financial front, and no one can confidently suggest a way out. "Serious economic experts make predictions that come up inside out," observes Norman Mailer, "and no one can quite explain why they are wrong."[1]

The major parameters of economic well-being fluctuate up and down, up and down, while millions of people in the United States nervously await each new development. How did we ever come to this state of dependence on the economy? The question ought not to be "What are the economic statistics doing?" but instead "What are the economic statistics doing to us?" Is the economy freeing us physically and spiritually and granting us a financial margin with which to serve the purposes of God? Or are we being reduced to feverish bundles of nervousness, discontent, and greed?

In fact, the debt trap set for us has a sudden spring — one that cuts off financial margin at the neck.

"BEYOND OUR MEANS"

Our list of economic woes is a long one. The ever-expanding invoice of problems requires an ever-expanding ocean of money, yet our government — along with a huge percentage of its citizens — is flat broke. As explained by *The Wall Street Journal* economist Alfred Malabre, Jr., "For a very long time, we've been living beyond our means — for so long, in fact, that now, sadly, it's beyond our means to put things right, at least in an orderly, reasonably painless manner."[2]

1. Personal, corporate, national, and international debt levels are lofting through the stratosphere. "A mountain of debt has begun to move," explains investment counselor William F. Rickenbacker. "Like some mindless blob advancing over the landscape of a horror movie, it is suffocating everything it encounters." While each of these areas is cause for great concern, nothing generates both cynicism and pessimism quite as quickly as the massive federal deficit. "There never has been anything approaching this level of debt funding in the history of mankind in so short a period of time, even on a percentage basis," observes financial counselor and analyst Larry Burkett. "The effects of this will be felt throughout the U.S. and ultimately the world's economies."[3]

2. Bankruptcies are at record levels, nearly one million each year. The rate of bankruptcy in the 1980s was quadruple what it was even in the depression-plagued 1930s. Ninety percent of these are "just plain folks" like you and me. Bankruptcy is currently the number one growth area for law firms.

3. Real estate costs have inflated so alarmingly over the last two decades that increasing numbers of Americans cannot afford to enter the housing market, even despite the volatile market correction of the early 1990s. Homeownership percentage peaked at 66 percent in 1980 and has fallen steadily since. The average mortgage today requires over one hundred hours of factory labor a month to pay, compared to forty hours two decades ago.

4. College tuition costs have consistently outpaced inflation to the point where parents can no longer afford the fees. Student borrowing

has tripled in the last decade. At current rates of increase, a college education at the turn of the century is projected to cost fifty thousand dollars for public universities (currently enrolling 80 percent of the students) and one hundred thousand dollars for a private degree.

5. The savings-and-loan industry lies in shambles. Prior to deregulation in 1982 there were 4,600 savings and loans. A decade later, there are only half as many. The government bailout will eventually cost taxpayers several hundred billion dollars—the greatest such financial loss in our nation's history.

6. Banks joined the thrifts in a decade-long morass. In the 1970s, only eighty-three banks closed their doors. In the 1980s, this number rose to eleven hundred. Overleveraged corporate takeovers, the oil bust, collapsing commercial real estate values, the farm recession, massive Third-World debt, and our sluggish economy have left the banking industry in the worst shape in sixty years.

7. Scandal and greed rock the economic world at every turn. From the excesses of Donald Trump to the exploitation of Michael Milken to the hip-pocket senators of Charles Keating, public cynicism has given way to anger. Indictments roll off the presses like a daily newspaper: cocaine on Wall Street, savings-and-loan ripoffs, insider trading, illegal loans, influence peddling, money laundering. All costs eventually come out of the taxpayers' pockets.

8. Many cities, counties, and states are scrambling to avoid insolvency. Connecticut recently was forced to cut its work force by 40 percent, while Maine entered a state of emergency. New York City laid off twenty thousand workers, while Philadelphia and Detroit staggered ever closer to the edge. Bridgeport, the largest city in Connecticut, became the first major municipality to formally seek federal bankruptcy protection. The fifty largest U.S. counties ran a total deficit of $760 million in 1991, radically up from their combined $159 million surplus in 1989.

9. Congressional spending on welfare and social programs has risen 2,000 percent since 1960. Despite this level of governmental intervention, poverty rates either remained the same or increased. Currently, one of every five children is impoverished. Unemployment and homelessness have proven once again their inextinguishability.

10. Health-care spending continues to spiral out of control. Per-capita costs were $1,000 in 1980, $2,400 in 1990, and are expected to climb to $5,500 by 2000. Total health-care spending has exploded from

$27 billion to $600 billion in thirty years, far outstripping the consumer price index. Health-care costs are without question the business community's biggest concern. With the rapidly growing elderly population, Medicare consumes ever larger chunks of the federal budget—an aggression that cannot continue much longer. Meanwhile, Medicaid is straining many state budgets perilously near to the breaking point. Hospitals, mostly rural and inner city, are being forced to close in record numbers. Our nation's 31 to 37 million uninsured is a plight unparalleled in the Western world. A philosophy professor from the University of Alabama Medical School finally threw up his hands: "I once was a liberal about financing medical care, then I became a conservative; now I am a nothing. I once thought physicians' fees caused increases in medical costs, then I blamed large institutions; now I blame everybody and nobody. I once thought escalating medical costs were a problem, later I thought they were a crisis; now I think our system may collapse before the second millennium."[4]

We are not running out of urgent projects that need expensive attention, but we are quickly running out of funding resources. "Most Americans do not want to confront the painful idea that we are headed toward the wrong future," observes former Secretary of Commerce Peter G. Peterson. "We face a future of economic choices that are far less pleasant than any set of choices we have confronted in living memory."[5]

FAMILY INCOME

Despite the tremendous increase in liabilities listed above, we have no more money to pay for it all. The federal government, state governments, and families are all swimming in the same red ink. Most citizens have given up hope for any budgetary realism to come out of Washington or state capitals, for the kind of political courage necessary to solve these fiscal problems would be not only painful for the public but also unpopular at the polls. Few politicians are willing to die for their constituency the way Jesus was.

It is therefore not surprising that governments seem so incapable of fiscal restraint. But why do families have such difficulty balancing their budgets? It would seem that family-style microeconomics should be easier to solve than the macroeconomic complexity of a $1.3 trillion federal budget or a $5.7 trillion economy.

Part of the reason families are broke is due to their unparalleled love affair with consumption. People often get into debt and destroy their financial margin simply because they buy too many things they don't need. But before we are too harsh on John and Jane Doe, let's understand another reason families find themselves in trouble. It is a matter of first grade arithmetic: Real expenses have risen and real income has not.

Median family income (adjusted for inflation) has been stalled for two decades. According to a U.S. Department of Commerce publication, "There was no increase in family income between 1973 and 1990 in real terms."[6] Perhaps even more dramatically, Harvard political economist Robert Reich explains, "Over the past 12 years, the top 20 percent of income earners in the United States have increased their real wages in the neighborhood of 8 to 12 percent. The bottom 80 percent have fallen steadily behind."[7] Understanding this, we are not surprised to discover that "the typical family now spends 30 percent of its income on debt service, compared with 20 percent a decade ago."[8] The number of families in debt counseling has tripled over the last decade.

It is little wonder that lack of money is the leading stressor among families. According to family researcher Dolores Curran, 58 percent of married men, 66 percent of married women, and 87 percent of single mothers list finances as the top stressor in their family.[9] When income stagnates yet expenses keep rising, financial margin vanishes along with the dreams.

DEBT WRONG

Significant controversy exists among economic experts concerning the advisability of debt. Some, such as Milton Friedman, argue that debt is the only effective restraint on congressional spending—and in that he is most certainly correct. Additionally, many economists believe that as long as indebtedness does not grow faster than the gross national product, it can prove beneficial to the performance of the economy. This is especially true if the debt, rather than wasted on consumption, is invested in our future, such as research and development, infrastructure improvement, and education.

Others remain unconvinced. Debt, they say, unavoidably imprisons the future, and the "buy now, pay later" mentality too often corrupts into "binge now, pain later."

Debt-sponsored economic theory has only been around for about sixty years. Deeply troubled by the unemployment of the Great Depression, Britisher John Maynard Keynes began urging governments to abandon Adam Smith's laissez faire approach and to become more active in regulating the economy, especially to avoid or reverse downturns. This led to the notion that it is acceptable and even fiscally wise for borrowing, credit, and interest to fuel an economy. President Franklin D. Roosevelt had no objection, for after all, we were only borrowing it from ourselves.

As a result, the national debt began its growth in the 1930s, followed by corporate debt after 1945. Shortly thereafter, personal debt began to swell. And in the mid-1980s, our international trade deficit turned negative for the first time since 1917. So popular has borrowing become that currently our total national indebtedness from personal, corporate, and governmental sources is double our gross national product. This number is alarming. Whether in the personal, corporate, or national arena, so much capital is being siphoned off for interest payments that the entire economic system is increasingly threatened with paralysis.

For my part, I don't like debt. Debt is a noose, and I don't like having my neck in a noose. I don't like my future being imprisoned. I don't like the idea that my children and my children's children will hold me to blame for their suffering. But I am not in charge, and by now, debt— that sworn enemy of margin—is everywhere.

"Let no debt remain outstanding, except the continuing debt to love one another," the Apostle Paul reminds us in Romans.[10] "God doesn't prohibit borrowing," explains Larry Burkett, "but He certainly does discourage it. In fact, every biblical reference to it is negative."[11] Why? Because, as Proverbs explains, "The borrower is servant to the lender."[12] After God paid so dearly to free us, He would prefer we not become slaves again except to righteousness.[13]

I am not an economist and can feel Luther Hodge's breath on my ear: "If ignorance paid dividends most Americans could make a fortune out of what they don't know about economics." But I would be less than honest if I didn't admit that the practice of chronic indebtedness at such levels seems unwise to me. Admittedly, this rather old-fashioned conviction might never lead to riches, but then, I don't remember Christ signaling me in that direction anyway.

PLASTIC AND THE PIT

Spending more than we make is one of those modern plastic privileges of dubious advantage. Much of this deficit spending on a personal and family level occurs because buying has become a national mania. According to studies, one-third of all shoppers experience an "irresistible compulsion" to buy. Many buy strictly out of impulse. They go to the mall with nothing in mind other than recreational shopping. Not only is it entertaining, but it makes them feel better — an antidepressant of sorts.

The average consumer enters the store carrying seven credit cards, while the average household credit-card balance is nearing $2,000 (in 1980, this figure was $550; in 1990, it rose to $1,833).[14] There are bank cards, retail cards, entertainment cards, oil cards — easy to obtain, easy to use, and hard to pay off. A recent television ad showed a Yuppie looking at his long string of credit cards and saying, "All these cards, and I'm maxed out on each one." Then comes the reassuring voice: "Now there is a new card! You cannot be excluded from obtaining it, there is no maximum on how much you can charge, and we will send it to you even if you are recently bankrupt!"

On the front side, this kind of credit is seductive. Out the back door, it is treacherous. The innocent-appearing plastic card draws its life from our financial margin, becoming more powerful as we sink deeper into debt. Soon we find ourselves looking up from a deep hole, surrounded by possessions we do not really own. "We can be poor because of the things we *have*," suggests William T. Snyder. "In debt and committed to the hilt, living from one paycheck to the next means a person has no room to wiggle!"[15]

Our love affair with plastic is one of the main reasons we have "no room to wiggle," that is, no margin. Yet we have lost interest in the discussions about caution and restraint. When it comes to fiscal matters, our skills at rationalization are so well developed we scarcely wince when God's Word counters us. We may soon learn that we followed the wrong piper, not to Paradise but to the pit.

WEALTH

"Money," the Yuppie maxim goes, "is life's report card." Our society is so captivated with earning money, having money, and spending money that we can think of little else. And what better way to gain a financial margin than to earn more money! But just as riches are not righteousness, so money is not margin.

Nothing in Scripture and in the chosen lifestyle of Christ could be clearer: Wealth is not an objective of the spiritual life. When we encounter money along the path of life, we are encouraged to do one of three things with it: turn and walk in the other direction; pick it up and give it away; or if needed, use it for the necessities of daily living. Any other interaction risks adverse spiritual consequences.

"Do not store up for yourselves treasures on earth. . . . But store up for yourselves treasures in heaven," Jesus taught. "For where your treasure is, there your heart will be also."[16] He, in fact, spent a great deal of time expounding on the issue, discussing it even more than the topic of prayer. If the ultimatum "You cannot serve both God and Money" was relevant for ancient Israel, how much more for our modern world?

Paul adds his warning in the strongest terms:

> People who want to get rich fall into temptation and a trap and into many foolish and harmful desires that plunge men into ruin and destruction. . . . Some people, eager for money, have wandered from the faith and pierced themselves with many griefs. But you, man of God, flee from all this, and pursue righteousness, godliness, faith, love, endurance and gentleness.[17]

Again and again the Word instructs us in explicit terms to distrust money. It is not that money is evil, but that the love of money leads to all kinds of evil. With sufficient wisdom and discipline, money can glorify God and be a blessing to many. But wisdom and discipline are not exactly our long suit.

THE INVESTMENT FIRM OF JOHN AND JOHN

I am not a wealthy man, and I will never be a wealthy man. This statement arises not from an inability to generate wealth. The medical profession has well-recognized income-generating abilities. I am not *unable* to be wealthy, but rather I am *unwilling* to be wealthy. Why would I—or anyone, for that matter—wish to fall into a trap, be plunged into ruin and destruction, be pierced with many griefs, and risk wandering from the faith?

Linda and I have no savings. There is an involuntary pension plan through the medical school, and our two sons have a college fund, but in our own personal account we have nothing. This, however, does not present a hardship. Quite the contrary, it represents freedom. For even as we have no savings, we also have no debt.

Please understand, I am not recommending this approach in a universal way. Most Christian financial counselors would probably gasp if I did. Given the uncertainties of our day, a savings plan is recommended for most, and I respect that opinion. Saving for housing, children's college education, and health care is not inherently wrong (or at least is not clearly wrong).

But in my own heart, where these things must ultimately be decided, I feel deeply the words of the Apostle John: "If anyone has material possessions and sees his brother in need but has no pity on him, how can the love of God be in him?"[18] That particular verse has dwelt with Linda in a closely bound friendship since her college days. Additionally, we are convicted by the example of John Wesley, who said, "If I leave behind me ten pounds for which I have no use I am a thief and a robber." It just seems to me that, according to the investment firm of John and John, the way we are doing things is the right way for us.[19]

Yes, we have financial margin because I make more than we need and our expenses are significantly less than my income. We don't buy new cars. We seldom buy new clothes. Our house is paid off. So what do we do with our margin? We like to plow it back into the fields of the Kingdom as quickly as possible.

FOR THE FUN OF IT

Any discussion of financial margin would be incomplete without mentioning the pure joy of it. There are three reasons for this joy.

First, by lowering expenses below income you live with far less stress and pressure. If the refrigerator breaks down, you don't. If your car needs new tires, you simply go out and get them. Without margin, life struggles and staggers and stumbles. But when margin is present, life flows. And flowing is more enjoyable than staggering.

Second, having financial margin allows beneficence toward others. This is one of the most rewarding of all human activities, and I am convinced it is a subset of love. Meeting the needs of others delivers us from the world of selfishness and into a world of grace and gratitude.

These two sources of joy are sufficient grounds to recommend margin. But there is yet a third, even greater, source of joy. It is a transcendent kind of pleasure that comes neither from within nor without but from above. It comes from the source of all that is right, and when you approach it you feel its warmth even from a distance. In giving, you are ushered into a world where cynicism and hatred have been banished. You are considering others before yourself. You are choosing Heaven as the place you will put your treasure. You are doing what God asked you to do, and what He did Himself. In giving, you are pleasing Him.

"It is more blessed to give than to receive," Jesus taught us through Paul. These words are not talking about a future-tense, theoretical blessing waiting for us beyond the eternal horizon, reserved there as compensation for the excruciating pain of giving today. Instead, this is a kind of joy that begins with the *thought* of giving, with the declaration of freedom in your soul that indeed you belong to God. And the joy culminates in the act of giving, often a secret except for the spotlight of Heaven.

The German existentialist Friedrich Nietzsche once claimed that Christians have no joy. But joy is mentioned over five hundred times in Scripture and clearly ought to be a part of the normal Christian life. If you wince because Nietzsche's dagger finds a joyless heart, restore your financial margin and then give it away.

RESTORING FINANCIAL MARGIN

Many see no way out. They have been treading water so long that they can't remember what it was like to have money left at the end of the month. They are controlled. Mammon, it seems, has won.

For all such weary debtors, take hope. A solution for our many economic burdens is possible; otherwise, God is not God. Let's see how we might go about restoring margin to our finances.

Rx: 1   Travel in the Right Direction
When making a journey of known destination, it is obviously important to start out on the right road headed in the right direction. In this case, our destination is restored financial margin. But before beginning our trip, the Father has some travel instructions for us.

If consulted, God would probably vote in favor of each of the previous three margins: emotional energy, physical energy, and time. Regarding financial margin, however, He would furrow His brow, look us in the eye, and then respond, "It depends." The issue hinges on whether or not the desired financial margin honors Him. Although each of the four margins discussed can be misused for self-serving goals, destinations involving money are particularly famous for dishonoring God. He wants to be sure before casting His vote with us.

In dealing with money, settling the issue of lordship is a mandatory first step. Otherwise, we find ourselves headed off in the wrong direction and mired in a spiritual morass that I want no part of. So, to clarify, we are not talking about restoring financial margin for the purposes of pride, of wealth, or of meeting our security needs in a way that bypasses the Father. Instead, we are talking about the kind of financial margin that honors Him.

To reach this kind of financial margin, which direction do we travel? For such an important question, contemporary Christians spend far too little time considering their answer. The choice of nearly the entire Western world is to travel down the economic road. We must realize, however, that *the economic road is not and has never been the road Jesus called us to travel*.

Economists and politicians of the past fifty years have honestly believed that economic advancement was the solution to the problems of humankind—a view shared nearly universally today. The conveniences I enjoy make me a beneficiary of such thinking. Yet if we are honest with ourselves, we should admit that the economic road was never suggested to us by Christ.

The economic answer is not the answer to our problems. Economics will solve some of our suffering, but nothing more. And solving our suffering is not the goal of the Christian life; walking in righteousness is. If we suffer, then we suffer—it is only for a season. But the economic road is not the road. The proverbial "bottom line" is not, after all, the bottom line.

If we are to restore margin to our finances, we must put first things first. Only then will we be able to break the power money holds on us and *use it instead of being used by it*.

Rx: 2   Break Its Back

Money is powerful—very powerful. It is so powerful, taught Jesus, that it competes head-to-head with God. "For Mammon's work is the exact opposite of God's work," explains French sociologist Jacques Ellul. "Given this opposition, we understand why Jesus demands a choice between Mammon and God. He is not speaking of just any other power, just any other god; he is speaking of the one who goes directly against God's action, the one who makes 'nongrace' reign in the world."[20]

Before we can accomplish anything righteous with money, we first need to understand this power, confront it, and with the help of God, demolish it. How is it possible to break the substantial power money holds over us? Very simple—give it away. "There is one act par excellence which profanes money by going directly against the law of money, an act for which money is not made," explains Ellul. "This act is *GIVING*."[21]

When we give money away, we not only neutralize its power over us, but we also bring it under the domain of the Kingdom of Light. Nongrace is turned into grace. God is honored, and His lordship is confirmed.

Rx: 3 Counter Culture

Once we are headed in the right direction and have, with the help of God, broken the power money holds over us, then we find yet another important battle in front of us: We must break the power of culture. Before we will be able to succeed in reestablishing financial margin, we must free ourselves from the dominating influences that surround us.

The way of the world is not a benign force, but instead a dictator that tells us how much education we should have; what kind of job we should seek; what kind of house, car, and clothes we should buy; who is "beautiful" and who isn't. It is rare to meet a person who isn't owned, bound, or trapped in destructive ways by a multitude of controlling cultural forces. If we remain controlled by such a culture, we will have little chance of achieving God-honoring financial margin. That same culture will demand we buy its wares and live by its rules. Acquiescing to such demands inevitably leads to margin erosion.

Willingly and knowingly we wrestle control from culture and set our orientation in the opposite direction. It is wonderful if a righteous community of believers can support one another in making such countercultural decisions. But don't wait for your friends or fellow churchgoers to lead the way or even to give you permission. This is a battle you must fight, and unfortunately, often you will have to fight it alone.

Rx: 4 "Live Within Your Harvest"

As the proverb suggests, make do with what you have. And, should you care to venture further into grace, not only make do with what you have but accept what you have. *More than a strategy, this is a conviction, the kind where you drive a stake and declare it so.*

Living within your harvest is possible—it just isn't popular. It conveys that we have boundaries and that we are willing to confine ourselves within the scope of these boundaries rather than pine for the putative greener grass on the other side of the fence.

Contentment and simplicity are invaluable friends in this effort, as we will see in the next two chapters. Content yourself with what God sends your way and live a simple life of righteousness. Then God, honored by your devotion, will in turn tend to both your margin and your harvest.

Rx: 5 Discipline Desires and Redefine Needs

There is great confusion abroad as to how we distinguish needs from desires. The list of what we call "needs" today is certainly much longer than the list was in 1900, which in turn was much longer than the list at the time of Christ. If the list expands each year, is this an expansion God approves of? "The cultivation and expansion of needs is . . . the antithesis of freedom," teaches economist E. F. Schumacher. "Every increase of needs tends to increase one's dependence on outside forces over which one cannot have control."[22]

It is wise to clarify this distinction between needs and desires and to be honest about it before God. Our true needs are few and basic: We need God, love, relationships with fellow human beings, meaningful work, food, clothing, and shelter. Most of the rest of what we call needs are instead *desires*, relative to the age and location in which we live.

Let me quickly state that I don't think God limits us to only our needs. He is a generous, gracious God who allows us many of our desires. So if I want carpeting in my house, I should not attempt to deceive God or myself by calling it a need. But I should also realize that God is generous and might well grant the desire.

The issue is knowing when God says "Thus far and no more." For me, when there is pride, ostentation, laziness, waste, or excessive comfort involved, then it is a desire I don't even try to bring before God.

In this process, we are greatly aided if we tune out advertisements, which are nothing more than artificial "need creation." If you listen to them and believe them, your financial margin will tend to disappear as you chase a satiation you will never find. The best advice is to turn them off. After twenty years with a small portable black-and-white television, we finally bought a color set with remote control—simply so we could turn off advertisements.

If you want to have financial margin, redefine desires and needs, using God's definition. In the process, don't listen to advertisements.

Rx: 6 Decrease Spending

Coming now to perhaps the more practical aspects of this topic, there are three ways to increase our financial margin: decrease spending, increase income, or increase savings. Among these choices, the best is to simply reduce our spending. It sounds easy, but as we all know, in practice it is hard to sustain. The context of our culture screams against restraint, and every message we receive—from the ads on television to the specials in the newspaper to our coworker's new sweater to our neighbor's new van—all urge us to cave in.

A friend, who at one time owned a catalog store, offered this interesting explanation of customer spending patterns: "When people run out of money, they stop shopping. But this only lasts about six weeks. Then, whether their financial situation has improved or not, they start buying again."

Doesn't that match what you know to be true about human nature— whether in dieting or exercise or no-shopping resolves? Understanding this simple fact of human psychology leaves us in a stronger position than we were before. *We now recognize that even our best resolves usually last only a short time and require conscious renewal on a regular basis.*

There are two facets of decreased spending: short-term and long-term. Even a short-term spending freeze—a day, a week, a month—is helpful in reestablishing financial margin. In contrast, the long-term approach requires a vastly different level of commitment and is better thought of as a lifestyle change. Short-term resolves are considerable in number but limited in effect; long-term resolves are limited in number but considerable in effect. For example, a moratorium on eating out for a month is probably sustainable and would improve the average family's financial margin by $140. But a decade-long moratorium on eating out would be very difficult for most families, even though it would improve their financial margin by over $16,000.

Rx: 7 Increase Income

Increasing income by increasing work hours is a common approach used to solve financial-margin problems. In some instances, this approach is appropriate. In most, however, it compounds marginless living. As we saw in the last chapter, most of us already have a shortage of discretionary time and are not looking to increase work hours. Yet desperation and a perceived need to consume more drive people to do strange things.

We see farmers who are now milking three times a day in an effort to increase production; service-sector workers who volunteer for overtime or weekends; spouses who violate their personal convictions to enter the dual-wage-earner role; executives who accept a promotion they don't really want; medical residents who moonlight covering emergency rooms. In each instance, these workers would rather have more time margin than more work. But their financial margin has been so eroded by the circumstances of the last two decades (stagnant family income and rising expenses), as well as personal consumption practices, that they seem to no longer have a choice.

Here we need to reconsider the problem of needs versus desires. Many people work extra and then four months later buy a new car. They have made their choices and do not have my sympathy. Others have indeed trimmed both needs and desires to bare bones. For them, increasing income seems the only option left.

The tendency of choosing more work hours in order to increase *financial margin* has a significantly negative effect on our *time margin*. On occasion, we observe that our quest for margin collides with itself, one need against the other.

Rx: 8 Increase Savings

Increasing savings is yet a third way of maintaining a financial margin. If, for example, you currently have no savings and pay expenses from a checking account that is monthly drained dry, what happens if there is an emergency—for example, medical expenses of two thousand dollars? You would need to take out a loan and enter into debt. But if you sustained a savings of three thousand dollars, you would have margin against such emergencies.

Unscheduled and unpredictable breakdowns will happen, and we should consider having some margin for them to happen in. Appliances, automobiles, lawn mowers—all wear out, usually on their own timetable. Sickness, unemployment, and sudden travel expenses are other unanticipated events. With personal and family budgets already stretched to the limits, such emergencies often result in a fiscal crisis.

The issue comes in deciding two crucial questions:

- ▶ How much savings should we have? Is one thousand dollars enough? Is fifty thousand dollars too much?
- ▶ What should the savings be spent on? What if you have a savings of twenty-five thousand dollars and God has need of it? Do you give it back to Him?

Most Christian financial counselors recommend a regular savings program: for children's college education, for exceptional medical expenses, for housing costs, for retirement. In addition, some advisors recommend setting aside a contingency fund equal to three to six months of your usual spending for unexpected emergencies. I personally do not follow this rule, preferring to live a little closer to the edge of faith. There have always been needs within the community that have taken priority over a savings program.

In the final analysis, the issue is not savings but hoarding. Moderate savings is probably acceptable to God and a good component of financial margin. Hoarding, however, is never acceptable. He is trusting us with certain resources; He as owner and we as stewards. We should never pretend that we have rights to what is not ours.

God is honored by funnels and dishonored by sponges. Be a conduit of His blessing, not a dead end. Some increased savings for known future expenses and unknown contingencies seems acceptable. But dead-end hoarding or empire building is not the kind of financial margin I have in mind.

Rx: 9   Make a Budget

Making a budget has the distinction of enjoying the most universal recommendation of all financial-margin suggestions. The scope of this book does not yield itself to the specifics of how to make a budget, and there are other books available to teach that. (I would recommend the works of Larry Burkett and Ron Blue.) But if you have trouble in the area of financial margin, the first thing you should do (that is, after solving the spiritual questions involved) is to set up a budget.

Rx: 10   Discard Credit Cards

The second thing is to cut up your credit cards. The majority of American families would probably be better-off if credit cards disappeared from the face of the earth tomorrow. They can be extremely dangerous. To be honest, I do not believe all credit cards need to be thrown away, and I personally have a credit card. I use it because I seldom carry cash and because I know I can pay it off each month.

I would strongly recommend against having credit cards if you are prone to impulse buying, if you already have excessive amounts of consumer debt, and if you cannot pay off the balance each month.

For a fairly large percentage of people, nothing would regain their financial margin faster than the simple act of destroying all their credit cards and instead paying cash for purchases. Simply stated, avoid debt.

Rx: 11   Don't Mortgage the Future

According to Christian financial counselor Larry Burkett, do not assume a mortgage of more than 40 percent of your net spendable income. (The net spendable income equals the gross income minus the taxes and tithe.) Included in this percentage are not only the mortgage payments but also the real estate taxes, insurance, utilities, and repairs.[23]

Obviously, the smaller the percentage you spend on mortgage and other associated housing costs, the larger your financial margin. Forty percent is a ceiling. Also, if you have other concurrent nonmortgage debts, this percentage may need to be decreased.

Far too many people, especially young couples, take on a mortgage that effectively deprives them of any financial margin for decades to come. When the hard reality sets in, they worry, they develop conflicts in their marriage, they begin overworking to try to make ends meet, and they deprive themselves of the joy of giving to the unexpected needs God sends their way.

Rx: 12   Resist Impulses

A large percentage of purchases are made on sheer impulse. Stores know this and stack impulse items near the cash register. These are the things you didn't go to the store to buy, but bought anyway.

If you want financial margin, don't buy on impulse. Buy only those things you know you need and can use. If you have difficulty in this area, make a list of needed items before going to the store and don't deviate from it.

It goes without saying that big-ticket items, such as a car, boat, or house, should never be bought on impulse . . . never, *never*, NEVER!

Rx: 13 Share, Lend, Borrow

Part of the reason we have our love affair with shopping and consumerism is because we think we need to personally own everything we use. This is not true. We need to develop a new depreciation of things and a new appreciation of people. Things are to be used, and people are to be served. To not allow someone to use something we own places more importance on the thing than on the person. It is a common error in our society, and one that particularly dishonors God. He feels our neighbors are so valuable that He sent His Son to die for them. But we think so little of our neighbors that we won't let them use our lawn mower. These attitudes are literally an eternity apart.

When I brought my chain saw in for repairs several years ago, the attendant offered his philosophy on lending: "Never loan out your chain saw. Other people don't take care of it." Nonsense. I haven't seen my chain saw now for the last twelve months. And I'm not worried a bit. As a matter of fact, I can't think of anything I own that I would not be willing to lend to another person. Of course, I have somewhat of an advantage in that I do not have fancy or expensive things, making me all the more willing to loan them out.

If we are willing to loan out our things, then others will not need to purchase similar items, and they will have more left over to use as financial margin.

Rx: 14 Emphasize Usefulness over Fashion

The mindless, out-of-control fashion games we play also rob us of freedom, destroy our peace, and deprive us of financial margin. Some fool or group of fools halfway around the world proclaims we must wear purple shirts and blue tennis shoes this year. Like robots we respond in unison.

Someone has to give permission for people not to follow fashion. The opinion levied over and over again by culture says that if you wear plain clothes and drive a rusty car, you should feel embarrassed. But God never said such a thing at all. As individuals and as churches, we ought to be saying the same things that God says. Does your church give people permission to live simply and not feel embarrassed? If not, then begin doing something about it. I don't mean in an institutional way that would risk legalism. Instead, begin doing something in a personal way. Go to the cross, take the embarrassment yourself, and start allowing others to follow your example of simplicity in fashion.

Rx: 15   Fast

It is healthy to periodically separate from the things of the world and do without. In traditional thinking, such fasting pertains to food. But in the context of financial margin, it is good to fast from shopping for periods of time. Use up what you have in the refrigerator and freezer. Wear out whatever clothes you have in the closet. Get along on whatever you have in the house. Remember the sampler on Grandma's kitchen wall: "Use it up. Wear it out. Make it do. Do without."

The world does not stop nor the family fall apart when we unplug from the treadmill of consumerism for a period. About the only momentous thing that will happen is your finances will be resuscitated by a much-needed transfusion of margin.

Rx: 16   Kingdom First

Jesus was distinctly unambiguous when teaching about priorities: "But seek first the kingdom of God and His righteousness, and all these things shall be added to you."[24]

All margins—in emotional energy, in physical energy, in time, and especially in finances—ought to fall within this context. All margins ought to be first to honor God. All margins ought to be made available for the purposes of His Kingdom.

Money belongs to God. Wealth belongs to God. The Kingdom belongs to God. We belong to God. Margin belongs to God.

Only the choice belongs to us.

PART THREE

THE
PROGNOSIS:
HEALTH

ELEVEN

Health
Through Contentment

Some public health authorities estimate that only 10 percent of the indicators of health are influenced by physicians, hospitals, and medicines. What, then, influences the other 90 percent?

This book is about the building of a new, integrated health paradigm, beginning with margin.

Margin—its presence or absence—influences health. Restoring margin is a huge first step in the health direction. At least we can breathe again.

But margin cannot survive standing out there on its own. Too many forces come against it. Attempting to build a margined life without support is like attempting to build a tree house without a tree. The tree house might be just what you need for protection against the dangers of the jungle. But it must have a tree.

Contentment is willing to lend support to margin. So are simplicity, balance, and rest. Without each of these, margin has little chance of surviving. These four builders of health, however, are not very popular today. They are meek and unpretentious, greatly overshadowed by the flamboyant power of progress. So they have all been asked to eat dust.

"INEXTINGUISHABLE DISCONTENT"

Half a century ago, my grandfather might reasonably have predicted that advances in affluence, technology, education, and entertainment would bring a commensurate increase in contentment. Such has not been the case. Instead, observes historian Arthur M. Schlesinger, Jr., our society is marked by "inextinguishable discontent." For the average American, discontent has become a way of life. When we are told this is "the age of envy," the indictment does not sting. When E. F. Schumacher accuses our economic system of using "greed and envy as its motive power," our usual response is to yawn and dial our broker.

Contentment is a cause without a constituency, a virtue without a voice. No one talks about it, let alone recommends it. Books dedicated to it are rare. I cannot recall the last sermon I heard addressing it. It is understandable that secular society would not broadcast an endorsement, for secularism and contentment are enemies. But why isn't it emphasized within the church as it is in the Scriptures?

Discontent as a driving force for a society might make that society rich, but it will bankrupt it in the end. As the coffer fills, the soul empties. It's like planting a garden with weeds. Come July there will be plenty of green, but in September we'll have nothing to eat.

THE SECRET

Contentment is not only a good idea, it is our duty. If God recommends something, we *ought* to do it. If God requires something, we *must* do it. As J. I. Packer has emphasized, contentment is both commended ("Godliness with contentment is great gain") and commanded ("Be content with what you have").[1]

Such a forceful endorsement by the Almighty should make contentment a prominent concern for each of us. Instead, we make it a secret concealed by our indifference to it. When the Apostle Paul wrote, "I have learned the *secret* of being content," his use of the word *secret* was intentional.[2] Those things we expect to bring contentment surprisingly do not. We cannot depend upon it to fall into place through the progressive evolving of civilization, for contentment arises from a different source.

Most of us do not know how to uncover this secret and have never seriously tried. Our quest is usually not for *contentment* but for *more*.

This quest brings us into an immense maze, where before us lie dozens of avenues. Some are wide, luxurious, downhill, and tempting, and we see a rush of our friends entering them. They lead to beautiful houses, comfortable cars, exotic vacations, and affluence. Other avenues, equally popular, lead to prestigious colleges, distinguished jobs, important friends, and power. Still others direct us to beautiful spouses, beautiful children, deep tans, and popularity.

All the while, off to one side, courses a narrow uphill road, unadorned and unpopular. It is dusty from its sparse use and lonely from lack of travelers. The sole treasure at its end is an elusive commodity called "godliness with contentment."

Godliness is an attitude whereby what we want is to please God. *Contentment*, explains J. I. Packer, "is essentially a matter of accepting from God's hand what He sends because we know that He is good and therefore it is good."[3]

Contentment is the freedom that comes when prosperity or poverty do not matter: to accept what we have and "to want but little," as Thoreau advised. The more we choose contentment, the more God sets us free. The more He sets us free, the more we choose contentment.

FORTY LASHES MINUS ONE

The Apostle Paul lived in such a state of freedom, but that did not spare him pain. He suffered much for his faith—even more than most other martyrs. "It seems to me," he writes, "that God has put us apostles on display at the end of the procession, like men condemned to die in the arena. We have been made a spectacle to the whole universe. . . . We are weak. . . . We are dishonored! To this very hour we go hungry and thirsty, we are in rags, we are brutally treated, we are homeless. . . . We have become the scum of the earth, the refuse of the world."[4]

Comparing himself to those who boast of their spirituality, Paul further points out that he had worked harder, been in prison more often, been flogged and exposed to death many times. He had received forty lashes minus one on five occasions, been beaten with rods, three times been shipwrecked, been in the open sea overnight, been hungry, thirsty, cold, and naked, and gone without sleep again and again.[5]

Despite his suffering, this same Paul teaches us about the secret we need but know little of. From prison he writes,

I have learned to be content whatever the circumstances. I know what it is to be in need, and I know what it is to have plenty. I have learned the secret of being content in any and every situation, whether well fed or hungry, whether living in plenty or in want.[6]

Paul emphasized the importance of contentment on two occasions (Philippians 4 and 1 Timothy 6). Yet somewhere between his theological teaching and our lifestyle application, a fog rolled in.

WHAT CONTENTMENT IS NOT

In our propensity to get things wrong, we have attributed to contentment attitudes and feelings that have nothing to do with it. Contentment isn't denying one's feelings about unhappiness, but instead a freedom from being controlled by those feelings. It isn't pretending things are right when they are not, but instead the peace that comes from knowing that God is bigger than any problem and that He works them all out for our good.

Contentment isn't the complacency that defeats any attempt to make things better, but instead the willingness to work tirelessly for improvement, clinging to God rather than results. It isn't a feeling of well-being contingent on keeping circumstances under control, but instead a joy that exists in spite of circumstances and looks to the God who never varies. It isn't the comfortable feeling we get when all our needs and desires are met, but instead the security in knowing, as A. W. Tozer reminds us, that "The man who has God for his treasure has all things in One."[7]

Finally, contentment isn't that pseudovirtue of the "American dream" where we claim solidarity with Paul from the easy chair of middle-class America. We profess to having learned the secret of contentment in all circumstances, yet we've never experienced forty lashes, stoning, shipwreck, hunger, thirst, homelessness, or imprisonment. Perhaps none of us should presume maturity until the truer tests have been endured. To snuggle up alongside Paul and profess contentment without having known want seems a bit impudent on our part. Paul's contentment in need and plenty is mostly of interest because of the need. Until we know true need and survive the test, we must not presume to be his companion.

THE LAST SHALL BE FIRST

I believe Mrs. Nguyen Thi An (a fictitious name) can claim a rightful companionship with Paul. Though she has lost everything, she has all things in One. They have taken her husband, her home, and her belongings, yet her contentment they cannot take.

Mrs. An's husband was a pastor in Vietnam. When their church was closed by police, he was thrown into prison. Without official papers, she and her children were forced to live on a balcony outside an apartment. Yet her faith has forged a sanctuary out of her surroundings, from which she greets us:

My Dear Friends,

. . . You know around here we are experiencing hardships, but we thank the Lord He is comforting us and caring for us in every way. When we experience misfortune, adversity, distress and hardship, only then do we see the real blessing of the Lord poured down on us in such a way that we cannot contain it.

We have been obliged recently to leave our modest apartment and for over two months have been living on a balcony. The rain has been beating down and soaking us. Sometimes in the middle of the night we are forced to gather our blankets and run to seek refuge in a stairwell.

Do you know what I do then? I laugh and I praise the Lord, because we can still take shelter in the stairwell. I think of how many people are experiencing much worse hardships than I am. Then I remember the words of the Lord, "To the poor, O Lord, You are a refuge from the storm, a shadow from the heat" (cp. Isaiah 25:4), and I am greatly comforted. . . .

Our Father . . . is the One who according to the Scriptures does not break the bruised reed nor put out the flickering lamp. He is the One who looks after the orphan and the widow. He is the One who brings blessings and peace to numberless people.

I do not know what words to use in order to describe the love that the Lord has shown our family. I only can bow my knee and my heart and offer to the Lord words of deepest

thanks and praise. Although we have lost our house and our
possessions, we have not lost the Lord, and He is enough.
With the Lord I have everything. The only thing I would fear
losing is His blessing!

Could I ask you and our friends in the churches abroad
to continue to pray for me that I will faithfully follow the
Lord and serve Him regardless of what the circumstances
may be?

As far as my husband is concerned, I was able to visit
him this past summer. We had a 20-minute conversation that
brought us great joy. . . .

I greet you with my love.

Mrs. Nguyen Thi An[8]

Would that she could finish this chapter, and I could be her student.

THE RELENTLESS POWER OF DISCONTENT

Despite her impoverished circumstances, Mrs. Nguyen Thi An races far
ahead of affluent America. Why is contentment so hard for us? For one
thing, it's slippery. Contentment is not at all like cutting down a tree,
which, when it is done, is done. It's more like trying to pick up mercury
with tweezers—it keeps squirting away. It's like the carrot suspended
two feet in front of our face that moves every time we do. We keep chasing, and it keeps dodging. "Give a man everything he wants," declared
Immanuel Kant, "and at that moment, everything will not be everything."

Beyond its slippery nature, contentment is difficult to achieve
because of the relentless power of discontent. The battle waged
between contentment and discontent is often subtle but never soft.
When we enter the material world for our contentment, it pulls us in
deeper and deeper, and the pull is deceptively strong. That for which I
long becomes that to which I belong.

In addition, contentment is difficult because it is a relative state—
at least the world's practice of it is relative. A number of factors influence this relativism: the age in which we live, the local culture, and the
lifestyle of family members and friends. If you live in New York City
and all your neighbors drive Mercedes, you might feel embarrassed if
you drive a pickup. Living in rural Wisconsin where many people cut
firewood, however, you would find a beat-up truck more acceptable.

If we were to draw one line representing ALL THERE IS TO HAVE and another representing WHAT WE NOW HAVE, the gap between these lines would be, in most cases, proportional to our level of contentment.

——————— ALL THERE IS TO HAVE ———————

(education, looks, money,
job, marriage, family,
house, cars, toys,
prestige, power, friends,
athleticism, etc.)

——————— WHAT WE NOW HAVE ———————

As the top line rises, the gap between what we now have and all there is to have becomes greater. Often our discontent becomes greater as well. *One of the dubious advantages progress has given us is the relentless raising of the top line.* Progress perceives this as its duty—to give us more and more. Were we free to select among the opportunities without pressure or comparison, perhaps these abundant choices would be acceptable. But humans are not like that, or at least our society is not like that. Life in the United States has become essentially a comparative experience.

With the invention of air conditioning, for example, progress raised the top line. Before the arrival of air conditioning, no one was discontented to drive in sweltering heat without it. People were miserable because of the heat, perhaps, but not discontented, because you cannot be discontented about something that doesn't exist. Yet when progress invents it for us, the level of expectation rises, and with it the level of discontent.

Living in Texas without an air-conditioned car today, you would likely be discontented. Fifty years ago you would not have been. Some might retort, "Before air conditioning people were miserable, and now, some are discontented. Isn't it about the same?" No. To be miserable with the heat is not a sin.

SET-POINTS

The relativism of contentment can be illustrated using the concept of a "floating set-point." This set-point, somewhat different for each person, is positioned at that level where you are content. If your circumstances match this set-point, you are temporarily satisfied. Once additional possibilities enter your awareness, however, your set-point floats to a new level. Then you buy a bigger house, get a better-paying job, move south, or undertake a multitude of other "improvements," and again you are temporarily satisfied.

This contentment set-point is free to float upward without limitation. There is no ceiling, and we have not tried to establish one as a matter of public policy, let alone common sense. Instead, we have fueled our economy by stimulating the set-point to rise even faster than it normally would. While this set-point is free-floating, it moves almost always in the upward direction. To see it fall voluntarily in a person's life is a wondrous thing, almost miraculous; I might even say, suggestive of godliness.

THE PROSPERITY LADDER

Another erroneous measure of contentment is the prosperity ladder. Most of us look "up the ladder" and notice that the wealthy have more than we do. This, of course, strikes a near fatal blow at one's contentment. If, instead, we reversed our gaze and looked down the ladder, our gratitude would thrive and opportunities for sharing would abound.

The pettiness of my own sources of discontent would be amusing were I not so repentant about them. I have been known to grumble when our house temperature drops to sixty degrees, yet there are untold millions in the world who do not have shelter. I have been known to complain if the day is rainy, yet a large segment of the world's land is shriveling up in drought. I have been known to groan if I miss my dinner, yet thousands who go to sleep tonight without food will not awaken in the morning. Christ came to save me from sin—not from sixty-degree homes, rainy weather, and delayed dinners.

This relativism, where the grass is greener on your neighbor's lawn, can be remedied, but first it must be confessed. We need to quit staring at those who have more than we do. We need to override the set-point by spiritual maturity, to look down rather than up the ladder, and to fix our contentment on godliness rather than relativism. It helps immeasurably if we are surrounded by a community of like-minded friends rather than a society where envy has been normalized.

THE AGE OF ENVY

The normalization of envy is yet another reason why the achievement of contentment is difficult. Historian and author Herbert Schlossberg explains why Helmut Schoeck calls this the "age of envy": "By that he means that fewer people than ever are ashamed of being envious, apparently believing that the fact of their envy is proof that social injustice has been done."[9] The cultural message is strong: Why shouldn't we want what others have? We have rights, including the right to enjoy the good life. This, of course, is precisely the kind of logic that so efficiently destroys not only contentment but margin as well.

Is covetousness no longer a sin? In business we rename it ambition, making it not only dignified but exalted. "When children grab things from each other and declare, 'This is mine,' parents try to teach them to share," points out simplicity author Art Gish. "When these children grow up and grab for themselves, we praise them for being industrious."[10]

The advertising industry deserves a great share of the blame for consciously stimulating a chronic state of discontent. Were everyone in the United States to adopt a scripturally authentic lifestyle of contentment, we would much less often need new clothes, new toys, new furniture, and new automobiles. As a consequence, our discontent-dependent, debt-sponsored economy might well collapse on our heads.

MANUFACTURED NEED

The only way to avert this economic breakdown is to continually convince the American public that more and better is desirable. If this "need creation" is successful, it will guarantee not only economic stability but possibly even growth. Somehow in the process we forgot scriptural admonitions. I am not aware of a single person who takes seriously these words of Paul at their deepest level: "If we have food and clothing, we will be content with that."[10]

Two broad types of advertising deserve mentioning. The first reminds or informs: "We are having a sale this week," or "When looking for good fried chicken, don't forget us. We serve nightly until 9:00 p.m." The second type stimulates or manipulates need: "All the best athletes use Ajax breath mints," or "Use Jake's *new and improved* fishing lure and you will never have another boring minute of fishing." Nearly every advertisement that interrupts my consciousness (I do not seek them out—they trespass) is of the latter type.

At first, the lying was subtle, and we overlooked it. Then it became progressively more blatant, wrapped in entertainment. Today, the lying is at absurd levels but goes largely unnoticed. Thus we have the intentional stimulation of covetousness through the telling of shameless lies, both of which Scripture condemns. Yet we sit in rapt attention.

The advertisers use many additional strategies—visual stimulation and sexual innuendo are but two of the more prominent—yet all these are *methods*. What we really need to understand is the *message*. My point is, the message we are given is that we need something. That we really do not need much at all is viewed by advertisers as an obstacle to overcome. They must manufacture need.

If we actually needed the thing, advertisers would not have to convince us of it. "The fact that wants can be synthesized by advertising, catalyzed by salesmanship, and shaped by the discreet manipulations of the persuaders shows that they are not very urgent," notes economist John Kenneth Galbraith. "A man who is hungry need never be told of his need for food."[12] We are not a hungry society; we are, in reality, overfed. Need must be created, and discontent must be stirred up. Our fallenness plays collusively into the hands of the enemy, and we are easy prey.

POISON VERSUS PEACE

These manufacturers of need have been eminently successful, which has been helpful for the economy but troublesome for veracity. In truth, discontent has so many disadvantages one wonders why it is popular. It can suffocate freedom, leaving us in bondage to our desires. It can poison relationships with jealousy and competition. It often rewards blessing with ingratitude as we grumble against God. "Discontent will destroy your peace, rob you of joy, make you miserable, spoil your witness," warns Packer. "We dishonor God if we proclaim a Savior who satisfies and then go around discontent."[13] And when it has done its work, discontent abandons us, leaving us no comfort in our indebted, marginless, friendless self-pity.

The advantages of contentment, on the other hand, are many: freedom, gratitude, rest, peace—all components of health. They who are content do not have to worry about the latest styles or what to wear tomorrow. They can rejoice in their neighbor's good fortune without having to feel inferior. They do not fret with wrinkles or graying because they accept what comes. They do not have to worry how they might buy this or that because they have no desire for this or that. They are not consumed with how to get out of debt because they have no debt. They have time for gratitude even in small things. They have time for relationships because possessions and the bank do not own them.

Do you see how a life of contentment both enables and supports margin? And do you see how a life filled with contentment and margin both enables and supports healthy relationships?

CONTENTMENT AND RELATIONSHIPS

God commanded contentment because He knew we would need it to anchor right relationships.

We *relate better to God* when we are satisfied with what He gives. We might say words of worship, but if our heart is not resting in the contentment of His presence, He is not fooled. "The Christian position from the beginning," contends Schlossberg, "has been that people are satisfied by becoming reconciled with God, not by acquiring wealth."[14]

We *relate better to self* when contented with our circumstances. If allowed to write a prescription redesigning our body, personality, or station in life, most of us would grab at the chance: smarter, funnier, richer, better looking, taller, thinner, more athletic. Yet none of these requests would even be an issue were it not for our comparisons with others. If we were all alone with God (which, in regard to contentment, we are), we would have a different set of values than the one society offers.

We *relate better to others* when the relationship is stabilized by contentment. If every encounter with my neighbor reminds me of something I covet, that relationship becomes tenuous. Envy makes it hard to have friends—everyone I know has something I do not.

CONTENTMENT AND MONEY

Our relationship to money is another area where contentment is essential. The poor envy the rich, while the rich envy the richer. Money gives a thrill but no satiety. The rich soon sense this and are perhaps surprised by it, but then go back to making more money anyway. Satisfaction will come later, they speculate, and if it never comes, at least there is the thrill.

Money *does seem* to meet our needs in the short term. It buys us food, shelter, vehicles, and experiences. It does not, however, meet any of our long-term needs: love, truth, relationship, redemption. This short-term deception is difficult for us to understand and is one of the reasons God spent so much time instructing us concerning money and wealth. Money is treacherous, we are told, and riches are deceitful. It is not a sin to be wealthy, but it can be dangerous. "God is merciful and can deliver the rich from the danger of being rich," observes John White. "But many of us do not want to be delivered."[15]

Many of today's rich are faced with the same depression, meaninglessness, alcoholism, suicide, and fractured relationships we see in the poor (or, for that matter, the middle class). The poor are not surprised by their plight. The rich, however, have run the rainbow out to its end and have found it an unexpectedly empty journey.

"To Americans usually tragedy is wanting something very badly and not getting it," observed Henry Kissinger. "Many people have had to learn in their private lives, and nations have had to learn in their historical experience, that perhaps the worst form of tragedy is wanting something badly, getting it, and finding it empty."[16]

Millions, as Kissinger hints, have had to discover that they can't find true contentment in important jobs and that the advertised contentment of cars, houses, and wardrobes is but a short-term hoax. The things one can buy with money are never the things that last. "Keep your lives free from the love of money and be content with what you have," we read in Hebrews, "because God has said, 'Never will I leave you; never will I forsake you.'"[17]

Did your car, your house, or your wardrobe ever say, "Never will I leave you"?

While earning money is necessary at some level, the Apostle Paul taught that seeking *wealth* would threaten us with devastation. People who want to get rich, Paul wrote in 1 Timothy 6:9-10,

> ◗ Fall into temptation.
> ◗ Fall into a trap.
> ◗ Fall into foolish desires.

▶ Fall into harmful desires.
▶ Are plunged into ruin.
▶ Are plunged into destruction.

And some people eager for money

▶ Have wandered from the faith.
▶ Have pierced themselves with many griefs.

Do you want to be plunged and pierced? Nor do I. But that doesn't seem to stop us from wanting to get rich. Were Paul's message not included in the biblical text, it would be out of print. No readership remains, even within the church.

THE THEOLOGY OF ENOUGH

We need contentment to relate correctly to money and, in a similar way, to possessions. The rules here are simple:

1. God comes first and possessions come second.
2. Possessions are to be used, not loved.

One of Jesus' most frightening warnings to contemporary America is His rebuke of the rich landowner in Luke 12. When the fields yielded a great harvest, the landowner proudly built huge barns and stored up his treasure for the years to come. Now, he thought, life will be easy and secure.

God's judgment was quick: "You fool!" That night the man's life was taken from him.

"Watch out!" warns Jesus. "Be on your guard against all kinds of greed; a man's life does not consist in the abundance of his possessions" (Luke 12:15). Tragically, for many Americans today, their empty lives do indeed consist in the abundance of their possessions.

"Within the human heart 'things' have taken over," asserts A. W. Tozer. "God's gifts now take the place of God, and the whole course of nature is upset by the monstrous substitution."[18] Why hasn't the Church stood against this popular error? Why hasn't there been a clear expression of a "theology of enough"? Perhaps it is because things are not evil, as stealing and adultery are; only the *love* of things, like the *love* of money, is evil. It is easy for us to say, "I don't love this thing; it's just that I *need* it." God is what we need; things are what we use. In the words of one Christian journalist, "Contentment lies not in what is yours, but in whose you are."[19]

BOREDOM AND SUFFERING

Contentment is also helpful in enduring boredom and suffering. Children today use the word boring frequently. It is intended as the ultimate verbal scourge, and basically it means, "I'm discontented. Entertain me." The prevalence of this word is an unsettling indicator of where our children are in relation to contentment.

As I was growing up, we used our imagination and creativity to make our own fun. Today, electronic entertainment rides a nonstop conveyer belt directly into the dormant souls of the young. It is not a favorable development. I cannot be optimistic that this trend will miraculously result in a mature sense of contentment in later years. Over time, a decaying log will not turn into a house. All you get is a bigger pile of rot.

> A man said to the universe:
> "Sir, I exist!"
> "However," replied the universe,
> "The fact has not created in me
> A sense of obligation."[19]

In his famous poem, Stephen Crane reminds us of an important truth: God is not indebted to us. If life is boring, then it is boring. We work to make it better, but our duty throughout the working is contentment. If life is tough, so it is tough. Our duty is contentment. If there is suffering, why would we expect anything different? Our duty is contentment.

Life can be painful. Most people do not choose this pain; it comes with living. Contentment, however, is different. Contentment or discontent is a matter of the will, a choice. When we choose obedience, God, in His wonderful way with surprises, can redeem the pain and suffering in our lives and can turn the destruction into benefit.

DON'T WAIT — WORK

No formula exists for finding contentment other than obedience. Remember, it is a secret. It won't make sense to worldly thinking, and it won't be discovered by scientific study. First you must seek it. Then it will be revealed to you.

This, of course, is no excuse to sit around waiting to hear from Heaven. There are steps you can take, acts of your will, which point you in the right direction. You always have a better chance of discovering the secret if you're in the vicinity of its hiding place. The following nine steps will start you on your way.

1. Get to work. The conflict between contentment and discontent is a struggle format. It requires much effort on our part. You cannot get from New Orleans to Minneapolis on the Mississippi except by paddling.

2. Divorce your thinking from society's relativistic standards. God says, "Be content," not "Be content if . . ." Never allow the affairs of others to influence your contentment.

3. Turn off the ads and tune out the lies. If you wish to preserve your financial margin, cast your lot with contentment.

4. Defer to God's opinion concerning your family relationships. How often, particularly in modern America, have we seen the devastation visited upon families through the "if only" syndrome? Emotional margin is an early casualty with such discontent as, "If only my wife were more appealing or more sexually interested," or "If only my husband made more money or had more hair." Infidelity, even in thought, is greener grass only because it's been spray painted by the Deceiver himself. Contentment keeps our eyes on the right side of the fence.

5. Set new standards for your contentment using the truth of Scripture. God has long desired to teach us these principles, but it has not been an easy task for Him.

6. Develop "counter-habits," as John Charles Cooper calls them. Instead of getting, try giving. Instead of replacing, try preserving. Instead of feeling covetous, try feeling grateful. Instead of feeling inferior before men, try feeling accepted before God. Instead of being ruled by feelings, try enjoying the freedom of contentment.

7. Subtract from your needs. Make a list of all the things you need and then start crossing things off. It might at first be painful, but after a while it becomes fun. "There are two ways to get enough," G. K. Chesterton has pointed out. "One is to continue to accumulate more and more. The other is to desire less."

8. Accept from God's hand that which He gives—not resignation, not complacency, but contentment. All that is needful He will supply.

Even pain and suffering that seemingly cannot be corrected, He can redeem.

9. If you still do not feel the stirrings of contentment within, argue with yourself and tell yourself the truth. We discover contentment, according to Packer, "by learning to talk to ourselves in a good Christian way. You listen to God in Scripture and then tell yourself what He said. If your emotions disagree, you argue with your emotions. And if you find unbelief in your heart, you argue with that unbelief and drive it out by appeal to God's truth."[21]

DISLOCATION OR DELIGHT?

Is contentment, then, a move in the health direction? Let's ask the masters.

"Discontent doth dislocate and unjoint the soul, it pulls off the wheels," advises Thomas Watson in *The Art of Divine Contentment*. "Discontent is a fretting humour, which dries the brains, wastes the spirits, corrodes and eats out the comfort of life."[22]

"*Christian contentment*," counters Jeremiah Burroughs in *The Rare Jewel of Christian Contentment*, "*is that sweet, inward, quiet, gracious frame of spirit, which freely submits to and delights in God's wise and fatherly disposal in every condition.*"[23]

When I get sick, I want to go to their clinic. They never knew about penicillin. But they sure knew a lot about health.

TWELVE

Health
Through Simplicity

Though it has been variously commended and practiced for centuries, simplicity has seldom been more needed than it is today. Health requires it. Sanity demands it. Contentment facilitates it. "Simplicity is crucial to progress," observes complexity expert Duane Elgin, "for without simplicity we will be overwhelmed by massive social and material complexity."[1]

If overload is sabotaging our equilibrium, simplicity can help. If we find ourselves being detailed to death, simplicity can restore life. If we find ourselves overextended in our emotional, financial, and time commitments, simplicity is one of the best ways to reestablish margin. "Do not underestimate the delight of real simplicity in your life style," advises stress expert Hans Selye, M.D.[2]

GETTING AWAY FROM IT ALL

We hear frequent talk about the rat race and the treadmill, about stopping the world to let people off. Many fantasize about walking away from their jobs, throwing away the television, and moving to a cabin in the woods. Indeed, in the last few decades, many have acted upon the fantasy. "Former city dwellers are said to be opting out by the hundreds of thousands in search of clean air, safe streets, more time for family—in short, a simpler, slower pace of life," reports John Naisbitt.[3]

The reasons people feel like "getting away from it all" have already been explored. Given the complicated, rushed nature of daily life in modern America, it is not surprising that many are looking for the exit door. The solution, however, for our stress-overload-pain triad is not so much escaping as it is transcending: The solution is simplicity. Simplicity does not guarantee margin, but it is helpful.

NOT A MODERN INVENTION

In our age of frenzied distress, large numbers of contemporary thinkers have begun discussing and writing about the concept of a simple lifestyle. We encounter with regularity such phrases as "the plain life," "plain people," "intermediate technology," "intentional communities," and "contrast culture." We are enamored by the Amish lifestyle, wanting to tour their villages, eat their food, and bring home their quilts. Even the popular "country look" in home decorating has become, at least in part, a manifestation of the nostalgia many share about things simple and past. In much of the United States now, glitz and gaudiness are out; fireplaces, rocking chairs, and cross-stitch are in.

Despite its attractiveness and timeliness, simplicity is not a new concept. The spiritually minded have long sought it as a way of facilitating the contemplative life. The monastic orders and the Desert Fathers practiced simplicity, often including vows of poverty, extreme asceticism, and complete separation from the world.

Through the seventeenth and eighteenth centuries, many of those who traveled to the New World in search of religious freedom, from the Puritans to the Quakers, sought a simple, godly lifestyle. America of the nineteenth century also saw its simplicity movements. Perhaps the most lasting impressions were made by the Transcendentalists, a group who were in many ways spiritually motivated but not within the context of orthodox Christian doctrine. Two of their number, Ralph Waldo Emerson and Henry David Thoreau, were articulate prophets for this "plain living and high thinking," and their legacy continues to influence many today.

The modern era has witnessed such simplicity causes as the hippie communes and cultural dropouts. In addition, there has been significant activity within the Church, although not always mainstream. From the International Consultation of Simple Life-Style to the Mennonite Central Committee, some in the Church seek to find the posture of proper theological balance in an age of affluence and complexity.

Austere separatists such as the Amish, once widely scorned for being so backward, now garner more respect. "We should look again at the life styles and beliefs of the Brethren, Mennonites, and Amish," encourages author John Charles Cooper. "They do not pollute the earth. They do not waste food. They concentrate on the care of the earth and the care of their families. They have no ambitions for wealth or status. They harbor no political lusts to control the lives of their neighbors. All they ask for is the right to live simple, godly lives. The joy of these plain people lies in their communion with Christ and with one another."[4]

CHRISTLIKENESS

Even if I were not a Christian, the notion of stepping off the treadmill would sound attractive. Yet for adherents of Christianity, a stronger pull motivates: To be a follower of Christ means we should *follow* Him. No one lived a simpler, more unencumbered life than He. His birth was in spartan conditions, and His life was free from the ties of possessions or money. He was born with nothing, lived with little, and died with nothing. His simplicity was not accidental. Jesus could have chosen any standard, yet He chose to live simply.

In the Sermon on the Mount, Christ told us not to worry even about food and clothing and not to worry about tomorrow. That He did not seek luxury is a statement to us who follow Him. When He demonstrated servitude by washing the feet of His disciples, He explained, "I have set you an example that you should do as I have done for you. . . . No servant is greater than his master."[5]

The Apostle Peter instructs us to walk after the example of Christ in enduring suffering.[6] Paul teaches us to follow after Jesus' example of humility.[7] "Does the Bible infer that we are to live like *a king* or like *the King*?" asks Rev. Tom Allen. "The simplicity, sacrifice and servanthood of Jesus Christ should be our way of life, too."[8]

INTERNAL ANCHOR, EXTERNAL JOY

All external manifestations of the Christian life require internal foundations, and simplicity is no different. The external practices are important, but the internal requirements are essential. For simplicity to bring us the lifestyle rest we are searching for, the internal truths must be confirmed by our own will. They have to do with the lordship of Christ. This means seeking the Kingdom first, thus giving over our plans, our expectations, our future, our family, our reputation, and our possessions to Him. Once these conditions are met, then we are free to begin seeking the external practices.

With the internal issues settled, the external practices are a joy. Loaning or giving away our possessions is not anxiety-producing because we are only stewards anyway, and the true Owner has told us to give generously. We are free to wear older clothes or to live in modest homes because God doesn't care. We no longer need to impress. With the internal truth anchored, the external simplicity of our lives is a celebration. Without this anchor, however, the external workings become a chore, a set of rules, and often degenerate into legalism.

WHAT IT IS

Simple living over the centuries has been variously defined. "The precise meaning of the simple life has never been fixed," explains historian David Shi. "Rather, it has always represented a shifting cluster of ideas, sentiments, and activities."[9] Certain common threads, however, can be identified. The simple life is:

Voluntary — If the simple life is forced, it ceases to be simple. Involuntary impoverishment, for example, makes it difficult for people to choose simplicity. This is not to say it is impossible. But the plain life is far more profitable when it is chosen as an act of the will.

Free — One of the key features of simplicity and, at the same time, one of its principal advantages is that it is a life of freedom. It is free from anxiety — about our reputations, our possessions, our tomorrows. It is being controlled by that which is life-giving and refusing to be controlled by that which is destructive.

Uncluttered — Realizing that psychological and material clutter impedes our journey, simplicity seeks to unclutter. Emotionally, we release our worries, we reconcile our relationships, we forgive our enemies, and we begin anew each day. Materially, instead of possession gluttony, we practice de-accumulation. Like runners of old, we strip down to that which is authentic so that we might run the race effectively.

Natural — We respect the natural order — the things God has created and the job God has given humankind within that order. We don't just return to nature; we return to the God who created nature.

The simple life understands that natural beauty exists and that it penetrates deeper than the adornments of humankind. The real beauty of another human exists within the spirit and consists of virtue and purity.

Creative — Life is not boring just because it is simple. Simplicity sets the imagination free to work and to enjoy. Passive entertainment can dull the sense of wonder God has placed within us. The simple life, however, affords an opportunity to rediscover the joys of creativity.

Authentic — A simple lifestyle must distinguish between the spiritually authentic and spiritually inauthentic aspects of life and be devoted to the former. Biblical authenticity includes those things God has told us to focus on, those things that have eternal, God-assigned value: people, love, service, worship, prayer, self-denial, relationships, contentment, freedom, rest.

Focused — Understanding the significance of spiritual authenticity, we focus on it. We lock in on what is good and true. We bind ourselves to that which has eternal value. This does not mean we do not wash our car or take out the garbage. But it does mean that we understand who God is and what His priorities for our lives are — and then follow them. It does mean that we focus intensely on seeking the Kingdom first, and on loving God and man. Without such focus, we drift.

Margined — Because the simple life is focused, it is able to distinguish the things that truly matter from the imposters. It can tell the difference between the authentic and that which is only attractive. Thanks to such visionary wisdom, simplicity recognizes the importance of margin and seeks to protect it. Together margin and simplicity are allies in a hostile world. Like a team of oxen straining against the storm, they will not be beaten back by the forces that seek to crush them both. The pace might plod. But they are a reliable team, always pulling together. Given time, the work will get done. Thanks to their efforts, health has a better chance to reach its final destination — relationships.

Disciplined—Restraint is necessary for successful living, and all the more for simple living. Comfort is not a legitimate primary goal—authenticity is. Understandably, then, those seeking simplicity may experience discomfort. Doing without is often necessary. Inasmuch as the simple life is an obedient life, and obedience requires discipline, we will not be able to thrive without it.

Diligent—The simple life knows how to rest, but it also knows how to work. One of the benefits of simplicity is a return to human labor. It is time to rethink the notion that small-scale, labor-intensive production is undesirable. It is good to be physically active. It is good to work with our hands. Human energy, unlike coal, natural gas, or oil, is renewable and nonpolluting. It is good to start and end the work ourselves and to have pride in the process and the product. It is good to plant our own food, to sew our own clothes, to cut our own wood, to walk to work.

Healthful—A life voluntarily chosen and lived in freedom; a life uncluttered and natural; a life that is focused, diligent, and disciplined; a life characterized by creativity and spiritual authenticity—is not this a healthy life?

WHAT SIMPLICITY ISN'T

Misconceptions abound about the simple life. We can clarify simplicity as much by explaining what it isn't as by delineating what it is. And it is not:

Easy—Many equate "simple" with "easy" and become disillusioned with simple living when they find out how hard it can be. To bake your own bread or cut your own wood is not always the easiest way to provide food and warmth. But doing these chores yourself allows an often hard-earned independence that can facilitate simplicity.

Legalistic—Legalism is the trap I dread more than any other. Those who choose to live a simple lifestyle often set a standard of judgment for the lives of others. Such legalism does not liberate; it kills. It destroys the joy of both the accuser and the accused. The message of simple living is better spread by invitation than by judgment.

Proud—While simple living is intended to be a vehicle for virtue, it can deteriorate into the vice of pride. This we might call "reverse pride." It is possible, and even tempting, to wear patches on your clothes as self-awarded badges of righteousness. It is possible to practice self-exaltation for the rust on your car or the stone-ground whole-wheat bread in your oven. All of these highly visible "sacrifices" serve to elevate your (perceived) righteousness level several notches above that of your inferiors. Jesus, of course, dealt with this attitude in Matthew 6 (giving, fasting, praying) and no new teaching is needed.

Impoverished — Taking a vow of poverty does not guarantee that spiritually authentic simplicity will follow. Simplicity does not reject money and ownership — it merely subjugates it. All money goes quickly to the purse of the Father for use in our lives and the lives of others according to His wishes. We don't seek wealth as a goal in itself, not only because it is sinful to do so, but also because money cannot buy what we need. Yet money is received and used, for the Father knows how to control it for the purposes of His Kingdom.

Ascetic — Asceticism rejects all possessions and argues that "things" are spiritually handicapping. While it is true that things can become spiritually inauthentic, they are not an a priori evil. God is a good Creator, and He has created a whole world full of good things. It is not wrong to use them — they were made to be used. But our material appetites must be controlled.

Neurotic — Some adherents live a simple life but know nothing of its freedom. They tilt toward spartan asceticism because they feel unworthy of any blessing or they feel responsible for all the poverty in the world. Such a guilt-driven lifestyle is not simplicity. It is neurosis. God blames us only for what we are to blame for, and He took it all away when we asked Him to. Now that the slate is clean, we choose simplicity, not out of guilt but out of sensitivity and devotion.

Ignorant — Simple livers are not to be simpletons. We don't achieve such a lifestyle by burning our books and burying our heads. On the contrary, one of the main advantages of such a life is the opportunity it provides for study, discussion, and meditation. God created our brains just as surely as He did our hearts, and He expects us to use them both for His glory. Ignorance is not the essence of simplicity — it is an enemy.

Escapist — "The grass is greener on the other side of the fence" is 98 percent lie. We don't attain the simple life by throwing away our cars and phones and running off to live in the woods. Clearly, for some people the simple life is facilitated by moving from an overmortgaged house or departing a traffic-paralyzed city. But simple living is not a location; it is an attitude. It is not escaping; it is transcending. It is not separation; it is sanctification.

A RETREAT TO THE PAST?

Many among us might wish to turn back the clock, to retreat to a simpler, easier time. We long for the quiet of nature rather than the blast of rock music and car horns. We want to be more directly involved in the elements, whether planting the seed that feeds our family or digging the worms that catch our fish. Perhaps we even long to raise our own animals or build our own log home.

Much debate continues over such nostalgia. Is it healthy, or is it escapist? Is sentimentality an ally or a deceiver? We often forget the horrid problems of the past, and in the process, also overlook the blessings of today. "Too often the past seems far more virtuous, simpler, and happier than it actually was," reminds historian Shi.10 Our historical memories are selective. To pine for a misrepresented dreamland is not a spiritually authentic thing to do.

In addition to calling such nostalgia irresponsible, some argue we could not reverse the process of history even if we wanted to. These critics maintain that the forces which have steamrolled us to this point are far too strong to be turned back. Such a longed-for retreat to the past is not only irresponsible—it is impossible. Progress, they say, cannot be stopped.

Progress *is* very strong. Yet we must be careful here. To say that history and progress must flow in only one direction is to give those forces the power of gods. In exposing such thinking, Herbert Schlossberg points out, "One of the most common examples of historicism is the saying, 'We can't turn back the clock.' The progressive connotations of this saying are wholly illusory. . . . In refusing to believe that an identified historical trend may be challenged, the historicists have divinized history."11 Nothing is so embedded that it cannot be dislodged. No momentum is so great that it cannot be redirected. Otherwise, God is not God.

When Art Gish was confronted with the question of turning back the clock, his answer was enlightening: "The analogy of a clock is not helpful. It is not the question of a clock, but a compass. The issue is not chronology, but direction. And that we can decide. . . . We are not retreating, but looking ahead to perceive what is important.

Simplification implies leaving things behind and moving to a new future."[12]

Progress *can* be suspended and reversed on an individual level, and, for that matter, even on a societal level (although admittedly, with great difficulty). But is that the best direction for our simple-life search? Instead of escaping, can we not transcend? Selectivity is an important concept here. Can we not hold on to what is good and reject what is destructive?

THE DIFFICULTY OF SIMPLICITY

What factors make the simple life hard to obtain? If we embark on this journey, let's first decide how much of the currency of fortitude we need to bring with us. There will be tollbooths all along the route, with the costs often quite steep.

No sooner have we started out the gate then we encounter our first problem: society's disrespect. If we choose to ignore fashion and status, we will not gain the admiration of our peers. From the outset, we need to decide who it is we are trying to please.

To further illustrate this roadblock called social respectability, let me suggest a story and then ask a question. Suppose one day you went exploring in a cave near San Francisco. When you came out, shockingly you discovered that everyone had disappeared from the face of the earth, transported away by invading aliens. As you search for an automobile, you find that they too have been removed. By linking your cam-recorder to a fax machine and then running both through a satellite dish, you cleverly locate the only two cars left in the United States. The first, a ten-year-old Chevrolet with ninety thousand miles, is near San Diego and could be reached in three weeks by walking. The other car is the same model Chevy, only brand-new. It is on the outskirts of New York City and would require six months of walking to reach. Which would you choose?

Perhaps you already suspect my point. Given this scenario, virtually all of us would be content with the older car. We would not walk an extra 161 days just for a shiny paint job and new interior. Yet this is commonly what we do in our society—work six months for a new car instead of three weeks for a functional older one. Why do we do this? Is it because we get tired of paying for repairs? No. We buy new cars primarily for one reason: *because of the presence of other people.* We desire respectability in the eyes of others. Appearance — not function — rules us.

Continuing down the narrow road of the simple life, we keep encountering another problem: our expectations. After decades of convenience and affluence, we not only desire but expect ease and satiation. Gratification of our appetites has become a widespread goal not seriously challenged by the church. If we do not reprogram such expectations, we will experience recurrent frustration in our search for simplicity.

Our lack of discipline presents us with yet another obstacle. We have not needed much discipline during this era of abundance, and we have lost interest in it as a component of lifestyle. Most of us have grown soft. But the simple life is not easy, and discipline is necessary.

Finally, our own mistaken opinions of how things ought to be also trip us repeatedly. Theological confusion has permitted us first to look at what we want and then to build a theology that justifies it. For example, very little money is needed to live a fully God-honoring life. Yet somehow we have incorporated the presumed need for money into our theological construct. True enough, we need a lot of income to live as our society does, to partake in the many benefits of our age. But it is not true that we need a lot to live on.

SUGGESTIONS

The following are suggestions that will assist in simple living. Beware of the distinction between suggestions and rules, for if you make them rules, you will have converted simplicity into legalism and defeated its purpose before even beginning.

Possessions and Finances

- Cultivate contentment, desire less.
- Resist covetousness.
- Resist consumerism.
- Wage war against advertisements.
- Buy things for their usefulness rather than their status.
- De-accumulate.
- Develop the habit of giving away.
- Share possessions.

- Offer the use of your possessions—don't make others ask.
- Develop a network of exchange.
- Avoid overindulging—for example, toys, food, movie viewing, etc.
- Avoid impulse buying.
- Don't buy anything if the time and money spent on it compete with family, service, and God.
- Avoid debt if possible.
- Don't buy now, pay later.
- Avoid credit cards if they are a problem.
- Reject fashion, especially fads.
- Deemphasize respectability.
- Simplify your wardrobe—give away excess.
- Learn how to make do with a lower income instead of needing a higher one.

Pace and Atmosphere

- Slow down.
- Do not exhaust your emotional bank account.
- Lie fallow.
- Say no.
- Enjoy peaceful music.
- Control/restrict/eliminate television watching.
- Get a remote control set and turn off advertisements.

Relationships

- Cultivate a closeness with God.
- Schedule "simple" dates with your spouse.
- Teach your children.
- Enjoy family field trips.
- Practice regular hospitality.
- Help each other, emphasize service.
- Encourage others.
- "Always speak the truth and you'll never be concerned with your memory."
- Don't judge.
- Learn to enjoy solitude.

Appreciation

- ❱ Send cards of encouragement and appreciation when others are not expecting it.
- ❱ Be grateful for things large and small.
- ❱ Emphasize a joyful life.
- ❱ Appreciate creation.

Spiritual Life

- ❱ Make the Word central.
- ❱ Meditate, memorize.
- ❱ Pray.
- ❱ Encourage simple worship.

Activities

- ❱ Make your commitments simple.
- ❱ Don't overwork.
- ❱ Fast periodically from media, food, people.
- ❱ Elevate reading, go to the library.
- ❱ Simplify Christmas.
- ❱ Write down those things you need to remember and forget everything else.

Nutrition and Exercise

- ❱ Exercise.
- ❱ Bike or walk.
- ❱ Make your recreation active rather than passive.
- ❱ Develop healthy sleep habits.
- ❱ Avoid overeating.
- ❱ Frequent a co-op.
- ❱ Whenever possible, buy food directly from those who grow it.
- ❱ Garden.

FAD OR THE FUTURE?

Is simplicity a trendy fad? Will it fade in significance as did the hippie communes, or is it destined to grow in importance? Simple lifestyles, or something approximating that idea, will only continue to increase in importance. Our age is ever becoming more complex and diffusely overloaded, and simplicity is a movement whose time has come.

One hundred years ago, the most popular spokesman for simple living was the writer John Burroughs. Naturalists and students, journalists and politicians (including Theodore Roosevelt) wore a path to the door of his rustic New England cabin. Humble and self-effacing, he was an eloquent spokesman for unencumbered living.

> I am bound to praise the simple life, because I have lived it
> and found it good. When I depart from it, evil results follow.
> I love a small house, plain clothes, simple living. . . . To see
> the fire that warms you, or better yet, to cut the wood that
> feeds the fire that warms you; to see the spring where the
> water bubbles up that slakes your thirst, and to dip your pail
> into it; . . . to be in direct and personal contact with the
> sources of your material life; to want no extras, no shields;
> to find the universal elements enough . . . to be thrilled by
> the stars at night; to be elated over a bird's nest, or over a
> wild flower in spring—these are some of the rewards of the
> simple life.[13]

Do these strike you as sentiments that future generations will scoff at—or yearn for?

I agree.

WHAT DOES THE LORD REQUIRE?

The simple life will not sound attractive unless you are in love with the Truth. If you have such a love, however, anything that distracts you from it is gladly cut adrift. Then, after you have been freed to pursue your path unencumbered, you will not desire more from your days on earth than simply to act justly, to love mercy, and to walk humbly with your God.[14]

THIRTEEN

Health
Through Balance

The human body is a universe. Made up of 1028 atoms, we each contain millions of times more atoms than there are stars in space (1020). Ninety percent of these atoms are replaced every year, and virtually 100 percent are replaced every five years. Thus our physical beings are continuously tearing down but also continuously building up. From dust we have come and to dust we return—continuously.[1]

Veritable factories that never shut down, our bodies exhibit a complexity beyond human comprehension. We each are made up of trillions upon trillions of working units, all perpetually moving, metabolizing, combining, interacting, adjusting, purifying, purging, building, and decaying. Yet everything must function in balance. If this balance is disturbed, disease is the result. We get sick. We feel pain.

When organ systems are functioning in a balanced manner, physicians say they are "compensated." To be decompensated—that is, out of balance—is to be ill. Likewise, in the area of mental health, when someone is functioning poorly, he or she is said to be "unbalanced." For physiology to avoid becoming pathology, balance is essential. It is no different in the broader context of life.

THE BALANCING ACT

The balanced life today seems inaccessible: too many activities, too many choices, too many decisions, too many commitments, too many expectations, too many people, too much hurry, too much change. Overload, stress, complexity — all are unbalancing pressures. Their effect is to cause ever-increasing disequilibrium in systems and people. Of the many problems compounded by this mischievous triad, imbalance is prominent among them.

The average conscientious American wants to be committed as a spouse, responsible as a parent, faithful in the church, successful in the workplace, and active in the community. Family, church, community, self — each one is a legitimate pull. Indeed, life is full of tugs:

Work	Leisure
Action	Meditation
Leading	Following
Speaking	Listening
Handwork	Headwork
Productivity	Recreation
Intensity	Idleness
Serving	Waiting
Giving	Receiving
Applying	Learning
Structure	Spontaneity
Assertiveness	Submissiveness
Confidence	Humility
Judgment	Grace
Analysis	Synthesis
Specialization	Integration
Society	Solitude
Laughter	Solemnity
Duty	Freedom
Joy	Sorrow
External life	Internal life

How does one find the balance? When life is so correctly constituted of both sides, by what criteria do we make decisions? Is balance appropriate? Is it possible?

As we have illustrated, medicine has become very specialized. More and more is known about the details of health and disease, and specialists are required for such detailed understandings. Yet the kind of investigation that dissects organs and cells will never lead to an understanding of *the person*, and generalists are needed to put it all back together. Specialization versus integration, analysis versus synthesis—how do we balance?

Are we to pray or to serve? To work or to rest? To rejoice at the goodness in people and the great goodness in our Creator, or to sorrow at the pain so evident all around? Life requires both. Balance has always been necessary and will always be necessary. It is just becoming more difficult.

BALANCE OR EXCELLENCE?

Much is made today of the virtues of excellence. But what does this mean? Often the excellence described is only in one narrow corridor of life: virtuosos who exist only for their music, or corporate executives who live at the office.

What do these passionate high achievers think of balance? For many, it is an enemy. Single-minded fervency is their standard. One-hundred-percent effort is the minimum, and those who question such asymmetrical dedication are distrusted and unpromoted.

While undivided devotion to one cause can bring great success and vault a person into prominence, such a priority structure often leaves the rest of that person's life in a state of disorder. Thus it is not uncommon to discover a physician who fails as a parent, an entertainer who fails as a spouse, a pastor who neglects personal health, or an executive who fails at all those other areas. Traditional wisdom has told us not to put all our eggs in one basket. Yet, in pursuit of excellence, we often discard this basic wisdom. Balance is not the goal; preeminence is the goal.

I am not advocating halfheartedness and mediocrity, for we always ought to do our best. But "doing our best" has limits. Our rush toward excellence in one quadrant of life must not be permitted to cause destruction in another. "We need," as Norman Cousins explains, "to be more proportionate."

Those who go all out for success in one endeavor, points out physicist/engineer Richard H. Bube, risk failure in other important areas of life. "Not only is the ability to exhibit excellence in other fields decreased, but in several fields the net consequence is to produce what we may colloquially call 'negative excellence.'" Bube recommends "a more balanced approach."[2] This principle is demonstrated in figures 13.1 and 13.2 (adapted from Bube).

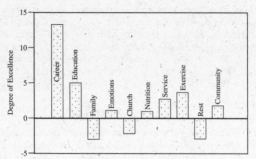

Figure 13.1 - Excellence Plus Failure

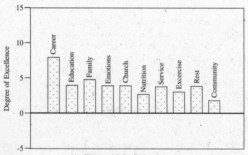

Figure 13.2 - Balance

Schematic illustrations of choice patterns in major fields of a persons endeavors. The ten bars represent individual areas that require time and effort and in which it is possible to establish excellence. (a) This set of choices represents those made by a person who strives for such a high degree of excellence in one area that other areas may actually experience "negative excellence." i.e. failure. (b) This set of choices represents those made by a person who strives to avoid failure in any area and therefore does not achieve quite as high a degree of excellence in any one area as the person represented in (a). Limitations of time and resources make it necessary for every person to choose between some degree of (a) and (b).

The person in figure 13.1 has chosen to strive for such a high degree of excellence in one area that other areas reveal little excellence or even "negative excellence" (that is, failure). Consequently, this person has achieved excellence in the career area but, at the same time, has suffered failure in the other important areas of family, church, and rest.

In contrast, the person in figure 13.2 has chosen to live a balanced life and has therefore avoided "negative excellence" in any area. As a consequence, no outstanding level of excellence has been achieved. On the other hand, no failure has been experienced either.

If you wish to achieve excellence but also to have life balance, beware. Those who advocate excellence at all costs often do not believe in "outside interests" and may not tolerate them. Family, friends, church, as well as margin in personal time and emotional health — all are luxuries that may compete with a stellar performance in a single area. If, then, we are forced to choose between excellence or balance, how do we choose? Once we understand that God expects us to act responsibly in each area of life, it is easier to discern the problems associated with one-track excellence.

A MATTER OF PRIORITIES?

If we accept that balance is important, especially in light of avoiding "negative excellence" in any area of life, how do we achieve it? Since each of us lives according to a set of priorities — whether we are aware of it or not — perhaps that is the place to start.

What does your priority list look like? For those committed to ultraexcellence, one goal stands alone on the top — perhaps wealth, power, athletic success, academics, or political victory. Sequentially beneath this exalted goal are myriad subordinate goals. These form a constellation of priorities for each person. If written down, one list might look something like this:

1. God
2. Spouse/marriage
3. Children
4. Self
5. Work
6. Church

7. Friends, neighbors
8. Health
9. Security
10. Civic duty

Does creating such lists help us solve our problem and lead us to biblically authentic decision making about balancing priorities? I think not. "A list of priorities doesn't make sense!" observes J. Grant Howard in *Balancing Life's Demands*. "No matter how you define and describe your particular approach, if it is a sequential approach, it is loaded with contradictions."[3]

We cannot achieve balance by stacking our priorities one on top of another, even though this is a common practice. As Dr. Howard goes on to advise, it fits better to think of God as *central* to everything and then build outward from that point. We do not love God, *then* spouse, *then* children, *then* self, *then* church. We love God, spouse, children, self, and church all at the same time. Similarly, we do not love God 100 percent, spouse 95 percent, children 90 percent, church 80 percent. God's standard requires that we love all of them all of the time.

One of the interesting things about love is that it is not a mathematical entity. When divided, love multiplies. However we attempt to factor it, love remains an intact whole. For example, if we have one child in our family, we might be singularly devoted to that child and love him or her 100 percent. If we have a second child, does that mean we love each child only 50 percent? Of course not. We would love each child 100 percent even if there were ten of them.

God has suspended the laws of mathematics in allowing love to expand infinitely. In so doing, He has delivered us from the need to prioritize our love sequentially.

THE APPORTIONMENT OF TIME

It does not make sense to have sequential priorities in terms of love or even in terms of commitment. We love each person fully. Additionally, we are committed to doing good in all areas of life. Priority thinking is appropriate when we speak of *time*, however.

Time is the context within which we all must work. In any given year, no one is granted more time than another person, and no one is granted less. Time cannot be stretched or borrowed. It is a universal given, and it is in apportioning this time that balance and priorities become very important.

Time, then, is the key. When we couple it with our goals, desires, and responsibilities, we have some priority decisions to make. It is unwise to give all our time to work and family, but none to personal health. God created us to need health, and it is not wrong to seek it. Likewise, God created us to need each other in relationship. It is not wrong to dedicate time for that. He created us with duties toward nature, work, and government, and it is not wrong for us to focus on these duties. *But the time devoted must be balanced, for if we give too much in one area we neglect our duty in another important area and fail God's requirements for balanced living.*

RESTORING BALANCE

Partitioning our time is probably the most important practical issue in achieving balanced living. Yet rationing it wisely presents a dilemma for each of us. How do we do it? First and most important, balance cannot be achieved unless we are willing to say no.

It is not easy to say no. Anyone who has eaten in a buffet restaurant knows what it is like to face a long table of inviting foods: salads, potatoes, gravy, rolls, corn, chicken, shrimp, roast beef, and pie. It is difficult to go down this line without saying yes to too much. In life, as in the buffet, our plates fill up sooner than we realize. In attempting to be sociable we try to accommodate everyone's invitations. In attempting to live a full life we taste every experience. In attempting to be good parents we try to give our children more opportunities than we had. In attempting to be compassionate we want to help with everyone's problems. In attempting to be good providers we accept extra work assignments.

At this point we need to remember discussions from earlier in the book. With each passing year, modern-day life spontaneously becomes more stressful, more overloaded, and more complex. No one controls all this change—it is simply the way progress unfolds. As we are presented with more decision and activity overload within an increasingly complex and stressful context, balance becomes more difficult. We cannot resolve this problem without saying no—even to some very good things. Saying no, then, is the first step. But what comes next?

What follows are four additional steps to restoring balance.

1. It is important that we gain control over our own lives, for only then will balance be a possibility. If our schedules are ruled by the urgent and tyrannical, we will not have the control necessary for substantive changes. Each of the chapters in parts 2 and 3 is intended to help us gain a measure of control and reorient our lives in a God-given rather than society-driven direction.

2. We must place God at the center of all things, and build outward from there, rationally and consistently. We know which areas of living God has told us to focus on—in particular, loving relationships. Making our choices in the light of accepted limits, we reassess regularly and defend each area of importance against the onslaught of other demands.

3. We must beware the trap of trying to solve the problem of imbalance by becoming even more imbalanced. Sometimes it feels like we are in a Chinese finger trap—the harder we try to pull free, the worse we become entrapped. If already maximally scheduled, we cannot give added attention to one area unless we subtract from another area. "We respond to our sense of imbalance by committing more time and energy to an area in which we feel deficient," warns physician George Rust.4 Yet when the rain barrel is full, it is full. We cannot put another drop in unless we first take a drop out. As elementary as this principle is, its application escapes the majority of modern-day people.

4. We must accept the no given us by others. We ought not to feel offended when another person is merely attempting to achieve God-honoring balance and margin. Let's beware of forcing our expectations upon our friends. Give them the freedom to maneuver within the complicated context of their own lives. "Be kind," someone once said, "for everyone you meet is fighting a hard battle."

If we insist on unbalanced living (for example, working fourteen-hour days or being involved in six church programs simultaneously), at least we should allow those around us to seek balance should they so desire. Even as we reap the rewards for our area of excellence, we will also reap the penalties for the areas of negative excellence. Others might not desire this same scenario.

A FEW SHELLS

One of the most charming books written about balance and simplicity is a small volume by Anne Morrow Lindbergh. Well known as wife of the famous pilot Charles Lindbergh and daughter of the diplomat Dwight Morrow, Anne Lindbergh was a celebrity in her own right as aviator and author. Probably her most famous book, *Gift from the Sea*, was written during an island retreat off the New England coast. Our personal copy is a 1957 edition, and by that time—two years after first publication— more than one-half million copies had been printed. She wrote,

> For the natural selectivity of the island I will have to substi-
> tute a conscious selectivity based on another sense of val-
> ues—a sense of values I have become more aware of here.
> Island-precepts, I might call them if I could define them,
> signposts toward another way of living. Simplicity of living,
> as much as possible, to retain a true awareness of life.
> Balance of physical, intellectual, and spiritual life. Work
> without pressure. Space for significance and beauty. Time
> for solitude and sharing. Closeness to nature to strengthen
> understanding and faith in the intermittency of life: life of
> the spirit, creative life, and the life of human relationships.[5]

GOD UNDERSTANDS

Balance is necessary and attainable. Not easy, but possible. When we understand that we are finite and that it is okay to be finite, then we can begin to accept our limits with comfort.

God expects us to perform well in many areas of life. But when He gave us the limits of time and finiteness, at that moment He also built in the necessity of balance. We work hard to please our Master, but we also rest confidently knowing that He understands our condition.

What we do we do well—but we do not do it all.

FOURTEEN

Health Through Rest

Three-year-olds seldom sit still. Bundles of energy tightly wound, they dash from here to there, leaping over toys and ricocheting off walls. Church services—as every parent knows—were not designed with these squirmers in mind. Each Sunday the rear of the sanctuary witnesses the sixty-minute ritual of parent against child; the one trying to survive, the other trying to escape.

My eldest son, Adam, was once such a wiggly three-year-old, and I was more than once the embarrassed parent. A particular service stands out vividly. His restless noisiness was not in the least malicious, but it was distracting nevertheless. Attempting to maintain quiet, I lifted him onto my lap and held him loosely in my arms. The wiggling, however, did not stop. Now, instead of random wiggling, there was willful wiggling. He and I were soon doing battle. Adam was intent on freedom. I was intent on containment.

Finally, after twenty minutes, that blessed moment arrived. As if someone had thrown a switch, he suddenly melted into my arms and fell asleep. The tug of war ended. Adam had yielded and was now at rest. As the struggling ceased, my attitude also changed. The frustration of the previous moments vanished, and in its place was a deep protective love.

This, I thought, is as it should be—not striving, but nestling. I would have moved mountains at that moment to defend him.

Rest. In the arms of a loving Father.

WEARINESS

The patients who come to my office do not seem rested. For that matter, neither do most physicians. The medical residents I teach often are five minutes away from collapse. Many people I meet look haggard and worn-out.

Often-used descriptors of our society include active, busy, driven, fatigued, tired, exhausted, weary, burned out, anxious, overloaded, or stressed. But seldom do you hear our society described as "well rested." We are a tired generation, one for which Matthew Arnold's "hurry sickness" has become a way of life. Our carburetors are set on high, and our gears are stuck in overdrive. Our lives are nonstop.

We have leisure but little rest. The pace, the noise, the expectations, and the interruptions of modern life have not soothed the soul nor brought refreshment to the burdened spirit.

FROM JET TO DONKEY

Earlier in the book we took a short trip abroad, visiting Africa and the Caribbean. Let's again pack our bags and head off on another fact-finding mission, this time watching closely for signs of cultural and personal restedness. Even though we board a DC-10 in New York, be prepared to disembark from the back of a camel in the middle of nowhere.

The first thing we notice is that the pace of life in such places is decidedly slower than ours. The people have much more time to visit with their neighbors, walk to town, or stop and leisurely watch the children rolling a hoop down the middle of the main street. No one seems in a hurry (except, that is, when they drive).

Just your presence in town brings the entire society to a curious halt. The children flock around and almost all of them are giggling. In the market, everyone is talking—but only a fraction of the exchange is commercial. If you ask for directions, you will have twelve volunteers.

On the main street, men sit on barrel tops and talk. Women lean out of shop windows to visit with the closest passerby. Kids try to hawk their trinkets or beg for money—but often with just the hint of a smile at the corners of their mouths. If you go to the bank for a transaction, you might wait interminably for even the smallest request. But no one else seems to mind, and no one looks at the clock. Oh, the frustration we feel when our paperwork is processed with the speed of a glacier.

Despite such an accumulation of anecdotal evidence, sociologists will still want more hard data. And skeptics will scorn my sentimentality. In fairness, I want to be honest. When abroad in more primitive conditions, I often miss modern conveniences—like a cold glass of milk or bathrooms without cockroaches and tarantulas. But what I don't miss are telephones, televisions, stoplights, video games, watches that beep during pastoral prayers, and boom boxes on the beach.

I have not gone so far as to suggest that the way of life in developing countries is superior or preferable to that of developed ones. I am only making the observation that these refreshingly gracious and hospitable people are not exhausted, in body or spirit, whereas we often are. Those who would maintain that progress brings rest are wrong. We may have education, affluence, technology, leisure, and conveniences—but the only experience many of us have with rest today is the first half of restless.

God, however, has commanded us to rest. A biblically authentic and balanced life will include time to be still, to remember, to meditate, to delight in who He is and what He has made. But a large obstacle stands in our way: There is no glory in rest. No social acclaim. We are never a hero because we rest. We can only be still and better wait upon the Lord. We can only meditate upon the Word more. We can only have more margin with which to serve our neighbor. These things, however, are not socially reimbursable.

BURNING UP THE ENGINE

The healthiest lifestyle comes equipped with four gears. The first is *park* for the contemplative times. This gear is to be used for rest and renewal. It is the gear we use to recharge our margin batteries. This is where we do much of our thinking about values and spirituality, as well as much of our Scripture study and prayer. It is the gear we plan to use as we pick up a novel and head for the hammock, or as we sit on a stump and watch the wildlife.

The second gear is *low.* This gear is for relationships, for family and friends. This is the gear we use when talking with someone, and it prevents us from being distracted and nervously moving on to the next activity while still in the middle of a conversation. This is the gear we use when the children ask for a story or a back rub. Or when they ask about the death of pets, or sex, or God. No hurry here: just quality.

The third gear is *drive*. This is our usual gear for work and play. This gear uses lots of energy, and the faster speed feels good because it is productive. It gets us from place to place quickly. This is the gear we mow the lawn in or exercise in.

The fourth gear is *overdrive*. This gear is reserved for times that require extra effort. If we have a deadline coming, we kick into this gear. If we are playing a basketball game, we call upon overdrive to energize us. This is the gear I use during flu season when my schedule is double-booked. This is the gear most families use getting ready for church.

Unfortunately, many in our society do not shift down from overdrive. Our cars are not meant to race at high speeds continuously—the engine would burn up. Neither are our bodies or spirits. Yet to slow down for some is unthinkable and for others, impossible.

- In our everyday lives, most of us need rest in three areas:
- Physical rest, the least important of the three.
- Emotional rest, more important by several orders of magnitude.
- Spiritual rest, which, though widely neglected, is of supreme importance.

PHYSICAL REST

Constant activity is a characteristic of our age. If we are not active, we feel slothful. If we are not productive, we feel guilty. A healthy twenty-eight-year-old man sitting on a lawn swing for an entire Sunday afternoon would more than likely feel the need to apologize to his neighbors should they discover him.

Such busyness does not come because our bodies can't help themselves. We cannot blame our thyroid or adrenal glands. Nor does it result from a theological teaching. It comes from a cultural value system that idolizes productivity.

I am not saying that productivity is wrong. I am only saying it must not be idolized. Productivity has no more spiritual value than does rest and, as a matter of fact, probably less. Industriousness might be good for an economy, particularly one like ours. But that does not mean it is healthy in all respects.

As a physician, I clearly affirm that physical activity is not only good, it is necessary. But so is physical rest. Our bodies were designed to need rest. Sleep is the clearest example, and one that cannot be violated. Many Americans, however, get the activity-rest cycle out of balance. Millions get too little activity, and millions more get too little rest. Type As, as an illustration, refuse to rest: to them it is an enemy. Also, those around them are made to feel weak if they desire a pause. Consequently, life is lived full speed ahead. They work hard, they play hard, and they even Sabbath hard.

Restless Work

Work in our culture often dominates other areas of life. To be sure, work is very important. But other activities are more important. The people who work the hardest and rest the least naturally rise to the top, from where they drive the entire work system. They set the rules, which maximize productivity. Even love and relationship come far down the list. Little wonder rest cannot find a resting place.

"People in the Western world have leisure. We do not need to slave every minute in order to eat. But only a few appear to have rest," observes Mennonite author Doris Longacre.

> Profit-making work began to swallow Sundays and holidays. No wonder everyone has been getting so tired.
>
> Obviously much of this fatigue takes place in the name of making more money, even though the pantry's already stocked. After all, by burning a little more gas and working one more evening a week, it is possible to chase down one more account, open another store, or farm another field. But it may not be possible to love a spouse, children, and the friendless poor at the same time.[1]

God has instructed us that life is more than work. It includes relationships, worship, and yes, even rest. "A rest-less work style produces a restless person," notes Gordon MacDonald. "We do not rest because our work is done; we rest because God commanded it and created us to have a need for it."[2]

Lethal Leisure

Leisure might be the name we give our time away from work, but it is not a synonym for rest. Many can't understand why they are so tired after a vacation. The reason is because our vacations and weekends have ceased to be restful. "It is ironic that our society, so addicted to pleasure and 'leisure,' knows so little of what it means to rest," observes lawyer and pastor Jim Buchan. "We are often more tired after the weekend is over than before it started. We come back from our vacations feeling as if we need some time to rest."[3]

Americans do not tolerate an activity vacuum well. The slow, contemplative life is largely foreign to our experience. Therefore, when "leisure time" appears on our schedule, we select from the many activity options society offers. This is not inherently wrong. Neither is quiet, introverted reflection always right. But when we work hard and then play harder, no wonder we feel fatigued so often.

Technology does not answer our need for physical rest. Laborsaving devices help in some respects, but curiously, those cultures that have the most laborsaving devices are the most hectic and the least rested. We often wonder why the homemaker remains so tired despite all the household appliances and conveniences. We forget to calculate that for every minute of time saved, our society offers hours of new activities, each with noise, expectations, and complexities of its own.

Although progress may not approve, *it is okay to rest physically.*

EMOTIONAL REST

More important to our overall health than physical rest is the resting of our emotions. Ask physicians about the frequency of anxiety or depression they find in their patients, and you will be stunned to learn how few in our midst are emotionally healthy and well rested. We worry about our jobs, our marriages, our children, our looks, our age, our health, and our future. The unacceptably high rate of tranquilizer use is a reliable indicator of our lack of emotional rest.

Physical rest and emotional rest often go hand in hand, but we have no guarantee the resting of our bodies will produce rested psyches. The stilling of outward activity does not always assure a commensurate quieting of inward activity. Nevertheless, if we would rest our emotions, a wise first step would be to seek out quiet. Unfortunately, Walden is rarely found; lights and noise are to our right, people and action are to our left. With each successive decade, the ambient environmental noise level increases. Even within the four walls of home, televisions blare seven hours a day. Rock music has defrauded an entire adolescent generation out of anything even approximating emotional rest.

The majority of each day is spent with people. While that is exactly where we should be most of the time, it can be quite draining. For many, occasional solitude is a prerequisite for emotional resting, but where does one find privacy and silence?

Even the privilege of royalty doesn't always assure the privacy of rest. Near the end of his reign, England's King George V was asked what he would do if he could do whatever he pleased. "He replied that he would take his biggest car and drive and drive as far as it would take him. There he would find a little farmhouse, and in the farmhouse there would be a small, clean, whitewashed room, furnished only with a bed and an open fire. He would lie down on the bed, and lying so, alone in the small, clean room, he would look at the glowing coals of the fire, and the flames playing blue about them—and so he would rest. For once in a royal lifetime he would rest."[4]

Contemporary Commotion

If you think about it, you can find many reasons for the absence of emotional rest in our midst—so many, in fact, that it would be surprising to discover true restedness among us. Noise deprives us of rest, yet we have more noise today than ever before. Activity overload deprives us of rest, yet we are busier than ever. Inappropriate expectations deprive us of rest, yet our culture advertises: "You *deserve* the best." Pride deprives us of rest, as we worry about every wrinkle we have and every piece of clothing we wear. Discontent and covetousness deprive us of rest, yet our culturally sanctioned advertising intentionally stimulates discontent. "The proud man and the covetous man never have rest"; noted Thomas à Kempis, "but the meek man and the poor in spirit live in great abundance of rest and peace."[5]

Preoccupation with success deprives us of rest—always climb a little higher and get a little more. So does preoccupation with power. Yet success and power are two cogs of the "American dream," and we are reluctant to let them go. Debt deprives us of rest, yet our debt is at unprecedented levels. We worry about our image and our reputation until we have no rest.

As A. W. Tozer observed, "The heart's fierce effort to protect itself from every slight, to shield its touchy honor from the bad opinion of friend and enemy, will never let the mind have rest."[6]

Restless Relationships

Perhaps the greatest root cause for the absence of emotional rest in our society is fractured relationships. When there is fighting in the workplace, contention in the community, bitterness in the church, and combat in the home, we won't find rest. The saddest of these, of course, is the home. It was intended by God as a haven of peace and security. But when strife enters, rest flees.

"If we don't deal with our unresolved conflicts, they'll deal with us," counsels Tim Kimmel. "Are there people whom you need to forgive? Do yourself a favor. Give them something they don't deserve but desperately need. Give them the gift of forgiveness. It's a gift that, once given, offers something in return. Your spirit gets a rest."[7]

If we would avoid the many unexpected pains of our day, we must discipline our expectations, tame our discontent, and mend our relationships. For *it is important to rest emotionally.*

SPIRITUAL REST

When our bodies find rest, we feel refreshed. When our emotions find rest, our countenance is lifted. Yet relaxed muscles and minds are of little worth unless our souls also find rest in the acceptance of God. Such a rest transcends the problems of our world and shelters us where no injury can follow. As the psalmist tells us, "He who dwells in the shelter of the Most High will rest in the shadow of the Almighty. I will say of the LORD, 'He is my refuge and my fortress, my God, in whom I trust.'"[8] The shadow of the Almighty is impregnable; His rest ultimately the only dependable rest.

We should be concerned with at least two types of spiritual rest. God calls us to *Sabbath rest.* And He offers us *surrendered rest.*

Sabbath Rest

Someone once remarked, "God rested—and He wasn't tired." After creating, even the Almighty rested: "God blessed the seventh day and made it holy, because on it he rested from all the work of creating that he had done."[9] He looked on what He had made and delighted in it, and He has commanded us to do the same.

At Sabbath rest we don't simply rest the body—although that is important. Also, we don't primarily rest the emotions—although we would be wise to discover such rest in our Sabbaths. Instead, *it is a remembrance*. Moses writes, "Remember that you were slaves in Egypt and that the LORD your God brought you out of there with a mighty hand and an outstretched arm. Therefore the LORD your God has commanded you to observe the Sabbath day."[10] This same God who rescued the Israelites from their slavery in Egypt is the One who rescues us from our bondage to sin. Remember.

At Sabbath time we suspend dominion work and instead worship the dominion-Maker. We cease reaping for our own cupboards and instead bring an offering to Him. We rest not because we are tired. We don't cease our labor because it is finished. We don't worship because now there are grapes on the vine and cattle in the stalls. We rest and worship one day in seven simply because He is the Lord.

Remembering, worshiping, and resting are acts of contemplation. Yet churches today, for the most part, have not developed a practical theology of contemplation nor a practical theology of rest. "It is my own conviction that the church, and humanity at large, neglects inwardness at its own peril," warns philosopher Nicholas Wolterstorff. By inwardness Wolterstorff means contemplation. "It seems to me that amidst its intense activism, the Western world is starved for contemplation."[11]

The Sabbath rest is an opportunity for contemplation, an opportunity to remember our roots.

Surrendered Rest

"Softly and tenderly Jesus is calling"—but the world is shouting and waving its hands. Sometimes, over the din, it is hard to hear His invitation: "Ye who are weary come home." The Sabbath rest is a rest He *calls* us to, but the surrendered rest He *offers* to us. The Sabbath rest we enter out of obedience; the surrendered rest we enter out of our need. The Sabbath rest arises from the good and perfect law of God; the surrendered rest arises from the good and perfect grace of God. The Sabbath rest is remembrance; the surrendered rest is meekness. Both provide soothing, God-ordained healing.

High on my list of favorite scriptures are Jesus' words in Matthew 11:28-30: "Come to me, all you who are weary and burdened, and I will give you rest. Take my yoke upon you and learn from me, for I am gentle and humble in heart, and you will find rest for your souls. For my yoke is easy and my burden is light." These words draw weary people everywhere. Yet, per usual, Jesus leaves us scratching our heads. What does He mean, to take His yoke? I'm not sure that sounds restful. It sounds more like hard work and suffering. "I see pastors wanting to follow Christ and taking up his yoke, but somehow not finding the rest," pastoral counselor Louis McBurney points out. "Instead of a lighter load, they have a heavier one."[12] Where is rest hiding?

MEEKNESS

The answer lies in meekness. In this passage, Christ calls Himself "gentle and humble"—meek. He came not to judge but to die. He came not to shout and defend the honor of the Father but to die. He came not to fight but to die. No persecution could disturb Him for He came to suffer. Yet all the time He was suffering, He knew He was winning.

We, too, can suffer and win. We can live with love even when others hate—all the time knowing that love wins. We can respond with grace when others fight, knowing that grace wins. When we come to Him and surrender, accepting His yoke, we accept full vulnerability to the onslaught of the world. Yet, at the same time, we are assured that nothing can separate us from the victorious love of Christ. This rest is a self-weakening unto God-strength. It is a self-emptying unto God-fullness. It is the rest of full surrender.

"Jesus calls us to His rest, and meekness is His method. The meek man cares not at all who is greater than he, for he has long ago decided that the esteem of the world is not worth the effort," teaches Tozer. "The rest Christ offers is the rest of meekness, the blessed relief which comes when we accept ourselves for what we are and cease to pretend. It will take some courage at first, but the needed grace will come as we learn that we are sharing this new and easy yoke with the strong Son of God Himself."[13]

In an age of strife and unrest, when our bodies are weary and our spirits are frenzied, "Don't worry, be happy," will not rescue us. I prefer Corrie ten Boom's "Don't wrestle, just nestle." Even when I feel inferior, even when I have been victimized, even when the pace and pressures of life bring me to the point of collapse, Christ brings me to His rest. When my surrender is completed and His yoke is accepted, then my soul will find rest. And *it is imperative, in such an age as ours, that we rest spiritually.*

FIFTEEN

Pain, Margin, Health, and Relationship

History is something that happens to people; what happens is always different from what people would rather have done. . . .We have made great progress—for which we also have paid a price.[1]

—Claude Levi-Strauss, French anthropologist

Humans are passive agents. It is true that, from time to time, we make small and even a few large changes attempting to improve matters. But mostly our lives are filled with passivity.

At this juncture, however, allowing history to just "happen to us" is unforgivably foolish. For no matter what their ideological bent, the trend watchers are united in one opinion: Something is afoot. Along with much of the rest of the world, the United States is in a period of profound disequilibrium. Having never been through a disjuncture of such dimension or consisting of such particulars before, we are not quite sure in what condition we will find ourselves when it leaves off.

In this unfolding of historical change, we have been guided by the process of history called progress. In many respects, progress has done a good job, bringing us places previously reserved for fantasy writers. And at such speed! But progress has been especially painful of late.

WHAT TO DO WITH PAIN

At times it appears as if the cumulative weight of suffering and sorrow will sink the entire world. People hurt, families hurt, friendships hurt, churches hurt, communities hurt, nations hurt. Some hurt more than others, but nearly all hurt to some degree. Many have hurt for so long it seems as if the pain will never end. What should we do about all this pain?

First, let's thank God for it. Anything that redirects us to Him is of benefit.

Second, let's repent. Not the "ineffectual, unfervent prayer of an unrighteous man availeth little" kind of repentance, but the kind that means something and costs something. The kind of repentance where you conduct business with God and whereafter life has actually changed and you are headed in a different direction.

Third, let's do some surgery. There is a lot of pruning that needs to be done and abscesses that need draining. Let's prune away the time cancers, amputate the energy tumors, and drain the debt abscesses. Don't cringe — God is a great physician, and it is good to be pruned and drained. We ought to do it more often. For without surgery, margin and health will not return.

Fourth, let's cooperate with God. Our hope for the future is only valid because of one fact: God is still around, and what's more, He's still interested. Our success or failure will hinge on our cooperation with Him. "When this little life is over, nearly all that makes the headlines in the newspapers or fills the bulletins on the radio will seem to be of purely temporary significance," notes J. B. Phillips. "But the work of those who have cooperated with God will remain, for it is part of his everlasting purpose."[2]

SHORT TERM, LONG TERM

When we contact God to tell Him we are ready to cooperate, He will give us a two-term plan: short and long.

For the short term, we need worry only about today. Isn't that good news? Isn't that hopeful? Plan for tomorrow, to be sure. Be concerned for tomorrow. But worry only about today.[3]

You see, our responsibility is to do what is right today. Of course the future is important; of course we are concerned about what kind of society we end up with; of course we must plan intelligently and prayerfully. But we can only get there one day at a time, and today is the day to do what is right.

Today we must begin valuing the things God values and cease valuing those things of no value to Him. Today we must agree that our choices *do* make a difference—whether we live without margin, work two jobs, build an expensive house, overload a friend, don't spend time with our children. Today let's decide to invest in relationship, to encourage someone. Today decide to love, the sacrificial-service kind of love. Today forgive someone who should have been forgiven long ago. Today light one little candle and stop cursing the darkness.

For the long term, God would have us set about rebuilding using the instructions previously given. He has already told us what to do— now we just have to do it.

Let me tell you another hopeful secret about God's plan. He wants us to reclaim society, but not necessarily as the first order of business. Redeeming what we can of progress will be a huge job, but we can work on that tomorrow. For now, we have enough work at home to keep us occupied. So put away the newspaper, turn off the nightly news, and *forget about the despair of problem mountain*. We will return to them later. It is time to put on the work clothes and report for duty in the front yard.

Here God awaits us, with the confidence of a Leader who has been through it all before. As we become teachable—even desperate—what will be His advice? He has, of course, already given us lots of instructions, all of them valuable. But if we were to boil them all out, one principle would rise to the top: the priority of relationship.

GOD'S REPORT CARD

If God's greatest commandments are as inclusive as I believe they are, when life is over and we receive our report card, it will have only one category—relationship. There will be three lines:

▶ How did we relate to God?
▶ How did we relate to ourselves?
▶ How did we relate to others?

We know that relationship is so important to God because *He does all His work there. That is why progress missed Him.* Progress kept telling us to search for buried treasure inside bank vaults, while all the time God had it buried in the heart of our neighbor.

Even if we have little time for healthy relationships, we all instinctually understand their importance. Due to the antagonistic influences of marginless living, however, they are an increasingly rare commodity. Overloaded contemporary life attempts to de-relationalize us, which is perhaps the English equivalent of the German word *Zerrissenheit*— "torn-to-pieces-hood." Today, it is possible to live in a city surrounded by one million people and be alone for a lifetime. We become a number, and no one ever loved a number. The systems of modernity swallow us alive. Bureaucracies, corporations, institutions—all conjure up images of structures that inhale people and exhale cement.

God, however, is a personal God, and relationship is very important to Him. He created us as relational beings—not because He had to but because it suited Him. We are relational and dependent whether we acknowledge it or not, whether we want to be or not. We ought not kick against this, however, for it was meant as a gift. God gave us to each other for reasons of benefit, not torture.

RELATE TO WHOM?

How do we know that God's report card contains three categories? Jesus told us so. When asked outright by the Pharisee, Jesus answered that, of course, the Shema was the greatest commandment: "'Hear, O Israel, the Lord our God, the Lord is one. Love the Lord your God with all your heart and with all your soul and with all your mind and with all your strength.'" However, He did not stop there: "The second is this: 'Love your neighbor as yourself.' There is no commandment greater than these!"[4]

In so answering, Christ laid out for us the greatest imperative of eternity: to love God, our neighbor, and our self. This commandment must be the first guideline for all of life's decisions and actions. Nothing is to come before it.

Love the Lord your God. God is our Creator, which means we were related to Him even before birth. He yearns for our broken relationship to be reconciled. He went 99.99 percent of the way and extends a nail-pierced hand for us to grasp. His patience has given us much space to repent. We live in a world that promotes distance, builds fences, buys locks, and doesn't talk on elevators. But God, in Christ, says, "Come."

Love yourself. God assumes we love and care for self. Some people, however, have no relationship with themselves. To leave them alone in solitude for a day would be punishment. That we are worthy of love is demonstrated by the fact that God loves us. His love validates our worth and, as a matter of fact, provides the only basis for it. Without that validation we stand undeserving. Some are so broken by this unworthiness that they get stuck in it. The concept of unworthiness is a wonderful thing to grasp and is the first step in setting things right. But getting stuck in it is a spiritually neurotic thing to do and is not God's will. The call to spiritually accurate self-love is not a denial of our unworthiness but is instead the result of a journey that goes through unworthiness to God.

Love your neighbor. Created incapable of meeting all our own needs, God gave us others, in relationship, to help. Despite the fact that each individual is of more value than all the careers, education, and money in the universe added together and multiplied times infinity, right relating to others seems to be the most difficult item on the contemporary agenda.

QUIET KINDNESSES

God has shown us the road to health, the path to blessing—it is the way of relationship. Do you see now why careers, degrees, and estates can never quite get the job done? Somehow we just keep taking our expensive automobiles to our posh offices to make another hundred thousand dollars, while all the time our relationships vaporize before our eyes and our loneliness deepens.

But we are not helpless. Progress does not own us. We do not have to let history "happen to us." We are free to change. And God is still interested in lending a hand.

We can focus on relationship and create a margin for it. We can simplify and balance our lives so that relationships have some space. We can invest ourselves in other people. When we don't feel like it, we can still do it. Even when we can't find anyone else interested in friendship, we can always start spreading around quiet kindnesses, *expecting none in return.*

Soon, love will begin to flow out from us, and with the flow there will also come a flowing back. For love, you see, is "the most excellent way."[5]

LOVE

All the commandments in Scripture reduce to Christ's Great Commandment, and the Great Commandment reduces to one concept: love.

God is in love with His creation. The creature has something of the Creator in him, and God has loved us from the beginning. Even when the creature turned his back on Heaven, yet God loved him: "I made you, and I will carry you. I don't hold anything against you. Let me rescue you."

The history of the world reduces to this: your being pursued by love. He courted you; He followed you; He loved you. If you go to work or school or church, He is there. If you go to the edge of the universe or to the borders of hell, He is there. If you go deep inside yourself, He is there. In the dark of the night, in your depression, He is there. On your deathbed, when you don't want anybody to leave you, He is there. If you look behind you or before you, He is there, waiting to be allowed entrance into your life.

In the economics of eternity, God paid a great price. If we only better understood the cost, we would also better understand our worth.

THE ECONOMICS OF THE RELATIONAL LIFE

Love is the currency of the relational life. In the relational life, we spend love and receive love. That was God's idea from the beginning. It is what He taught us, and it was what He showed us. God wants us to spend love freely, even generously. When we do, everyone becomes rich. It is the primary currency of God's economics.

As you can see, love is not like other resources. There is an infinite supply. You can use it and use it and use it. Yet there will still be more left over. As a matter of fact, *the more it is used, the more its supply increases*.

Some guard their supply of love, doling it out in portions. But this kind of thinking works with money, not with love. With money, the more you hoard, the richer you become. But *with love, the more you spend, the richer you become*.

Spending and receiving love is the best part of Kingdom work. It is also the best part of doctoring.

FLOWERS FROM THE OTHER SIDE OF THE GRAVE

Eileen was sixty-three years old and already had advanced cancer when I first met her. Following surgery, there was little that could be done.

She healed nicely from her operation but, some months later, developed a persistent cough. "It is probably the tumor, Eileen," I said. "We should get a chest X-ray to be sure."

"No, doctor," she replied. "I don't want to know anything about it." Soon, however, her shortness of breath left us no choice but to investigate.

"It's as we suspected," I said. "Your X-ray shows a large amount of fluid in the right lung. If you would like, we can make you more comfortable by draining some of the fluid off here in the office. It really doesn't hurt much, and you should be able to breathe easier."

Under normal circumstances, tapping the lung is always followed by an X-ray to make sure the lung has not been punctured or deflated during the procedure. But after three uneventful taps in the clinic, I decided to deviate from protocol and do the procedure in Eileen's home. By now, she was having great difficulty getting around.

Each time I went to her home, I would first sit on the bed and we would talk. Then I would examine her lungs, position her for the procedure, paint her with Betadine, and introduce the needle into her chest.

On the third visit, I held her hand for a while, and together we looked out the open window. Perhaps we both sensed the end was near.

"Those are beautiful lilacs," I said, noticing for the first time the flowers hardly a foot or two outside her open window. They were just coming into full bloom, and the room was full of their fragrance.

"Lilacs are my favorite," she replied. "That is why I wanted to be down here, close to them. I love them."

After draining another quart of fluid off her lung, I left the house for the last time. A week later she died.

Shortly after Eileen's death, her daughter came to the clinic carrying a huge bouquet of deep purple lilacs in a blue mason jar. She asked the receptionist to bring the flowers to my office, explaining that it would be too hard for her to see me just then.

This note was with the lilacs:

> Words do seem inadequate to express our thanks for all you have
> done for our family. Because of your kind, caring ways Mom
> was able to stay in her home and be as comfortable as possible.
>
> Mom wanted the "Best Doctor in the World" to enjoy
> her special lilacs. God bless you!

I have received many expressions of thanks from the relatives of
deceased patients. But this was the first time I had been given flowers
from the other side of the grave.

I am not the "Best Doctor in the World." But at least for a moment,
I felt like it. Medicine can be a grinding profession when money is the
only reward. But when love is the currency of exchange, gratitude alone
can pay the debt in full.

MUST WE LOVE?

I did not drain the fluid off Eileen's lung because I am a technician who
enjoys doing procedures. I did not visit her in the home because I am a
businessman looking for increased revenue. Instead, I cared for her
because I allowed her ache to enter my heart.

Eileen was suffering, and I had the skills to help. I reached out to
her, not as a proceduralist or a profiteer, but as a physician. My reaching is what I call love. Why should I work just for money when I can
work for love? And from the other side of the grave, Eileen reached
back. I call that love too. Relational economics.

Somehow, we just can't wrap our minds around this idea of love.
We can't nail it down and say, "There, I've got you." Yes, love is strange.
It is weak yet tough, vulnerable yet strong. It chooses to lose but can
never be beaten. It puts itself last yet always leads the way. It is mysterious, yet it came in flesh and stood before us. It is death—yet it is life.

God's love is commonly undervalued and always underestimated.
No virtue can compete with it, and no vice can defeat it. God ordained
that it should be so, and He stands guard to see that no one changes the
order of things.

Must we love? That is a nonsensical question. It is like asking,
"Must we breathe?" No, we do not have to breathe, and no, we do

not have to love. But the consequences of both those decisions will be the same.

ARE YOU READY?

Pain surrounds us all. Much of this pain comes from progress's blatant disregard for our need of margin. And much of this pain—far too much of this pain—is because of neglected and broken relationships. It is difficult to be healthy in a society where relational, emotional, and spiritual sickness is endemic. If you live in a swamp, malaria has a head start.

But do you know what? Malaria can be treated, and so can pain. Margin can be restored. Broken relationships can be healed. It takes work. It takes love. It might even take going to the cross. But healing is worth it. I have never seen a truly healthy person who didn't derive that well-being from the benefits of intact, loving relationships.

Are you ready to commit to relationship in love? This is not like asking, "Would you go to the store for some milk?" but more like, "Are you ready to lay down your life for your friends?"[6]

If you are, then do everything you can to travel in the health direction. If stress crushes your spirit by poisoning you with despair, then either conquer stress or walk away—but don't stop relating. If overload destroys your relationships, then dispatch overload to the far side. If that malignant, universal enemy of relational health, marginless living, leaves you panting for air and desperate for space, then go and take margin back. Hack it out of your cultural landscape. And guard it for the sake of your God, yourself, your family, and your friends.

Health cannot be far behind.

Appendix: Graphs

The graphs on the following pages visually demonstrate the rapid and unprecedented changes within American society. A few guidelines will help make their interpretation easier and more accurate.

The slope—It is important to note the slope of the curves. As explained in chapter 3, curves that slope upward rapidly are called exponential. Some of the graphs appearing here are true exponential slopes, while others only approximate exponential slopes for a period of time. The point is, all these graphs illustrate rapid, radical change.

The reason margin disappeared as quickly as it did is because of the type of exponential slopes found on these graphs. Remember: straight line graphs represent historical transition; exponential curve graphs represent historical disruption.

Extrapolation—If you want a glimpse into the future, take the most recent portion of these curves and extend it for another twenty-five or fifty years. For example, if you were to do this with the graph of health-care costs it would become quickly apparent why so many people are worried.

S-curves—Several of the curves (for example, divorces) already demonstrate a tailing off, and this is reassuring. Nevertheless, during the time when these slopes were climbing rapidly, the amount of change experienced in our society was dramatic.

Time frame — Most graphs have a standardized time frame, from 1900 to 2000. A few, however, go back much farther.

Not all are negative — Not all of these graphs represent problems — for example, the number of new books or the gross national product. Most of the graphs, however, have at least some negative repercussions.

Logarithms — With two of the graphs, the change was so dramatic that it had to be scaled logarithmically. I have provided some additional explanation with these graphs to help in understanding the startling dimensions involved.

Generic graphs — The first three graphs listed are generic: *complexity, information,* and *change.* The type of data represented by these topics is hard to quantify. Nevertheless, I believe them to be in essence true.

Graphs Illustrating Increase

Despite the absence of objective parameters for the y-axis, generic graphsare perhaps the most important in the appendix to understand. The slopes here represent my estimates, and some would take issue with the exact shape of the curves. Butno one can deny that each of these areas has experienced rapid and historicallyunprecedented increases over the last century.

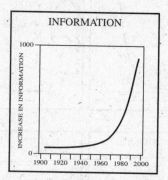

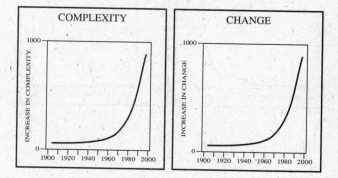

Graphs Illustrating Rapid U.S. Economic Change

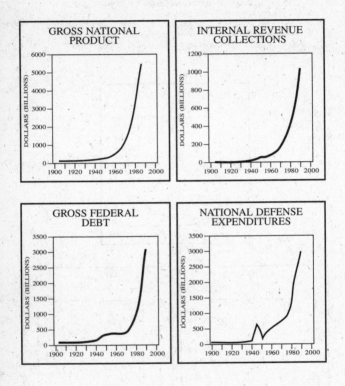

Graphs Reflecting Financial and
Economic Difficulties

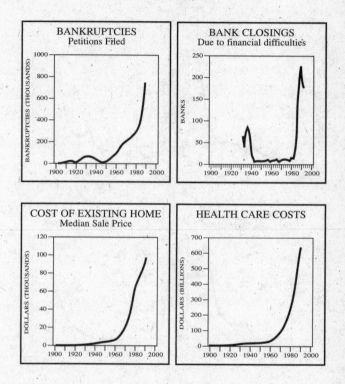

Graphs Reflecting Various Social Problems

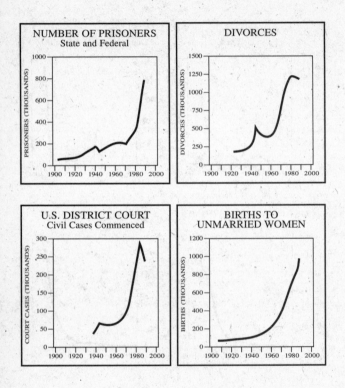

Graphs Illustrating Change in the Mail
and the Media

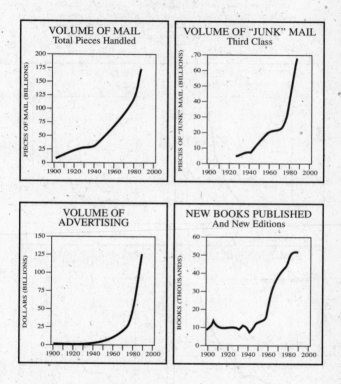

Graphs Illustrating Change in Travel and Mobility

Note that the graph representing passenger cars registered is actually morelinear than exponential. It is included, nevertheless, out of respect for thetremendous role the automobile has played in dissipating margin and bringing aboutunprecedented societal change.

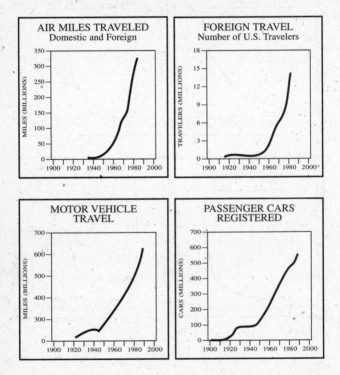

Graphs Reflecting Various Demographic Changes

Note the different time frame on the x-axis.

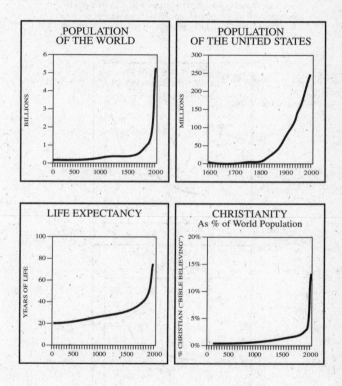

Logarithmic Graphs Illustrating Technological Power

These two graphs are the most dramatic of all those in this appendix, which iswhy the logarithm scale is necessary for the y-axis. As you can see, the maximumspeed of vehicles has increased over one thousand times, while the explosive power ofweapons has increased nearly ten billion times!

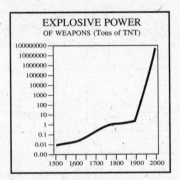

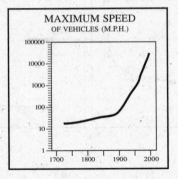

Notes

CHAPTER 2—THE PAIN OF PROGRESS

1. Robert Nisbet, *History of the Idea of Progress* (New York: Basic Books, 1980), pages 4-5,7.
2. Nicholas Wolterstorff, *Until Justice and Peace Embrace* (Grand Rapids: Eerdmans, 1983), pages 64 and 25.
3. David H. Hopper, *Technology, Theology, and the Idea of Progress* (Louisville, KY: Westminster/John Knox, 1991), pages 126-127.
4. Nisbet, page 9.
5. Christopher Lasch, *The True and Only Heaven: Progress and Its Critics* (New York: W. W. Norton, 1991), page 13.
6. Jeremy Rifkin, Entropy: *A New World View* (New York: Bantam, 1980), page 3.
7. Dennis Meadows, et al., *The Limits to Growth* (New York: Universe Books, 1972), page 23.
8. Mihajlo Mesarovic and Eduard Pestel, *Mankind at the Turning Point: The Second Report to the Club of Rome* (New York: New American Library, 1974), pages 1,129.
9. Robert L. Heilbroner, *An Inquiry into the Human Prospect* (New York: W. W. Norton, 1975), page 22.

10. Alvin Toffler, *The Third Wave* (New York: Bantam, 1980), page 350.

11. Mark Rosin, "The Family of the Future," *Parents*, March 1982, page 67.

12. John Naisbitt, *Megatrends: Ten New Directions Transforming Our Lives* (New York: Warner Books, 1982), pages 279,283.

13. Norman Mailer, Interviewed, "Something Has Been Stolen from Us That We Can't Name," *U.S. News and World Report*, 23 May 1983, pages 73-74.

14. Mesarovic and Pestel, page 11.

15. Harry Schwartz, "Solzhenitsyn Without Stereotype," *Saturday Review World*, 20 April 1974, page 24.

16. Lasch, page 168.

17. Karl Löwith, as quoted by Bob Goudzwaard in *Idols of Our Time*, trans. Mark Vander Vennen (Downers Grove, IL: InterVarsity, 1981), pages 12-13.

18. Goudzwaard, pages 50-51.

19. Robert N. Bellah, et al., *Habits of the Heart: Individualism and Commitment in American Life* (New York: Harper and Row, 1985), page 277.

20. Micah 6:8.

21. Bellah, page 284.

22. E. F. Schumacher, *Small Is Beautiful: Economics as if People Mattered* (New York: Harper and Row, 1973), page 157.

23. William Wilberforce, *Real Christianity: Contrasted with the Prevailing Religious System* (Portland, OR: Multnomah, 1982 first published 1829), page 91.

24. "This is what the LORD says: 'Let not the wise man boast of his wisdom or the strong man boast of his strength or the rich man boast of his riches, but let him who boasts boast about this: that he understands and knows me, that I am the Lord, who exercises kindness, justice and righteousness on earth, for in these I delight,' declares the LORD" (Jeremiah 9:23-24).

25. Wilberforce, page 123.

CHAPTER 3—THE PAIN OF PROBLEMS

1. Alvin Toffler, *Future Shock* (New York: Bantam, 1970), page 186.

2. Mark A. Noll, George M. Marsden, and Nathan O. Hatch, *The*

Search for Christian America (Colorado Springs, CO: Helmers and Howard, 1989), pages 152 and 148.

3. Harry Clay Blaney III, *Global Challenges: A World at Risk* (New York: New Viewpoints, a division of Franklin Watts, 1979), page 8.

4. J. Scott Armstrong, *Long-Range Forecasting: From Crystal Ball to Computer* (New York: Wiley, 1985), page 102. Note: A piece of construction paper is .016 inches thick. If doubled ten times, the pile of paper would be 16.38 inches thick. If doubled another ten times, it would be 16,777 inches, or 1,398 feet. If doubled another ten times, it would be 1,431,552 feet, or 271.1 miles. And if that were doubled ten times, the result would be an amazing 277,606 miles! The distance to the moon is 250,000 miles.

5. Barry B. Hughes, *World Futures: A Critical Analysis of Alternatives* (Baltimore: The Johns Hopkins University Press, 1985), page 149.

6. Hughes, page 4.

7. Robert N. Bellah, et al., *Habits of the Heart: Individualism and Commitment in American Life* (New York: Harper and Row, 1985), pages 285 and 277.

8. George Gallup, Jr., with William Proctor, *Forecast 2000* (New York: Morrow, 1984), page 12.

9. Gallup, pages 155,156.

CHAPTER 4—THE PAIN OF STRESS

1. Richard Trubo, "Stress and Disease: Cellular Evidence Hints at Therapy," *Medical World News*, 26 January 1987, page 26.

2. Christiaan Barnard, M.D., "Medicine Negated," *Living in the Future*, ed. Isaac Asimov (New York: Beaufort Books, 1985), page 226.

3. Hans Selye, M.D., *Stress Without Distress* (New York: New American Library, 1974), page 14.

4. Selye, pages 93-94.

5. Selye, pages 28-29,94-96,136.

6. David Elkind, *The Hurried Child: Growing Up Too Fast Too Soon* (Reading, MA: Addison-Wesley, 1981), page 26.

7. Eileen Rockefeller Growald and Allan Luks, "Good Samaritan Has Big Heart, Healthier Body," *St. Paul Pioneer Press Dispatch*, 21 March 1988, section B, page 1.

8. Selye, pages 73-74.

9. E. F. Schumacher, *Good Work* (New York: Harper and Row, 1979), page 25.

10. Allan V. Abbott, M.D., and Ruth K. Peters, "Type A Behavior and Coronary Heart Disease: An Update," *American Family Physician*, November 1988, pages 105-108.

11. Quoted in Thomas B. Graboys, M.D., "Stress and the Aching Heart," *The New England Journal of Medicine*, 30 August 1984, page 595.

12. Carol Tavris, "Coping with Anxiety," *Science Digest*, February 1986, page 51.

13. Jon Johnston, "Growing Me-ism and Materialism," *Christianity Today Institute*, 17 January 1986, page 16-I.

14. Ann Tyndall, *Longevity Lifestyle* (San Bernadino, CA: Borgo Press, 1986), page 111.

15. Selye, page 68.

CHAPTER 5—THE PAIN OF OVERLOAD

1. Bob Sakamoto, "Bear Secondary First Rate," *Chicago Tribune*, 13 October 1990, section 2, page 1.

2. Alvin Toffler, *Future Shock* (New York: Bantam, 1970), pages 351-352.

3. *Resident Mental Health* (Kansas City, MO: American Academy of Family Physicians, 1988), page 6. The human function curve is found in *Stress and Women Physicians* (New York: Springer-Verlag, 1985) by Marjorie A. Bowman, M.D., and Deborah I. Allen, M.D. Used by permission.

4. John Townsend, *Hiding From Love: How to Change the Withdrawal Patterns That Isolate and Imprison You* (Colorado Springs, CO: NavPress, 1991), page 77.

5. Richard J. Foster, *Freedom of Simplicity* (New York: Harper and Row, 1981), page 91.

6. Edward Wenk, Jr., *Tradeoffs: Imperatives of Choice in a High-Tech World* (Baltimore: The Johns Hopkins University Press, 1986), page 51.

7. Quoted by Mihajlo Mesarovic and Eduard Pestel, *Mankind at the Turning Point: The Second Report to the Club of Rome* (New York: New American Library, 1974), pages 151-152.

8. Philippians 4:13, NKJV.

9. Roberto Vacca, *The Coming Dark Age*, trans. J. S. Whale (Garden City, NY: Anchor Books, 1974), page 8.

10. Robert Banks, *The Tyranny of Time: When 24 Hours Is Not Enough* (Downers Grove, IL: InterVarsity, 1983), page 45.

11. Arthur M. Schlesinger, Jr., "The Modern Consciousness and the Winged Chariot," *The Personal Experience of Time*, eds. S. Gorman and A. E. Wessmann (New York: Plenum, 1977), page 269.

12. Toffler, page 269.

13. J. Grant Howard, *Balancing Life's Demands: A New Perspective on Priorities* (Portland, OR: Multnomah, 1983), page 144.

14. Aleksandr I. Solzhenitsyn, *A World Split Apart: Commencement Address Delivered at Harvard University, June 8, 1978* (New York: Harper and Row, 1978), page 27.

15. Vacca, page 111.

16. Terri Lackey, "Churches Can Add to Family Stress," *Twin Cities Christian*, 13 December 1990, page 9A.

17. Louis McBurney, M.D., with David McCasland, "The Danger of Aiming Too High," *Leadership*, Summer 1984, page 30.

18. Theodore Berland, *The Fight for Quiet* (Englewood Cliffs, NJ: Prentice-Hall, 1970), page 200.

19. Ronald A. Taylor, "What All That Noise Pollution Is Doing to Our Lives," *U.S. News and World Report*, 16 July 1984, page 50.

20. Donald A. Norman, "Infuriating by Design," *Psychology Today*, March 1988, page 53.

21. J. D. Runions, as quoted by J. R. Kriel, M.D., in "Le Syndrome Du Bon-Dieu: A Fatal Malady Affecting Doctors," *Christian Medical Society Journal*, Winter 1983, page 26.

CHAPTER 6—MARGIN

1. Russell D. Robinson, *An Introduction to Helping Adults Learn and Change* (Milwaukee: Omnibook, 1979), page 38. Idea credited to Howard McClusky.

2. Mildred Tengbom, "Harried Lives: If You're a Frenzied Mess, It's Time to Decide What's Really Important to You," *Focus on the Family*, October 1985, pages 11-12.

3. Robert F. Greene, M.D., "True Confession: I Enjoyed My Year

Abroad as a Short-Term Missionary," *Christian Medical and Dental Society Journal*, Winter 1990, page 17. Reprinted by permission. The Society is a fellowship of Christian physicians and dentists representing Jesus Christ in and through medicine and dentistry. P.O. Box 830689, Richardson, Texas 75083-0689.

4. John W. Burnside, M.D., "A Piece of My Mind: Deserted Island," *The Journal of the American Medical Association*, 265, 6 February 1991, page 589.

CHAPTER 7—MARGIN IN EMOTIONAL ENERGY

1. Louis H. Evans, Jr., *Covenant to Care* (Wheaton, IL: Victor, 1977), pages 80-81.

2. "Attempted Suicide Among High School Students—United States, 1990," *Morbidity and Mortality Weekly Report*, 20 September 1991, page 633.

3. Alvin Toffler, *The Third Wave* (New York: Bantam, 1980), page 365.

4. Tom Sine, *The Mustard Seed Conspiracy* (Waco, TX: Word, 1981), page 81.

5. Jack Dreyfus, *A Remarkable Medicine Has Been Overlooked* (New York: Simon and Schuster, 1970), pages 26-27.

6. Nancy Livingston, "Out of the (Agent) Blue Come More Suicide and Depression," *St. Paul Pioneer Press Dispatch*, 13 January 1987, section C, page 1.

7. Gerald L. Klerman, M.D., and Myrna M. Weissman, "Increasing Rates of Depression," *The Journal of the American Medical Association*, 261, 21 April 1989, page 2234.

8. Walter E. Afield, M.D., "Managed Mental Health Care: Curbing Costs in the 1990s," *Medical Interface*, March 1990, page 26.

9. Frederic Flach, M.D., *Resilience: Discovering a New Strength at Times of Stress* (New York: Fawcett Columbine, 1988), page 35.

10. "The LORD is close to the brokenhearted and saves those who are crushed in spirit" (Psalm 34:18).

11. "God opposes the proud but gives grace to the humble" (James 4:6).

12. Willard Gaylin, as quoted by Bill Moyers in *A World of Ideas* (New York: Doubleday, 1989), page 120.

13. "Laughing Toward Longevity," *University of California, Berkeley Wellness Letter*, June 1985, page 1.

14. In research conducted at the University of Pittsburgh, Margaret T. Crepeau studied 137 males and females to determine both atti- tude (meaning) and behavior with respect to weeping. Three groups were included: healthy patients, colitis patients, and ulcer patients. The healthy patients scored higher (at a statistically sig- nificant level) on both the meaning scale and the behavior scale than did the ulcer or colitis patients.

15. John Townsend, *Hiding From Love: How to Change the Withdrawal Patterns That Isolate and Imprison You* (Colorado Springs, CO: NavPress, 1991), pages 80-81,82.

16. Quoted by Arthur F. Holmes, *Contours of a World View* (Grand Rapids: Eerdmans, 1983), page 12.

17. S. D. Gaede, Belonging (Grand Rapids: Zondervan, 1985), page 56.

18. Thomas à Kempis, *The Imitation of Christ*, trans. Richard Whitford (New York: Washington Square Press, 1953 1424), page 3.

19. 1 Corinthians 13:13, emphasis added.

20. Flach, page 259.

21. Armand Mayo Nicholi II, "Why Can't I Deal with Depression?" *Christianity Today*, 11 November 1983, page 40.

22. Nicholi, pages 40-41.

23. Diogenes Allen, *Christian Belief in a Postmodern World: The Full Wealth of Conviction* (Louisville, KY: Westminster/John Knox, 1989), pages 5,126.

24. Romans 5:2-5.

25. Colossians 3:14.

26. Hans Selye, M.D., *Stress Without Distress* (New York: New American Library, 1974), page 124.

27. 1 Corinthians 13:13, emphasis added.

CHAPTER 8—MARGIN IN PHYSICAL ENERGY

1. Judd Allen and Robert F. Allen, "From Short Term Compliance to Long Term Freedom: Culture-Based Health Promotion by Health Professionals," *American Journal of Health Promotion*, Fall 1986, page 40.

2. Quoted in Don R. Powell, *A Year of Health Hints* (Emmaus, PA: Rodale Press, 1990), page xxi.

3. Marcia F. Goldsmith, "Risk Assessment, Management Addressed at 'Prevention 85,'" *The Journal of the American Medical Association*, 254, 20 September 1985, page 1421.

4. Arthur J. Barsky, M.D., "The Paradox of Health," *The New England Journal of Medicine*, 318, 18 February 1988, page 414.

5. James O. Mason, M.D., "From the Assistant Secretary for Health," *The Journal of the American Medical Association*, 263, 26 January 1990, page 494.

6. Susanna McBee, with Sarah Peterson, "How Drugs Sap the Nation's Strength," *U.S. News and World Report*, 16 May 1983, page 57.

7. Armand M. Nicholi, Jr., M.D., "The Nontherapeutic Use of Psychoactive Drugs," *The New England Journal of Medicine*, 308, 21 April 1983, page 931.

8. Byron J. Bailey, M.D., "Tobaccoism Is the Disease—Cancer Is the Sequela," *The Journal of the American Medical Association*, 255, 11 April 1986, page 1923.

9. Jimmy Carter, "Closing the Gap: The Burden of Unnecessary Illness," *The Journal of the American Medical Association*, 254, 13 September 1985, page 1359.

10. Martin Shaffer, *Life After Stress* (New York: Plenum Press, 1982), pages 91-92.

11. Shaffer, page 92.

12. Anastasia Toufexis, "Drowsy America," *Time*, 17 December 1990, page 84.

13. "Woes of Night Work Vary Among Patients," *Medical World News*, 10 August 1987, page 22.

14. Toufexis, page 78.

15. John Kenneth Galbraith, *The Affluent Society* (New York: Mentor Books, 1958), page 103.

16. David Hilfiker, M.D., *Healing the Wounds: A Physician Looks at His Work* (New York: Pantheon, 1985), page 137.

17. Psalm 127:2.

18. Quoted by Doris Janzen Longacre, *More-With-Less Cookbook* (Scottdale, PA: Herald, 1976), page 15.

19. Karen Walsh, "Exercise Can Be the Great Escape," *Wisconsin Week*, 26 November 1986, page 3.

20. Kenneth H. Cooper, M.D., Aerobics (New York: Bantam, 1968), pages 62,107.

21. Don R. Powell, *A Year of Health Hints* (Emmaus, PA: Rodale Press, 1990), page 96.

22. Cooper, page 158.

23. Powell, page 94.

CHAPTER 9—MARGIN IN TIME

1. Quoted by Daniel J. Boorstin, *The Discoverers* (New York: Random House, 1983), page 25.

2. Boorstin, page 39.

3. Nancy Gibbs, "How America Has Run Out of Time," *Time*, 24 April 1989, page 59.

4. Gibbs, page 58.

5. Jeremy Rifkin, *Time Wars* (New York: Simon and Schuster, 1987), page 19.

6. Quoted by Frank E. James, "Battle of Miniature Cellular Telephones Heats Up with Launch of Motorola Model," *The Wall Street Journal*, 8 May 1990, page 30.

7. E. F. Schumacher, Good Work (New York: Harper and Row, 1979), page 25.

8. Douglas LaBier, *Modern Madness: The Emotional Fallout of Success* (Reading, MA: Addison-Wesley, 1986), page 98.

9. Juliet B. Schor, *The Overworked American: The Unexpected Decline of Leisure* (New York: Basic Books, 1991), pages 21-31.

10. Gibbs, page 60.

11. Richard Phillips, as quoted in "The New Workaholics," *St. Paul Pioneer Press Dispatch*, 5 January 1987, section D, pages 1,3.

12. Quoted in Robert Banks, *The Tyranny of Time: When 24 Hours Is Not Enough* (Downers Grove, IL: InterVarsity, 1983), page 66.

13. Dolores Curran, *Stress and the Healthy Family: How Healthy Families Handle the Ten Most Common Stresses* (San Francisco: Harper and Row, 1985), page 157.

14. Quoted in Gibbs, page 61.

15. James Dobson, *Dr. Dobson Answers Your Questions* (Wheaton, IL: Tyndale, 1982), pages 27,28.

16. Alex Kotlowitz, "Changes Among Families Prompt a Vanishing

Sense of Community," *The Wall Street Journal*, 11 March 1987, section 2, page 33.

17. Jean Fleming, *Between Walden and the Whirlwind: Living the Christ-Centered Life* (Colorado Springs, CO: NavPress, 1985), page 40.

18. Gordon MacDonald, *Restoring Your Spiritual Passion* (Nashville: Oliver-Nelson, 1986), pages 24-25.

19. Fleming, page 43.

20. Nancy Yanes Hoffman, "Meyer Friedman: Type A Behavior Cardiovascular Research Continues," *The Journal of the American Medical Association*, 252, 21 September 1984, pages 1392-1393.

21. Tom Sine, *The Mustard Seed Conspiracy* (Waco, TX: Word, 1981), page 129.

22. Bruce Larson, *There's a Lot More to Health Than Not Being Sick* (Waco, TX: Word, 1981), page 114.

23. Dietrich Bonhoeffer, *Life Together* (New York: Harper and Brothers, 1954), page 99.

CHAPTER 10—MARGIN IN FINANCES

1. Norman Mailer, Interviewed, "Something Has Been Stolen from Us That We Can't Name," *U.S. News and World Report*, 23 May 1983, pages 73-74.

2. Alfred L. Malabre, Jr., *Beyond Our Means: How America's Long Years of Debt, Deficits and Reckless Borrowing Now Threaten to Overwhelm Us* (New York: Random House, 1987), page xii.

3. Larry Burkett, *The Coming Economic Earthquake* (Chicago: Moody, 1991), page 121.

4. Gregory E. Pence, "Everyone's Entitled to Blame for Soaring Health Costs," *The Wall Street Journal*, 22 December 1983, page 24.

5. Peter G. Peterson, "The Morning After," *The Atlantic Monthly*, October 1987, pages 58,64.

6. U.S. Department of Commerce, Bureau of the Census, *Money Income of Households, Families, and Persons in the United States*, 1990 Series P-60, No. 174, August 1991, page 9.

7. Robert Reich, as quoted by Susan Dentzer in "Harnessing Human Capital," *U.S. News and World Report*, 22 April 1991, page 46.

8. Mortimer B. Zuckerman, "The Free Ride Is Over," *U.S. News and World Report*, 15 October 1990, page 136.
9. Dolores Curran, *Stress and the Healthy Family* (San Francisco: Harper and Row, 1985), page 62.
10. Romans 13:8.
11. Larry Burkett, *Major Purchases* (Chicago: Moody, 1991), page 19.
12. Proverbs 22:7.
13. Romans 6:18-19, 1 Corinthians 7:23, Galatians 5:13.
14. Jo Ann Tooley, "Database," *U.S. News and World Report*, 22 October 1990, page 16.
15. Doris Janzen Longacre, *Living More with Less* (Scottdale, PA: Herald, 1980), page 97.
16. Matthew 6:19-21.
17. 1 Timothy 6:9-11.
18. 1 John 3:17.
19. Additional verses that speak to this issue are found in Proverbs 3:27-28: "Do not withhold good from those who deserve it, when it is in your power to act. Do not say to your neighbor, 'Come back later; I'll give it tomorrow'—when you now have it with you."
20. Jacques Ellul, *Money and Power*, trans. LaVonne Neff (Downers Grove, IL: InterVarsity, 1984), page 88.
21. Ellul, page 110.
22. E. F. Schumacher, *Small Is Beautiful: Economics as if People Mattered* (New York: Harper and Row, 1973), page 33.
23. Burkett, *Major Purchases*, page 53.
24. Matthew 6:33, NKJV.

CHAPTER 11—HEALTH THROUGH CONTENTMENT

1. 1 Timothy 6:6, Hebrews 13:5.
2. Philippians 4:12.
3. J. I. Packer, "The Secret of Contentment," Address given at Wheaton College, Wheaton, Illinois, 27 February 1984.
4. 1 Corinthians 4:9-13.
5. 2 Corinthians 11:23-27.
6. Philippians 4:11-12.
7. A. W. Tozer, *The Pursuit of God* (Harrisburg, PA: Christian Publications, 1948), page 20.
8. Nguyen Thi An, "A Letter Written to a Vietnamese Friend in

Canada," *Alliance Life*, 10 December 1986, page 17. Used by permission.

9. Herbert Schlossberg, *Idols For Destruction: Christian Faith and Its Confrontation with American Society* (Nashville: Nelson, 1983), page 103.

10. Arthur G. Gish, *Beyond the Rat Race* (New Canaan, CT: Keats Publishing, 1973), page 130.

11. 1 Timothy 6:8.

12. John Kenneth Galbraith, *The Affluent Society* (New York: Mentor Books, 1958), page 128.

13. Packer, "The Secret of Contentment."

14. Schlossberg, page 136.

15. John White, *The Golden Cow: Materialism in the Twentieth-Century Church* (Downers Grove, IL: InterVarsity, 1979), page 61.

16. Quoted by L. S. Stavrianos, *The Promise of the Coming Dark Age* (San Francisco: W. H. Freeman and Company, 1976), page 165.

17. Hebrews 13:5.

18. Tozer, page 22.

19. Doug Trouten, "Discontent Is the New Spirit of the Age," *Twin Cities Christian*, 13 September 1984, page 6.

20. Joseph Katz, ed., *The Poems of Stephen Crane* (New York: Cooper Square Publishers, 1966), page 102. Originally published in Stephen Crane's book of poetry entitled *War is Kind*, 1899.

21. Packer, "The Secret of Contentment."

22. Thomas Watson, *The Art of Divine Contentment* (Glasgow, Scotland: Free Presbyterian Publications, reprint of 1855 edition), pages 16,22.

23. Jeremiah Burroughs, *The Rare Jewel of Christian Contentment* (Edinburgh, Scotland: The Banner of Truth Trust, 1987 1648), page 19.

CHAPTER 12—HEALTH THROUGH SIMIPLICITY

1. Duane Elgin, *Voluntary Simplicity* (New York: Bantam, 1981), page 16.

2. Hans Selye, M.D., *Stress Without Distress* (New York: New American Library, 1974), page 142.

3. John Naisbitt, Megatrends: *Ten New Directions Transforming Our Lives* (New York: Warner Books, 1982), page 136.

4. John Charles Cooper, *The Joy of the Plain Life* (Nashville: Benson, 1981), page 106.
5. John 13:15-16.
6. "To this you were called, because Christ suffered for you, leaving you an example, that you should follow in his steps" (1 Peter 2:21).
7. "Your attitude should be the same as that of Christ Jesus" (Philippians 2:5). "But made himself nothing, taking the very nature of a servant, being made in human likeness" (verse 7).
8. Tom Allen, "Living Like the King," *Alliance Life*, 10 June 1981, pages 5-6.
9. David E. Shi, *The Simple Life: Plain Living and High Thinking in American Culture* (New York: Oxford University Press, 1985), page 3.
10. Shi, page 18.
11. Herbert Schlossberg, *Idols For Destruction: Christian Faith and Its Confrontation with American Society* (Nashville: Nelson, 1983), page 15.
12. Arthur G. Gish, *Beyond the Rat Race* (New Canaan, CT: Keats Publishing, 1973), pages 73,74.
13. Quoted by Shi, page 200.
14. "He has showed you, O man, what is good. And what does the Lord require of you? To act justly and to love mercy and to walk humbly with your God" (Micah 6:8).

CHAPTER 13—HEALTH THROUGH BALANCE

1. David M. Baughan, M.D., "Contemporary Scientific Principles and Family Medicine," *Family Medicine*, 19, January/February 1987, page 42.
2. Richard H. Bube, "On the Pursuit of Excellence: Pitfalls in the Effort to Become No. 1," *Perspectives on Science and Christian Faith*, June 1987, pages 70-71. Used by permission.
3. J. Grant Howard, *Balancing Life's Demands: A New Perspective on Priorities* (Portland, OR: Multnomah, 1983), page 37.
4. George Rust, M.D., "The Balancing Act," *Christian Medical Society Journal*, Winter 1983, page 8.
5. Anne Morrow Lindbergh, *Gift from the Sea* (New York: Pantheon, 1955), page 120.

CHAPTER 14—HEALTH THROUGH REST

1. Doris Janzen Longacré, *Living More with Less* (Scottdale, PA: Herald, 1980), pages 210-211.
2. Gordon MacDonald, *Ordering Your Private World* (Nashville: Oliver-Nelson, 1984), pages 166,174.
3. Jim Buchan, "Grinding the Gears," *Focus Ministries*, March 1984, page 4.
4. Marjorie Barstow Greenbie, *In Quest of Contentment* (New York: McGraw-Hill, 1936), page 57.
5. Thomas à Kempis, *The Imitation of Christ*, trans. Richard Whitford (New York: Washington Square Press, 1953 written in 1424), page 13.
6. A. W. Tozer, *The Pursuit of God* (Harrisburg, PA: Christian Publications, 1948), page 112.
7. Tim Kimmel, *Little House on the Freeway: Help for the Hurried Home* (Portland, OR: Multnomah, 1987), pages 63,66.
8. Psalm 91:1-2.
9. Genesis 2:3.
10. Deuteronomy 5:15.
11. Nicholas Wolterstorff, *Until Justice and Peace Embrace* (Grand Rapids: Eerdmans, 1983), page 146.
12. Louis McBurney, M.D., with David McCasland, "The Danger of Aiming Too High," *Leadership*, Summer 1984, pages 34-35.
13. Tozer, pages 112,116.

CHAPTER 15—PAIN, MARGIN, HEALTH, AND RELATIONSHIP

1. Claude Lévi-Strauss, as quoted by Linda Rogers, "'Passive' Progress," *World Press Review*, December 1983, page 41.
2. J. B. Phillips, *For This Day*, ed. Denis Duncan (Waco, TX: Word, 1974), page 180.
3. "Therefore do not worry about tomorrow, for tomorrow will worry about itself. Each day has enough trouble of its own" (Matthew 6:34).
4. Mark 12:29-31.
5. "Now I will show you the most excellent way" (1 Corinthians 12:31).
6. See John 15:13.

Index

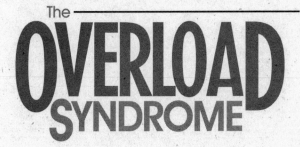

The OVERLOAD SYNDROME

Contents

*To my wife, Linda, and
to our children, Adam and Matt*

Daily, you make it all worthwhile.

Acknowledgments

Although much of my study and writing is done in "solitary confinement," scores of people rightfully deserve credit for significant contributions.

Don Steffen provided timely advice and a providential game-saving tackle. Don Simpson continues to inspire with his nobility. Bill and Gail Thedinga contributed helpful materials. The staff at several libraries—most prominently Dennis Olson and Lelah Lugo—lent valuable assistance. Ruth Swenson and Genevieve Wilson sent resources that fit perfectly into the text. Wilbur and Dan Hutchinson generously provided tapes.

The Bochmans, through their Hospitality House, provided a temporary sanctuary for in-depth work. Darlene Bochman once again demonstrated secretarial skills unsurpassed on this planet— the only person I have ever met who can finish transcribing before I finish dictating.

The NavPress staff has been gracious in encouragement, guidance, and resources. Terri Hibbard was patient and thorough in her editing, leaving the book better for her unflagging efforts.

My wife, Linda, helped more than I can recount. It would require another chapter to catalog her many contributions, including copy-editing, reading and research, handling administrative details and running errands, phoning and E-mailing, and so on, to say nothing of her nonstop affirmation. Adam and Matt contributed with their patience, and, of course, by simply being our children.

Jack and Diana Stimmel, Remy Diederich, Joanne Natwick, Joan Mecusker, Hector Cruz, Caroline Miller, Marcia Borgie, Warren and Karen Swenson, Becky Folkestad, Opal Harstad, Aggie and Tonya Wagner, as well as many other family and friends—all have contributed through both prayer and practical help along the way.

To each, please accept my heartfelt gratitude.

Introduction

Time to Rest, Space to Heal

Life in modern-day America is essentially devoid of time and space. Not the Star Trek kind. The sanity kind. The time and space that once existed in the lives of people who regularly lingered after dinner, helped the kids with homework, visited with the neighbors, sat on the lawn swing, went for long walks, dug in the garden, and always had a full night's sleep.

People are exhausted. Like the mother of four from LaGrange, Illinois, who said: "I'm so tired, my idea of a vacation is a trip to the dentist. I just can't wait to sit in that chair and relax."

People are stressed. Like the neurosurgeon who quit medicine to open a bagel shop. People are breaking the speed limit of life. Like the man who confessed: "I feel like a minnow in a flash flood."

People are overloaded. Like . . . me. Or at least I was. But that is the story of this book. If overload is sitting on our collective chests and blowing smoke in our faces, what can we do about it? Where is the pause button for the world?

We need more time. We need more space. We need more reserves. We need more buffer. We need, in short, more margin.

A FLAWED FORMULA FOR THE PERFECT LIFE

There was a point in my life when, of necessity, I decided to investigate a more margined way of living. Everything seemed out of control. I remember one day in particular—a Tuesday in 1982. I was finishing an evening meeting across town and beginning a migraine at the same time. Meanwhile back home, my wife, Linda, went for a late evening walk. Along the dark street, her crying could be in private.

My headache and Linda's crying were both manifestations of the same illness: overload. We were not only working, we were overworking. We were not only committed, we were overcommitted. We were not only conscientious, we were overly conscientious. We were not only tired, we were exhausted.

Everything had become a burden: medicine and patients, caring and serving. How could so many good things bring such pain? We were not involved in anything that was bad—nothing unsuccessful, nothing selfish, nothing evil. We were meeting needs everywhere we turned.

Yet life was obviously out of control. Joy dried up and blew away. Buoyancy sank. Enthusiasm evaporated. Rest was a theoretical concept. My passion for medical practice shriveled to the size of a dehydrated pea.

Frankly, I was mystified. No one had taught me about this in medical school. Nor in residency. Nor in church. If fifteen years earlier I had written a formula for the perfect life—I had achieved it all. I had a prestigious career, a generous income, grateful patients, supportive colleagues, a great clinic, a brand new hospital, a wonderful town, a loving family, a vibrant church, and a growing faith.

But if we had such a perfect life, why was I getting all these headaches? Why was Linda crying? Why was it so hard to get out of bed in the morning? Why did I dread looking around the next corner?

If we had such a perfect life, why did we live so far from Utopia?

SIMPLE PLEASURES

At the same time, good friends of ours were going through a financial nightmare. Steve, who had started his own business, had an outstanding reputation and was well-liked by both employees and clients. Still, the economic realities of the early eighties—with sky-high inflation and equally high interest rates—had a strangle hold on his company. Our dear friends were actively being crushed by the resultant financial destitution.

One summer day—again, in 1982—my wife saw Steve and Lisa walking down the street hand-in-hand. She stopped to greet them, finding out they were on their way to buy a small ice cream cone. Two miles each way. Walk and talk. Total time: two hours. Total cost: fifty cents. It was the kind of date they could afford.

Linda was pleased to see them enjoying the weather and each other's company. Yet, at the same time, she couldn't help feeling a little envious. Oh, to have the time to walk and talk! To have the pleasure of an uninterrupted afternoon together. Why was it so hard to find the simple joys we knew when first married? Our world was like a pinball machine, and we were careening through life like unhappy electrons that had jumped their orbits. It was time to reconsider some basics.

AN EXAMPLE TO FOLLOW

Perhaps the turning point came when I decided to examine more closely the practice style of the Great Physician. How did Jesus care for people? He focused on the person standing in front of Him at the time. In my case, however, the person standing in front of me was often an obstacle to get around or over in order to get where I was going—even if that person was Linda or one of our two sons, Adam and Matt.

If Jesus had chosen to live in modern America instead of ancient Israel, how would He act? Would He have consulted a pocket calendar? Would He have worn a watch? Would He have carried a beeper? Can you imagine Him being paged out of the Last Supper?

When I look deeper at the life of Christ, I also notice that there is no indication He worked twenty-hour ministry days. He went to sleep each night without having healed every disease in Israel—and He apparently slept well. Neither did He minister to everybody who needed it. Neither did He visit or teach everybody who needed it. There were many needs that He simply chose not to meet. Even when Lazarus became sick, Jesus was shockingly slow to mobilize. I would have had a helicopter there in twenty minutes. But Jesus delayed for two days.

Is this to imply that He was lazy or didn't care? Of course not. But it is to imply that He understood what it meant to be human. Jesus was fully God and fully human, and His fully human side understood what it meant to have limits. Jesus understood what it meant to prioritize and to balance in light of those limits and how to focus on the truly important. We can learn a lesson from Jesus—it's okay to have limits. It is okay not to be all things to all people all of the time all by ourselves. At any given moment, the most important thing in life is the person standing in front of us.

When I finally learned these lessons about availability and prioritizing, life changed. For the first time in my life, I recognized the importance of leaving a margin. The more I understood the phenomenon of margin, the more I realized its importance. And the more I understood its importance, the more I yearned for its freedom in my own life.

Carefully, and even forcefully, Linda and I carved out margin in four areas: emotional energy, physical energy, time, and finances. As we did, ninety percent of our pain disappeared. Life came alive again. My passion for medicine returned in full force.

We remain busy, to be sure. But we are no longer chronically overloaded. We still serve, teach, and help with a full investment of passion and enthusiasm. But always within the context of limits.

REDESIGNING LIFE

I will never forget the evening when Linda and I, on our living room floor, decided it was time to make substantive changes. Together we took out a pad of paper and sat down before the fireplace. "Let's start by pretending everything in our lives is written on this paper," I suggested. "Every attitude, every activity, every belief, every influence.

"Then let's erase it all. Tear up the paper and throw it in the fire. Wipe the slate clean. Erase away all our beliefs, everything we have been taught by parents, friends, society, church. Remove all our hopes and dreams. Remove all our possessions. Nothing should remain. Then let's give the pencil to God and ask Him to redesign our lives by that which is fully and spiritually authentic."

It was an exciting evening. An exhilarating sense of freedom swept over us. As we wrestled control of our lives away from the world, we felt the elephant slipping off our backs. And as we turned and handed control over to God, no spiritualized elephant took its place. The Father, we instantly sensed, had in mind much more than our survival. It was an indescribable feeling.

Our redesigned life was simpler. That decision reduced our income significantly, but the freedom, the time, the rest, and the balance have been well worth it. We have never looked back.

Today, because of margin, I no longer dread getting up in the morning or looking around the next corner. Today, when I hang out the "Gone Fishing" sign on my door, I don't worry about the opinion of the world. Now, as I head down the road with my family, I know that the same God who invented both rest and relationship is wishing us a good catch.

MARGIN, LIMITS, AND OVERLOAD

Margin is the space that once existed between our load and our limits. Margin is the space between vitality and exhaustion. It is our breathing room, our reserves, our leeway. Margin is the opposite of overload, and therefore the antidote for that vexatious condition.

Yet overload has recently become the majority of American experience. Because of the rapidly changing conditions of modern living—largely due to progress always giving us more and more of everything faster and faster—we are exceeding our limits in scores of areas all at the same time. From activity overload to choice overload to debt overload to expectation overload to information overload to work overload, we are a piled-on, marginless society.

The contemporary American axiom is to *maximize everything*. We push the limits as far as possible. Then we push some more. This has become not only business dogma but also standard operating procedure for nearly every sociological experience. We spend ten percent more than we have—and it no longer matters if one is talking about time, energy, or money. We work hard, play hard, and crash hard.

For many of us, that once popular axiom is no longer working. It is time to consider replacing it with a new axiom: *leave a margin*. Most of us need some time in which to rest and some space in which to heal. Our relationships desperately need some margin in which to be revitalized.

LEAVING A MARGIN FOR ERROR

If you were flying from Minneapolis to Boston, would you leave just two minutes to change planes in Chicago? (I tried it once. Not recommended.) If you were going 65 miles per hour on the interstate, would you leave a mere two feet between you and the car ahead? If you were interviewing for an important job, would you show off your understanding of management principles by arriving "just in time"? Political observer Peggy Noonan comments, "I think the essential daily predicament of modern Americans is this: There is no margin for error anymore."[1]

To illustrate the practical importance of margin, let me relate a story. Several years ago, a medical colleague became engaged. Having taught this delightful young physician, I was pleased to receive an invitation to the wedding.

They were to be married on an August afternoon at 3:00 P.M. As our home is a half-hour from the church, at 2:25 P.M. I loaded my family into the car and headed east. By my calculations, we would have thirty minutes to get to the church, five minutes to find a pew, and zero minutes to waste. The organ would start, the bride would begin down the aisle. . . .

As planned, we arrived in the church parking lot at precisely 2:55 P.M. Perfect timing. So far, so good. There was only one problem. The parking lot was empty. Completely empty. Not as in *I'm early* empty, but as in *I've got the wrong church* empty. There were seventy other churches in the city, and I had five minutes to find the right one. Normally a good problem solver, I came quickly to a plan. Linda, too, had a plan. The trouble was her plan and my plan were not the same plan. And, of course, neither would get us to the church on time.

I am not an irritable person, and Linda is even less so. But I was irritable right then. It was hot, and I was starting to perspire. Linda and I exchanged conflicting suggestions for solving our dilemma and redeeming what was left of the wedding. Meanwhile our two delightful boys were in the back seat discussing how incompetent their parents were.

We finally found the church—but, of course, arrived twenty minutes late. Squeezing into a back pew, I had worked up an uncomfortable sweat. Somehow our anticipation of a delightful afternoon spent with friends celebrating the highlight of a life had not quite turned out as hoped.

We had left no margin for error. And we had paid the price.

BENEFITS VERSUS DRAWBACKS

Being marginless means that we are expended, depleted, and exhausted with no oasis in sight. Having margin, however, means that when we are drained, we have someplace to go for our healing. Many people, desperate for something other than their daily diet of stress and overload, yearn to regain margin in their lives.

The margined life has much to commend about it.

Joy

As a result of a very unscientific survey, I have noticed that people, in general, do not like being marginless. On the other hand, most people do like having margin. The vast majority of Americans simply do not enjoy living at one hundred and twenty percent all the time. Most of us would jump at the chance to slow down and give joy an opportunity to gain a new foothold.

Service

Margin permits service to the needs of others. Research demonstrates that people involved in helping others are themselves healthier. But who has time to serve? When Colin Powell convened the Volunteerism Summit in Philadelphia, *USA Today* headlined: "Overstressed, Overworked: Who Has Time to Volunteer?" The modern marginless lifestyle is toxic to service.

Health

Margin is health enhancing. Our bodies are enormously self-correcting. But they must be given a chance. Margin allows both the soma and the psyche a chance to heal. It gives our immunological equilibrium a chance to right itself. Even the best crew can't fix a race car when it is going 200 miles per hour. Neither can our bodies perform needed repairs in the midst of a hyperliving lifestyle.

Relationships

Margin nourishes the relationships most important to us. It allows time to communicate and grants space in which to reach out. My advice: Don't trust the vitality of your relationships to the normal flow of culture, because right now, culture isn't helping.

Availability

Margin allows availability for the purposes of God. When God taps us on the shoulder and asks us to do something, He doesn't expect to get a busy signal. "In the spiritual life," explains theologian Henri Nouwen, "the word discipline means 'the effort to create some space in which God can act.' Discipline means to prevent everything in your life from being filled up. Discipline means that somewhere you're not occupied, and certainly not preoccupied. In the spiritual life, discipline means to create that space in which something can happen that you hadn't planned or counted on."[2]

Without margin, we are self-protective, painfully uninterested in an opportunity to serve our neighbor. Without margin, we tread water and hang on by our fingernails, trying to survive another day. Without margin, we are chronically exhausted, chronically late, chronically rushed. Without margin, we are overloaded.

Margin, on the other hand, tells us to guard our reserves. Create buffers and fortify them. Carve out some space between our load and our limits. Don't be chronically overloaded, overcommitted, and overwhelmed. Give ourselves space to rest, room to breathe, freedom to move, time to adapt, and money to spare. Only then will we be able to nourish our relationships. Only then will we truly be available and interruptible for the purposes of God.

What about you? Have you lost your joy and passion? Do you suffer from work dread? Are your relationships strained from stress? Do you wish you could check into a hospital just to sleep?

Understand that you are not alone. These symptoms are not a figment of your imagination. Instead you are suffering from a virulent new disease: the overload syndrome. Welcome to the new majority experience.

In this book we will examine the syndrome that is taking our margin away. Where does overload come from? What does it look like? What will it lead to? Most importantly, what can we do about it? With each overload, prescriptions will be offered that can counteract its effects, restoring needed time to rest and space to heal.

Defining
and
Understanding
Overload

■ ■ ■ ■ ■ ■ ■ ■

CHAPTER 1

Overload and the Reality
of Human Limits

In his famous story, "How Much Land Does a Man Need?,"[1] Tolstoy
tells of the ambitious peasant Pakhom, who, after gaining ever
greater plots of land, finally heard of a wonderful deal in a far-off
country. He traveled to the land of the Bashkirs and negotiated with
the village elder, who seemed a fool. The elder told Pakhom that he
could have all the land he wanted for a thousand rubles a day.

Pakhom did not understand. "What kind of rate is that—a
day?" he asked. "How many acres could that be?"

"We don't reckon your way. We sell by the day. However much
you can walk around in one day will be yours."

When Pakhom expressed that a man can walk around much
land in one day, the elder burst out laughing. "And all of it will be
yours!" he replied. But there was one condition: If Pakhom didn't
return to the starting point by sundown, the money would be forfeited.

Ecstatic, Pakhom spent a sleepless night. Rising at dawn, he
went with the villagers to the top of a hill where the elder put down
his hat. After placing his thousand rubles on top, Pakhom began

21

walking, digging holes along the way to mark his land. The going was easy and he thought, "I'll do another three miles and then turn left. The land's so beautiful here, it would be a pity to miss any."

Pakhom hurried throughout the morning, going out of his way to add more land. But at noon when he looked back at the hill where he had begun, it was difficult to see the people. *Maybe I have gone too far,* he worried, and decided he must begin to make shorter sides. As the afternoon wore on, the heat was exhausting. By now his bare feet were cut and bruised, and his legs weakened. He wanted to rest, but it was out of the question.

Pakhom struggled on, walking faster, then running. He worried that he had been too greedy and his fear made him breathless. On he ran, his shirt soaked and his throat parched. His lungs were working like a blacksmith's bellows, his heart beat like a hammer. He was terrified. *All this strain will be the death of me.*

Although Pakhom feared death, he couldn't stop. *They'd call me an idiot,* he thought. When he was close enough to hear the Bashkirs cheering, he summoned his last ounce of strength and kept running. As he finally reached the hill, everything suddenly became dark—the sun had set. Pakhom groaned. He wanted to stop, but heard the Bashkirs still cheering him on. He realized that from where he was at the bottom of the hill, the sun had set—but not for those on top. Pakhom took a deep breath and rushed up the hill. Reaching the top, he saw the elder sitting by the hat, laughing his head off. Pakhom's legs gave way, and he fell forward grasping the cap.

"Oh, well done!" exclaimed the elder. "That's a lot of land you've earned yourself!"

Pakhom's worker ran up and tried to lift his master, but Pakhom was dead. The worker picked up Pakhom's spade, dug a grave, and buried him—six feet from head to heel, exactly the amount of land a man needed.

THE AUTOPSY

In a modern setting Pakhom would have fit in nicely on Wall Street. Or Main Street. Perhaps he even stares at us each morning from our bathroom mirrors. By asking post-mortem questions about Pakhom, let's see if we can't catch a glimpse of what is wrong with our own lives.

Pakhom most likely died from a heart attack or a heat stroke brought on by overexertion. But on another level, did he die of running? Does this mean that running is bad for you? Of course not. Running is good for you. Unless, of course, it is *too much* running. *Too much* running can be bad. It can even be fatal.

Did Pakhom die of ambition? Does this mean that wanting land is unhealthy? No, unless it is *too much* land. That, too, apparently can kill.

It is not wrong to run, to have ambition, to want a farm, to expand the farm, to dig holes. Still, Pakhom died. Stone, cold dead. He died from overload.

Overload is that point when our limits are exceeded. Tolstoy's story is a powerful illustration of the reality of limits and the health implications of exceeding them. The Bashkirs knew that Pakhom's body had limits—but his greed did not.

In the same way, today many are harming themselves through the temptation to do more than their limits will allow. Walking, running, and ambition are not necessarily unhealthy. *Too much,* however, is universally unhealthy.

Overload is like that. The problem is not with *load*. The problem is with *over*.

Generally speaking, *loads* are a good thing. We would be hopelessly bored without them. As a matter of fact, even though this is an *anti-overload* book, I am a *pro-load* person. Load is not the enemy. Overload is.

UNIVERSAL LIMITS

Do you have a well-developed psychology of human limits? Perhaps even more importantly, do you have a well-developed theology of human limits? To clarify this issue, let's examine two questions:

1. *Do we have limits?*
2. *If we have limits, where did they come from?*

Do We Have Limits?

Do we? All of us? Of course we do. Every person has limits—no exceptions. We see limits everywhere we look. One could even say there is a law of limits, both in our human experience and in the physical universe.

Yet many people act under the illusion that there are no human limits. Many managers grow quickly impatient with such talk. Many employers continually insist that those under them do more and more with less and less. Many Type A's (a personality type that is driven and hypercompetitive, with carburetors stuck on high) live in chronic denial. Many Christians assume that God has, in fact, given them a special exemption.

It is true, of course, that many individuals have accomplished stunning feats. One person, for example, memorized the non-repeating number pi to thirty thousand digits. Some climb Mt. Everest without oxygen. Some run a marathon in Nepal at an average elevation of fourteen thousand feet. Dramatic stuff.

After reading of such accomplishments, we might be tempted to assume that humans have almost unlimited powers. But when we take such an assumption at face value and adopt it as a life motto, we can find ourselves in deep trouble—heart attacks, work dread, ruined relationships, exhaustion, depression, and burnout. Many are already there. And many more are dangerously close.

Recently I mentioned to a friend that humans will never run a one-minute mile. He paused briefly and then said, "Never say never."

Think about this. With whom do you agree? Do you agree with my friend and insist that someone might eventually run the mile in one minute, as unlikely as that seems? Or do you agree with my assertion that it is humanly impossible?

If you paused to consider the possibility, I am sympathetic to that pause. It is right to consider whether this assertion seems true or not before answering. But just the fact that we are willing to even consider the possibility of a one-minute mile in itself illustrates the fact that we have a problem truly accepting our limits.

Of course we all wish to be careful making such pronouncements as "the one-minute mile is humanly impossible." In the past, people have made predictions and then ended up looking foolish when later proved wrong. But I want to force you into a position here. If you refuse to make the statement that we will never be able to run a one-minute mile, then let's push further. How about thirty seconds? If you still hold out, then how about five seconds? Eventually, you will have to agree that we have limits.

The position I am taking is not always popular. We are so accustomed to pushing the limits—even exalting that push—that we often completely skip over the fact that we do, in fact, have limits. We all do. It is undeniable. Everything on earth has limits.

Again this is not a popular argument to make. Many of our leaders, thinkers, inventors, and motivators are teaching us to think big, to think of all the possibilities, to assault the impossible. And that's good. But we must be careful and we must be precise, for there is another side to this issue that often remains unexpressed. When we start to pretend that somehow we don't have limits, we get ourselves mired in painful consequences.

For many well-meaning Christians, my argument almost sounds like heresy. I recently saw a T-shirt that said "No limits," with three or four Bible verses backing up the slogan. But the Bible never says that we are unlimited. It says that God is unlimited. There is a difference. This brings us to our second question.

If We Have Limits, Where Did They Come From?

Are limits the result of the Fall or were they God's idea? In other words, did limits come into the world with sin and death or did God create them intentionally?

Limits were God's intention from the beginning. He decided early on that limits were not only good but necessary. It was His way of preempting any ambiguity about who is God and who is not. He is the Creator—the One without limits. We are the created—the ones with limits.

The fact is, we often get into all kinds of trouble by inflating our role in the drama of life. Perhaps this is one of the main reasons why God created limits. He knew that without limits, we would overreach, swell with pride, and become independent. We would get priorities all messed up, and life balance would be neglected. He would have been right. So to address that problem preemptively, He created limits.

We are not infinite. None of us has more than twenty-four hours in a day. We do not have an inexhaustible source of human energy. We cannot keep running on empty. Limits are real and, despite what some stoics might think, limits are not even an enemy. Overload is the enemy.

As the author of limits, God put them within us for our protection. We violate them at our peril. God is under no moral obligation to bail us out of our pain if we attempt to do more than He asks.

GOD THE CREATOR . . . OF LIMITS

For some, to say that we have limits seems to limit God. But saying that *we* have limits in no way suggests that *God* has limits. And to say that all the spiritual work in the kingdom must be done with human effort misses the point of God's power altogether. It is very freeing to realize that God has the resources to get the job done, and that rest is still a part of His will for us. Conversely, it is lack of faith—coupled with an inadequate view of God—to think that we have to work twenty-hour days to get everything done. Far from dishonoring God by acknowledging human limits, it dishonors Him to *deny* limits. It insults His creation wisdom.

I am not out to thwart our accomplishments or encourage us toward mediocrity. Mediocrity and I are not friends. Instead, I am only warning us not to trust our own strength but to give God full credit for the fact that He gets the work done. It is, after all, His world, His work, and His power. "But we have this treasure in jars of clay," explained the apostle Paul, "to show that the all-surpassing power is from God and not from us."[2]

NO EXCEPTIONS, NO EXEMPTIONS

Over the past decade I have given hundreds of presentations on margin, human limits, and overload. If I had a nickel for every time someone asked me about the role of personality variation on perceived overload, I could make a down payment on the solar system.

Personality, genetics, culture, values, expectations, ethnic background, family system, work ethic—all play a tremendous role in determining how the topic of overload applies to each individual life. Therefore, the issue of the variability of human personality must be an important aspect of the discussion whenever attempting to have a balanced view of overload on the individual level.

There are two generalizations we can make about this topic:

1. *Everyone is different.* These differences must be taken into account when we talk about the issue of human limits.
2. *Everyone is the same.* Limits exist, and the universality of that fact ultimately holds sway over all dissenting views.

Everyone Is Different

God created us extraordinarily diverse. We are all variations on a theme and the variations are endless. God invented chromosomes and genetics and decided to use the human genome to accomplish His creative human artistry.

Each nucleus of each cell has twenty-three pairs of chromosomes. If we were to combine all the chromosomal material from one cell together, we would have the human genome. Imprinted on our human genome is everything about our physical nature, as well as much about our personality and emotional makeup. In each cell, this human genome contains eighty thousand genes. They are all encoded on tightly coiled DNA and three billion base pairs per cell. This human code is unique to each person.

God did something quite remarkable along the lines of diversity, and it seems to me that we ought, at minimum, to acknowledge it. Instead of kicking against it, we should recognize this, accept it, even celebrate it.

Someone once said that foreign travel is when we pay a lot of money to go to a place where things are different and then complain because they aren't the same. In many ways, God made us different for a reason, yet we complain incessantly because others aren't the same as us. I have a feeling God was right to make us different from one another. Imagine how boring the world would be if everyone were a clone of me. *I* wouldn't even want to live there.

Everyone Is the Same

On the other hand, all of the billions of people on the earth are the same in one important dimension—we all have limits. No one is infinite. We all need to sleep, to eat, to exercise, and to rest. The extent to which we need to do these things varies tremendously. Yet we all hit our personal limits at some point. Despite our enormous diversity, we are all bound together by this similarity of limits.

For every limit there is a threshold. Somewhere a line can be drawn for every human being to represent such a threshold. True, we would have to draw this line in a different place for each person, but the fact remains—we can draw such a line *somewhere*. Even people who never thought they would reach their limits are hitting the wall under the fast-paced conditions of modernity. That threshold, which once seemed so distant and theoretical, is now a painful reality for us all.

Combining these two generalizations, we see that for each person we can draw a line that represents the threshold of his or her personal limits, but for each person that line will be drawn at a different place compared to others.

Exceptional People Maybe—but No Exceptions

What about those extraordinary people who seem to accomplish so very much and never get weary? People who only sleep two hours a night, or who create a hundred million dollar business in just five years, or who have ten children and a sixty-hour job as a corporate executive, yet get voted "parent of the year"?

Indeed such stories are breathtaking. But this does not mean that I should feel guilty if God has not given me those same abilities. We should not be in the business of telling God how He should arrange the personalities in His kingdom. It is, after all, His kingdom, and He has the right to do with it as He wants.

These exceptional people are interesting and their accomplishments laudable. But remember, even exceptional people have limits. Unfortunately if we follow many of them into the future, we often would find the same painful consequences of chronic limit violation the rest of us experience: physical illness, emotional burnout, relational strain.

THREE CASES

Let's examine three different circumstances to learn what they can tell us about how personalities and beliefs influence our discussion of overload.

Highly Productive People (HPP)

At one end of the spectrum are those in our midst obviously wired for a higher level of involvement, activity, and achievement than the rest of us. They get by on less sleep, always seem to have energy to spare, rise to the top of organizations, and in general, lead the charge into the future. For purposes of simplification, let's simply call them highly productive people (HPP)—those in the top ten percent of productivity. They have several specific things to teach us about overload—both positive and negative.

The highly productive person accomplishes a great deal. These extraordinary people accomplish more before 9 A.M. than the rest of us do all month. Much of our national success can be attributed to their efforts. They do much of the work, make most of the decisions, develop most of the new products, and create most of the wealth that the rest of us have grown to depend on.

The highly productive person has a remarkable work ethic. The work ethic practiced by HPPs is extraordinary. They have a special capacity for putting in long hours, staying focused, and still maintaining energy and passion. Persistent and persevering are often good descriptors.

The highly productive person often has great vision. Even in the midst of the smoke and fire of overload that disable the efforts of others, HPPs can see where they need to go and are determined to get there. They have the vision of an eagle and the jaws of a pit bull. Once they sink their teeth into a project they believe in, they are not about to let go.

The highly productive person often lacks good warning signals. All of us lack adequate warning signals for overload and do not realize that we are overloaded until we feel the pain. Unfortunately HPPs often find themselves at an even greater disadvantage. While others might be able to tell that something is wrong when they are at one hundred and ten percent, HPPs often don't realize they are seriously overloaded until they are at one hundred and forty percent. And by that time, there is nothing left to do but crash and burn.

The highly productive person sometimes sets up unrealistic standards for others. Because achievement comes so easily to HPPs, they will often set the bar high and then kill themselves trying to live up to it. That may be okay for them. But often they will require this same level of unrealistic commitment from others. Trying to motivate others is a good goal, but when we are trying to motivate others to join us in a high-energy lifestyle, we need to be sure that we are indeed speaking for God.

The highly productive person often doles out acceptance based on performance. We get paid for what we do and that is the way it should be. And if we don't do anything, we will never go anywhere. It is called justice. The performance-based approach to life contains in it a certain reality that is undeniable. However, HPPs often have an inflated sense that performance is *all* that matters.

When the world they control becomes structured in this way, those who do not have high energy and productivity tend to linger further behind. Or they will experience chronic overload trying to keep up with people who are wired more advantageously.

Performance deserves to be *one* criteria by which acceptance is handed out. But it should not be the only criteria—or even the main criteria. We must always be careful to value most what God values—things like love, compassion, service, justice, faithfulness, purity, prayer, obedience, kindness, and gentleness.

Highly Sensitive People (HSP)

On the other end of the spectrum from the high-energy, highly productive people are the highly sensitive people (HSP). (This is not to imply that they are unproductive, but just that their personality structure is very different from the HPP.) The highly sensitive person has been well described by psychologist Elaine N. Aron in her 1996 book by that title.[3] HSPs, we could perhaps say, are in the top ten percent of sensitivity (Aron uses the figure fifteen to twenty percent). They often find themselves chronically overwhelmed by excessive sensory input.

The highly sensitive person has antennae up for social discord or discomfort. They can feel the pain in the room. They can read the faces. Even with subtle indicators, they can tell when the social hierarchy is being unkind. They are also particularly susceptible to the insults and violence on television and in other media.

The highly sensitive person sometimes seems antisocial. Because they pay a price for social interaction, they don't venture out as much. They might be more socially isolated. It takes longer for them to heal. Their batteries are discharged by all of this continuous and chronic sensitivity vigilance. It does not mean that they are truly reclusive, but just that they are worn down by the requirement of excessive sensitivity.

The highly sensitive person is often creative. They live in a world in their heads. They are good company for themselves on long car trips, and they don't mind solitude. They dream a lot. They don't try to control others' lives, because they intuitively understand how complicated that process is.

The highly sensitive person is more susceptible to overload. They pay a higher emotional price for almost everything. It is like the world's loudspeaker is always on for them. They wear down more quickly. They must pay special heed to the words of this book. These interesting people make a special contribution to the world, but often at a greater emotional price than others. They give something that no one else can in quite the same way—sensitivity.

A Christian Exemption?

Finally, let's consider one other category—Christians. Are believers equipped with some kind of stress exemption? Do they ever burn out? These might sound like heretical questions. Nevertheless, the issue is important to consider. Because if we answer the question incorrectly—in either direction—there will be significant consequences.

Many people with great faith assume that God gives them a

special exemption to stress, overload, and burnout. It therefore comes as a great surprise when they, too, hit the wall.

How could this happen to me? I must not have had enough faith.

Disillusionment sets in. Then discouragement. We stop ministering. We have no permission to tell others of our pain. What to do? Sadly, we sometimes find ourselves trapped in a system that provides no comfort—only judgment.

Overload, just like influenza, is a nonsectarian pathogen. It strikes indiscriminately. Believers experience overload just like we experience the flu when it comes to town. We have the same limits and susceptibilities as everyone else.

As it turns out, salvation solves the lostness problem—of incalculable value. But it does little to solve the overload problem. This is not to say we don't have deep spiritual resources. But in some ways, we also have a heightened sensitivity to the pain and brokenness of the world around us. And often that hurts unbearably.

God had His reasons for not delivering us from this pain. It is best to trust His heart in the matter.

FAITH OR PRESUMPTION?

Sorting through the broad applications of the stress-limits-overload issue takes time. Unfortunately, our practicality and theology have not yet had the opportunity to catch up to the rapid changes all around us. We are still trying to figure out where to draw the line between faith and presumption. It is a very important line.

Beware of the presumption of overextending. What happens if we are out on a limb, doing one hundred and fifty percent of what we ought and then get into trouble? We cry out to God, "Help!"

But God replies, "When you come back to where you belong, then I will help you. Remember: *You* are the creature. *I* am God. Use My power, not your own."

Nevertheless, because this is such a difficult lesson for us to learn in our performance-driven, activity-oriented culture, we see people working eighteen-hour days for laudable causes, neglecting their relationships . . . only to have their spouses leave or their children become alienated.

We see others doing wonderful service for God and humankind but depriving their bodies of sleep, nutrition, exercise. Then comes the heart attack at age forty-eight.

We see delightful, well-meaning servants who overcommit and then wonder why they have no joy.

We see physicians who are so chronically overworked that they resent their patients for being ill.

And on it goes. And on . . . and on. . . .

FATAL FLAW

Ultimately the driven notion that we must relentlessly pursue activity every waking minute is fatally flawed—both practically and theologically. If we insist that we must be "all things to all people all the time all by ourselves"; that God requires no less than total, all-out, burnout effort; that it would insult Christ's sacrifice for us to rest; that there are too many opportunities for us to slow down—then we will find ourselves backed up against a logical juggernaut. If these arguments hold, then how could we defend ever ceasing our efforts?

For example, if after a productive, busy day you finally quit at midnight, I would go to your house and greet you on the front step. The conversation might go like this.

"Are you done for today?" I would ask.

"Yes. Finally. A long day—seventeen hours. But all important things. It was an exhausting day—but a good one."

"Why are you quitting now?" I would ask.

"Well, because it's midnight."

"So it is. Does that mean that all your work is done? Isn't there *something* that you could be doing? Isn't there some good that you could still pursue? Isn't there some need you could work on? Some studying . . . or perhaps letters of encouragement to write?"

"Give me a break!" you would say. "What do you expect?"

Exactly my point. Whenever we quit for the day, it is always arbitrary. The world is not yet perfect—but we ceased our efforts? There is still more to be done—and yet we are going to sleep? The fact is, whenever we quit we are abandoning the job unfinished.

Because *the job can never be finished.*

Life is always a process, and it is the *process* that God is concerned with more than *productivity*. He knows perfectibility is not possible and that all our labors are feeble against the brokenness of the world. When we overly emphasize *productivity* (a typically American thing to do), we often pervert the *process*: instead of faith, we substitute work; instead of depth, we substitute speed; instead of love, we substitute money; instead of prayer, we substitute busyness.

God does not give out monthly productivity sheets. All He asks is "Do you love Me?" Such love is not measured by units per hour (productivity), but rather by consistently loving the person standing in front of you at the moment (process). It does not have to do with the past nor the future, but the present. Right now. Are you bringing the kingdom of God to bear on whatever you are doing—right now?

Let's take the world of medical practice as an example. A productivity model would say that if I see thirty patients a day rather than twenty, I am a better doctor. Rewards will follow. Does this mean that seeing fifty patients is better than thirty? One hundred patients is better than fifty? Obviously, as *productivity* is pushed to extremes, *process* begins to suffer. I can tell you from experience that an overemphasis on medical productivity displaces caring, compassion, and service.

God does not have to depend on human exhaustion to get His work done. God is not so desperate for resources to accomplish His purposes that we have to abandon the raising of our children in order to accommodate Him. God is not so despairing of where to turn next that He has to ask us to go without sleep five nights in a row. Chronic overloading is not a spiritual prerequisite for authentic Christianity. Quite the contrary, overloading is often what we do when we forget who God is.

Our contemporary drivenness assumes that God never reaches down and says, "Enough, my child. Well done. Now go home and love your children. Encourage your spouse. Rest. Pray. Meditate. Sleep. Recharge your batteries. I'll have more for you to do tomorrow. And, by the way, don't worry. Remember who you are dealing with."

IT'S OKAY WITH GOD

Since God is the author and creator of my limits, then it is probably okay with Him that I have limits. He probably does not expect me to be infinite and is a little surprised when I try. It is okay with Him if I am not all things to all people all the time all by myself. As a matter of fact, it is probably *not* okay with Him if I assume otherwise.

You see, it is okay for me to have limits—God doesn't.

It is okay to get a good night's sleep—God doesn't sleep.

It is okay for me to rest—God doesn't need to.

It is probably even okay to be depressed—because God isn't.

We do not know a lot about what heaven looks like, but this much we know: God is not pacing the throne room anxious and depressed because of the condition of the world. He knows, He is not surprised, and He is sovereign.

It is okay if we have limits. He is able.

CHAPTER 2

■■■■■■■■

Blame Progress

During medical school, Linda and I traveled to India for a summer of hospital volunteering. Flying into Bombay, we knew it was monsoon season and expected to get wet. Our arrival at the airport was a soaking one. After collecting our bags, we peered past the teeming hoards to see that outside it was still raining hard. Actually, the density of rainfall looked more like someone had lifted the ocean a mile above Bombay and then dumped it on top of the airport.

Later, we learned that ours was the only flight to land that day. Roads were flooded and the traffic was paralyzed. A rare taxi took us as far as he could into town, charging exorbitant rates. We paid the inflated fare and stepped out of the cab into six inches of water mixed with—whatever. Taking off my shoes and socks, I lifted the suitcases to my shoulders. We surely made some sight—foreigners without a clue, sloshing down unknown Bombay streets with floating garbage bumping into our ankles.

So, this is summer in India! we thought. We had heard of monsoons and found it all quite adventurous.

The next morning's headlines, however, stunned us: "Eighteen inches in twenty-four hours—largest rainfall in eighty-five years!" It wasn't just a monsoon we had experienced the day before—it was an *unprecedented* monsoon. It wasn't just a rain, it was an *historic* rain. And even though we stood in the middle of it, we had no idea that history was being made at our ankles.

HISTORICALLY UNPRECEDENTED

Such failure to recognize the historic dimensions of current events is not unusual. Even when we experience the historic as it happens, most of us remain unaware of its significance. Even when we are being personally victimized by unprecedented events, still we do not understand. We assume today is "every day" when in fact it is "like no other day."

Let us now return to our discussion of overload and limits. Why, *at this point in history,* are we discussing limits? Is there something afoot that causes this discussion to be particularly timely and relevant? Indeed. Something is happening on our generational shift, and it is historically unprecedented. The universe has seizured, destabilizing everything at the same time. Yet we just keep eating and sleeping, buying and selling—all the time failing to realize that *this* deluge is different. These current developments are historically, experientially, mathematically, and spiritually unprecedented on a scale that staggers our thinking. Unfortunately, our day-to-day routine provides no frame of reference with which to assess such occurrences.

Perhaps an apt comparison would be a raft floating down a river. The raft is our life, its four sides defining the limits of our existence. Every morning we awaken to—the same raft. Of course, we are aware that there is water surrounding the raft, but every morning it also seems about the same. Our perceptions fail us here. For even though the raft stays the same, the river does not. First, the river picks up speed. Almost imperceptibility at first. Then the river gets deeper—but that is also unknown to us.

Then the river gets wider. Slowly at first, so we are not aware of day-to-day changes. Finally, the river gets rougher. The waves are higher than we remember them. The shoreline is barely perceptible and goes by in a blur. We begin to grow uneasy. Still, all we see is the raft.

Similarly, our lives float in a culture. Our lives continue to be the same twenty-four hours a day—work eight hours, sleep seven hours, eat three times. All the while, the cultural flow becomes faster, rougher, and blurred. Taking refuge in the boundaries of our raft, we pretend that because the dimensions of our raft have not changed, nothing else has changed either. There is, after all, "nothing new under the sun."

Until we plummet over the falls.

SUDDENNESS

Not only are these changes *unprecedented* in a way hard to imagine, but they are also *sudden.* Suddenness, perhaps, like the million-dollar house in southern California that burned to the ground in ten minutes. In the same way, historically speaking, contemporary overloading happened in the blink of an eye.

Before our current overload crisis I doubt most of us gave much thought to the issue of limits. Perhaps we assumed limits would arrive in a slow, discernible manner. We thought we would see the thresholds coming and could adapt to these interesting changes in a paced way. Unfortunately that has not been the case. The limits came at us too many, too fast. People hit the wall and then scratch their heads in confusion and disbelief.

Let me give you two mathematical illustrations to help you gauge what I am referring to.

First, a quiz about exponential change.

To support dairy farmers in our home state of Wisconsin, the loyal thing is to eat ice cream. If I were to double my ice cream consumption every year—one teaspoon of ice cream at age one, two teaspoons at age two, four teaspoons at age three, and so on—how much would I be eating at age fifty? Answer: Fifty-two tons per second.

Second, a quiz about big numbers.

If at a rate of one digit per second, you were to count to a million, how long would it take? Answer: Ten days. Now, counting at the same rate, skip a billion and count to a trillion. How long would it take? Answer: Thirty-two thousand years.

Our intuition is not capable of approximating the answers to these two questions. In the first instance, we do not know how to estimate exponential change—even though exponential change is happening all around us. (For a more complete discussion of this important phenomenon, see *Margin* Part One and Appendix for graphs.)[1] In the second instance, we do not understand big numbers and have no frame of reference by which to assess them. Our national debt, for example, is five trillion dollars—and there is not a person alive who knows what five trillion dollars means.

In many ways, these two illustrations describe both our experience and our problem. Fifty-two tons per second and thirty-two thousand years speak to the radical sudden dimension of change we are experiencing. So much has changed so fast that we lag significantly behind the curve in understanding both its dimensions and its practical implications.

MORE AND MORE, FASTER AND FASTER

If life is changing this dramatically, why is it happening? And why is it happening *now*? Many forces contribute to the overload of our age, but dominant among them—surprisingly—is progress.

Progress has been wonderful in many regards. It has given us thousands of advantages over earlier eras: education and communication, medical technologies and antibiotics, convenience and comfort—advancements almost beyond imagination. But, like everything else in a flawed world, progress has a downside. And that downside has much to do with overload.

Progress works by *differentiating our environment*. For example, if we cut down a tree, bring it into the garage, and instruct progress to differentiate the log, it would make tables, chairs, baseball bats, fruit bowls, and toothpicks—that is, many varied wood products. Understanding this *differentiation* is the key to understanding *progress*. And understanding *progress* is the key to understanding *overload*.

The functional result of such differentiation is that progress always gives us *more and more of everything faster and faster.* Getting more and more of everything is wonderful—as long as that is what we need. When saturated, however, getting more and more of everything faster and faster becomes a problem.

Most of us don't need *more.* And we certainly don't need it *faster.* Instead of being our friends, *more* and *faster* have now become our twin enemies. Instead of bringing benefit, more and faster often bring us pain—the pain of overload.

If thirsty, it would be unsatisfying to drink water through an eye dropper. That's too little water. We want more and we want it faster. But it would be even more unsatisfying to drink from a fire hose. That's too much, coming too fast! We don't need our sinuses irrigated—we just want a drink of water.

Progress is acting like a fire hose. And our sinuses have never been cleaner.

PUSHY PROGRESS

"Progress," someone once said, "is where we work very hard to make things as good as they used to be." Observed another critic, "Progress is the future you envisioned yesterday but didn't like when you woke up today."

Such sentiments have become commonplace at the turning of the millennium. But why do we express this ambivalence? A major reason for our cynicism: overload. People have been pushed to their limits—and beyond. Often, it was progress that did the pushing.

There are only so many details that can be comfortably managed in anybody's life. Once this number has been exceeded, one of two things happens: disorganization or frustration. Yet progress gives us more and more details every year—often at exponential rates. We have to deal with more "things per person" than ever before in the history of humankind. As a result, overload is not only real, it is pathogenic.

Every year we have more products, more information, more technology, more activities, more choices, more change, more traffic, more commitments, more work. In short, more of everything. Faster.

This ubiquitous overloading is a natural function of progress. It is automatic. If we sit meekly and do nothing about it, next year at this time, we will be even more overloaded than we are right now.

ONE-WAY STREET

Progress, in many ways, can't help itself. It has only been taught to go in one direction: differentiation. This is precisely what we have asked and expected of progress. Who in their right mind would expect progress to give us *less and less, slower and slower?* We have, therefore, built our way of life—and our economy—around this differentiation.

As a result, if we were to slow progress, our economy would fall apart. To date, that lacks bipartisan support. Yet, on the other hand, if we do not slow the tidal wave of overloading at the hands of progress, we will fall apart. That, too, lacks bipartisan support.

In such a tug of war between progress and the economy on the one hand, and the problem of overloading on the other, progress and the economy will win. Hands down. The economy *always* wins. Therefore, progress is not going to slow down. We can count on *more and more* from here on out.

It is time for an axiom: *Progress automatically leads to increasing overload, marginlessness, speed, change, stress, and complexity.*

- Overload: Most of us now live beyond the threshold of our limits, and progress is not going to reverse that trend.
- Marginlessness: Margin is the space between our load and our limits. Progress has taken this therapeutic space away.
- Speed: Every year, the speed of the treadmill goes faster. Buckle your seat belt.
- Change: Future Shock arrived some time ago, and there is no deceleration in sight.
- Stress: Stress is our adaptation to change. As change increases, so does stress.
- Complexity: The flow of progress is always in the direction of increasing complexity.

Because progress only knows how to travel in one direction, these six saboteurs of progress are not self-correcting. Mark them well— they are after you.

THE ROLE OF TECHNOLOGY

If progress is the train driving us to the land of overload, technology is the engine. They work hand in hand. Just as they have been partners in bringing us benefit, so they have partnered together in the crime of overload. Did you realize, for example, that the average American has to learn how to operate twenty thousand pieces of technology? What could better illustrate contemporary overload than that single statistic?

As we begin to examine specific overloads in Part Two it will become apparent how technology plays an integral role in each— and how *resisting* technology plays an equally important role in the suggested prescriptions. Accessibility overload, for example, is only possible because accessing technologies are now so mobile and miniaturized we have no excuse left for not being on-call for the universe. Media overload has exploded precisely because technology has given us a telecommunications revolution unprecedented in human history. There is now even a television set that can be worn on the head. (And you thought Walkmans were annoying.) Activity overload is only possible because the technologies of transportation and communication both stimulate and facilitate it.

If, as an illustration, you picture *progress* as the entire world, imagine *technology* as the Pacific Ocean, and each specific *overload* as an island within that ocean. Because progress runs our economy, and because technology propels the engine for so much of progress, don't look for either to slow anytime soon. Yet it is easier, on an individual level, to resist technology than it is to stand in the way of progress. Simplicity is still an option. We can't leave the earth. But we can always move away from the Pacific.

WARNING SIGNS

As progress and technology careen out of control downhill, increasing overload, marginlessness, speed, change, stress, and complexity will inevitably follow. Even the highest levels of privilege and power are not exempt. Recently, for example, I had the honor of speaking with some members of Congress about these concepts. In response to a question from one congressman about what symptoms accompany stress and overload, I listed about twenty: *psychological symptoms* such as anxiety, depression, confusion, negative thinking; *physical symptoms* such as headaches, unexplained fatigue, indigestion, increased infections; *behavioral symptoms* such as irritability, withdrawal, driving too fast. As I finished, another asked: "What does it mean if you have *all* of those symptoms?"

What are the warning signs that overload is upon us? How do we know when we are approaching the threshold line of our limits? To illustrate, let's look at three scenarios: eighty percent full (margined), one hundred percent full (maximized), and one hundred and twenty percent full (overloaded).

Eighty Percent Full

On the unsaturated side of our limits, we can be open and expansive. We can say yes to new opportunities and activities with enthusiasm because there is space to put them.

Our boss asks: "Can you work overtime this weekend?" *I'd be glad to! I enjoy my work, I've got the time, and besides, who couldn't use a little extra money?*

Our church asks: "Can you teach Sunday school?" *Sure. It's great fun to be around kids and a privilege to teach them.*

Our spouse asks: "Can we take the neighbors out to dinner and a movie?" *That would be great. We have wanted to get together with them for months now.*

Living on the unsaturated side of our limits allows space for involvement without the complicating burden of unnecessary self-protection.

One Hundred Percent Full

As we straddle the line that represents the threshold of our limits, decisions become much harder. A strange ambivalence arises about any new decision.

Our boss comes to us and says: "Can you work overtime this weekend?" *I'm not sure . . . let me think about it . . . I'll have to get back to you . . . Oh, I guess I can.*

Our church asks: "Could you teach Sunday school?" *You know, that is something I have always wanted to do. But I'm kind of busy right now. I had better think it over and let you know next week.*

Our spouse asks: "Can we take the neighbors out to dinner and a movie?" *I don't think so, honey. Not this week anyway. Let's think about it for next week.*

This new ambivalence is uncomfortable, and we can't really explain it. We have never felt this way before, and wonder why it is so hard to make decisions about things we have always felt positively about in the past.

One Hundred and Twenty Percent Full

As we cross into overload, we find the land of saturation downright painful.

Our boss comes to us and says: "Can you work overtime this weekend?" *NO. As a matter of fact, I QUIT! I'm tired of people dumping all their problems on me.*

Our church asks: "Could you teach Sunday school?" *Are you kidding? I hate kids!!!*

Our spouse asks: "Can we take the neighbors out to dinner and a movie?" *I've got a better idea. Let's just pull down the shades and pretend we're not home.*

Once our lives are saturated, the rules totally change. We can't factor anything more into our lives until we take something equally time- or energy-consuming away. As elementary as this principle sounds, it nevertheless escapes most of us most of the time.

RECOGNIZING AND ACCEPTING OUR LIMITS

When we are overloaded, how can we tell? We are not very adept at knowing where our limits are, and most of us have never seriously thought about them—certainly not in any objective or scientific terms. Unfortunately, God did not equip us with reliable warning signals. There are no indicator lights that blink at ninety-five percent; no alarms that blare at one hundred percent. Often the first sign we have is pain.

When overloaded, joy has a tendency to disappear. We might develop a variety of physical symptoms. We become self-protective and begin resenting people for needing our help. Irritability, often directed at those we love the most, further damages our attitude.

Overload reminds us of two important truths:

- We are only human. It is best not to forget it.
- God, the author of our limits, will use these same limits freely to remind us that we have need of Him.

PRESCRIPTIONS AGAINST THE PAIN

Part One of this book is important because diagnostic accuracy matters. As someone once observed: "Problem resolution always begins with correct problem identification." We will not solve our problems until we correctly understand them.

But now that we have diagnosed *overload* as the new universal constant, what can we do about it? Let's shine a light down each corridor of our lives, searching for prescriptions against the pain of each specific overload we encounter.

PART TWO

Relieving Contemporary Overloads

CHAPTER 3

■ ■ ■ ■ ■ ■ ■ ■

Accessibility

■ I am dying of easy accessibility. If Alexander Graham Bell
walked into my office, I'd punch him in the nose. If he
called, you can be sure I'd put him on hold.
—JAMES M. CERLETTY, M.D.

■ The good news is, you're always connected to the office.
The bad news is, you're always connected to the office.
—THE WALL STREET JOURNAL, FULL PAGE AD

■ Yuppie ear—A NEW SYNDROME WHERE PEOPLE ANSWER THEIR
CELL PHONES IN THE MIDDLE OF THE NIGHT AND
INADVERTENTLY STICK THE ANTENNA INTO THEIR EAR.

■ Beepilepsy—NEW NAME GIVEN TO THE MOMENTARY SEIZURE
OF PANIC SUFFERED WHEN ONE'S PAGER GOES OFF.

The future arrived yesterday, when the Starship Enterprise landed
in our backyard. Slick gadgets are strapped to every belt, plugged
into every socket, and stuck in every ear. Overhead, still more
gadgets swim in the heavenlies.

As telecommunications rapidly reshape the globe, we sit at the
beginning of a universal connectivity unprecedented in human history. Cell phones and pagers, videophones and video-conferencing,
telecommuting and fax machines, Internet and E-mail, satellites
and the information superhighway. Images of futuristic excitement,
to be sure.

But what will be the result of this incredible flurry of seemingly unstoppable activity—good or bad? Like most modern things,
it will be both. At exactly the same time. The wheat and tares are
growing side by side. On the "bad" side, the aspect of this development that disturbs me most is accessibility overload—the
absence of hiding places. Privacy is going, going, gone. Natural
solitude has disappeared.

INESCAPABILITY

A major unintended consequence of the flood of accessing technologies is that soon there will be no natural excuse for being unavailable. In the midst of our enthusiasm for the telecommunications revolution, we have not sufficiently discerned the horrifying psychic cost of what columnist William Safire has called *unrestrained reachability*. Don't get me wrong. I like people. Some of my best friends are people. But I also like to escape from time to time.

"Where were you all day? I tried to call you five times!" your boss or clients or in-laws or bridge partner will say. And because virtually everyone will carry tiny cell phones/pagers, you will have no excuse.

"I turned off my pager phone."

"You what?!!!"

What will this be like for exhausted pastors on vacation, maybe five states away, when a parishioner goes to the hospital? Do we disturb pastors for such occurrences? Most of us wouldn't. But some will—you can bet on it.

What if parishioners die? Do we interrupt pastors' much-needed vacations by requesting they return for the funeral? I spoke of this scenario recently at a Toronto pastors' retreat. Two of the pastors had agonized with this exact situation in the previous year. One returned home to do the funeral; the other didn't. The first disappointed his family and lost an important vacation. The second disappointed his church family and lost an important ministry opportunity. Both were victimized by progress and accessibility overload.

What about our employers? It goes without saying that most bosses are more invested in the job than the people they supervise. This often makes for a natural asymmetry between their expectations and those of the employees.

"Where were you yesterday?" the boss might ask. "I was trying to reach you all day!" Never mind that it was Saturday and we were camping with the children. Or that it was Christmas Day and we were halfway to Grandma's house.

The recent *Wall Street Journal* ad quoted at the beginning of this chapter flaunts this new and discomforting development. Both the good and the bad news is the same—we are always connected to the office. The advertisement, hawking a particular computer notebook, continues, "Being out of the office no longer means being out of touch. Connectivity has never been easier. Just think, your people will finally be able to stay connected around the clock. They'll just love that, won't they?"[1]

Lucent Technologies placed their own version of the same message, again in a full-page ad in the *Journal*: "A Formal Apology. Since inventing cellular and after introducing digital wireless, wireless office systems and cordless phones, it seems that anyone can get ahold of you no matter where you are. Sorry. Sincerely, Lucent Technologies."[2]

Physicians, who have been on-call since Adam broke his ankle chasing Eve, now find that requirement stretched to the insane extreme: "Telephones in our homes and offices, cordless phones in our backyards and cars, beepers, fax machines, and E-mail," complains Milwaukee physician James Cerletty. "It's enough to give you a stroke.... Albert Einstein said that the reason we are here on earth is for each other, but I don't think he envisioned how technology would erode our privacy.... What we have is an overload, a plethora, a supersaturation of communication. I'm dying of easy accessibility."[3]

PHONES

I don't recall always hating the telephone. But no ambiguity about that feeling exists today. How can one ever escape something as prevalent as mosquitoes and as audibly irritating as a chain saw?

"The telephone is one of those miracles one can discuss in terms either sacred or profane," explains Lance Morrow. "No one has yet devised a pleasant way for a telephone to come to life. The ring is a sudden intrusion, a drill in the ear.... The satanic bleats from some new phones are the equivalent of sound lasers.

"But the ring cannot be subtle. Its mission is disruption.... The telephone call is a breaking-and-entering that we invite by having telephones in the first place. Someone unbidden barges in and for an instant or an hour usurps the ears and upsets the mind's prior arrangements."[4]

Call Waiting

Call waiting, representing a "last-come, first-served" ethic, is like trying to choke out noxious weeds by planting thistles. But we don't like busy signals either. In a lifetime, the average American spends two years trying to call people who aren't in or whose line is busy. (Some of us, it seems, spend that much time annually.) So this is our choice: to be irritated by the busy signal or to be irritated by call waiting.

Answering Machines/Voice Mail

Answering machines are one of those things that we wish everyone else had but are sometimes glad we do not. My residential phone has never been graced with such a device. It is not that I wish to inconvenience those trying to contact us. But even less do I wish to return home at 11:00 P.M. and find out there are now five people I have to call. The answering machine slickly transforms *someone else's desire* to contact me into *my need* to return the call.

Junk Phone Calls

Unsolicited sales calls are yet another invasion of both privacy and sanity. Autodialing machines exist which can dial one hundred calls per hour in sequence, regardless of whether the phone is listed or not. My wife, Linda, recently received her fifth call asking us to become the proud owners of a GM Credit Card. Like the rest, it was refused. The notable thing about this call is that it arrived at 1:00 P.M. on a Sunday afternoon, just as we sat down to dinner. Monday through Saturday dinner—by now we are used to that. But Sunday dinner?

Menu-Driven Answering Systems

No discussion of modern telephone frustrations would be complete without mentioning automated menu-driven answering devices. Some have as many as ten options. I once tried calling America Online every day for thirty days to solve an on-line problem. Calling every hour of the day, including the middle of the night, the closest I ever came to reaching a living human being was thirty minutes ("If you wish to talk with our service department, the next available representative will be with you in . . . (pause) . . . thirty minutes"). Finally, after a month, I contacted a young relative in Illinois who solved the problem in five minutes.

CELL PHONES

More than fifty million Americans own cell phones, with a new one being sold or given away every three seconds. The best thing to remember about such time-saving technologies is that they usually don't. The people with the most "time-saving technologies" are the same people with the highest blood pressure and fastest pulse.

A friend from Vail told us of her attempt to take twelve members of the exclusive Young Presidents Club hiking in the Colorado Rockies. At the first break, while overlooking a beautiful vista, seven of the twelve pulled out cell phones and called their offices. In Alaska, an avid salmon fisherman took three brokers out on the Russian River at 3:00 A.M. Before they even caught anything, the brokers were on their cell phones working the world markets.

One local telephone company advertises: "You need a cellular phone. It can save your life!" True. But knowing this, people are now taking risks they should not be taking and bringing along a cell phone to bail them out. Increasingly, mountain rescues are required for hikers and climbers who find it easier to pack their Motorola rather than all that safety equipment.

E-MAIL

In 1996, for the first time, the volume of E-mail sent exceeded the total amount of surface mail delivered. E-mail is fast and cheap. In many ways, it is a guy's stationery. To write a letter, first we have to find paper, pen, envelope, stamp, and address. And then we have to find the time. E-mail is much simpler.

As much as I dislike the phone, I like E-mail. It does not disturb me until I wish it to. I can answer it at my leisure and convenience. Sometimes (rarely) I do not answer it at all. But I recently heard of a man from California who was on vacation for a week.

When he returned, he had more than a thousand E-mail messages waiting for him. Just around the corner, this is the world waiting for us all.

Americans living abroad love E-mail. Except when they hate it. "Sometimes I feel that all I do is answer the mail," complains Dan, a missionary from Mexico. "When I travel for a few days, it's not uncommon to come back and get as many as one hundred messages that have to be read and answered." Susan, stationed in Mozambique, figures E-mail costs her about three dollars a page to receive. "That really adds up," she says, "especially for messages that aren't critical.

"One thing that bugs me is the short turnaround time churches expect," says another missionary. "I once received a three-page questionnaire to fill out with the request that I send it back within twenty-four hours for their missions conference. I received the E-mail at 5:15 P.M. Friday, and they wanted the information to compile on Saturday afternoon so they could use it on Sunday morning."[5] This is NOT to say that we should stop E-mailing our friends abroad—mostly this new technology has been a stunning success. But as with everything else, we should be both discerning and sensitive.

PAGERS

A few years back, my pager died from old age. Before I could celebrate, one of the graduating residents gleefully threw me his instrument. The pager number? 666. My first inclination was to throw it like a hand grenade. Then I thought it was perhaps a demonstration of God's sense of humor.

Do you worship in a church with physicians? If so, you undoubtedly have experienced the sound of a pager going off during the pastoral prayer. Beepers in church, in the movie theater, in weddings, in funerals—I have heard it all. Pager signals are one of the most dreadful noises ever invented to shake the brain loose from its tentative moorings. The beepilepsy startle is an involuntary reaction to which I have never accommodated.

Thankfully, many beepers today use the quiet vibrating mode.

This helps not only the sanity of the "beepee," but the rest of the world as well.

"I remember the days when there were signs outside our medical institutions that said: *Hospital Zone—Quiet Please,*" reminisces Dr. Cerletty. "Nowadays . . . beepers, monitors, and other noises make hospitals sound like a warmup act for a heavy metal rock band. Beepers burst onto the medical scene almost twenty years ago. The early models let out a sound so shrill that any dog within a two-mile radius began howling like a fifty-year-old with renal colic. Once doctors learned that calls could just as easily be from a used car salesman as a sick patient, beepers began to be 'inadvertently' misplaced or lost."[6]

HACKING, SPYING, STALKING, AND THE EVAPORATION OF PRIVACY

Telecommunication technologies have contributed to a deprivation of privacy unprecedented in human history. To date, much of this concern is more theoretical than actual. But the infrastructure exists, and the erosion of privacy has turned from a intermittent drip to a steady flow.

Joshua Quittner is the fully-wired news director of Time, Inc.'s information mega-mall. Recently, he was victimized by a prankster who rerouted the Quittner's home telephone to an out-of-state answering machine. Callers trying to reach them heard a voice identify himself as Mr. Quittner, who then said some extremely rude things. Next, the voice requested people to leave messages. This went on for several days until finally the ruse was suspected and phone service restored.

"It seemed funny at first. But the interloper continued to hit us again and again for the next six months. The phone company seemed powerless. Its security folks moved us to one unlisted number after another, half a dozen times. They put special PIN codes in place. They put traces on the line. But the troublemaker kept breaking through. . . .

"I remember feeling violated at the time. . . . Someone was invading my private space and there was nothing I or the authorities could do . . . it struck me that our privacy—mine and yours—has already disappeared."[7]

Let me say that I am not paranoid. Then let me point out that both you and I are being watched—either actually or potentially—every time we buy prescription drugs with company insurance, browse the Web, use a cellular phone, use credit cards, take out life insurance, register to vote, give our social security number, use an ATM, make a phone call, get checked out with a supermarket scanner, enter sweepstakes, use electronic tollway passes, send E-mail at work, or walk before a surveillance camera (which the average New Yorker does twenty times a day).[8]

Beginning with only your name and address, within a few hours any talented computer sleuth can find out what you do for a living, the names and ages of your spouse and children, what kind of car you drive, the value of your house and how much tax you pay on it, plus a detailed map of how to get to your home.

PRESCRIPTIONS FOR RESTORING PRIVACY TO OVER-ACCESSED LIVES

What can be done to counteract the accessibility overload syndrome's ill effects? How can we reestablish the needed privacy and solitude that permits a later reengagement with our needy world? Many steps can be taken—some to begin the process of restoration, others to guard against future erosion of important privacy needs.

Rx 1 *Be Discerning*
In a fallen world, all new technologies will have both positive and negative consequences. Our responsibility is to understand clearly this dynamic and then make day-to-day decisions regarding which consequence dominates.

It is not enough to look only at how much the technological trend is helping. We must, more importantly, also understand how much it is hurting. No amount of trendiness, pizzazz, or glitz should sway us. Nor should cultural or commercial pressure. Just because something is "good for business" is not sufficient reason to let it damage the spirit.

Rx 2 *Set Boundaries*

Caving in to demands that are emotionally overwhelming, relationally unhealthy, physically exhausting, and spiritually inauthentic is not the way to create the space and rest we all need. This dilemma is best solved by understanding and establishing boundaries.

The concept of boundaries suggests that it is acceptable and even desirable to erect and defend a perimeter around the private spaces of our lives. People have the right, for example, to establish the atmosphere in their own homes, regardless of the world's opinion on that issue.

In our family we have erected a sometimes loose boundary to protect the dinner hour: we do not answer the telephone during that time. Similarly, when the boys were young, we would not allow the telephone to disturb our evening routines of reading to them, praying with them, and tucking them in bed. No matter how important the phone call was, it could wait. As radical as this might sound, it is really simple common sense that has eluded us far too long.

Occasionally, when I am home alone and in a particularly drained state, I might not even answer the doorbell. After extensive speaking trips, I need to lie fallow, to do nothing, to recharge my batteries. It is not my desire to be rude or insensitive. But sometimes, I simply must rest.

Rx 3 *Control Interruptions*

The average middle manager in America, according to one study, is interrupted seventy-four times every day. Interruptions are a part of modern life, but with effort, they can be modified. Relocate to a quieter room. Go to the library to work. Work late at night or early in the morning. Have other people take messages for you and return them in a batched fashion. Control the telephone. Turn off the beeper. Employ technologies that block interruptions rather than cause them.

If interruptions were allowed during writing projects, I would give up in despair. An isolated setting away from home works best for me. Or when home, I routinely write through the night and then sleep after the sun comes up.

Rx 4 *Tame the Telephone*

Consider turning off or unplugging the telephone at selected times.

Consider getting an answering machine and letting it take calls when you are busy with more important things.

Consider using caller ID.

If you have call waiting, consider selectively turning it off before placing calls. Just press *70 and then enter the number you are calling. Call waiting automatically turns back on after each call.

For the more radically minded, consider getting an unlisted number. Forty percent of Californians have unlisted numbers, surely an accommodation to accessibility overload.

Even though our family has not gone to these lengths (except for turning off the phones, which we do often), I will not criticize those who choose these measures. Increasingly, in the face of advancing "unrestrained reachability," we will all develop an affinity for such protections.

Rx 5 *Deactivate the Answering Machine*

Just because we have an answering machine does not mean we have to leave it on all the time. If we find it overwhelming to come home to full voice mail, just turn it off. If the call is important, the person will call back.

Our family has never used an answering machine on our residential line. A second line to my study, however, has such a device. This second line exists primarily for the computer modem and sending faxes. However, not uncommonly I will give out this number so others can use the answering machine and not get caught playing "telephone tag."

Another suggestion—try this for your recorded message: "Please wait for the beep and hang up."

Rx 6 *Disconnect*

Consider selecting a personal or family "disconnect time"—a set time each day or a set evening each week. During disconnect time, shut out the external world. Announce to your friends, your relatives, your neighbors, your church, your work: "Every evening from 5:30 to 7:00, we are disconnecting. Don't try to reach us then because you won't be able to."

Rx 7 *Refuse Telephone Solicitation*

Set a consistent policy never to respond to telephone solicitations. Once you buy something from telemarketers, you're put on a "chump list" that's sold to other marketers. My advice—never buy.

Many pitches are for commercial products or services; other appeals are for charity. *When the call is for products or services,* politely refuse at the first instant without being rude. Then hang up. *When the call is for charity,* respond, "I'm sorry, but it is my policy to never respond to telephone solicitations. However, if you wish to send me materials in the mail, I will consider whether I should give to your cause."

Rx 8 *Remove Your Name*

Consider removing your name from many telemarketing and direct-mail lists. Write to:

(Telemarketing)	(Direct-mail list)
Direct Marketing Association	Direct Marketing Association
Telephone Preference Service	Mail Preference Service
P. O. Box 9014	P. O. Box 9008
Farmingdale, NY 11735	Farmingdale, NY 11735

To have your name and E-mail address removed from all electronic commercial mailing lists controlled by Cyber Promotions, send an E-mail with the words "Remove all" in the subject or message field to: remove@cyberpromo.com.

Rx 9 *Cell Phone—Take It or Leave It?*

I do not own a cell phone. After twenty years of being on call in medicine, I can't figure out why I should pay inflated rates to stay connected when I so desperately desire the opposite.

This, however, is not a sentiment shared by all doctors—nor should it be. A young female resident physician rose to the defense: "But I got a cell phone for Mother's Day and it's been great. Now, when I'm on call, I can take my baby for a stroller ride, or I can do an errand at the store." Exactly. If it serves your purposes and you are firmly in control, then use it. But if it is complicating and tyrannizing your already overloaded life, reject it.

In terms of safety—especially if you have young drivers—you may want to invest in a "pay-as-you-use" cell phone for emergency use only.

Personally, I'll buy one just after the Cubs win the World Series.

Rx 10 *Buy a Phoneless Cord*

Put a phoneless cord on your Christmas list. It could be the best gift you receive all year.

Rx 11 *Fix Your Cookie*

If computer security has you worried, rig your cookie. Your cookie is the little bits of code that identify you to cookie-catching websites. In other words, it is a software device dumped into your hard drive while you are visiting a website. The cookie continues to monitor your on-line activity even after you leave that site. It then feeds back information about your browsing habits the next time you reconnect to the parent website. Use your computer's Windows 95 "Find" command to get any file with the word "cookie" in its name. Look at it using a word-processing program to find out who is stashing cookies in your browser. To disable your cookie, go to website www.luckman.com and get a free "anonymous cookie," a program that disables cookies.[9]

Rx 12 *Retreat to a Motel*

Increasingly, overloaded people are checking into local motels just to escape. If you can afford it, this is a periodic option that the entire family might enjoy. Use an indoor pool during winter. Order a pizza, cuddle on the bed, and watch a family movie. Thirty years from now, it might remain as one of your children's most vivid memories.

In a variation on this theme, our church board sends our pastor out of town once a quarter for three days and two nights. He can tell no one where he is going; he has no agenda from the board; he goes alone or takes his wife; and he is to have no pulpit duties the following week. Our board does this because we appreciate our pastor. We want him to last. We feel that our church will have a healthier, more invested pastor for a longer period of time.

Rx 13 *Buy a Cabin*

Yes, this might decimate one's financial margin. But, on the other hand, it might also prevent a heart attack. Our family has never owned a second home, but several friends have purchased such "heart attack insurance." What might sound like a rationalization is really a sound emotional investment.

Buying a remote retreat with joint ownership might also present interesting possibilities for a church to build community. Inviting people to get away together for a weekend not only allows for needed escape but also accomplishes more relationship building in two days than might otherwise happen in ten years.

Rx 14 *Seek Solitude*

As accessibility overload arrives through the front door, *natural solitude* departs out the back. Fortunately, for the determined, *intentional solitude* is still attainable.

Use solitude for rest. Solitude is also of value in long-term creative projects. "To think and create," explains Janna Malamud Smith in her book *Private Matters,* "people often need solitude because its privacy allows not only mental continuity, quiet, and relief from feeling noticed, but latitude to experiment with half-formed ideas and ridiculous solutions."[10]

Use solitude to build a deeper relationship with God and self. If we do not make friends with God and self—if we do not cultivate an inner life—our aging will be fraught with loneliness. "It is solitude and solitude alone," observes theologian Dallas Willard, "that opens the possibility of a radical relationship to God that can withstand all external events up to and beyond death."[11]

Jesus practiced and found strength in periodic solitude. Yet today, many are frightened by solitude. Perhaps the more the idea threatens us, the more we ought to consider it. "I don't know of any answer to busyness other than solitude," says Willard. "Or tragedy."[12]

■ ■ ■ ■ ■ ■ ■ ■ ■

CHAPTER 4

Activity and Commitment

■ Some people can't say no. They enroll in too many courses, hold down too many jobs, volunteer for too many tasks, make too many appointments, serve on too many committees, have too many friends. They are trying to be all things to all people all at once all by themselves.—DR. J. GRANT HOWARD

■ When we do two things simultaneously, we take about thirty percent of our attention off the primary task.
—RICHARD THIEME

■ It now takes twenty-to-thirty phone calls in the average church to get the same number of volunteers as it used to take two-to-three calls.—DR. JENNIFER GLASS, UNIVERSITY OF IOWA

■ God will not guide us into an intolerable scramble of panting feverishness.—THOMAS KELLY

Busy. Perhaps the primary descriptor of modern living. "Whenever two people meet today, one or the other is sure to mention how busy he or she is," observes author John Charles Cooper. "No one seems to have any free time."[1] Booked up weeks in advance, we try to do two or three things at the same time in an attempt to squeeze still more in. If in 1950 we had ten activities to choose from, today—compliments of progress—we have a thousand. Further complicating matters, most of these activities are either fun or worthy, and overload descends upon us in an avalanche.

Activity is a most excellent thing. So is commitment. It is good to be involved, vital, and energetic. On the other hand, inactivity, by its very name, connotes laziness, idleness, and lethargy.

Even activity overload can, at times, be appropriate and normal. But *chronic* activity overload is a toxic condition. Nearly every individual and family I know is afflicted.

Activity overload takes away the pleasure of anticipation. Suddenly the activity is upon us, and we must rush to it. We also lack the delight of reminiscing, for we are immediately on to new activities.

Activity overload also leads to agenda overload. People's schedules are so full that one does not often see shared agenda. Friendships which formerly were solidified by shared activities are now divided asunder by activity overload.

Activity overload also leads to exhaustion, of which we have no shortage. Consider this church's experience:

"Two summers ago, we had a schedule bordering on the insane. Besides two 'work days' each week to help construct our new sanctuary, we hosted three choir-and-mission teams, two volunteer building teams, held a week of vacation Bible school [and] two weeks of day camps, supervised two college-age summer missionaries in a full slate of youth and children's activities, and conducted two old-fashioned tent meetings.

"About all we reaped that summer was an exhausted leadership and a listless congregation for the next six months. Even our most dedicated members were peeking from behind their curtains to make sure no one was coming to recruit them for a new project."[2]

BUSYNESS, DRIVENNESS, VALUE, AND GUILT

Despite most people's abundant personal—and painful—experience with activity overload, it is interesting to see how we have normalized such a state. We have come to believe that *activity* is all that counts, everything else being sloth. If we are not busy, we are not of value. Where did this notion come from? And why is it so strongly resident within us?

The associated guilt that comes from inactivity, in turn, feeds nicely into the prevalent value system of driven people. "Driven people operate on the precept that a reputation for busyness is a sign of success and personal importance," explains Gordon MacDonald. "Thus they attempt to impress people with the fullness of their schedule. They may even express a high level of self-pity, bemoaning the 'trap' of responsibility they claim to be in, wishing aloud that there was some possible release from all that they have to live with.

But just try to suggest a way out!"[3]

In addition to the guilt of inactivity, there is an associated pride that comes from being busy. "When in high school, I prided myself on the outrageous number of extra-curricular activities I participated in," one graduate student in therapy told me. "I used to joke with people that we could get together provided they used some of my free time between 2:00-4:00 A.M." The tighter the schedule, the better driven people feel about themselves and their achievement. They often push themselves to the breaking point before realizing the danger of overload.

From a missionary who served in East Africa comes a contrasting view: "I think back to the nine years our family enjoyed on the lower slopes of the Kilimanjaro," reminisces Mildred Tengbom. "There, while our work was sometimes tense, the pace surely resembled more a walk than a run. There were plenty of green trees to sit under and a conscience that allowed us to sit down under them. We weren't constantly being told that our value depended on how 'active' or 'involved' we were."[4]

Which notion is correct? In fact, God created both activity and rest, and commends both to us. It is an essential cycle now so distantly lost it seems only ancient historians and archeologists can dig up the memory.

THE ACTIVITY-REST CYCLE

As Americans, we tend to equate the will of God with busyness. But God is actually interested in both sides of the equation, and the extreme imbalance we currently live under is a fairly modern development.

Augustine talked of the active life and the contemplative life. While both had an important role to play, the contemplative life — being the domain of reflection, mediation, and prayer — was considered of greater value.[5]

If a patient has rheumatoid arthritis, in addition to important medications, two therapeutic measures are essential: activity and rest. Rheumatoid patients need daily activity or their joints will freeze up. But they also need well-defined times of rest or their joints will be destroyed.

Our lives are similar to that of the rheumatoid patient. Activity and rest. Together. Balanced. Both important. Both of God.

Even though progress will be forever giving us more and more activity, faster and faster, God is not the sponsor or supporter of this development. In the midst of it all, He wants us to find Him, to live in Him, to rest in Him. "Our heavenly Father never gives us too much to do," claims pastor and author Charles Shedd. "We assign ourselves an overload, but never the Lord."[6]

Busyness is not a synonym for kingdom work, it is only busyness. And busyness is sometimes what happens to us when we forget who God is.

PRESCRIPTIONS FOR CALMING THE ACTIVITY STORM

What steps can we take to bring balance and sanity to our hyperactive and overly committed lives?

Rx 1 *Reestablish Control of Your Life and Schedule*
Most of us are hemmed in by scores of societal influences and pressures. The first thing we need to recognize is that we have more control than we think. We should never completely relinquish our schedule to the unpredictable, commercialized, spiritually inauthentic, and sometimes ruthless whims of the world.

Be *active* in self-examination and *intentional* in correction. Abandon self-pity. Nobody is locked into anything. We *can* accomplish the needed changes if we want them badly enough. Live as simply and as slowly as needed in order to make the necessary changes.

Rx 2 *Prioritize Activities and Commitments*
Inherent in the understanding about overload is the need to prioritize. If we have more to do than we can possibly do, then we must choose. And we must choose wisely according to God-honoring criteria.

Many people do not consciously realize what their priorities are. The following are principles I have attempted to use:

■ Get priorities from the Word of God.
■ Look through God's eyes, and then act on what is seen.

■ Seek *first* the kingdom of God, and everything else *later.*
■ People are more important than things.

Rx 3 *Practice Saying NO to Good Things*

Once we clearly understand our priorities, the next step is learning how to say *no.* It is only a two-letter word and yet one of the most difficult to speak.

Regaining margin and control in our lives will never happen unless we develop the ability to say *no*—even to good things. It is easy to say *no* to bad things—like a root canal, an IRS audit, or a flexible sigmoidoscopy. But it is hard to say *no* to things we enjoy.

Practice. Stand in front of the mirror and say *no* over and over again until you get good at it. Take lessons from a two-year-old.

Saying *no* is not an excuse for noninvolvement, laziness, or insensitivity. Instead, it is purely a mechanism for living by our priorities, allowing God to direct our lives rather than the world, and preserving our vitality for the things that really matter.

One pastor told me that in his church, *no* is a holy word. Theologian Thomas Kelly encourages us to find that group of people who are so centered in the things of eternity that "*No* as well as *yes* can be said with confidence."[7]

"Bombarded with requests?" asks Dr. J. Grant Howard. "Learn to say no! Already overcommitted? Cut back! See something else that needs to be done? Delegate it!"[8]

Rx 4 *Consider Doing Less, Not More*

If most of us are already too busy, then we have some cutting back to do. Determine to do less, not more. But also determine to do the *right things*—another decision that requires a clear understanding of priorities. All activities need to be assessed for their spiritual authenticity.

The problems of the world will not be solved by our accomplishing another ten percent more in life. Consider doing ten percent *less.* Decide what is most important and concentrate on that.

Rx 5 *Protect Open Spaces*

Don't saturate your schedule. There is no need to feel guilty if your calendar has empty dates and open spaces. On the contrary, it is abnormal and unhealthy to have none. This is the precise message of margin—we need some space to heal and time to rest.

"My life in Connecticut . . . there is so little empty space," lamented Anne Morrow Lindbergh. "There are so few empty pages in my engagement pad, or empty hours in the day, or empty rooms in my life in which to stand alone and find myself. Too many activities, and people, and things. Too many worthy activities, valuable things, and interesting people. For it is not merely the trivial which clutters our lives but the important as well."[9]

Create space. Then guard it against the overloading pressures of the world at your door.

Rx 6 *Periodically Prune Activities*

Every year the apple trees in my front yard sprout new branches without even being asked. It would seem that these branches might increase the health and yield of the trees. However it is only when I actively prune away unnecessary growth that the trees flourish.

In the same way, every year our lives sprout new "activity branches"[10] without our intending it. There are always new meetings, committees, concerts, lectures, plays, parties, musicals, dinners, and sporting events that add themselves to our lives. Many activities are self-perpetuating even when we lose interest in them.

All activities, according to time management author Robert Banks, "should come up for periodic review and be required to justify their continued existence."[11] So mark your calendar, and prune on schedule.

Rx 7 *Limit Long-Term Commitments*

Since humans are limited, the number of our long-term or ongoing commitments should be limited as well. We can only spread ourselves so thin. If we are on the board of education in town, the infection control committee at the hospital, and the building committee at church, when will we find time to serve on the CPR committee for our marriage?

Rx 8 *Work to Establish and Maintain Balance*

An unexamined life will drift toward imbalance. This is the way the modern world works. And an unbalanced life will not be kind to us in the area neglected. If God has instructed us to perform in a certain area—even at the decent minimum level—then we will not thrive if we disobey.

Listen to God's advice. Take control of each area in your life where He has given explicit instructions. When we bring our balancing problems to God, we discover that He never assigns us twice as much as we can possibly do. Instead, the Father shows us the appropriate priorities to use and then always provides whatever time and resources we need to accomplish His will.

Rx 9 *Guard the Dinner Hour*

In biblical times people worked hard in the fields all day. When they came home, as darkness settled in, they reclined for the evening meal and spent hours eating and discussing. Then they went to bed.

In stark contrast, for most American families the concept of a family dinner hour has all but disappeared. We perhaps have not yet realized the magnitude of our loss.

I don't want to be a strict legalist, for it is neither practical nor possible to guard this hour rigidly. But try to establish *some* protections for the dinner hour. Try to eat at least four meals together a week. And refuse activities that would invade this time, simply because the family dinner hour is more valuable than these other commitments—no matter how valuable they might seem.

Rx 10 *Restore the Practice of Sabbath Rest*

When speaking to a group of stressed-out congressional staffers, one attractive young lady raised her hand with an unexpected and insightful question: "If we had held to the notion of a Sabbath rest, is it possible we would not be in this state of national exhaustion?"

I responded, "Yes. I think you are right. I suspect that if we unplugged one day in seven from the frenzy of the world, the amount of restedness might prove sufficiently therapeutic to spread over the rest of the week."

When our culture started to let the Sabbath slip (for example, Sunday morning soccer leagues), it was the beginning of a flood of complicating problems. In a survey of *Working Mothers* readers, ninety-five percent of people look forward to weekends to rest. But fifty-two percent were more exhausted at the end of the weekend than they were before.

Use the Sabbath both to rest from busyness and to remember God's great deeds on our behalf.

Rx 11 *Fast; Lie Fallow*

Imagine a one or two week fast — total shutdown — from activities. It would be an interesting experience. Perhaps *jarring* would be a better word. For most moderns, the experience would be so foreign that we could not tolerate it.

For the first few days, we would probably be so disoriented that we would feel the experiment is not working. As with any withdrawal there might be a nervous feeling, akin to panic. Just because it feels so uncertain is no reason that we should judge prematurely. Remember, it takes time to learn right living — just as it takes time to learn how to ride a bike or detoxify from alcohol.

Go to the mountains and lock yourself in a cabin for a week. Don't bring any electronics. Just sleep when you get tired and wake when you have slept enough.

Even a regular day away can be beneficial. "I've learned the necessity of stepping back, looking where I was going, and having a monthly quiet day to be drawn up into the mind of God," says theologian John Stott.[12]

Rx 12 *Remember Who It Is That Gets Things Done*

God is the multiplying coefficient for our labors. We might only do fifty percent of all that we had planned tomorrow and yet *accomplish* five hundred percent more in terms of eternal significance — if our efforts are sensitive to the promptings and empowerment of the Holy Spirit.

Someone has said, "God can do in twenty minutes what it takes us twenty years to do." Let's trust more and do less.

Is it busyness that moves mountains. . . or faith?

CHAPTER 5

■ ■ ■ ■ ■ ■ ■ ■

Change and Stress

- The only trouble with success is that the formula for achieving it is the same as the formula for a nervous breakdown.—CHUCK SWINDOLL

- Although people will pay to fix their stress, they are not about to change the lifestyle that is causing it. —DAVID C. MCCASLAND

- Stress may be the spice of life or the kiss of death. —ROBERT ELLIOT, M.D., CARDIOLOGIST

- Things get worse under pressure.—MURPHY'S LAW OF THERMODYNAMICS

52 years

William Shakespeare was born in 1564. When he died in 1616, the world around him was not very different from the world he was born into. The occupational spectrum was the same, lifestyles were unchanged, disease and life expectancy were the same, family makeup was the same. And so it has been, from generation to generation, for century upon century, that life has been slow and static, with the most accurate descriptor being *same*, not *changing*.

But at the beginning of this century, change picked up momentum. It has continued to accelerate through the last few decades, and the acceleration is not linear but exponential. Change is like a massive tidal wave that sweeps us up and dominates us by its own independent and autonomous strength. As a direct consequence, it has given birth to an unprecedented stress epidemic that has taxed our capacity for adaptation.

For millennia, change was slow, controlled, assessable; now it convulses at warp speed. There has been more change from 1900 to present than in all of recorded history prior to 1900. And there is no deceleration in sight.

Change and stress reside together in the same equation. The key to understanding stress is understanding change.

CHANGE OVERLOAD

In the sixties, Bob Dylan alerted us to the fact that "the times, they are a-changin'." In 1970, Alvin Toffler proved it. Toffler had written other books, but it was *Future Shock* that put his name on tongues across America. The book sold millions, became an overnight classic, and was not only required reading, but required mentioning.

Toffler was concerned about not only rapid change, but more importantly, the astounding increase in the rate of change. Future Shock, maintained Toffler, is a "roaring current of change, a current so powerful today that it overturns institutions, shifts our values and shrivels our roots. Change is the process by which the future invades our lives . . . unless man quickly learns to control the rate of change in his personal affairs as well as in society at large, we are doomed to a massive adaptational breakdown."[1]

Toffler saw more clearly than Dylan. We were not merely a-changin'—we were explodin'. And, predictably, it has only increased. We no longer live in a place planted on a firm foundation but instead on an ever-shifting, ever-changing continuum of uncertainty that keeps everyone off balance.

Change has been pervasive in all areas of our society. In our personal lives, we change jobs between seven to ten times in our lifetime and careers three times. Women, on average, change jobs every 5.8 years and men every 7.6 years.[2]

We change residences even more frequently. "In the United States a man builds a house in which to spend his old age, and he sells it before the roof is on," wrote Alexis de Tocqueville in 1835. Today the average American occupies twelve or thirteen residences in the course of a lifetime, twice as many as the average person in Britain or France and four times as many as the typical Irish.[3] In a five-year period, between forty and fifty percent of Americans will change addresses. Part of this is due to the U.S. divorce rate, the highest in the world—another modern change with its own set of stressful consequences.

With job and address changes, the kids change schools and friends, while the entire family changes neighbors, churches, insurance, doctors, dentists, and grocery stores. If we don't move, our neighbors do. Even without a move, we may change doctors because of insurance mandates.

This change dynamic affects the local church also. With the average family moving once every five years and senior pastors changing churches on the average of every four years, instability ensues. Even people who don't move to a different town still change churches on average every four years. We also increasingly change church traditions. In the 1950s only four percent of church members in the average church had grown up in another denomination. By 1993, the figure had risen to forty percent.[4] And then the pew Bible is likely to change to a new translation chosen from among 450 English language versions.

The profound social and moral changes of the past half century have devastated traditions, reconfigured families, rewritten rules, and upset moral structures. The ripple effects have turned into shock waves, affecting virtually every quadrant of our social experience: governmental spending, poverty statistics, parenting and day care, birth control and sexuality, medical ethics, beginning and end of life decisions, music, movies, and television. All of which prompted historian William Manchester, when comparing 1930 with 1990, to write "One can almost say that everything that was then is not now, and everything that was not then now is."[5]

"But now we must face the fact that we all live in radically different times," explains psychiatrist Dr. Frederic Flach in his book *Resilience.* "It is one thing to go through periods of personal disruption and recovery when the world around us is relatively stable. It is quite another to have to do so when the rate at which change is taking place throughout the world has become incredibly accelerated and whole cultures find themselves on the verge of disarray. More and more, each of us is at greater risk. We have little choice but to take responsibility for weathering change very much unto ourselves."[6]

These conditions represent a change dynamic unprecedented in human history. By God's design, we were created remarkably adaptable. But adaptability has limits.

STRESS OVERLOAD

Stress is directly related to change. Three hundred years ago, people did not have much stress. Yes, they had pain, tragedy, destitution, hardship, and suffering — but they did not have much change, and therefore, by definition, they did not have much stress. Today's conditions, however, are vastly different. The flood of change sweeping over every quadrant of our existence has brought with it unprecedented stress. Vintage overload.

Stress is an internal physiologic adaptation to any change in our environment. This *stress response* was God's idea, placed within us at Creation. Despite the generally negative connotation of stress, the stress response is value neutral.

Would you like a stress-free life? If you are wise, you would not accept that option — no matter how tempting it might sound. If we do not have change, challenge, and novelty in our lives, we would literally die.

How about a *low-stress* life compared to a *high-stress* life? Surprisingly, studies reveal that most people would prefer the high-stress scenario. Having little memory of what the low-stress state feels like, most of us can't recall being bored. To remind you, it's . . . boring.

Without at least some change and stress, we languish. But if, on the other hand, there is too much change and stress, our adaptational mechanism breaks down. Because of our contemporary turbo-charged change dynamic, most of America is in a hyperstress environment.

Stress contributes to a myriad of illnesses. Some patients exhibit cardiovascular symptoms, such as racing pulse or chest pain. Some experience gastrointestinal problems such as hyperacidity, irritable bowel, or diarrhea. Some break out in rashes or develop tics. Headaches, as well as other musculoskeletal aches and pains, are common. Some people experience immunological compromise, resulting in more infections, or possibly even higher risks for cancer. Still others have insomnia, anxiety, depression. . . . The list is endless.

When stress is pushed to the extremes, burnout results. Next time you go into a forest, take a small sapling and bend it over. When you let go, the tree will straighten back up again. Now take that same sapling and bend it until it breaks. When you let go, it cannot straighten back up. This is a picture of burnout. In the same way, in our lives, we adapt and adapt and adapt—and then something inside of us snaps. When this happens, healing comes slowly. I personally do not believe we ever get back the same level of enthusiasm, innocence, and passion that we previously had. Yes, there is life after burnout. But most of the healing is by scar formation.

PRESCRIPTIONS FOR CONTROLLING CHANGE AND BLUNTING STRESS

While we cannot completely stop change or eliminate stress, there are practical steps we can take to control these areas of overload.

Rx 1 *Slow the Rate of Change*
Much of our personal change stems from broader societal trends around us, and make no mistake, these are powerful forces. Nevertheless, a significant component of every person's change index is a direct result of personal choice.

If you are stressed out, slow the rate of change. If you have been future-shocked, hunker down for a spell. Put that job decision on hold for six months. Don't move. Let the kids finish the school year. Keep your church, your pastor, your friends. If you are stressed out, you will need them more than you might think.

If you choose *not* to slow the rate of change, consider obtaining a life-change score from a counselor. A life-change index assigns points to various changes (everything from getting a pet to losing a loved one). This will allow you to quantify both the positive and negative changes in your life, each of which contribute to your overall score. If the numbers rise too high, seriously consider putting a moratorium on any significant change for six to twelve months. Otherwise, you face a high likelihood of physical or emotional illness.

Rx 2 *Move Less Often*

Make a conscious decision to sink in roots—one house, one town, one church—for one decade. Plant a one-foot-high apple tree in your yard, and don't move until it yields a bushel. Better yet, plant an acorn, and don't move until the grandchildren build a tree fort in its branches.

Not only does this slow the adaptational response—which is equivalent to stress—but it also encourages us to invest in relationships and learn to deal with issues over a longer period of time.

Also we should make note of the stress involved in building a home. Although I have not seen studies, there is plenty of anecdotal evidence. One physician's wife told me, "If your marriage can survive building a house, it can survive anything." Be forewarned.

Pastors are often called to relocate frequently. While this can be involuntary, at other times there is a prominent element of volition involved. But there is much to commend pastoral longevity in a church.

Rx 3 *Don't Overvalue Newness*

Just because something is new doesn't mean it is better. We tend to want the newest, automatically thinking it is best. Yet how often do we find some forty-year-old garden utensil at a garage sale which is more functional than the one we bought at the hardware store yesterday?

In medicine we are continuously being encouraged to try the "newest" medications. This means, however, we must now learn the dosage and side effects, and the patient has to adjust to a different regimen. Often these drugs are much more expensive and prove to be no more effective than the older, cheaper medicines we have been using for decades.

Change is sometimes improvement, but it is often pure novelty. If it adds to your stress level, see past the novelty and think twice.

Rx 4 *Establish Stability Zones*

When the only seeming constant is change, most of us can benefit from having areas in our lives where change is minimized and where stability and reliability are assured. "In the face of rapid change and over choice, a 'personal stability zone' is an important source of security and anchorage," observes stress author Walt Schafer. "A personal stability zone is any object, place, activity, belief, person, or group that is stable and constant through time, regardless of other changes."[7]

Safe havens become a valuable respite from a chaotic and otherwise unpredictable world. They can be as simple as a favorite spot for meditation or prayer, as predictable as a routine annual vacation spot, or as accepting as a long-term small group. Such friendly and comfortable points of reference become familiar harbors in stormy seas.

Rx 5 *Put More Control in Your Life*

The control issue is of central importance in determining the destructiveness of a stress experience. The first thing we should tell ourselves in any stressful situation is that we have more control over circumstances than we think. This is especially true of our *response* to the stressor. Before external stressors can make us miserable, they must first have our permission. If we can learn to rise above stressful circumstances, we will have discovered a key not only to stress, but also to spiritual maturity.

A helpful equation is E + R = O (Event + Response = Outcome). You might not have control over the Event, but you do have control over the Response.

Rx 6 *Develop a Network of Caring Friends*

Studies consistently reveal a link between nurturing friendships and personal well-being. If I am hurting and go to a caring friend, empathy is in itself therapeutic. Researchers have studied what is called "the disclosure effect." If I have a frustration inside and am able to reveal my heart to a safe friend, simply "disclosing" the problem will improve my well-being in measurable ways. It is not necessary for my friend to fix the problem—all he or she has to do is listen.

Unfortunately, the rushed, stressful, marginless lifestyles so typical of modern living are toxic to friendships. It is very difficult to maintain mutual nurturing friendships in our nanosecond, change-overloaded culture.

Rx 7 *Spread Goodwill*

According to Dr. Hans Selye, the father of stress research, one of the greatest buffers against the ravages of future stress is to spread goodwill in the lives of other people. When stress comes to visit us, these people will surround us with their affirmation and support.

"Earn others' goodwill by helping them, and you will help yourself" might sound self-serving. But from another perspective, it is simply God closing His own feedback loop.

Rx 8 *Learn to Laugh*

The therapeutic benefits of laughter are well established in modern medicine as state-of-the-art, stress-reducing therapeutics. We don't yet fully understand *why* laughter works, but we do know that people who laugh heal faster.

The peak age of laughter is age four. I don't know if God is behind this symmetry, but four-year-olds laugh once every four minutes, or four hundred times a day. Adults, on the other hand, laugh fifteen times a day. If we were to follow four-year-olds around and laugh every time they do, positive things would happen to both our bodies and spirits. Laughter lowers the pulse and blood pressure and seems to improve immune functioning. One psychiatrist recommends thirty minutes of therapeutic laughter every day. Some people call this "inner jogging." Another laughter consultant calls it a cerebral enema.

The ability to laugh at oneself is perhaps most valuable. "Blessed are those who laugh at themselves, for they will never cease to be amused." In addition, laughing at our own problems has a way of putting them into perspective. One person, after a hurricane in southern Florida devastated his house, put a sign up in the front yard: "Open House." It didn't help him rebuild, but it surely helped him weather the storm.

Rx 9 *Play Music*

Seventy-five percent of Americans use music to de-stress. In response to the increasingly stressful conditions of everyday life, music therapists are emerging all across the United States. Studies reveal that surgeons who can choose their own music in the operating room have improved cardiovascular parameters during stressful surgeries. If, on the other hand, the music was chosen *for* them, there was no such benefit.

When God created music, He somehow ordained that it would be able to penetrate through superficial layers of our consciousness and go straight to the depths of our spirit. It has been my own experience, during times of significant stress, that music has helped me when nothing else could.

Find the music that ministers most precisely to your need and play it over and over. Massage your soul with a divine, supernatural balm, directly from the creative loving heart of God to yours.

Rx 10 *Rest*

"Come to me, all you who are weary and heavy burdened," offered Jesus, "and I will give you rest."[8] Just because He said this two thousand years ago doesn't mean it doesn't apply today. We can listen to culture when it says that rest is an idle waste; or we can listen to Christ when He says that rest is a divine gift. I've already cast my vote.

Rx 11 *Breathe Deeply*

Inhaling slowly, take a deep breath as you count to eight. Now, hold it for another eight seconds. Then exhale very slowly for the count of eight. This simple 8-8-8 breathing exercise is low-tech but highly effective. It forces us to slow the hurry for a brief time and to think about our breathing instead of our stress. Through physiologic mechanisms I don't fully understand, it seems to melt tension.

Rx 12 *Exercise It Away*

Many people "sweat to forget," finding it highly effective. Of course, our overloaded lives often don't allow time to exercise, and our emotional exhaustion makes it seem distinctly unappealing. But at least one study revealed a jogging program equal to antidepressants in treating depression.

Rx 13 *Stress Switch*

If engaged in a stressful activity—for example, attempting unsuccessfully to balance the checkbook—don't set it aside and lay on the couch thinking about the problem. This would penalize the mind with continued frustration. Instead practice "stress switching." Do something physical, something enjoyable. For example, I cut and stack wood or mow the lawn. I enjoy garden and lawn work and find this therapeutic. Others use sports or jogging. Even a short amount of stress switching seems to work. Any kind of diversion, representing a voluntary change of activity, is often better than inactively ruminating on the stressor.

Rx 14 *Limit Your Time with Negative People*

Negative people can be draining and one of life's greatest stressors. They usually do not want to get well. No matter how much you invest in them, they often do not improve.

It is a good idea—and a healthy exercise of boundaries—to limit time with such people. If you nevertheless feel you want to reach out to them, please do so. But be careful. Don't be naive. Attempting to "rescue" such people often does not objectively improve their life, it only exhausts yours.

Rx 15 *Don't Worry*

Most of us realize that worry is senseless. The saying "Worry does not empty tomorrow of its troubles—it only empties today of its strength" is succinct and fully accurate.

Beyond this commonsense knowledge, we now realize that worry can be medically harmful. A recent study in the medical journal *Circulation* reveals that people who had increased measurements of worry have poorer health outcomes.[9]

Jesus advised, "Do not worry about tomorrow for tomorrow will worry about itself. Each day has enough trouble of its own."[10] Even though many believers have heard this verse for decades, nevertheless they freely worry as if the Bible were silent. How strange it has not occurred to us that such worry is sin! "I had to learn that worry is sin," confesses Corrie ten Boom, "before I could get rid of the worry."[11]

Rx 16 *Reduce Stress*

Many books and seminars emphasize *stress management*. This is an important concept to teach, as we can blunt the ill-effects of stress by changing our reaction to stressors. Certainly our *perception* of the event matters a great deal, and our *response* to that perception matters even more. As was written even in ancient times: "Men are distressed not by things, but by the views which they take of them."

However, it is also important to recognize that if we live in a hyperstressed environment, *reducing* stress is just as important as managing it. Those who suggest our total approach should be "management" are not being realistic. If living in extraordinarily stressful circumstances day-in and day-out, the sanest thing a person could do is to change the circumstances, not just adapt.

Rx 17 *Problem Solved*
Even though God did not give Christians a magical stress exemption, He did remove forever the most important stressor in the universe. When we are feeling overwhelmed, it is good to remember that our biggest problem—larger than all the problems in the world added together and multiplied by infinity—was solved at the Cross. Forever. Freely.

"In the world you will have tribulation," said Jesus. "But be of good cheer; I have overcome the world."[12]

CHAPTER 6

■ ■ ■ ■ ■ ■ ■ ■ ■

Choice and Decision

■ The right to choose is as American as apple pie (or pumpkin pie, or Boston cream pie, or pecan pie).
—ROBERT KANIGEL

■ One of the tenacious paradoxes of technology is that we have more choices, but less time to choose.
—EDWARD WENK, JR.

■ We are, in fact, racing toward "overchoice."
—ALVIN TOFFLER

■ While incarcerated prisoners make twenty decisions a day, those of us walking the streets make one hundred and twenty decisions a day.—PRISON FELLOWSHIP

While writing *Margin* in the early 1990s, I rented a winter cabin in the lonely Wisconsin north woods. In a fortress guarded by snow and cold I would frequently spend two weeks at a time there, writing nights and sleeping days. During that creative interlude I came to appreciate the solitude and simplicity of rustic living.

When it came time to buy supplies, the tiny town of Birchwood was my only destination. The grocery store was a small, spotless IGA with hardwood floors and few customers. I grew to love that store and its clean simplicity. While the average supermarket today swells with thirty thousand different products, this IGA perhaps had fewer than two thousand. But I needed only five, maybe ten. Why wander miles of aisles?

The store had six choices of cereal. Not hard choices—I was satisfied with any of them. Back home I curiously inventoried the cereal variety available at our family grocery: 184 different kinds. Even when I knew the specific cereal I wanted, it still took time to find it amidst so many competing varieties and sizes.

That small rural grocery illustrated for me a valuable lesson: Just because we have increased choice does not automatically mean we have increased benefit. If choice is a freedom, it can also be a burden. Yet the breadth of choices will only continue to proliferate. "Ironically, the people of the future may suffer not from an absence of choice, but from a paralyzing surfeit of it," explained Alvin Toffler. "They may turn out to be victims of that peculiarly super-industrial dilemma: overchoice . . . the point at which the advantages of diversity and individualization are canceled by the complexity of the buyer's decision-making process."[1]

Writer Robert Kanigel understands about such overload and limits. "Here's the problem: While choices multiply, we stay pretty much the same. Our bodies and minds remain the bottleneck through which choice must pass. We still have the same brains our forebears did, still only twenty-four hours a day to use them. We still need time and energy to listen, look, absorb, distinguish, and decide. The opportunity to choose among many options is, of course, a good thing. But maybe you can have too much of a good thing? Even of choice itself? . . . Each choice saps energy, takes time, makes a big deal out of what isn't."[2]

So much of daily living is now involved with the making of trivial decisions based on this incredible profusion of choice. As Thoreau wrote in *Walden,* "Our life is frittered away by detail."

To illustrate, here are some statistics compiled over the past fifteen years researching societal trends. Some are very current, others perhaps not. Nevertheless, they accurately convey the magnitude of the problem involved in contemporary choice and decision overload.

> 55 medical specialties
> 60 different kinds of Muzak ("elevator music")
> 80 different blood pressure medicines
> 93 brands of bottled water at an Amsterdam boutique
> 125 kinds of yogurt
> 126 different types of subcompact cars
> 177 kinds of salad dressing

184 kinds of breakfast cereal
249 kinds of soap
250 kinds of toothpaste
450 English language versions of the Bible
500 different bachelor's degrees being offered in college
551 kinds of coffee
752 different models of cars and trucks sold in the U.S.
1,200 new business books every year
1,500 movies per month to choose from with a satellite dish
1,500 insurance payers in the American system
2,500 types of light bulbs—in one store alone
3,000 different medications in the Physician's Desk Reference
4,500 new children's books every year
5,000 magazines to choose from
30,000 different products in the average grocery store
58,000 new books or new editions every year
1,000,000 titles from Barnes & Noble on-line
25,000,000 different versions of automobiles when all possible combinations of styles, options, and colors available are taken into account

Missionaries returning from abroad routinely comment on the staggering and almost gluttonous selection of goods and services available in American stores. For example, Oreo cookies—now you can buy mint, double stuff, chocolate dipped, giant, or regular. I don't remember any crescendo of discontent responsible for this new proliferation.

Toothpaste is available in 250 different varieties. As I approached the Crest display recently, I found not only regular but also mint, gel, kid's gel, tartar control regular, tartar control gel— all in both pumps and tubes, not to mention a multitude of sizes.

Milk now comes in whole milk, reduced-fat milk, low-fat milk, non-fat milk, buttermilk, acidophilus milk, calcium-fortified milk, soy milk (plain), lactaid, goat's milk, carbonated milk, and milk with juice. And ice cream? . . . the hundreds of flavors include avocado and shrimp. "Recently, I was in an ice-cream parlor in San Francisco that served the sort of fresh-fruit drinks sometimes called smoothies," observes columnist Calvin Trillin, "and I noticed that the add-ins you could get in your smoothie (most of them for an extra fifty cents) were listed as follows: *spirulina, bee pollen, brewer's yeast, calcium, ginseng, lecithin, protein powder mix, vitamins & minerals, and wheat germ.* In Kansas City, people would pay a lot more than fifty cents to have any of those things removed from whatever they were eating and replaced with Betty Lucas' chicken batter."[3] Obviously, not everyone has the same tastes—part of the reason for choice I suppose.

On top of this are the 327 *billion* discount coupons published annually in the U.S. People now wander through their ultra-mega-supermarket, purses and pockets stuffed with coupons, with little thought that their minutes and hours are increasingly being consumed by the trivialities of modern commercialism. Personally, I can think of better ways to invest my time than browsing among thirty kinds of toilet paper.

DECISION STRESS AND PROGRESS

Where did this mountainous avalanche of choice come from? "The most fundamental reason we moderns are plagued with an over-abundance of choices," explains sociologist S. D. Gaede, "is that we are a choice-seeking people. We want more alternatives, more options, more possibilities."[4]

His observation is true, yet there is a deeper reason: progress. As we have already seen, progress works by differentiating our environment, automatically giving us more and more, faster and faster. Progress relentlessly results in choice. And *choice* requires *decision*.

"Because of the rapidity of change occurring in our society . . . leaders are faced with the need to make more decisions than ever, and to make them more quickly than was expected previously," observe researchers George Barna and William Paul McKay.[5] Not only have decisions proliferated, but the context of the decisions is often more burdensome. It is one thing to decide whether to get rippled barbecue chips or unrippled sour cream and onion; it is entirely another to decide to unplug the respirator of a loved one.

The simple decisions don't cost us much, and we make them easily: "I'll have a Big Mac, fries, and a Coke." But modernity has brought us new choices which are not so easy: whether to have children and how many; whether to buy a house and how big a mortgage to assume; whether to move and how often; whether to change jobs; whether to change churches; whether both spouses should work outside the home or not; whether to put Grandpa into the nursing home.

The psychic stress associated with decision overload contributes much to our exhaustion. In medicine, we encounter it daily. Some days I come home from the clinic so fatigued that I crawl into the house. "What should we have for dinner?" Linda asks. "I don't know and I can't afford to think about it," I say. "I'll eat the silverware . . . the china. But please don't ask me to make another decision."

In 1947, the first *Physician's Desk Reference* (PDR) contained three hundred pages. Fifty years later it has swollen to nearly three thousand pages. How does one choose from the scores of anti-hypertensives or the hundreds of antibiotics?

One year, I received 461 invitations to medical conferences. One conference I attended in Anaheim listed over three hundred workshops or events to choose from in three days. Six months later, I attended another conference in San Diego where, again in three days, I had 511 options for involvement. It seems I spent half my time there trying to decipher the conference brochure.

ANALYSIS OVERLOAD

Choices require decisions. And decisions require analysis. The increased analytical burden required by choice and decision over-load appeared on our psychological agenda almost overnight. Yet even if analysis overload sneaked up on us and remains largely unidentified, it nevertheless results in enough daily complexity to cross a rabbi's eyes. Sales, payment options, fast food menus, IRS rules, administrative decisions, computer software. . . . Choices must first be analyzed and understood before they can be decided.

For example, AT&T (or Sprint or MCI) sends an advertisement proposing a new way to save money by reconfiguring my long distance service. It sounds good. It looks good. But is it? Really? Who knows. And even though I have a physics degree and have won math awards, I do not have the capacity to investigate. Why does AT&T want to save me money anyway? Money currently going to their pocket they now wish to switch to my pocket? Right.

When paying his phone bill, Leonard Laster, M.D., was struck with the same problem. Suspecting he was paying more than the advertised rates, he called the company to check. The woman who answered informed him he was free to investigate their various plans and choose the one that best suited his usage pattern. "When I told her that my postgraduate training in analytical mathematics was inadequate to meet such a challenge, she said that if I wished, she would enter my billing data into a computer program and perform the analysis for me. I said that I wished, and before long she determined that I had been overpaying for some time.

"She transferred my account to a more appropriate plan, and made a 'courtesy adjustment.' . . . I attempted to explore with her— but got nowhere—why the company hadn't alerted me to this situation earlier, and why the burden of the cost-benefit analysis had been covertly shifted on to my rather meager decision-making capabilities."

Following that encounter, Laster began reflecting on the growing number of analytical assignments required by the routine activities of daily living. "Are you off to lunch in a fast-food restaurant? You will be confronted with an array of menu packages— a hamburger, drink, and dessert at one price; french fries and chicken dish, with or without dessert, at another. You will have to determine the most financially effective buy, but not to worry: a simple multi-factorial variable systematic analysis will point you in the optimal direction."[6]

Analysis overload—from credit card deals to catalog sales to travel promotionals—has become an integral part of living in a choice-overloaded world. "How can you sort through preschools,

HMOs, retirement plans, or roofing contractors with equanimity intact?" asks Kanigel. "Each present difficult choices, riddled with complexities, uncertainties, places to go wrong. Maybe you're smart. And maybe you're well-educated. But you can't have a Ph.D. in *everything*."[7]

A soloist once gave a concert in our church, and just before the break, announced that tapes would be available for six dollars each, or three for twenty dollars. No one laughed. Probably no one had the energy to do the math.

PRESCRIPTIONS FOR EASING CHOICE OVERLOAD AND DECISION STRESS

We cannot escape: choices requiring decisions requiring analysis are here to stay. Some simplifying principles, however, will help ease the distress and confusion along the way.

Rx 1 *Simplify Your Decision Making*

Decide to limit choices rather than continuously expand them. Why buy more clothes, for example, when you already have an abundant choice?

When I got tired of deciding what to wear to the office each day, I settled on a simplicity-based solution: either brown or blue pants, and either a white or blue shirt. Everything matched, and I could get dressed in the dark.

Similarly, when traveling, I have a "speaking uniform": gray slacks, a blue shirt, and a blue blazer. I don't own a suit. Einstein, it seems, owned several outfits exactly the same. On his way to discovering relativity, he did not wish to waste time deciding among trivialities.

Rx 2 *Simplify Meal Choices*

During college, I studied in Switzerland for a year, living with a Swiss physician's family. Although enjoying the highest standard of living in the world, it was interesting to witness how simply the Swiss often chose to live compared to the average American family.

Take mealtime. Every morning, we had plain homemade yogurt and dense German bread . . . the kind that if it fell off the table, it would break your foot. For the evening meal, we had the same dense bread with cheese or jam.

For the noon meal, we all sat leisurely around the dinner table for two hours (the phone never rang, and they did not own a television), while my Swiss mother served the meal. She prepared and rotated only six or seven menus. Why have more? We loved each of the options she provided.

There is no need to have fifty different kinds of foods. Decide on a dozen or so that the family really enjoys, and then stick with this routine until it is time to change. Remember, most of the world eats the same thing three times a day—and prefers it that way.

A pediatrician from Alabama wrote me after working short-term in an impoverished Central American clinic. One of her routine habits was to ask children their favorite thing to eat. Every child gave the same answer: food.

"Plan meals with your family's likes and dislikes in mind," write authors Mimi Wilson and Mary Beth Lagerborg, "but once you've set the menu, try this rule: Today's Menu—Two Choices: *Take It or Leave It.*"[8]

Rx 3 *Develop Enjoyable Routines*

Routines can, at times, be boring. But they can also be comforting or even delightful. For example, many people have an established routine for Saturday or Sunday morning breakfast. To simplify our Sunday mornings when the boys were growing up, we would have "Sunday cereal" each week—a more expensive kind of cereal that the boys enjoyed. It would vary, depending on what was on sale. But it was always something they looked forward to. And it simplified that busy morning for the entire family.

Most people drive to work over the same route each day, use the same parking spot, buy gas from the same store, and shop for groceries the same day every week.

Some people have hamburgers every Wednesday or fish every Friday. Some buy donuts every Saturday morning, have pot roast every Sunday dinner, or bake stollen every Christmas.

These routines might not add spice to life, but they do add a much needed and pleasurable *stability*. These routines are called programmed decisions, and they cut down greatly on decision stress. The vast majority of our daily decisions are "programmed" in a healthy way. Routines work.

Rx 4 *Make Decisions and Stick with Them*

Making decisions costs us in both time and energy. There is seldom a compelling reason to revisit the decision frequently. If you have decided against cable, don't redecide weekly. If you decide not to attend R-rated movies, then stick with it. If your insurance costs too much, then research the options and make an informed decision. But not quarterly—that's too much decision stress.

We have already seen how fasting, twentieth-century style, can play an important role in addressing overload. Consider fasting from choices for a period, to better concentrate on the deeper truths of life. One of the purposes of fasting is to concentrate on the transcendent. Consider shutting down the trivial to give depth a chance.

Rx 5 *Value Traditions*

Traditions are called traditions precisely because they form a link to the past. One value of tradition is that it is a celebration of sameness, not change. And when you do not change, you do not have to make a choice. "The value of a tradition is that it obviates the need for a decision," explains sociologist S. D. Gaede. "We need them because a life empty of tradition is a life void of its past and incapable of producing a meaningful future. It is a life of impoverished freedom."[9]

Identify those traditions in your personal, family, and church life that have special significance and protect them vigorously. There is nothing shameful about *old-fashioned* if the tradition represents a rich heritage and contains vital connections to the past. We need only to remember the festivals and remembrances instituted by God to understand that "sameness," in the opinion of the Almighty, can be a valuable anchor for the soul.

Rx 6 *Be Wary of Advertisements*

All ads should come with a disclaimer: "Caution: Faulty logic ahead." Ads are not trying to be helpful; they are trying to be convincing. Ads will complicate, not simplify, your decisions. And they will bias you toward purchases you will later regret. When making choices, trust your own judgment.

Rx 7 *Ignore Marketing Gimmicks*

If a company is encouraging you to reconfigure your current service or try a new one, ask yourself one simple question: Why? Once you understand the answer, your decision making is made simple.

Forget it. Don't even go through the math. Be assured that *they* have already done their math and it comes out advantageous for them.

Maybe I've grown cynical. But it simplifies my choices, my decisions, my analysis, and my life to simply ignore marketing gimmicks.

Rx 8 *Keep "Good Enough" over "Better"*

We often decide against something simply because fashion dictates tell us it is outmoded. Carpet, curtains, clothes. Why place the extra burden of decision upon us in this arena when we should perhaps be saving our strength for those decisions of greater import?

Unless they are really important to you, forget about the bells and whistles. Do we really need that new car simply because it has a new option? Or that new computer—when our current computer has fifty times more power then we will ever need? Even Microsoft, in an advertisement, claims, "Think about how many features you have in all of your software. Hundreds of them just waiting to do your bidding. If only you knew how to use them all. Because if you're like most busy people, you simply haven't got time to learn every feature in every program." Therefore, they reason, buy this Microsoft Office Upgrade.

My answer: Thanks, but what I have is already "good enough."

Rx 9 *Look Beyond the Glitter*

It is hard in the midst of a ricocheting life to choose the best things, the right things—they don't glitter as much on the surface. We eat what tastes sweetest at the time, not what ultimately digests the healthiest. There is the immediate and then the delayed—and in choosing the immediate we often sacrifice the wisdom of choosing what is best for the delayed.

When young physicians ask advice about choosing their future practice locations, I advise them to look beyond the honeymoon. The first six months of practice seems great, no matter where you go. But far more important is the first six years. "The validity of a decision is best judged on the basis of long-term consequences," observes engineer Edward Wenk, Jr. But under stress, he goes on to warn, we tend to discount the future.[10]

Decide with the future in view. You will want to live there someday.

Rx 10 *Choose Appropriate Load, Not Overload*

Although people don't always regard it as such, choosing too much to be involved in is indeed a choice. Yes, culture is responsible for much of the overload that is swamping us. But we can choose to create a margin if we want it badly enough. All it takes is a sufficient amount of counter-cultural intent.

Remember: When we insist on living overloaded lives, this choice not only damages our own well-being, but also inflicts damage on those around us.

Rx 11 *Own Your Decisions*

Many people bemoan how trapped they are in life: the boss expects too much, the family demands too much, the debts mount too fast. But ultimately we live in a world of our own choosing—even if we don't "feel" like the choice is ours. "The loss of felt choice is an everyday experience," explains psychologist Larry Crabb. "But we must state clearly that loss of *felt* choice does not mean loss of *actual* choice."[11]

"We who lived in the concentration camps can remember the men who walked through the huts comforting others, giving away their last piece of bread," recalls the late Viktor Frankl, in perhaps his most famous quotation. "They may have been few in number, but they offer sufficient proof that everything can be taken from a man but one thing: the last of his freedoms—to choose one's attitude in any given set of circumstances, to choose one's own way."

Ultimately, we are emotionally healthier and relationally happier if we own our choices. "One's philosophy is not best expressed in words. It is expressed in the choices one makes," observed former First Lady Eleanor Roosevelt. "And the choices we make are ultimately our responsibility."

Rx 12 *Pray for Wisdom in Decision Making*

We should probably pray for *all* the decisions in our lives, small or large. But at least, as a first step, we need to pray more for the important decisions, those requiring resources beyond our understanding. God promises wisdom for those who ask and trust.[12] Many times we lack this wisdom simply because we do not pray for it.[13]

I once saw a banner on the back of a church where I was speaking that stopped me in my tracks: "A life without prayer is a boast against God." Not a wise way to make decisions.

Rx 13 *Daily Re-choose the Things of God*

Just before he died, Moses reminded people of the need to choose carefully, for much is at stake. "This day I call heaven and earth as witnesses against you that I have set before you life and death, blessing and curses. Now choose life, so that you and your children may live, and that you may love the LORD your God, listen to his voice, and hold fast to him."[14]

Joshua, following Moses, declared his choice: "But if serving the LORD seems undesirable to you then choose for yourselves this day whom you will serve. . . . But as for me and my house, we will serve the LORD."[15]

Do we daily choose righteousness? Haddon Robinson talks about a "glad surrender" to the things of God. God, it seems, owns it all anyway. Our time belongs to God. So does our money. So do our careers and our possessions. Our families belong to God, we belong to God, our future belongs to God.

Only the choice belongs to us.

CHAPTER 7

■■■■■■■■

Debt

- ■ We will loan you enough money to get you completely out of debt.—SIGN IN A LOAN OFFICE

- ■ More than a billion people around the world live on less than a dollar a day.—RON SIDER

- ■ Interest works night and day, in fair weather and in foul. It gnaws at a man's substance with invisible teeth.
  —HENRY WARD BEECHER

- ■ There are two times in a man's life when he should not speculate — when he cannot afford it, and when he can.
  —MARK TWAIN

Economics has gained a dominant ascendancy over the affairs of the human race in a very short time, staggering even economic thinkers. For millennia, people were destitute, but largely self-sufficient in their destitution. If they needed a house, they built it. If they needed clothes, they made them. If they wanted bread, they baked it. Even at the time of the Revolutionary War, when ninety-two percent of Americans earned their living on the farm, independence and rugged individualism were the rule of the day. But in the same year the United States declared its independence, Adam Smith published his treatise on *The Wealth of Nations* and the world changed forever.

Smith, the father of modern economic science, taught that *free enterprise* was a higher state of historical evolution than was *government-constrained enterprise*. In this laissez-faire capitalism, humans "naturally" seek self-betterment through the economic system. As forces of competition are played out in the marketplace, an "invisible hand" translates the entire process into benefit for all by adjusting costs, goods, and labor.

In reaction to the unemployment and the Great Depression in the 1930s, John Maynard Keynes deviated from Smith's laissez-faire by urging governments to take a more active role in helping to regulate the economy, especially to reverse downturns. This led to the notion that it is acceptable for borrowing and credit to fuel such economic interventions. With such thinking in place, the U.S. national debt began to grow in the 1930s, followed by corporate debt in the 1940s. Shortly thereafter, personal debt began to swell, and by the mid-1980s, our international trade balance turned negative for the first time since 1917.

Today, our lives are addictively intertwined in the economic system, and the credit-debt mentality has been fully normalized. "Someone has described a modern American," wrote pastor and college president Paul Billheimer, "as a person who drives a bank-financed car over a bond-financed highway on credit card gas to open a charge account at a department store so he can fill his Savings and Loan financed home with installment-purchased furniture."[1]

This economic ascendancy has seen remarkable successes but equally vexatious problems. In 1997, for example, health care costs for the first time exceeded one trillion dollars—$3,759 for each person in the U.S. Health care economist Paul Starr observes that from 1948 to 1990, the amount businesses paid for health care increased fifteen and six tenths percent per year—clearly not sustainable. Health care has become so costly that millions of self-employed workers are paying as much as eight thousand dollars per family annually for coverage, and more than forty million Americans have no insurance at all.

College tuition represents a second economic predicament, rising at double the rate of inflation and increasing far faster than median family income. Today, only one out of thirteen families can afford to pay full college costs.[2] Home costs are yet another large ticket item. Even with the market correction in some regional areas, we have never recovered from the huge real estate run-up in the 1970s and 1980s.

On top of this, our consumptive notion of the Good Life has dug another debt hole. Even though eighty-two percent of Americans believe "most of us buy and consume far more than we need,"[3] the vast majority of us haven't attempted to modify our earn-and-spend lifestyles. We work harder to pay for the American Dream's debt, and even with two wage earners in the marketplace, a larger number are falling farther behind.

DEBT

Consumer debt currently stands at 1.4 trillion dollars. The amount of debt households must service has grown to its highest share of income in twenty years.[4] Still, with America awash in available cash, financial institutions are encouraging easy credit. Even though some of these loans will default, the profits from the good loans off-set the bad.

We are witnessing a fundamental restructuring of the economic system, borne primarily by the middle class, and people are using credit for types of debt they previously used banks and cash for. Easy borrowing is now so available and people's debt levels so high that many are accessing the credit market for daily expenses. "In the past, families would borrow to buy a car or send kids to college. Today, they're borrowing to gas up the car or send kids to the pediatrician," observe journalists Karen Gullo and Vivian Marino.[5]

Recently a new—and even more worrisome—credit market-ing strategy has emerged: the one-hundred and twenty-five percent loan. It allows borrowers to take out a second mortgage which, when combined with the first, can total as much as one-hundred and twenty-five percent of a home's approved value. "For consumers who own homes it's one more way to keep spending," observes economist Maury Harris.[6] Consumers are, in turn, using this bor-rowed money to pay off credit-card debt, lower monthly mortgage payment (due to longer maturity and lower finance charges), and to provide still *more* buying power. "These risky loans break the time-honored mortgage-lending standards that require banks to lend no more than eighty percent of a home's appraised value," explains *The Wall Street Journal's* Fred R. Bleakley. "History shows that a telltale sign that an economic expansion is nearing its end occurs when lenders start making riskier loans."[7]

One consequence of our mountainous debt is a resurgence of

pawn shops. Twenty-nine million people frequent eleven thousand pawn shops across the U.S. Rather than offering the traditional thirty percent of an item's value in pawn, the new philosophy is to offer fifty percent. The profit comes not by reselling the item, but by repeat customers (increasingly well-to-do) willing to pay twenty-five percent monthly interest charges.

Financial adviser Russ Crosson teaches that, aside from the spiritual implications, debt is unwise for at least two reasons: it is three times as hard to get out of debt as to get into it, and it sentences us to a lower lifestyle in the future. Yet, aside from these individual and family concerns over debt stress, there is a growing systemic concern that this amount of consumer debt will deepen the next recession. Can this debt-sponsored credit gamble pay off indefinitely? "Given a choice between building your business on large debt or facing a firing squad . . . choose the firing squad," advises businessman and author John Capozzi. "There's a chance the firing squad might miss."[8]

CREDIT CARD PUSHERS AND USERS

A huge shift in the debt-credit strategy over the past twenty years has come through the widespread use of credit cards. Up to eighty percent of the population holds at least one major credit card. More than one *billion* are burning holes in wallets and purses in the United States. Yet, even with this level of saturation, 2.5 billion new credit card offers are mailed each year. Each individual receives, on average, twenty offers per year.

Today, we can obtain specialty cards not only through our banks, department stores, gas stations, and phone companies, but also from our union, grocery store, and on-line service. The Association of Trial Lawyers has a card, as do fans of Frank Sinatra. Even sixty-two percent of college students have credit cards.

Meanwhile, reflective of our deeper consumer debt, credit-card debt is doubling every five years and credit-card delinquencies are at the highest level in twenty-four years. Even though only two or three out of one hundred accounts will default, only one in three accounts pay off the balance each month.

One man had twenty credit cards all charged to their limits, and yet was holding on to twenty more "just in case." Even when people go bankrupt, they still receive several credit-card solicitations every month. Some even come preapproved.

BANKRUPTCY

With such easy credit and high levels of debt, it comes as no surprise that we are setting bankruptcy records. In 1996 and again in 1997, we surpassed one million bankruptcies, each a new record. At more than twenty thousand families per week, this is a rate greatly exceeding the Great Depression. In the Great Depression, one out of every 215 people filed for bankruptcy. But if current trends hold, as many as ten percent of America's one hundred million households will declare bankruptcy in the 1990s.

How did this trend pick up such momentum? "The battle to save people from going headlong into debt was lost decades ago when lending shifted to a reliance on income rather than on assets as collateral," explains a *Forbes* article. "This democratization of credit helped fuel the growth of the economy, but it let many people get ever deeper in the credit hole."[9] When asked how people go bankrupt, author Ernest Hemingway easily answered, "Two ways: gradually, then suddenly."

Bankruptcy is largely a white, middle-class problem. Though the popular bankruptcy image is of an undisciplined spendthrift, in fact most bankruptcies are triggered by serious career, marriage, or health problems. The average bankruptcy filer is thirty-something, divorced, with one year of college, and an annual income of around $40,000.

Some say that bankruptcy has followed divorce and illegitimacy in being destigmatized, and we ought to put more shame back into it. Others blame bankruptcy lawyers, with their *Solve your debt problems quick and easy!!* ads. "Bankruptcy has become the latest entitlement in this country," complains MasterCard economist Lawrence Chimerine—not exactly an unbiased observer.[10] Others say that it is not so simple. The average bankrupt person has debt (excluding home mortgages) equal to twice his or her yearly income. And the experience still hurts. How would you like to lose the hundred-year-old family farm on your generational shift?

Prescriptions for Defeating Debt Overload

If culture has one hand around your wallet and another around your throat, these prescriptions will help loosen the grip.

Rx 1 *Commit to a Budget*

For anyone experiencing difficulty with debt, particularly chronic debt, the first step is to set up a budget. The scope of this book does not permit details about budgetary techniques and procedure. There are several excellent and practical books in this area, and I would recommend those by Larry Burkett or Ron Blue and Co.

Before you can set up a budget, you need to know where and how you are spending money. Start now by recording all expenses and retaining all receipts for three months.

Rx 2 *Avoid Future Debt*

The first rule of holes is this: When you are in one, stop digging. Resist the consumptive lifestyle. Say *no* to new purchases. Avoid impulse buying. Don't even go to stores, especially malls. Throw away catalogs. Don't buy now and pay later.

Relax—it isn't so bad. According to studies, "Eighty-six percent of those Americans who have voluntarily cut back their consumption say they are happier as a result."[11]

Rx 3 *Pay Off Debt Systematically*

Make a plan, and stick to it. One idea consists of a four-step process: First, list all debts in order, from the smallest to the largest. Be sure everything is included. Second, make sure to pay at least the minimum payment on each debt each month. Third, double payments on the debt at the top of the list whenever possible. Fourth, as each debt is paid off, apply that payment plus the minimum payment toward the next debt.

Rx 4 *Dispose of Credit Cards*

If you have a debt problem, chances are fairly good that you also have a credit-card problem. If credit cards control you, control them instead. Cut them up and throw them away. Have a ceremony and burn them in the fireplace. Don't try to "modify" credit-card habits, as it often doesn't work. The best approach is cold turkey.

Rx 5 *Develop an Accountability Network*

Any lifestyle change is greatly assisted if an accountability structure is involved. We all cheat on ourselves. But when we bring in the spotlight of scrutiny from another objective person, many of our rationalizations wilt. Find another person or a group and discuss expenditures at least once a week.

Rx 6 *Examine Your Motives for Spending*

What is your psychology of spending? If we better understood why we spend, it will bring us halfway home in our quest for freedom from debt. There are many different motives, not all of which we care to confront. Do we spend because we simply enjoy buying? Do we spend when depressed? When bored? Are we addicted? Do we attempt to buy our way into the hearts of others? Do we buy because of peer pressure from those around us? . . . those at work? . . . those at church? . . . those in our neighborhood? If we own forty pairs of shoes or six automobiles, there is something beneath the surface that needs to be understood before it can be corrected.

Rx 7 *Make Spending Need-based*

If we are honest, only a small minority of our purchases are need-based. Instead, most of our purchases are desire-based, interest-based, pleasure-based, or cash-flow based. Just because we get a raise or a hefty tax refund is no reason to increase spending.

To make certain something is a *need,* don't buy on first pass. Wait. Think about it for a day or a week. Pray about it. If it is a clear need, there will be no ambiguity. But if it is instead a desire, another desire will arise to take its place, thus clarifying the true status of need versus desires.

Rx 8 *Develop Self-sufficiency*

In comparison to previous eras, today we are neither independent nor self-sufficient. We know how to make money—but that is all. When our money-making capacity is threatened or taken away, we must borrow for every aspect of daily living. Our assault on debt will be aided by learning to do for ourselves.

Learn to change your own oil. Grow some of your own food. Sew some of your own clothes. Learn to cut hair. Linda has done this for our family for decades, saving us thousands of dollars and hundreds of hours.

Rx 9 *Integrate Lifestyle Simplicity and Contentment*

Getting out of debt is one thing; staying out is a separate matter entirely. Deeply integrating lifestyle simplicity and contentment is helpful in countering our culturally normalized debt mentality. If we are content with the things God freely gives us, expecting little and rejoicing in whatever comes our way, debt loses its fangs.

"Although less income may result in more financial pressures . . . ," observes Russ Crosson, "income is often not the reason for financial pressures; lifestyle is. Therefore, control your lifestyle, live within your income, and be content in the vocation God has called and equipped you for."[12]

This message is not an easy one. But be encouraged that millions of Americans are discovering such a newfound counter-cultural freedom. Scripture warns us to avoid conformity to the world and entanglement with its affairs.[13] Burdensome debt is in violation of these commands; biblical simplicity and contentment help set things right.

Rx 10 *Move Down*

Many people take on home mortgages that deprive them of financial margin for decades. To make payments, they overwork. Exhaustion coupled with high debt creates interpersonal problems.

Consider moving to a smaller home. Obviously, this is an important decision that should be made with care and consensus. But for some, it will solve most—or all—of their debt problems overnight.

Rx 11 *Let Appliances Die in Your Arms*

Appliances often wear out in a predictable pattern, yet other times they prove astoundingly resilient. My father, a heating and air conditioning contractor, once commented that it's frustrating when people delay replacing an old furnace until it fails in the middle of the night in the middle of a snowstorm in the middle of the winter. I gently reminded him of the clothes dryer he replaced because it was "on its last legs." Still in medical training, we willingly took the dryer off his hands—and it gave us an additional fourteen years of service. "That," I suggested, "is probably why people don't want to pay for a new furnace when the old one might have some life in it."

Rx 12 *Stop Venerating Automobiles*

If we were to examine the issue honestly, most people pay more for automobiles than is necessary and the resultant auto loans play a significant role in their overall debt picture. I wonder—how much would Jesus pay for a car?

Personally, in our family we have never paid more than $4,000 for an automobile. Obviously, if you are not careful you can get some regrettable vehicles. But mostly, we have had reliable, adequately appealing cars that are satisfactory in every way.

One person reported he sold his favorite collector's car after hearing me speak. Quite frankly, hearing such reports is distressing, because I don't want responsibility for other people's decisions. When I expressed this view, he responded, "But you don't realize how great it feels to get out from under some of our debt load. It's wonderful!"

Rx 13 *Simplify Your Meals; Eat Out Less*

Expensive grocery bills are partly required and partly chosen. If you could discipline your taste buds to accept simplicity, you would eat healthier while spending a fraction of your usual food budget. Double your rice portion and cut your meat portion in half. Your wallet will thank you; your body will too.

In addition to high grocery bills, a large number of us eat out regularly. It is a common, delectable, and socially sanctioned experience. But it is also expensive and unhealthy. In the interest of health and debt reduction, eat in.

Rx 14 *Shop for Good Deals*
If we can slow down the treadmill and not have to buy our way out of hurriedness, it becomes much easier to look for sales and bargains. Decide not to pay full price unless necessary. Realize that not all purchases need to be new—buying at thrift shops, garage sales, and Goodwill has eased financial burdens for millions.

At our house, we keep a "gift box." When we find something on sale, we make the purchase and put it in the box as a future gift. This way we buy good gifts at less price and less hassle. Once on our way to a bookstore, we passed a children's close-out sale. Linda bought three hundred dollars worth of children's clothes for thirty dollars.

Simplicity author Paul Borthwick suggests that we remember the bargain shopper's motto: "*Everything* will eventually go one sale." But he also cautions, "Discount outlets and bargain basements can be a blessing and a curse." On one hand, they sell for less, reducing our costs. On the other hand, bargains can create a destructive, materialistic attitude by leading to many unnecessary purchases.[14]

Rx 15 *Simplify Christmas and Birthdays*
Because other people are involved, making the decision to cut costs in celebrations and gift giving is a difficult one. Within your family, if your children are small, begin the process early. Explain the real meaning of gift giving, and do not let it slide into commercialism. Put thought and love into the occasion more than money. One family set a limit—$100—for the entire celebration of Christmas. If Christ walked into our community December 24th, I'm thinking that might be the home He'd prefer to visit.

Rx 16 *Enjoy Free Activities*
If we have the time to be creative and imaginative, many things in life can be enjoyed absolutely free. Borthwick gives the following suggestions:

- Catch up on the latest magazines at the local library
- Check out a video instead of renting one
- Read a book rather than shop
- Visit a free museum
- Take a bike ride
- Go sledding or skating
- Work on a hobby
- Exercise for free
- Play basketball at public courts or swim at a community pool
- Walk the stairs
- Barter child care or swap baby-sitting[15]

Often we might find these alternative options not only financially helpful but also healthier physically and relationally.

Rx 17 *Respect the Potential of Economic Volatility*

It is hard to write about economics today, because before the ink is dry the news is old. In this globalized world with electronic money flying at the speed of light, a hiccup in Asia can cause a seizure in Europe. More than one trillion dollars in foreign exchange routinely changes hands each day, far outstripping any central bank's ability to exercise control. A scandal in the Middle East can affect Wall Street — or vice versa. With the world fully wired and tightly coupled, volatility and vulnerability are everywhere. Don't get too ambitious leveraging the future with debt-sponsored schemes — they might sour before tomorrow morning's alarm clock goes off.

Rx 18 *Be Suspicious of Economic Answers*

Economics is entrenched as the most powerful force in Western society. The near universal advice we receive is that the economic road is the direction we should travel in order to solve our many problems. But God has an eternal feud with the power of money, and He begs to differ. The simple life is greatly facilitated if we agree with God on this matter. Money is perhaps the answer to some of life's problems. But the money solution is never transcendent, and money is never the answer for the most important issues of the human condition.

Rx 19 *Use Debt as an Opportunity for Growth*

Mark Twain once quipped, "A person who has had a bull by the tail once has learned sixty to seventy times as much as a person who hasn't." As teachers, a bull and a debt have much in common. If debt has beaten us down, why not learn from the experience? If we will accept debt as being a valuable teacher of spiritual lessons, perhaps no better instructor exists.

Ask important and penetrating questions: Why did I get into debt in the first place? Am I controlled by my culture? Is my contentment linked to a consumerist lifestyle? Does my debt have spiritual implications? What would God have me learn through this process? If pain gets our attention, we should never waste the opportunity to grow.

Rx 20 *Change Your Measuring Stick*

Money is not the measure of all things. Perhaps it is time to remember "we live in a society, not an economy."[16] This same idea led economist E. F. Schumacher to write *Small Is Beautiful*, and to subtitle the book, *Economics as if People Mattered*. Before I had even opened the cover, I had learned from him.

Russ Crosson advises that we use a standard different from money for deciding our values. "Measure wealth not by the things you have, but by the things you have that you would not take money for."[17] If we could identify such a standard and integrate it practically into our everyday decision making, it would change most of our lives beyond recognition—*always* for the better.

CHAPTER 8

■■■■■■■■■

Expectation

- If you can dream it, you can do it. Now there's no limit to your ability.—PRUDENTIAL

- Your world should know no boundaries.—MERRILL LYNCH

- Life, liberty, and the pursuit of just about anything you please. Volvo—a car that can not only help save your life, but help save your soul.—VOLVO

- We thought the way up is up. But with God, the way up is down.—WELLINGTON BOONE

A medical colleague bounded up to me, announcing,"I finally discovered the best way to get through the day. In the morning, I say to myself *This is going to be the worst day of my life.* Then when the day is only half horrible, I'm happy!" It was offered somewhat tongue-in-cheek, but along with the humor comes a good dose of wisdom: Our happiness and contentment are dependent on the expectations we bring to the experience. As progress gives us more and more benefits, it raises expectations. This, in turn, often makes it harder to find the happiness and contentment we seek.

One clear *advantage* of progress is that we have learned that life *can be* improved. But one clear *disadvantage* of progress is that we have come to expect that life *will be* improved. The expectation tends to rise faster than the improvement. Happiness versus unhappiness, satisfaction versus dissatisfaction, contentment versus discontentment are all contingent on expectation, not the actual improvement. If, for example, we expect one car and receive two, we are ecstatic. But if we expect three cars and receive two, we are crushed. In each case, we received two cars. The emotional result, however, was polar opposite.

Expectation overload is one of the most difficult to control. Our affluent, media-saturated age has spawned a rising tide of expectations. We expect health, wealth, and ease—and are discontent if more doesn't come, no matter how well-off we are. "The life of people on earth is obviously better now than it has ever been— certainly much better than it was 500 years ago when people beat each other with cats," reflects political observer Peggy Noonan. "This may sound silly but now and then when I read old fairy tales and see an illustration of a hunchbacked hag with no teeth and bumps on her nose who lives by herself in the forest, I think: People looked like that once. They lived like that. There were no doctors, no phones, and people lived in the dark in a hole in a tree. It was terrible. It's much better now. But we are not happier. I believe we are just cleaner, more attractive sad people than we used to be."[1]

GREAT EXPECTATIONS

Expectation overload. People everywhere are crumbling under the weight of it. In some ways, it is the most devastating of all overloads, driving the entire train of overload trauma. We are expected to be smart, or at least well educated; to be beautiful, fashionable, and athletic; to drive a nice car (without rust) and to live in a nice house (always picked up); to own nice things (at least as nice as the Joneses); to be the perfect parent and spouse. And lest we refuse to accept the terms and conditions of the first set of expectations, there is a final expectation standing guard over all the others: *We are expected to conform.* Let's examine some specifics.

Automobiles

The admission price to the good life expects that we drive a nice automobile—certainly befitting our career, income, and social status. One day when I worked my rotating shift at the Student Health Center in our university, my car was ticketed: "Please move your car. This spot is reserved for the physician." Why did the officer write this note if not for an obvious cultural expectation that an M.D. would not drive a car like mine?

Homes
Over the past forty years, Americans have doubled the square footage in our homes even though families are smaller. Partly, as we will see, this is because of possession overload. But expectation overload is also to blame. Debt is not the determining factor in home size anymore—expectation is.

Fashion
Fashion has completely overwhelmed function—are we sure this is okay with God? If functionality were our only concern, most of us could survive on ten percent of our clothes budget. "Why exactly do we put on our 'Sunday best' to head out to church?" asks editorialist Doug Trouten. "The most common explanation is that we do it to honor God. Buried behind that explanation is the unspoken assumption that God is somehow going to feel honored because we're nicely dressed. But Isaiah tells us that to God 'our righteous acts are as filthy rags.' If that's how God feels about our righteousness, what makes us think He's going to like our suits?"[2]

Income
A dangerous expectation is that we need a lot of money to live on. Actually, the profound truth is that we need very little income to live a totally *God-honoring life.* Yes, perhaps we do need a huge cash flow to partake of the many benefits of our age. But people now struggling to make it on $100,000 could honor God completely with an income of $20,000. The rest is consumed purely in fulfillment of cultural expectation.

Careers
We expect our jobs to be stable, our careers to be faithful to us, our benefit packages to insulate us, and our company morale to meet our emotional needs. But in this era of downsizing, millions have been disappointed, displaced, and depressed by occupational insecurity and financial uncertainty.

Retirement

The expectation of retirement is a distinctly modern notion, historically speaking, and some predict it is transient. Indeed, they say, there is only a short window of time in only a few countries when such a luxury was possible at all. Yet we see people today who have retirement plans with millions of dollars who are nevertheless panicked that the money will not last. This is, of course, directly related to expectations.

Government

Big expectations have also encumbered big government in the form of rising entitlements: Social Security, Medicare, Medicaid, Welfare. Many social dilemmas have been appropriately addressed with these programs, and much societal suffering has been relieved. But, on the other hand, with each entitlement comes a commensurate expectation. And this expectation often traps people in dependency even as it traps government in untouchable budgetary spending.

Medicine

Expectations in medicine have risen to unattainable levels. We expect our doctor to know all the answers, our insurance to pay all the bills, and our body to heal all the ills. When these inappropriate expectations are not met, we look for someone to blame.

Plastic Surgery

Plastic surgery is yet another manifestation of our overblown expectations. Many, upset at nature for not giving them a perfect body, spend enormous sums attempting to buy one. If we didn't care how we (or others) looked on the outside, concentrating instead on the inner qualities of integrity, virtue, and purity, perhaps we would mature beyond our fixation with looks.

In Argentina, people openly boast of recent plastic surgeries, showing off their bandages and bruises around the eyes, and ask each other on television "Where did you have your nose job?" The president of the country flaunts his six plastic surgeries. I don't want to stigmatize it, but do we really wish to normalize it?

Mental Health

One modern expectation was that progress would solve our mental and emotional suffering through the benefits of education, wealth, technology, health care, and convenience. Such has not been the case. This profound disappointment has, in turn, made our depression and anxiety even more painful.

Education

Society expects us to get an education. And holding a degree, we expect that life will magically unfold. But, of course, many college students don't have a clue what to study, can't get a job in their field, and are surprised when an education does not prepare them for such all important real-life events as relationships, emotional well-being, and spiritual fulfillment.

Sports

Professional players get multi-million dollar contracts but seem less happy and more self-absorbed than ever. One recent NBA player, two years out of high school, turned down $17 million a year. While I don't completely condemn players for exploring fair market value, it is perverse to assume that happiness and contentment will come along with the expected top dollar.

Marriage

Our modern expectations of marriage are, at the same time, very low and very high. On the one hand, expectations are low in that we anticipate trouble. Even on the way to the altar, some are already wondering if the marriage can last. On the other hand, expectations are high in the sense that we place on our mate extraordinary demands to make us happy and meet our needs. In short, we demand more and put up with less.

Parenting

Parental expectations for our children often crush the child out of them. "The concept of childhood, so vital to the traditional American way of life, is threatened with extinction in the society we have created," writes child psychologist David Elkind. "Today's child has become the unwilling, unintended victim of overwhelming stress—the stress borne of rapid, bewildering social change and constantly rising expectations."[3] We begin hurrying them in education when they are still in the cradle, we want them to be beauty queens or football stars when they are six, and we insist on straight A's when they hit junior high. Whatever happened to unconditional love?

Traditions and Rituals

Why are modern weddings and funerals so outrageously expensive? Because the expectation bar has been raised impossibly high and no one has the fortitude to resist the flow. To be a good fiancé, one must show his love by purchasing the biggest diamond. To be loving parents, we must offer the most expensive wedding. To be good children, we must purchase a "respectable" casket. To be doting grandparents, we must flood the grandchildren with Christmas toys.

ADS, THE MEDIA, COMMERCIALIZATION, AND THE LAW

This extraordinary level of expectation derives from many different cultural forces, but chief among them are advertisements, the media, the commercialization of everyday life, and the legal system.

Everywhere we go, ads stare us down and draw us in. It is hard to avoid them, and as a matter of fact, we often are not even fully aware of their presence. Teenagers, on average, are exposed to 360,000 advertisements before they graduate from high school.[4] David Wolfe, creative director of a consulting firm, believes the communications explosion has "made it possible for everybody, even in the armpit of the outback, to know what cool is."[5] Movies are increasingly hawking products within the context of the plot.

Children, who daily watch up to five hours of television, including one hour of commercials, represent a manipulatable and recession-proof market. When confronted with Avon's line of Barbie cosmetics, critic Alex Molnar asked, "What's next, prenatal lipstick?"[6] One toiletry manufacturer is marketing solid deodorant for seven-year-olds—even though such children have no physiological need for the product until at least age eleven.

Additionally, products for children are increasingly sold on the basis of rebellion. "Just watch a Saturday morning's worth of TV commercials, and see how many products are sold by making the appeal that your parents won't like you to have this product," observes Kenneth Myers.[7] Yet the rebellion themes don't stop with children. Modern advertising is not only causing inordinate expectations but also driving the deeper problem of societal discord. Joseph Turow, a professor of communications, has discovered a "revolutionary shift" in the strategies and tactics of marketing companies, which, he says, "has been driven by, and has been driving, a profound sense of division in American society." Turow believes that advertisers, working in concert with conglomerating media companies, are forcing "a breakdown in social cohesion" in the United States.[8]

"Advertisers are focusing more and more on the emerging market of 'people who do only what they want to do,'" observes columnist John Leo, "that is, people who yearn to be completely free of all restraint, expectations, and responsibilities." Burger King offers, *Sometimes, you gotta break the rules.* A shoe company promises their shoe *conforms to your foot so you don't have to conform to anything.* Says Nike, *We are all hedonists and we want what feels good. That's what makes us human.* "The point here," explains Leo, "is that while everyone is aghast over blatant sex, violent movies, and gangsta rap, the ordinary commercial messages of corporate America are probably playing a more subversive role."[9]

No small contributor to the expectation problem, the legal profession must accept considerable blame. "There is some form of mass neurosis that leads many people to think courts were created to solve all the problems of mankind," accused former Chief Justice of the Supreme Court Warren Burger, saying many lawsuits are "an exercise in futility" best solved by other means.[10] Our national "victimization" epidemic is directly related to expectations exploited by the legal profession.

PRESCRIPTIONS FOR CORRECTING OUR EXPECTATION INFLATION

In light of ever-increasing societal expectations, what can we do to counteract these pressures? Many of the possible adjustments have to do with our mindset and lifestyle.

Rx 1 *Respect Limits*

We must realize our limits and become comfortable accepting them. We can't be superpastor, superteacher, or superparent all the time, and neither should we try. As a physician, I can't memorize all three thousand pages of the *Physician's Desk Reference*. Even Jesus didn't heal every disease in Israel.

Some have said, "Your God is too small." I agree! But I would also add, "We are too large." When we inflate our role in the drama of life and increase our own personal expectations beyond the realm of human possibility, we crash and burn against the Almighty's intentions. Remember, limits were His idea.

Rx 2 *Adjust Your Expectations*

"Expect more and you'll get it," says the MasterCard ad. Implicit in the message is that it is always *appropriate* to expect more. But as we adjust our expectations downward, we will discover less to be unhappy about.

If we always expect success and prosperity, we are destined to be chronically frustrated. But if we understand that humankind is fallen and life is difficult, we are more likely to be contented with the simple blessings God sends our way.

Rx 3 *Redefine Enough*

Perhaps the best way to deal with the expectation of always having enough is to diminish our definition of that word. For most of us, according to Vicki Robin, *enough* is "*more* than we have now." But if we instead defined *enough* as "*what* we have now," our expectations will be fulfilled. "It's the old idea that the less you want, the richer you are," says physician and marathoner George Sheehan, explaining the secret of his long career. "I try to make my life free of wants and restrict it to needs."[11]

Rx 4 *Compare Yourself to the Less Fortunate*

Expectations expand when we look at cars nicer than ours and friends who have swimming pools. Our well-being is sabotaged by envying movie stars with beauty and bodies to match. So, instead, let's look elsewhere. "After days of traveling in East

Africa, I was numb from witnessing the poverty," writes simplicity author David A. Sorensen. "'Are these people happy?' I
asked John, our Masai guide. 'They have much happiness here,'
he replied. 'It all depends on what you compare your own lifestyle
with, don't you think?'"[12] If they are happy in their destitution,
and we are unhappy in our affluence, perhaps we have some
recalibration to do.

Rx 5 *Beware the Trap of Winning*
Success begets increased expectations. "We not only have successes,
we become our successes," explains Henri Nouwen. "And the more
we allow our accomplishments . . . to become the criteria of our
self-esteem, the more we are . . . never sure if we will be able to live
up to the expectations which we created by our last successes. In
many people's lives, there is a nearly diabolic chain in which their
anxieties grow according to their successes."[13]

"People can become psychologically trapped by their own success as they race to keep up with the rising expectations bred by
each new achievement," observes psychologist Gilbert Brim. "With
each success they raise their level of difficulty, climbing up a ladder of subgoals, moving faster, raising aspirations and at some point
reaching the limit of their capacity.

"At this point, successful performance becomes difficult and
people begin to lose more often than they win. Their resources are
squeezed to the utmost. The business executive, promoted beyond
a level of just manageable difficulty, ends up being held together by
a thin paste of alcohol, saunas, and antibiotics."[14]

Let the "winner" beware. Even as you set high standards and
pursue lofty goals, always keep one eye on the threshold of your limits. Once success catapults you into the world of overload, the rules
of the game change. It is wise to make adjustments commensurate
with the amount of overloading.

Rx 6 *Tune Out Ads*
As we have seen, expectation inflation often comes from advertisements. Since most ads are nothing more than avenues of discontent
through "need creation," wage war against them. Perhaps the most

powerful way to accomplish this is to control the television. After twenty years of an old, black-and-white television, we finally purchased a color set because the remote control shifts the balance of power back into our hands as parents. When ads come on, we use the remote to switch the channel. Even though our children dislike this annoying habit, it accomplishes two things: It keeps us from seeing and absorbing the content of the ads, and it teaches our kids that we are serious about the false content of advertisements.

Rx 7 *De-emphasize Respectability in Fashion*

How often we change cars, wardrobes, furniture, and carpeting because of the burdensome assumptions about the opinions of others. Don't change fashion because someone else thinks it should be done. We are capable of judging function without the prejudicial expectations of others clouding our thinking.

Wearing only middle-of-the-road clothes, I virtually never make a fashion statement. But I have found great contentment in fashion mediocrity. Our fashion expectations are easier to fulfill when we buy things for usefulness rather than status.

Rx 8 *Simplify Holidays, Ceremonies, and Rituals*

In Pittsburgh, writes Chuck Colson, "all holidays from Thanksgiving through Christmas and New Year's have been blended into a gargantuan commercial celebration called *Sparkle Season.*"[15] I am not a scrooge, but my advice is this: Forget about Sparkle Season and all the obligatory trappings. Get back to the basics in ceremonies and celebrations: family, faith, friends. Some suggestions:

Christmas: Reduce the money expenditures. Simplify, simplify. Cut expectations to only those Christ Himself would endorse.

Engagements: Instead of a diamond for engagement, Linda and I decided on the Swedish custom of two gold bands—one for the engagement and one for the wedding. We still endorse the idea, twenty-seven happily married years later.

Weddings: One wedding in Boston was held in a garden where, instead of gifts, the bride and groom requested that people bring food for the reception dinner. Friends provided the music, served the meal, and took the photographs. Total cost? Chair rental.

Funerals: When my brother-in-law died prematurely at the age of fifty, his two sons built him a pine casket. It was wonderfully respectful, and all I would ever want myself.

Rx 9 *Resist Inflated Housing Expectations*

Just because we have the ability to buy an expensive home seems to convey a commensurate expectation that we will do exactly that. When a real estate agent handed Barbara and David Sorensen the keys to a downsized, 950 square-foot house, he said, "But I still don't get it. Why'd you buy such a small house, anyway?" Buying beneath one's ability seemed unusual to him. The Sorensens explained their desire for a simpler life, one more consistent with their values.

When the realtor described the extravagant house he was building, the Sorensens asked, "Why are you building such a big house?" He looked startled, not used to being challenged about such an obvious thing. "Well, because I can!" he replied.[16] If you want financial margin for decades to come, resist the expectation to buy bigger than you need.

Rx 10 *Free Others*

When we put too many expectations on others, they return the favor. In this hypercritical, grace-devoid, expectation-overloaded world, we need to set one another free. When we expect too much of others, we suffocate them. And when they do not fulfill our unreasonable demands, we frustrate ourselves. "Never, never pin your whole faith on any human being: not if he is the best and wisest in the whole world," advises C. S. Lewis. "There are lots of nice things you can do with sand; but do not try building a house on it."[17]

Rx 11 *Give Your Pastor a Break*

The pastorate has gone from a "low stress, high reward" job to a "high stress, low reward" job. Never was a job created with more conflicting expectations. Pastor's families are expected to be perfect, with spouses who have exceptional ministry gifts and children who are the most godly and best behaved. In addition, we expect modern churches to have endless programs for our ever-expanding needs. But of course, no one has time to volunteer—so guess who gets the job?

"Pastors can carry heavy loads, but there's a point at which it becomes too much," warns psychiatrist Louis McBurney, M.D. "Needs of the congregation combine with the pastor's own need to be needed, pushing the load beyond the breaking point."[18] If we want healthy, invested pastors, let's hire wisely and then set them free. Totally.

Rx 12 *Free Your Spouse*

Freedom is a key to any successful marriage. Not the narcissistic kind, the grace kind. As we relinquish control and lower expectations, the marital bond surprisingly solidifies. "If there is any area in our relationships as couples that controls our ability to gain inner rest, I believe it is the expectations we bring to our marriage," explains author Tim Kimmel. "As I counsel couples getting married—and couples trying to stay married—this is the one area I emphasize beyond all others. . . . What I need to do is come to a relationship with expectations that only cover *me*. After all, I'm the only person over whom I have control."[19]

Rx 13 *Love Unconditionally*

Give children a chance to grow up naturally, slowly, innocently. They should have paper dolls and earthworms at age six, not Latin tests and figure-skating competitions. The best way for making the entire parenting experience positive and peaceful is to give age-appropriate expectations, delivered with unconditional love.

Rx 14 *Don't Serve on a Silver Platter*

I fear for the future of today's children who have everything handed them on a silver platter. Many parents feel their children should experience all the benefits that progress has to offer. But I view the silver platter as a liability that greatly increases their expectation level in an uncertain future.

"For any happiness, even in this world, quite a lot of restraint is going to be necessary," explains C. S. Lewis.[20] That restraining process should gently begin at the hands of wise parents, who carefully hide the silver platter under the dish towel. But instead, warns sociologist Arlie Hochschild, overworked parents often overindulge their children out of guilt from absentee parenting.[21]

If you wish to invest in your child's future, don't raise their materialistic appetites and expectations. Instead, teach them the enormous secret found in biblical contentment.[22]

Rx 15 *Free Yourself from the Opinion of Others*

Perhaps the biggest burden we carry is our inordinate concern about the opinion of others. If we could free ourselves from that weighty expectation, we would find ourselves on freedom's road.

"The heart's fierce effort to protect itself from every slight, to shield its touchy honor from the bad opinion of friend and enemy, will never let the mind have rest. Continue this fight through the years and the burden will become intolerable," explains theologian A. W. Tozer. "Such a burden as this is not necessary to bear. Jesus calls us to His rest, and meekness is His method. The meek man cares not at all who is greater than he, for he has long ago decided that the esteem of the world is not worth the effort."[23]

Rx 16 *Deny Yourself*

If we want an expectation correction, try Christ. "If anyone would come after me," Jesus preached, "he must deny himself and take up his cross and follow me."[24] Denying ourselves is a normal and expected part of the Christian life. It is akin to fasting with this difference: Fasting is episodic; self-denial is lifelong. Christ did it for us. We do it for Him.

Yet, practically speaking, what do we deny ourselves? For many of us, the answer is virtually nothing. The requirement of self-denial is not for punishing us, but rather for focusing us and freeing us. It clears our head of the world and its many expectations, and points us in the direction of things that matter most.

CHAPTER 9

■ ■ ■ ■ ■ ■ ■ ■ ■

Hurry and Fatigue

■ Man is flying too fast for a world that is round. Soon he will catch up with himself in a great rear end collision, and man will never know that what hit him from behind was man.—JAMES THURBER

■ Drowsy drivers may kill as many people as drunken drivers.—BERKELEY WELLNESS LETTER

■ Fatigue makes cowards of us all.—VINCE LOMBARDI

■ I learned to tell time and now I'm always late.
—LILLY TOMLIN AS EDITH ANN

The world seems to have an automatically advancing speed rheostat, and every year the treadmill spins faster. American culture, reports editorialist Mortimer B. Zuckerman, "is strapped to a rocket whose velocity and range we can only faintly comprehend."[1]

"America. The land of the rushed," complains small town journalist Peg Zaemisch. "We have proudly defined our American lifestyle as 'life in the fast lane.' Now, we rush to construct passing lanes, so we can get around those pokie-schmokies in the fast lane . . . do they think we've got all day? We've become a country of out-of-breath-red-faced folks, racing around with our hair permanently blowing back." Zaemisch vows to tame her "catch-a-bullet-in-my-teeth schedule—just as soon as I get off this deadline."[2]

Even our sentences are peppered with such words as *time crunch, fast food, rush hour, frequent flyer, expressway, overnight delivery,* and *rapid transit.* The products and services we use further attest to our hurry: We send packages by Federal Express, use a long distance company called Sprint, manage our personal finances on

Quicken, schedule our appointments on a DayRunner, diet with SlimFast, and swim in trunks made by Speedo. "The society in which we live today would have us believe, or at least hope, that life will be okay if we can just get it packaged right and served to us on the run," observes publisher Bob Benson.[3]

In Montana, where speed limits are "reasonable and prudent," a man was clocked going 150 miles per hour. In the Nevada desert, a British speed burner set a new land speed record by going 764.168 miles per hour—breaking the sound barrier for the first time in a land-based vehicle. Elsewhere, an impatient Purdue engineer, frustrated with how long it took charcoal briquettes to light, decided to pipe in pure oxygen. It worked so well, he decided to use liquid oxygen—the kind used in booster rockets. That worked well too—he burned up all the briquettes and the grill in three seconds. "It was pretty bright," he said. "You didn't want to look at it."

BREAKING LIFE'S SPEED LIMIT

An eighty-nine-year-old man watched with dismay as his physician rushed breathlessly from room to room, patient to patient. Finally he reached out and grabbed the doctor by the arm. "Doc," he said, "you're goin' so fast you're passin' up more stuff than you're catchin' up to."

Although physicians know the syndrome well, our profession isn't alone in being plagued by this hurry sickness—the entire world seems caught up in it. Of course we all enjoy going fast, at least from time to time. But the enormous increase in the speed of daily life is clearly pathogenic. We live in a nanosecond culture, wheezing and worn-out.

Speed. Hurry. We pay a price for the pace at which we live. The late French historian Jacques Ellul commented, "No one knows where we are going, the aim of life has been forgotten, the end has been left behind. Man has set out at tremendous speed—to go *nowhere*."[4]

"These days, speed is of the essence," observes David Sharp of *USA Today*. "Anything that can't keep up becomes the cultural equivalent of roadkill."[5] Yes, the world is going faster. And yes, we in turn are also going faster. But the important question no one asks is this: When does *faster* become *too fast?*

Is there a speed limit to life? What happens when we exceed it? Does God give us a ticket? I have thought long and hard about the issue of speed and have come to believe that it is as much responsible for the problem of personal and societal dysfunction as any other single factor.

Virtually all of our relationships are damaged by hurry. Many families are being starved to death by velocity. Our children lie wounded on the ground, run over by our high-speed good intentions.

Why do we hurry our kids? Mostly, because *we* are in a hurry. "Parents were asked to go to the auditorium to hear the school band play some Mozart before we met the teachers," explained Elizabeth Berg about attending a school conference. "The musical director was careful to point out that the piece would take only two minutes. I looked at the expectant kids seated behind him, waiting to entertain us with their very best. The director said what he did because he could see us tight-lipped parents looking at our watches. I was deeply ashamed, and I thought, *If we don't have time for children playing Mozart, what do we have time for?*"[6]

God, I suspect, doesn't fit any better into our breakneck schedules than our children do. We walk fast, talk fast, eat fast, and then announce, "Sorry, I've got to run." The trouble is, God's not running after us. He knows that speed does not yield devotion. He knows that with all our running we're just opening an ever greater distance between where we're running to and where He's waiting for us. I think I would not be far wrong if I were to postulate that our sense of the presence of God is in inverse proportion to the pace of our lives.

Have you ever noticed that Jesus never seemed to be in a hurry? The Bible never says anything about Him running. Apparently, Jesus believed that very little of lasting spiritual or emotional value happens in the presence of speed. Jesus understood that busyness, productivity, and efficiency are speed words, not kingdom words. At times they are appropriate values—but they are never transcendent. Jesus understood that meditation, wisdom, and worship are slow, mellow, and deep.

FATIGUE OVERLOAD

When speed and busyness have matured, they give birth to fatigue. Americans are, if anything, exhausted. We are a nation of the *hard-wired and dog-tired*. Seminary president and author Chuck Swindoll claims our era is "the age of the half-read page, the quick hash and the mad dash, the bright night with the nerves tight, the plane hop with the brief stop, the lamp tan in a short span, the brain strain and the heart pain, the catnaps until the spring snaps . . . the land where the fun's gone."[7]

Fatigue, I should quickly point out, is a normal occurrence. It happens to all people and at all points in history. But that doesn't mean that all fatigue is equal. In many ways, today's "universal fatigue," as Swiss psychiatrist Paul Tournier called it, is a surprise. Progress, it was reasonable to expect, should lead to restedness and leisure. That we should have such weariness in body and spirit was not predicted.

Fatigue, of course, comes from many sources for many reasons. But contributing greatly to our current epidemic is our frenzied AWOL—"American Way of Life." In the context of this chapter, three common sources of fatigue—sleep deprivation, deconditioning, and stress—deserve special mention. Each is directly related to progress, overload, busyness, and hurry.

Fatigue from Sleep Deprivation

It is perhaps true that modern Americans get less sleep than at any other time in history. In 1850, for example, the average American got 9.5 hours of sleep per night. By 1950, that had decreased to 8 hours. Currently, it is 7 hours—and still declining. As a result, fifty to seventy million Americans (depending on which study you read) have sleep disorders.

Why, under the tutelage of progress, have the hours of sleep declined so dramatically? The answer is simple: electricity and the light bulb. We are now a twenty-four-hour-a-day society that seldom shuts down.

Fatigue from Deconditioning

Deconditioning is a second major cause of our fatigue problem, again, compliments of modernity. Once progress delivered us from the need to use our muscles in earning a living, we lost both strength and stamina. Now, we must artificiate ways to get the exercise we need. But who likes to sweat? Who likes the pain? And who has the time anyway?

Fatigue from Stress

There is no clinical doubt but that the mind writes prescriptions for the body and the body obediently complies. The greater the stress, the greater the feelings of tiredness, exhaustion, and burnout. While these feelings of fatigue are real, there is nothing for your physician to measure. The best antidote for this type of fatigue is a program of stress management combined with wise stress reduction.

PRESCRIPTIONS FOR HEALING THE HURRY SICKNESS

As the world around us accelerates, our energies wane. But we are not defenseless victims. The following suggestions will help replace frenzy with peace and rest.

Rx 1 *Consciously Slow the Pace of Life*

I recently saw a T-shirt that read: "It's not the pace of life that worries me. It's the sudden stop at the end." After contemplation, I decided the exact opposite is true. "The sudden stop at the end" means a home-going that, quite frankly, I look forward to. But *the pace of life is deadly!*

Is it possible to consciously slow our pace? Of course it is. We just have to say *no* more often. It is not easy, but it is necessary—and it is right.

Every year the world spins faster. So put on the brakes and obey the speed limit of your soul. The green pastures and still waters yet await us—but not in the direction the treadmill is spinning.[8]

As the "Old Negro Ballad" pleads:

Slo' me down, Lord
I'm movin' too fast.
Don't know my own brother
When he's awalkin' past.
Miss the best things o' life
Day by day.

Don't know a blessin'
When it comes my way.

Rx 2 *Make Technology Work For You and Not Against You*
Remember: Time-saving technologies don't save time. Instead, they
compress and consume time. Recognizing that technology is responsible for much of our time urgency problem, it is appropriate to be
skeptical. Clocks, watches, alarms, computers, answering machines,
cell phones, pagers, and fax machines often create more time problems than they solve. Use them judiciously.

Always make technology work *for you* and not *against you*. If
you can't control it, don't trust it. "The high-tech world of clocks and
schedules, computers and programs, was supposed to free us from
a life of toil and deprivation," explains technology critic Jeremy
Rifkin in *Time Wars*, "yet with each passing day the human race
becomes more . . . exploited and victimized."[9]

Leaving a workshop where I had just spoken, a dentist took off
his watch and flipped it into the swimming pool. You might not
wish to be quite this dramatic. But, then again. . . .

Rx 3 *Throw Away the Alarm Clock*
Psychiatrist Paul Meier provocatively asserts, "If you wake up to
an alarm every morning, there is a good chance that you are out of
the will of God." Radical thinking! But he is simply trying to shock
us into rethinking the will of God in light of the original equipment
provided at Creation. An alarm clock was not a part of the package.
Instead, God caused our bodies to generally wake up when we had
enough sleep. Now, however, that natural process never gets a
chance to complete itself.

Rx 4 *Repent of the Pride of Busyness*
The busier we appear, the greater the respect afforded us. While the
person sitting on a lawn swing is scorned, the speed-of-light jet
jockey is venerated.

"The clock dictates the tempo of our lives," explains Mayo Gilson,
M.D. "We all hurry, involving others in our hurry. Paradoxically, we
point to our lack of time with a certain pride, as if that lack has some-

thing to do with our importance as a person."[10] There is a trap here, and pride is its name. Before we can slow down and allow God to set things right in our hearts, we have some confessing to do. It is not busyness that we should honor in our midst, but love. Busyness and love are not the same. One is speed; the other is God.

Rx 5 *"Ruthlessly Eliminate Hurry"*

When John Ortberg moved from California to Illinois to assume a position at the rapidly growing Willow Creek Community Church, he first asked a wise mentor for advice. "You must ruthlessly eliminate hurry from your life," said his friend. Ortberg wrote down the advice and then waited for the next suggestion. "There is nothing else," explained the sage.[11]

I am struck by three aspects of this truth: how *simple* it is, how *difficult* it is, and how *ruthless* it is. *Ruthless* is indeed the best word to use in this context, because no other degree of intention is sufficient to accomplish such a goal.

Rx 6 *Take Your Time*

Persistence, the tortoise taught the hare, is more important than speed. Life is a marathon, not a sprint. The person who sprints wins the hundred-yard-dash — but loses the marathon. Business executive John Capozzi, in his best-selling collection of favorite maxims, illustrates the principle well:

- The race is not always won by the fastest runner but sometimes by those who just keep running.
- Measure twice . . . cut once.
- Avoid shortcuts. They always take too much time in the long run.
- To finish sooner, take your time.[12]

Rx 7 *Set an Earlier ETA*

Moderns do not like to arrive early and barely agree to arrive on time. We plan our schedules so that we can arrive "somewhere in the vicinity" — meaning give or take ten minutes. But then when traffic is snarled, or unexpected snow falls, or we get a late start, or the car is out of gas, we begin to hurry. And worry. The entire experience quickly erodes into yet another urgency-induced panic attack.

To short-circuit such routine disasters, plan to arrive early. With an earlier ETA (estimated time of arrival), you can slow down the driving, enjoy the day, and actually begin to anticipate with pleasure the event in front of you. The best way to accomplish an ETA, of course, is to have an earlier ETD (estimated time of departure).

Rx 8 *Turn Back the Clock*

Occasionally live one day in 1930, 1900, or 1850. You might be surprised at how delightful—and slow-paced—such an adventure turns out to be. When you commit to such an experience, use only the technology that existed during that era. This rule, of course, never precludes walking, reading, talking, or sleeping.

By eliminating our modern hurrying technologies—even for a day—it will quickly become apparent just how large a role these devices play in the unreasonable pace of life.

Rx 9 *Understand the Difference between Time and Time*

As it turns out, not all time is created equal. According to pastor Arthur Dunn, the Bible distinguishes between *kairos* and *chronos*. Kairos is *significant time*: meaningful, vertical, quality time—where Jesus lived. Chronos is *clock time*: linear, simple, chronological, measurable, quantity time—where we live.

While *chronos* is occupied with the linear measurement of the past, present, and future, *kairos* is occupied with nonlinear measurements that are event-conscious, life-focused, and meaning-sensitive. Busyness and productivity are usually activities of *chronos*, while spirituality and relationships are usually activities of *kairos*.

"Do people need help managing time because they are too busy?" asks Dunn. "Or do they need help managing time because they have lost the sense of the meaning of time?"[13] "The Bible calls us to live first by kairos [significant time]," explains author Ben Patterson, "and to let kairos dictate to chronos [clock time] what we will do and how we will live."[14]

I am convinced that if we understood this fundamental truth, both our hurry and our fatigue would disappear in the same holy breeze.

Rx 10 *Develop Healthy Sleep Habits*

Progress gave us the light bulb; the light bulb invaded the night; and sleep never recovered from the shock. Sleep was God's idea, and good sleep is restorative. Value sleep. *Choose* to get enough sleep. To be well-rested is a blessing, not a waste of time. Learn to enjoy a nap without feeling guilty.

Buy a good mattress—you will spend a third of your life there. I don't even mind if your mattress costs more than your car. Don't have disturbing conversations immediately before bedtime. Like the time Linda said to me, "Better get a good night's sleep, because there's something we need to talk about in the morning."

Rx 11 *Develop an Exercise Program*

In the first instance, progress took away exercise through technology and the subsequent automation of our lives. In the second instance, progress keeps exercise away through hurry and fatigue. But if given a chance, exercise works well to counteract fatigue overload.

Perhaps because exercise isn't our favorite activity, many of us conveniently never find time for it. But if we include it in a balanced budget of time usage, exercise will often reimburse us minute for minute. The increased vitality resulting from good conditioning allows more energy and efficiency for all other endeavors.

Rx 12 *Schedule Relational Time*

In our speed-driven lifestyles, relational health will not happen unless we intentionally make it happen. Hurry and intimacy are two entirely different things. Let's slow down so that our family and friends can be included in our schedules. "What they'll remember most about their childhood when they grow older are two things," explains educational consultant Buck Sterling. "How much love was in the home, and how much time you spent with them."[15]

Bob Benson came home late one night, but still made the rounds kissing his children in bed—a nightly routine. "I bent over and kissed Patrick on the cheek and quickly stood up and started out of the room. . . . His question stopped me cold and brought me back to his bedside. 'Why do you kiss me so fast?'"[16]

Begrudge not love its time.

Rx 13 *Schedule Margin Time*

"I believe that one of the supreme aims of a man's life should be to secure a margin," wrote Australian F. W. Boreham in 1915. "A good life, like a good book, should have a good margin. . . . The most winsome people in the world are the people who make you feel that they are never in a hurry."[17]

As we have seen, Jesus never seemed in a hurry. Time urgency was not only absent from His life, it was conspicuously absent. Creating a margin—that space between our load and our limits—is perhaps one of the best ways to allow Christlike spontaneity and interruptibility back into our lives. Margin blunts hurry and allows us to focus on the divine appointments God sends our way.

Margin tames hurry as few other forces can. But it works both ways. Hurry can also make short work of margin.

Rx 14 *Understand the Will of God*

Clearly understanding the will of God will solve both our hurry and fatigue overload in the same revelation. God is not so desperate for resources or power that He must assign us twice as big a load as we can possibly carry. Certainly, He will at times place extraordinary demands upon us. But this is for the purpose of refining us, not because His external objective is otherwise beyond His reach.

"We can be quite sure that whatever God wishes us to devote ourselves to He will grant us time enough in which to do it," explains Robert Banks. "Our responsibility is to find out exactly what He wants and hold resolutely to that. One of our greatest problems is that we misunderstand what God asks of us, either by adding all kinds of extra responsibilities or by possessing only a hazy idea of what He wishes. We will gain more time by properly understanding His will for us than by all the time-saving suggestions put together."[18]

Rx 15 *Wait*

Waiting on God has been a mainstay of theology for three millennia. Yet over the last thirty years, we have sacrificed this important truth and don't even have the wisdom to realize it's been a serious loss. If we are fatigued, exhausted, and hurrying to and fro with no rest in sight, is it possible that "waiting upon the Lord" is the answer to our problem? "They that wait upon the Lord shall renew their strength."[19]

"I found myself hurrying God," says author and pastor Henry Blackaby. "I just kind of fit Him in wherever He needed to be fit in. And one day God said to me, 'Henry, you're not going to hurry me any more. I'm not going to fit around your schedule—you're going to fit around mine.' That changed my whole life."[20]

If we will not recover the discipline of waiting, God is under no moral obligation to speed up His timetable to accommodate our urgency.

"Rest in the LORD and wait patiently for Him. . . ."[21]

CHAPTER 10

■ ■ ■ ■ ■ ■ ■ ■

Information and Education

■ If the most conscientious physician were to attempt to keep up with the literature by reading two articles per day, in one year this individual would be more than eight hundred years behind.—Octo Barnett, M.D.

■ The Library of Congress contains more than 100 million documents housed on 650 miles of shelving.

■ We're all overloaded. We're sending E-mail to somebody fifty feet away.—Diane Schwarz, Financial Systems Manager

■ [Information overload] is wild. It's killing people. In my office, I have fifteen televisions. I can't handle it all.—Ted Turner, described as the nation's No. 1 news junkie

Drowning in data is now an expected everyday part of corporate life, where having too much information is as dangerous as having too little. Information glut is causing off-the-chart stress levels and growing job dissatisfaction. "The synergistic evolution of computer and telecommunications technologies," explains journalist William Auckerman, "has created a world in which the quantity of information reaching our desks is growing exponentially, far surpassing the linear ability of the human brain to assimilate and process it."[1] Chalk up yet another casualty at the hands of progress.

"Unless we can discover ways of staying afloat amidst the surging torrents of information," warns psychologist Dr. David Lewis, "we may end up drowning in them."[2] The 1996 Reuter's study "Dying for Information" details the increasingly common symptoms of the *Information Fatigue Syndrome*: anxiety, self-doubt, paralysis of analytical capacity, a tendency to blame others, time-wasting, and in some cases illness.

Even though the respondents to this international survey of

managers claim they require high levels of information to do their jobs efficiently, forty-one percent said their working environments are extremely stressful on a daily basis, sixty-one percent report that their personal relationships have suffered, and ninety-four percent do not believe the situation will improve.

RUSH HOUR ON THE INFORMATION SUPERHIGHWAY

There are some who believe the rapidly emerging information super-highway will solve our problems. I don't. If our diagnosis were *too little information coming too slowly,* then the information super-highway would obviously help. But that is not our diagnosis. In fact, we already have too much information coming too fast. How do you put out a fire with gasoline?

As we have seen repeatedly, there are only so many details in anyone's life that can be handled comfortably. When that limit is exceeded, circuits begin to shut down. We refuse to process any more. Yet progress has given us more information in the past thirty years than in all the previous *five thousand years combined.*[3]

Francis Bacon, a contemporary of Shakespeare, is regarded by historians as the last person to know everything in the world. Since then, each of us learns a progressively smaller percentage of all the information that exists. As you might expect, with the explosive growth in information, the gap grows exponentially wider.

Furthermore, there is no reason to suspect that the situation will suddenly reverse, giving us a chance to catch up. Of all the scientists who have ever lived, ninety percent are alive today — each creating, processing, and distributing information. The doubling time of scientific knowledge is remarkably short. The rate at which information is discovered and disseminated exceeds — by many orders of magnitude — our limited ability to learn.

During residency orientation, I tell the young doctors that despite working eighty hours a week for three years doing nothing but learning, they will graduate from residency further behind than when they came. It is frustrating to work that hard, yet slip backward. But I also quickly tell them not to worry — most information exists in the form of pollution, of absolutely no use to them or their patients.

THE PERISHABILITY OF FACT

A surprising and discomforting aspect of this incredible information proliferation is that the more we know, the more certainty seems to recede. We had expected that with the progressive evolution of knowledge, we would hone in on a truth and finally nail it down. The opposite has happened.

Instead of becoming more certain about the truth, we become more insecure. I no longer believe there is a single right answer to a patient's problem. There is only *today's answer.* Don't misunderstand—I am not a therapeutic nihilist. Just a realist who has been around too long and outlived my informational innocence. The half-life of fact is not very long these days. Alfred North Whitehead observed: "Knowledge does not keep any better than fish."[4]

Physicians aren't fond of this development, even less, our patients. But, of course, such dislike doesn't change the universe's opinion of things. Nobody much likes the uncertainty principle, but that doesn't mean we get to repeal it. "Doctors are uncomfortable with uncertainty," explains psychiatrist Paul Fink, M.D. "In fact, our entire system of medical education is constructed as if everything were certain. The fact that what is certain today will be obsolete tomorrow has little influence upon faculties, students, and curriculum committees."[5] "Fifty percent of all we taught you is wrong," announced the President of Harvard Medical School at commencement. "The trouble is, we don't know which fifty percent."

Science is, after all, only "an orderly arrangement of what seem at the time to be facts."

DATACIDE

Everywhere you look, we are surrounded by data. The burgeoning amount of information available has strained all systems attempting to deal with it. A landmark edition of *The New York Times* (13 November 1987) was more than sixteen hundred pages long, contained more than two million lines of type comprised of twelve million words, and weighed twelve pounds. In Germany, the annual Frankfurt Book Fair is the world's largest, where seven thousand publishers from eighty countries show each other 350,000 titles.

According to David Shenk, author of *Data Smog,* paper consumption per capita in the United States tripled between 1940 and 1980, and tripled again between 1980 and 1990. In the average office, sixty percent of each person's time is spent processing documents. The typical business manager is said to read one million words per week.[6]

In one year, 230 journals, 3,200 journal articles, and 50,000 pages of material came across my desk. All of which were, of course, dutifully squirreled away for that illusory day when I will have the time to read them—especially that *New England Journal's* lead article, "Genetic Linkage of the Marfan Syndrome, Ectopia Lentis, and Congenital Contractural Arachnodactyly to the Fibrillin Genes on Chromosomes 15 and 5."

Using transistors etched onto microchips, computerization has thrown the information age into turbo gear. Every month, four quadrillion transistors are produced—*more than half a million for every human on the planet* and each costing far less than a staple. More than seven million transistors are etched on each tiny Pentium II chip, in lines one four-hundredth the thickness of a human hair.[7] It is now possible to cram 11.6 gigabytes of data into one square inch of disk space, which is equivalent to storing an eighteen-story stack of double-spaced typed pages on your thumbnail.[8]

How does one deal with such levels of information? We could perhaps use the document retrieval system recommended in this abstract of *The Journal of the American Society for Information Science*: "A probabilistic document-retrieval system may be seen as a sequential learning process, in which the system learns the characteristics of relevant documents, or, more formally, it learns the parameters of probability distributions describing the frequencies of feature occurrences in relevant and nonrelevant documents."[9] Excuse me for a minute while I blow my buffer.

Of course, no one *can* keep up, and we all increasingly realize it. But that doesn't stop us from trying—through more and more education. Which leads to yet another problem.

EDUCATION OVERLOAD?

I won't dispute the value of a good education. How could I? Upon graduation from senior high, I tell my two boys, my schooling was only half finished. After all, part of the Great Commandment is to love the Lord *with all your mind.*

But within the overload context, shouldn't the heretical question be asked: How much education is enough? How much education is too much? Every decade the educational level of the general populace rises. This is linked to better economic well-being and thought in general to lead to a better overall life. I don't disagree. But as the costs in dollars and years of life escalate, we should at least examine our premises. Is education the cure-all we have made it out to be? Or is information overload pushing us to the prophetic fulfillment of ever learning but never arriving at a knowledge of the truth?[10]

For many students, adolescence becomes nothing more than a strenuous competition to get into the best colleges. In an insightful *Newsweek* commentary, high school junior Elizabeth Shaw describes the driven tiredness many students experience.

After a short night's sleep, Elizabeth rises at 6:30 A.M. and stumbles to the bathroom, her eyes puffy. If lucky, she grabs a mouthful of breakfast before her forty-five-minute commute. She naps in class, learns mostly to pass tests, involves herself in an exhausting array of extracurricular activities, and arrives home around 8 P.M., where a lonely microwave dinner awaits. Then, she begins four hours of homework—not interested in understanding, just finishing the assignments. Sometime after midnight she crashes into bed for a few hours of sleep. Shaw relates:

> This cycle continues week after week, broken only by weekends full of homework and chores. . . . Why do we do this to ourselves? . . . Nearly every high-school student who works into the early morning hours is after one thing: acceptance to a "good" college. . . . School administrators, guidance counselors and parents make it seem as if my life will be over unless I get into a good college.

But recently, in talking to other adults, she discovered that most aren't working in their field of study anyway. Furthermore, many had regrets for not enjoying their high school days and their adolescent years when they had the chance. No wonder she asks, "Is This What Life's About?" in the title of her piece.[11]

Is there a difference between getting into a good university and being prepared to live a good life? I think so. Recently, a seventeen-year-old Californian achieved a perfect score on both sections of the SAT. When asked by a reporter, "What is the meaning of life?" she replied, "I have no idea. I would like to know myself."

THE ANTIDOTE FOR DATACIDE

If our brain cells are protesting and our desks are piled high, what can we do about it? Use the following suggestions as a surge protector against information overload and data distress.

Rx 1 *Increase Your Information Selectivity*

Obviously, we cannot read and process all the information we encounter—so how does one decide? Well-thought-out criteria are needed for sorting information into two great piles: that which interests us (or we know should interest us) and everything else. Sort these piles ruthlessly. The bigger the information overload, the more ruthless we need to become.

A high degree of selectivity works best for information services director Mike Rusk, who was receiving twenty technology publications per week. "It was causing me to be frantic. I saw technology moving so fast, at least on paper, and I couldn't keep up with it," he said. For sanity's sake, he decided to cancel all but two of the subscriptions. "I wanted everything to stop so I had time to digest it and see how it fit into our organization."[12]

Don't just wade indiscriminately through huge volumes of material. Be selective. "It is just as absurd for the user to tap the total collection of new material for his data as it would be for the jeweler to order six tons of gold-bearing ore when he wants to make a cufflink," advises Lewis Branscomb.[13]

Rx 2 *Use Interest as an Avenue for Learning*

When we study things we have no affinity for, learning is unavailable. But when we study things we most enjoy, learning is unavoidable.

"Learning can be seen as the acquisition of information, but before it can take place, there must be interest," explains information expert Richard Saul Wurman. "You can't get lost on the road to interest."[14]

The context of learning is all important. "Remembering does not happen as a matter of course whenever a person is exposed to information," states educational theorist Jeremy Campbell. "It does not even happen automatically if the person wants and intends to commit the information to memory. . . . Questions such as how much effort was spent in trying to store it in memory are of surprisingly little importance." Campbell summarizes by stating, "Clearly, meaning is an important ingredient in remembering."[15]

Rx 3 *It Is Okay Not to Know*

Give your brain a break—it is okay to be finite. It is okay not to know everything. For fifteen years my daily job was tutoring young doctors. When asked a question whose answer I did not know, it was always best to admit ignorance. Even when patients asked such questions, my standard answer was, "I'm not sure. Let me ask someone who is smarter than I am." Patients learned to trust me more, not less.

"By giving yourself permission not to know, you can overcome the fear that your ignorance will be discovered," observes Wurman. "When you can admit to ignorance, you will realize that if ignorance isn't exactly bliss, it is an ideal state from which to learn."[16]

Rx 4 *Pitch the Pile*

In nearly every home or office there is a stack of unread journals and magazines. Cancel publications you don't have time to read. Quit stockpiling journals, magazines, newspapers. If you don't have time to read them today, it is purely illusory that you will somehow have time next month.

"It is impossible, unproductive, and unhealthy to try to read everything," observes Marc Ringel, M.D. "In fact, one of the healthiest things you can do, when faced by an enormous, guilt-provoking pile of journals, is to throw them all out and start keeping up again from scratch. The consequences on your career of missing several months of journal articles will be unmeasurable, while the positive effects on your mental health may be considerable. Anything important that was reported in the pile of journals you tossed will reappear in the next pile."[17]

Swenson's suggestion: If the stack is more than six inches high, save the top inch and throw the rest away. If the stack is more than two feet high, throw the whole pile.

Rx 5 *Clear Your Desk*
The average desk worker has thirty-six hours of work on his or her desk and spends three hours a week sorting piles trying to find the project to work on next. Every year the amount of paper metastasizes without pity. We shuffle it around on our desks, stack it next to our easy chair, and pile it high on our shelves. If at all possible OHIO— Only Handle It Once.

A sure sign that you are too busy, according to Scott Buschschacher, is that you clear off your desk by putting everything in a box to look through it later—and you never see the box again. I have a few such boxes. Somewhere. I think.

Rx 6 *Use the Test of Time*
Publishers sometimes contend that the jar of mayonnaise in the refrigerator has a longer half-life than most books. Information pollution has a way of dying a fairly quick natural death. Understanding this, devote time to the works that have stood the "test of time." Read the Bible, the saints, the classics, the best of literature.

Step up a level or two—from data to information to knowledge to wisdom. There is a difference. The further up the line we ascend, the greater the possibility it will stand the test of time.

Rx 7 *Keep an Open Mind*
Some people are regrettably unwilling to deliberate beyond their decision-point. They regard thinking only as a short step on the

way to forming an opinion, and sometimes they bypass it altogether. As Matz's Maxim states, a conclusion is the place where you get tired of thinking.

Consider the following two thought lines:

Input ' interpretation ' thinking ' opinion ' end

Often this is the termination of thinking.

Input ' interpretation ' thinking ' opinion ' continued rethinking

This is the ideal case of an open mind.

It is right for us to form opinions and make decisions, but that should not be the end of thinking. We should continue to receive input and be willing to rethink the decision if that is indicated. "A closed mind is a sign of hidden doubt," contends theologian Harold DeWolf.[18]

Rx 8 *Stay Teachable*

As an educator it is possible to assess the teachability quotient of each student. As a pastor or psychologist you can assess the teachability quotient of the person seeking counsel. As a matter of fact, the entire world can probably be divided into two great camps: the teachable and the unteachable. The teachable hold such a massive advantage that I find it hard to measure both camps on the same scale. The unteachable will not grow or develop. The teachable, however, no matter where they began, will have a steady upward course—all the way to God.

Rx 9 *Don't Expect Truth from Information*

In our wired age, information and knowledge bring power and wealth. You can build a career and a fortune on them. But they are inadequate to build a life on.

Don't expect truth from information—they are not the same. Information can only take us so far. For example, when asked about faith, Bill Gates replied, "I don't have enough data on that."

Truth comes not from information, but from revelation. "Sanctify them by the truth," Jesus prayed. "Your word is truth."[19]

Rx 10 *Remain Humble*

Elitism, for me, is one of the most disappointing and discouraging of human sins. And I find it more associated with education than with wealth or politics. Once when I was working short-term in a developing country, another doctor (not American) revealed his disdain for the people we were serving. "Ignorance is the one thing I can't stand," he said. *Arrogance,* I thought, *is the one thing I can't stand.*

As the world increasingly divides into the haves and the have-nots, it will be important to hold the intellectual advantage with humility. Having access to education does not give us any extra credit with God—only increased responsibility.

Rx 11 *Study God's Opinion*

Some people are so overloaded processing information that they have no time left for the Scriptures. My advice is this: Absorb data and study facts, but never neglect God's opinion of the matter. And the journey down the road of God's opinion might lead to a humbling backfire of the intellect. "Do not deceive yourselves," the apostle Paul says. "If any one of you thinks he is wise by the standards of this age, he should become a 'fool' so that he may become wise. For the wisdom of this world is foolishness in God's sight."[20]

In our rush for an education, we all wish to appear learned in the eyes of our peers. But as British author G. K. Chesterton reminds us, "A man who has faith must be prepared not only to be a martyr, but to be a fool."

Rx 12 *Don't Neglect Education of the Heart*

How sad to see people who know the uttermost details of science or the liberal arts but who ignore the matters of the heart. IQ will seldom lead to happiness. Einstein, in fact, once commented, "Those who know the most are the gloomiest."

The Tin Man in *The Wizard of Oz* expressed it well: "Once I had a brain and a heart also. Having tried them both, I should much rather have a heart."

CHAPTER 11

■ ■ ■ ■ ■ ■ ■ ■

Media Overload

■ Right now television has the culture by its throat.
—NEIL POSTMAN

■ In the years ahead, we will live increasingly in fictions: We will turn on our virtual-reality systems and lie back, experiencing heavenly pleasures of sight and sound in a snug electronic nest. The real world will almost be totally blotted out from our experience.—WORLD FUTURE SOCIETY

■ At MTV, we don't shoot for the 14-year-olds, we own them.—BOB PITTMAN, FORMER MTV CHAIRMAN

■ There are no gatekeepers left at the networks.
—BOB GARFIELD, COLUMNIST AT *ADVERTISING AGE*

B y now, media in its various forms have penetrated all aspects of contemporary life. It is hard to imagine a life—or even a *single day*—that is not saturated start-to-finish with media. Much of this is acceptable, perhaps even laudable. Movies and television can inform, stimulate, and entertain. Newspapers and magazines keep us up-to-date. Music can lift our spirits, massage our souls, and stimulate our senses. The Internet can, at least potentially, do all of the above.

But everything in a fallen world has a downside. And, in that regard, media is as bad as it gets.

TELEVISION

Anchoring the top spot in the media winner's circle is, of course, the omnipresent television. It has reshaped every aspect of our society, from entertainment to news to political life to religion. It writes its own rules, only partially influenced by viewers.

In the average home, the television is turned on seven hours a day. The average viewer watches between twenty and thirty-six hours per week, depending on age and gender. It is hard to over-emphasize the impact of something so temporally dominating.

Some predictions estimate that early into the new millennium, satellite dish technology will be able to deliver five thousand channels. With such cable and satellite access, television's reach into our psyches has not yet peaked. And when you take into account the powerful attractiveness of new technologies such as big screen TVs with HDTV resolution and surround sound, our love affair is not about to end.

MOVIES

The younger the adult age, the more likely we are to be frequent movie attenders or to rent them in videos.

Who does *not* see a movie in the theater in a given month

18-24	seventeen percent
24-34	forty-seven percent
35-44	fifty-seven percent
45-54	sixty-three percent
55-64	seventy-three percent
65 and up	eighty percent[1]

According to media expert Dr. Ted Baehr, teenagers watch fifty movies a year in the theater and view another fifty a year on video. Eighty percent of these movies are PG-13 or R-rated.[2] Research has demonstrated that we store three trillion "videotape" images in our brain by the time we are thirty years old. But, worrisomely, we have no volitional control over selective forgetting. Once the images are there, we must then live with the consequences of that visual imprint. Realizing that the graphic content of R-rated movies is now irrevocably loaded into the memory banks of our youth gives us legitimate cause for alarm.

The easy accessibility of videos has both reshaped and inflated our movie viewing habits. A film is distributed through a sequence of exclusive windows—first in theaters, then in video, pay-per-view, pay TV (such as HBO), basic cable, and finally network television. Movie studios derive more than half of their revenues from video. Even though the video market is facing increasing competition from satellite TV, we rent 3.5 to 4 billion videos a year.[3]

Movies continue their slide in the direction of violence, nudity, and objectionable language. Many blockbuster movies now have elements of all three. The tendency in this direction has been mainstreamed and seems to hardly elicit a yawn.

Children at younger and younger ages are drawn into the movie/video habit, especially with the common use of videos for baby-sitting. As parents become more overloaded, it is simply too tempting to put in a video and place the children before the set. They are well behaved and even entranced. And for busy, stressed-out, exhausted parents, there is nothing so attractive as quiet children.

Toys are now commonly linked to movies that are R-rated. For example, the sci-fi movie *Starship Troopers* has graphic violence, nudity, and objectionable language. Alien bugs impale and behead humans, even sucking out their brains. (This from the same director whose last film was the pornographic NC-17 rated *Showgirls*.) Uninformed parents who see these alien bugs on toy shelves—labeled for kids four and up—are likely to think the movie is acceptable viewing. They would be mistaken.

RADIO, MUSIC, AND CDs

Radio can be a wonderful companion on the road, in the lonely hours of the night, or—for that matter—at *any* hour. Music, the mainstay of radio programming, is a special gift from the creative genius of God. Unfortunately, it has been counterclaimed by the Evil One, and the battle rages furiously for the heart and soul of a nation—especially our youth.

Records ruled the music world until 1982, when sales were eclipsed for the first time by audiocassettes. In 1992, CDs passed cassettes. The unique captivating power of music somehow results in discordant, strident melodies with shocking lyrics selling millions overnight, including such themes as sexual obsession, incest, rape, dehumanized sex, mutilation, cop-killing, torture, dismemberment, suicide, self-loathing, and nihilism.[4] (Specific examples are included in the Notes for those interested—and able to tolerate it.) How did we arrive at such a place? This much we know: Time Warner granted generous assistance along the way.

To assume that the average American teenager has not heard these songs is to be culturally naive. As Gerald Early has pointed out, "There is no innocence in childhood, only less mature depravities."[5] The average parent, however, remains blissfully unaware. "Teenagers receive at least two dozen forms of entertainment," explains media expert Bob DeMoss, "and most of it flies under the radar screen of adults."[6]

INTERNET AND COMPUTERS

Is the Internet (called *anarchy that works*) rightly considered a medium? Increasingly, the answer must be yes. It informs, entertains, advertises. And it is explosive. No one can completely predict how dominant it will become, just as no one really predicted its advent or its rapid ascension. Analysts expect forty-three percent of U.S. households to have some Internet capability by the year 2000.[7]

"Computer cost effectiveness has risen 100 millionfold since the late 1950s—a 100 thousandfold rise in power times a thousandfold drop in cost," explains technology expert George Gilder. "Three years ago, all the phone networks in the world combined carried an average of a terabit a second. Today, [individual] companies are sending three terabits per second down a single fiber thread the width of a human hair."[8] When you combine this stunning development with the anticipated growth in satellite technology—both geostationary (GEOs) and low-earth-orbiting (LEOs) satellites—estimates of Internet users vary from 300 million to 1 billion at the turn of the millennium.[9]

Kids can often navigate the Internet better than their parents, who never quite know what their children are into. Additionally, this trend can be socially isolating. In one survey, forty-six percent of respondents said their children prefer computers to their peers.[10]

Pornography over the Internet is, in my opinion, the greatest moral threat ever encountered in the pornography arena. It is more private than ever before and will prove to be far more devastating than most people can imagine. Speaking of the Internet, Bill Maher of television's *Politically Incorrect* explains, "Anything you can put sex into will be used for that purpose more than for anything else."[11] One adult entertainment website, ClubLove, reported an estimated 1.4 *billion* hits in 1997.

Computers once made great claims for the potential of CD-ROMs. But they are experiencing a type of overloading trouble all their own. With about ten thousand titles available, people simply do not have the time nor money to shop through these offerings. And even if they did, they do not have the time to use such a vast array of capacity. The essence of CD-ROM still shows great promise. But here, just as in any other area, too much is too much. Ultimately, overload brings us all to our knees.

EFFECTS OF MEDIA OVERLOAD

Media has reordered social thought and behavior in unprecedented ways. The widespread effects of this media profusion are broadly integrative, thus rendering the following discussion only partial.

Resets the Moral Acceptability Threshold

"Do the things that once offended you now entertain you?" asks media critic Al Menconi. "Are you able to enjoy the company of television programs, videos, and movies that have values diametrically opposed to yours? . . . Do you remember the first time you heard someone use profanity in a motion picture? I do. It was less than twenty years ago, in the movie "All the President's Men." I was shocked that they could use that word. Now we hear worse on television every night."[12]

This moral drift is important to understand, for it continues unabated. Extrapolate ten or twenty years into the future and it is frightening to imagine what media content awaits us.

Resets the Shock Threshold

In the past, if we saw blood, killing, or tragedies on the evening news, it would disturb us for weeks. Today, however, the rule of the newsroom is, "If it bleeds, it leads."

Movies are worse. Beginning about thirty years ago, succeeding waves of movies relied on more and more violence to attract crowds. Audiences became numbed to the repulsiveness of each level of violence, so directors had to enhance the horror to maintain interest. Such common fare no longer elicits anguish. To be sure, there is a temporary adrenaline kick—the kind that causes you to eat your popcorn faster. But no anguish.

Resets the Boredom Threshold

After one eight-year-old boy had been watching television all Saturday afternoon, his father politely asked him to turn off the set. When five minutes of silence had elapsed, the boy moaned, "But Dad, it's so lonely."

Results in Addictive Behavior

As a generalization, when media is available, people use it as a first option—the younger the age, the truer this principle holds. And once fully indoctrinated into this world of media, it is hard to break away. Media increasingly defines our world, and taking the media away is like taking our world away. When media is gone, there is seemingly nothing left—no inner reality, no relationships, no comfort, laughter, music, or security.

Gives a More Negative View of the World

The world is already in enough trouble and we don't need to make it appear any worse than it is. But in the world of media, bad news sells. According to media critic Ben Wattenberg, bad news is big news. Additionally, good news is no news. So if you want to get on the air, the formula is the simple: Say something terrible.[13]

Fictional programming isn't any better than the newscasts. The average prime-time TV schedule presents the viewer with 350 characters each night, seven of whom will be murdered on screen. "If this rate applied in reality, then in just 50 days, everyone in the United States would be killed," explains media critic Michael Medved.[14]

Increases Exposure to Sexual Material

The pervasiveness of media leads to an almost unavoidable exposure to sexually explicit material at ever-younger ages. Observes adolescent medicine specialist Victor Strasburger, M.D.:

> Teenagers watch an average of three hours of TV per day, listen to the radio for an additional one to two hours, and often have access to R-rated movies and even pornography long before they are adults. According to the best study from the late 1980s, the average American teenager views almost 15,000 sexual jokes, innuendoes and other references on TV each year. Fewer than 170 of these deal with what any sane adult would define as responsible sexual behavior. . . . Add to that the 20,000 commercials per year each teenager in America sees—with implicit messages that sex is fun, sex is sexy and everyone out there is having sex but you—and you have at least the possibility of a fairly important influence.[15]

WHAT IS AHEAD?

In the future, people will increasingly live in their home media centers where their alternative reality will be irresistibly more enjoyable than the stressful realities of work and relationships. They will have a seven-foot high, two-inch thick high-resolution screen hanging on the wall connected to their television/computer/Internet/phone/ cable/satellite complex. With easy and secure credit card payment mechanisms, they will be able to browse hundreds (or thousands) of television channels, call in any movie they wish when they wish it, surf the Internet, or shop to their heart's content.

Additionally, many will choose a virtual-reality sex life on demand. Health authorities and social welfare advocates might even propose cybersex as a cost-effective solution for the costly epidemics of unwanted pregnancies, abortion, sexually-transmitted diseases and AIDS.[16] If this scenario bothers you as much as it does me, begin preparing answers now. It will be here sooner than you think.

PRESCRIPTIONS FOR MODERATING MEDIA SATURATION

A passive approach to media consumption is not only unwise but increasingly irresponsible. The following are suggestions and guidelines that will help steer a healthy course through a risky minefield.

Rx 1 *Guard Against Media Constituting Your Only Barrier to Loneliness*

It is easy to lapse into a *media-saturated* existence, which eventually leads to a *media-dependent* existence. When lonely, bored, or stressed, the first thing we often do is activate our media surroundings—which usually means turning on the television. In a previous era, we would instead have perhaps visited a friend.

If you are lonely, get in the car and visit someone who would welcome the contact. Or get on the phone and call a friend. Write a letter of encouragement. Invite someone over. Make a coffee date.

This is not to say that all such media usage for loneliness is inappropriate. But if overused, it will result in more isolation, not less.

Rx 2 *Allow Boredom to Nourish the Imagination*

Don't fear boredom—it can be useful. People can't stand it for long. Boredom is a seed bed of imagination. To short-circuit boredom is to short-circuit creativity.

The temptation is to solve boredom with media. If the children are bored, don't always turn to TV, videos, or computer games. Let the boredom build. If boredom increases with no possibility of electronics, imagination will begin to surface. This is called "play." Play is the business of childhood. Let kids get bored and have to play their way out of it.

"What could have been long periods of super stagnation (stranded in a hayfield in the heat of August and cow-sitting!) forced us to hatch up our own amusements," explains Edna Hong, in describing her growing up years. "What we hatched proves among other things the creative power inherent in boredom, of being placed in a situation so boring that the most fallow imagination begins to improve."[17]

Rx 3 *Create Rather than Consume*

Life is meant to be participatory and relational. As James Coleman explained, "Life in general used to be experience-rich and stimulus-poor; now it has become nearer the reverse."[18]

Create entertainment, don't just consume it. Prefer active over passive. Play the football game yourself. Make your own music. Visit, bake, sew together. Travel. Don't live a vicarious virtual-reality existence. Instead, create a personal-experience reality.

Rx 4 *Establish Media Limits*

If media in all its forms continues to escalate in visibility and dominance, there obviously comes a point when we have to impose limits. Decide such limits as an act of intention rather than randomness.

For example, consider putting some limits on television. It is acceptable for TV to be an interlude, but it should not become a way of life. Have standard rules that make sense. Don't force yourselves into re-deciding every week. *Possible* suggestions (not laws!) might include:

- Allow up to seven hours of TV (including videos) each week.
- Require all viewing to be preplanned or intentional.
- No TV is allowed until homework or chores are done.
- One hour per day can be viewed only for approved shows.

Also limit the number of channels—be leery about expanding. More is not necessarily *better.* Limit the number of TVs as well. Although the majority of children today have a television in their own room (fifty-eight percent), mostly it is not a good idea. For one reason, we want to live as a family—otherwise "home is where we live alone together." For another reason, it is essential that parents keep an eye on what their children watch.

Beyond television, consider also establishing limits on Nintendo, Sega, Walkman, and Internet use.

Rx 5 *Have Non-electronic Children's Parties*

Consider not renting or viewing any electronics for birthdays or slumber parties. Cultivate other activities instead. For our boys' birthdays, we would always have two special events: marshmallow fights (they are safe and don't hurt) and darts thrown at balloons. Each balloon contained a small note with promises of a treat. The participant would pick up the note and immediately collect the treat. Later, we used an Ecuadorian blowgun instead of darts.

The point is, it is possible to have fun without the media dominating the scene. But once media is introduced, forget it. Nothing else can compete.

Rx 6 *Resist Advertisements*

Ads are omnipresent in our "engineered-message" lives. If we try to completely avoid them, we will not succeed. The next best thing is to discipline ourselves and train our children to be wary. Point out the falsehood and manipulation in each ad. Teach discernment. Distinguish between advertising "information" and "propaganda." Talk about the enormous cost of ads, thus their power. If ads don't influence, why are companies willing to pay millions of dollars for a few seconds of exposure? Discuss contentment versus discontentment. Talk about "need-creation." Ask yourself and the family, "If God were sitting on the couch with us, what would He think of this ad?"

My habit is either to turn the channel during ads, or mute it and get something else accomplished.

Rx 7 *Zap the Set*

Consider always having the remote nearby when watching television. Use it freely. Also use it as a threat and a teaching tool. If something objectionable comes on, hit the mute button, switch the channel, or turn off the set.

As violence screening chips (V-chips) were first being discussed, one man told me he had his own V-chip. He would sit on the couch with an open scissors, through which coursed an extension cord to the television. His children would stare at him with wide-eyed wonder, fearful that he might actually cut the power when inappropriate material came on the screen. I hope he does. Often. It would be a visible lesson the children would not soon forget.

Rx 8 *Disconnect Cable Selectively*

If you have cable—and most people do—there are some things best to avoid. Most cable operators will allow selective disconnection from those elements that you find objectionable. When I asked media expert Bob DeMoss if there was any reason people should have HBO and MTV in their homes, his answer was immediate: "None."

Popular movie critic Michael Medved agrees: "There is absolutely no excuse for MTV to be present in the home," he maintains. "It is one hundred percent negative."[19]

Call your carrier and request they selectively discontinue such channels from your cable package.

Rx 9 *Fast from the Media*

Throughout this book, the notion of modern *fasting* occurs often. Media is perhaps one of the most important kinds of fasts. Have a *no-television* week or month. Don't listen to the news perhaps for a week. Pray in the car instead of listening to the radio. Or simply enjoy the silence for a change. Cancel the newspaper or magazine. Create an intentional solitude.

Rx 10 *Regain Control of the Value System*

"Parents can no longer control the atmosphere of the home and have even lost the will to do so," asserted Professor of Social Thought Allan Bloom in *The Closing of the American Mind.*[20] Sadly, many of us have essentially and tragically lost control of the value system of our children—often compliments of the media. If we still hope to influence them in the direction of virtue, it is important to make our move early.

Spend time watching television and movies with your children. Be aware of what movies they are watching, what music they are listening to, what television programs are their favorites. Make an effort to understand their views and values. Discern their evolving worldview. (It *is* evolving—it's just that they don't always discuss it with their parents). Take pains to influence (without being overly paternalistic or preachy) while you still have the opportunity— you will lose control soon enough.

When your kids are young, have their friends play at your house so you can know what they are watching. Also let them know it is okay to call you to pick them up at any hour if they are at a friend's house and feel uncomfortable about the television or video selection.

Rx 11 *Be Aware*

We cannot effectively confront a problem in our society until we understand it. Yet to understand contemporary media requires that we watch and listen to very disturbing television, movie, and musical material. What to do? It presents a difficult dilemma plaguing many: either ignore the existence of such disturbing content, thus rendering ourselves ill-equipped to understand the needs of our children and neighbors; or expose ourselves to such content and thus subject ourselves to contamination. It is like asking: Should we eat garbage or go hungry?

Personally I have chosen to peruse some of what is out there, partly because of my work as a cultural analyst and futurist. For the general populace, however, I do not have an easy answer. Yet *somehow* we need to be more aware if we wish to understand and influence those around us.

Rx 12 *Hate Evil*

Evil, for reasons not completely clear to me, is always more interesting. This obviously is not a statement about the way things should be, but simply a statement of the way things are. Once we understand this, much that is mysteriously wrong in life becomes clearer. For example, if we had forty-nine stations broadcasting healthy, virtuous programming, and only one station broadcasting violent or sexual programming, most of America would be tuned into the one channel. Even church people. Evil is always more interesting.

Understanding the allure of evil explains why we watch so much of it, even when it is so clearly destructive. The sheer volume of evil our nation is exposed to on a daily basis is one of the most disturbing effects of the proliferation of media. The only remedy I know is two thousand years old: "Hate what is evil; cling to what is good."[21]

Rx 13 *Take the Internet Plunge*

It might surprise some to hear me suggest getting on-line. Internet access is virtually inevitable for all homes—just as were the telephone, television, and microwave. A balanced understanding of the age in which we live includes thinking through such new technologies rather than rejecting them out of hand.

The Internet will solve some problems and will exacerbate others. But there is no stopping it. We should not boycott it because of its downside but rather use it with care and discretion.

So sign on, but be careful. I have three main concerns:

- It can be a waste of time—set up guidelines.
- It can lead to addictive behavior—guard against it.
- It can give almost unlimited access to pornography in a much more dangerous way than ever before—install screening devices against inappropriate sites.

Rx 14 *Substitute Soothing Music*

Music fills the air and the ears of America, especially our youth. For many youth (perhaps most), music heroes have even greater stature than movie or sports stars. To simply tell these kids to stop listening is not realistic—they won't. But if we can give them an alternative, perhaps. . . . At least we can try. And hope. And pray.

Looking beyond the interests of our children to our preferences, there is a wide choice of what we might listen to. My advice: Listen to that which calms the spirit.

Rx 15 *Use a Movie Viewer Guide*

Many movies today are unfit for viewing—but which ones? To help discern, our family subscribes to a movie preview guide to make sure the movie meets our personal standards for acceptability. The guide lists acceptability ratings from -4 to +4, and entertainment ratings from 0 to 4. Their report also lists objectionable elements in each movie, so there are few surprises in the middle of the movie. We have established certain minimum acceptability guides. This way the boys' displeasure at our restriction is displaced onto the guide rather than on us. Having a concrete guide prevents a power struggle with each movie. It might seem a bit expensive, but we have found it invaluable.

Here are two possible guides to choose from:

- *Preview* comes out twice a month, and costs $33/year. 1309 Seminole Drive, Richardson, TX 75080 (Phone: 972-231-9910)
- *MovieGuide* comes out twice a month, and new subscriptions cost $15.95 for 6 months or $28.88 for one year. Address: Good News Communications, P.O. Box 190010, Atlanta, GA 31119 (Phone: 800-899-6684)

Rx 16 *Rent Videos*

Watching a movie together can be a valuable bonding experience. But at today's prices it costs $25 to $30 to take a family of four to the theater. Renting a video instead (or checking it out at the library for free or a minimal charge) has many advantages: it is less expensive; you can discuss the movie as it progresses; you can turn it off if it becomes objectionable; you can pause to get a snack or use the bathroom; and the popcorn doesn't cost $3.

Establishing a warm atmosphere in the home for such an event is a treat the children will long remember. In our family, we often will turn off the telephones, light candles, have a fire in the fireplace, enjoy special snacks, and push the sofas together.

Preview publishes an updated Family Video Guide of one thousand recommended videos. It provides a synopsis of the plot, suggested age for viewing, and entertainment rating.

Rx 17 *Encourage Reading*

Someone once said, "Having your book made into a movie is like having your oxen made into bouillon cubes." A good book well written is almost always superior to the corresponding movie. The book's language is more creative than the movie script, and the mind's imagination is usually more interesting than the movie set.

Consider reading the book together instead of seeing the movie. Or perhaps do both. The goal is not only to entertain, but to teach children a love for the written word. To accomplish such a lofty purpose in the face of overwhelming competition from movies and television requires more than coercion. It should be warmly relational as well. "It's the quality of interaction between the parent and child, or teacher and child, that motivates the kids in reading," explains psychologist Carrie Becker.[22]

In our family, the children were "invested" readers—meaning we bribed them. Not paying an allowance, we instead offered to pay a penny a page for reading books. After the title, author, and number of pages were recorded they were paid. When they wanted to make a special purchase, such as a bicycle or outdoor equipment, they would "read" for it. As a side benefit, avid readers usually limit their electronic media time.

Rx 18 *Create a Reading Evening*

Consider having a regular or episodic family reading evening. Go through a book or series together, such as C. S. Lewis's *Chronicles of Narnia* or J. R. R. Tolkien's *Lord of the Rings* trilogy. Or have each person reading his or her own book, but be together while doing it. Make it a special evening, with favorite food, snacks, soda, or juice. Create a warm, quiet, uninterrupted atmosphere. Announce it days in advance—don't spring it on the kids last-minute.

Rx 19 *Visit Used Bookstores*

More than two billion new books are purchased each year in the U.S., among them the 58,000 new titles that appear annually. But it can also be great fun to visit used bookstores. What a thrill to find an out-of-print classic for $1.50, or a recent twenty dollar hardbound best seller for three dollars. Linda has enjoyed searching for books by the British author Elizabeth Goudge, and we now are working toward completing our collection of her wonderful, otherwise unavailable works. Many libraries sponsor quarterly used book sales. One suggestion is to inquire about the sale dates and pencil them in on the calendar as a scheduled event.

Rx 20 *Have a Family Outing*

The library is as enjoyable a place to visit as the movies—but only if you start young enough. Our library is nestled on the shores of a beautiful lake, with window seats next to the water. It is hard to imagine a better setting to come for a quiet family outing. When the kids were younger, we also would go to used bookstores for family activities. They had no trouble entertaining themselves looking among the shelves that contained material of interest to them. Walks, hikes, fishing, museums, zoos, car rides into the country — all are satisfying alternatives for a life of media overload. Once the children are older, they will resist. That's okay, they will still have memories — an important legacy that will later serve them well.

Rx 21 *Include Only the Best*

Be selective about what media you allow in your home or into your life. There is so much to choose from and so much that is harmful, it seems unnecessary to even discuss the notion of choosing only what is best. But busyness and overload often overwhelm common sense, let alone discernment.

For television, choose only the best. For example, how can anyone go wrong with "Anne of Green Gables"? When our children were younger, we would watch *Little House on the Prairie* together. Even today these evenings remain as some of our fondest memories. Watch programming that models relational reconciliation and godly problem-solving. There is no controversy involved in watching the things that are noble and relationally powerful.

CHAPTER 12

■■■■■■■■

Possession

- In the next twenty-five years, the world's system will produce more goods than all of previous history of the world combined.—BARRY ASMUS, ECONOMIST

- Be content with what you've got; and be sure you've got plenty.—HAGAR'S TWO RULES FOR HAPPINESS

- He who buys what he doesn't need steals from himself.
  —SWEDISH PROVERB

- A man's life does not consist in the abundance of his possessions.—JESUS, LUKE 12:15

Years ago in Siam, if the king had an enemy he wanted to torment, it was easy: Give him a white elephant. The receiver of this gift was now obligated into oblivion. Any gift from the king obviously had to be cared for—it could not be given away without causing offense. Additionally, a white elephant was considered sacred and thus required the best nourishment and protection. Soon the extreme costs of caring for the gift drove the king's enemy to destitution.

Today it seems everyone in America is on the king's hit list. We are increasingly buried under mountains of possessions. Closets are full, attics are groaning, garages are bulging, storage space is saturated. Swollen houses lead to the three-car-garage syndrome: huge homes with spacious garages, yet all the cars parked in the driveway because the garages are already full.

If that little space left in your house is creating an annoying sucking sound, there is no shortage of consumer clutter waiting to occupy the temporary vacuum. For example, if you have $1.2 million to $75 million, you could buy a personal submarine over the Internet from the U.S. government (www.ussubs.com). Or you could buy a lighted Christmas wreath for the front grill of your car. If you want to light up the life of someone special, you can spend $400,000 for the Heartthrob Brooch. It has six rubies, seventy-eight diamonds, and chip-controlled, light-emitting diodes which flash with each beat of the wearer's heart. Or you could purchase the world's smallest working model railroad with a nineteen-inch attaché case for only $1,295 (battery included). If you buy sterling silver thermometer cufflinks for $98, you can take the temperature of your wrists.

If you can't find it at the mall, try mail order. *The Catalog of Catalogs* lists more than twelve thousand catalogs from which to order. "I hope you will not only find what you are looking for, but also hundreds of other teasers you'll want to send away for," writes the editor. "Don't resist the urge!" One of their best selling catalogs is "Things You Never Knew Existed"—*Items you can't possibly live without!*

CONSUMER ORGY

"Affluenza," states the PBS television special, "is an unhappy condition of overload, debt, anxiety, and waste resulting from the dogged pursuit of more." Affluenza turns the *good* life into the *goods* life. We now have more shopping malls than high schools, and in many communities, the mall has become the center of community life. Mall mania leads to recreational shopping, compulsive shopping, and therapeutic shopping. As many as one-third of shoppers express an irresistible compulsion to buy—often in reaction to stress, anxiety, or depression. Forty percent of these compulsive shoppers admit their closets are filled with unopened items. Thomas O'Guinn, professor of advertising, University of Illinois, believes that "consumers are in an endless, hopeless search for happiness through the acquisition of things."[1]

Not only do we want more—we want bigger. Not just quantity, but bulk. Houses are three rooms larger than they were twenty years ago, even though families are smaller. Our cars are bigger, shoes are larger, furniture is overstuffed, tubs are huge, and now they have a mattress one size up from the king. Plates even hold more, McDonald's tells us to *Supersize it!*, and 7-Eleven has a 64 ounce *Double Gulp*. "We're having a harmonic convergence for bigness," observes Jon Berry, editor of *Public Pulse*.

Florida attorney Stacey Giulianti is a case in point. "I've got a 61-inch TV, which, diagonally, is one inch bigger than my own mother," the twenty-nine-year-old lawyer said. "I've got an 11-speaker surround-sound system. I've got oversized plush couches and a monster-size kitchen with a huge bread maker and a commercial-size mixer. And I've got a large master bedroom with a walk-in closet that was the size of my bedroom in my old house." He has a soaking tub, twelve-foot cathedral ceilings and an enormous Infiniti four-by-four truck that they never drive off-road. "Life is messy," he points out, "and it's nice when you're done with your day to be able to come home and soak in the big tub, grill in your big backyard, and watch your 61-inch TV. It allows you to escape the daily stress. You work hard, you want to enjoy your comforts."[2]

Where is one to store this cultural largess? In ever larger houses, of course. Martha Stewart, after all, has to put her sixteen televisions someplace. One Californian mansion we saw from a distance has twenty bedrooms, twenty-five bathrooms, plus both indoor and outdoor Olympic size pools for a thirty-two-year-old man, his wife, and daughter. Ironically, he made a fortune in the mini-storage business.

Today, many garages are as large as entire houses were in the 1950s. Forget Martha's TVs; Jerry Seinfeld has to put his sixty cars somewhere.

INEXTINGUISHABLE NEEDS

I suppose there was a time, several decades back, when both manufacturers and retailers feared a theoretical saturation point—that threshold where consumers would say *enough* and stop buying. But if they ever feared the existence of such a theoretical point, by now the answer has declared itself: There is no such point of satiety. No matter how much people have, they still want more.

"The urgency of wants does not diminish appreciably as more

of them are satisfied," explained John Kenneth Galbraith in *The Affluent Society*. "When man has satisfied his physical needs, then psychologically grounded desires take over. These can never be satisfied or, in any case, no progress can be proved."[3] Forty years after he wrote those words, his economic theory still holds. "So long as the consumer adds new products—seeks variety rather than quantity—he may accumulate without diminishing the urgency of his wants" Galbraith summarizes.[4]

PRESCRIPTIONS FOR CURBING THE CLUTTER

If you are looking up at your mountain of possessions from a deep hole of debt, rather than rent another storage garage consider the following suggestions.

Rx 1 *See Owning as a Liability Rather than an Asset*

There seems to be a one-to-one relationship between the *possession of things* and *the consumption of time*. Everything we own requires a commitment of our work time to pay for it and our leisure time to use and care for it. Don't buy or keep anything if the time spent on it competes unfavorably with family, service, or God. Remember: Everything we own owns us. We are free in accordance with the number of things we can do without.

At the beginning of every day we are given assignments with eternal significance—to serve and to love. But when God issued these assignments, He wasn't intending that we serve things and love possessions. He was talking about people. The simpler our possessions, the more time for people.

Rx 2 *Unclutter*

Life is busy enough, days are interrupted enough, and space is crowded enough. Whenever we get a chance, it is wise to kick out the clutter.

"Getting rid of it all was a tremendously liberating experience," relates simplicity author Elaine St. James. "Once you begin to experience the exhilaration and the sense of freedom such an exercise generates, uncluttering will become easier and easier."[5] Until you come into that sense of exhilaration you may need a "clutter buddy," defined as "one who supports another person in sorting and discarding accumulated personal possessions."[6]

Rx 3 *Have a Birthday Party*

"I've proven that I can make what I need to make, buy what I need to buy," said New York writer Liz Perle McKenna. "What I own doesn't say who I am anymore." So for her fortieth birthday party, she asked her guests to come to her home and take something away.[7]

Rx 4 *Look Down the Ladder*

Instead of looking *up the ladder* at people who have possessions we lack, Joni Eareckson Tada teaches us to change the direction of our gaze — look *down the ladder* at the poor, the ill, the destitute. Imagine ourselves in their shoes. When, through compassion, we internalize their hardship, it will deliver us from our current bondage to envy. The *desire for more* is replaced by the *gratitude for enough*.

Rx 5 *Resist the Consumptive Lifestyle*

In modern America, living a consumptive lifestyle is as natural as breathing. To *shop till you drop* is thoroughly and thoughtlessly mainstream. People are temporarily pleased with their external purchases but chronically unhappy with their internal emptiness. To step off the treadmill requires a level of understanding, of intention, of resistance that is hard to come by. No one models it for us, and we don't have the time or energy to think through the implications and consequences on our own.

All that is rapidly changing. At an unprecedented pace, voluntary simplicity is gaining enthusiastic adherents. Is it possible that the most important answers for our most important problems are not consumption-based answers? Christ's chosen lifestyle two millennia ago gave a prominent hint as to God's opinion on this issue.

Rx 6 *Make a List*

A large percentage of purchases are bought on impulse. Fifty percent of hardware purchases, for example, are impulse decisions — as are fifty percent of grocery purchases. Impulse purchases are those things we didn't go to the store to buy—but we bought anyway.

Make a list of needed items *before* going to the store. Don't leave home without it and don't deviate from it.

Rx 7 *Be Creative*

One of the difficulties with our hyperliving, exhausted, chronically-behind lifestyle is that often we must buy our way out of hurriedness: quickly pick up that present at full price and pay to have it gift-wrapped; stop for fast food once again tonight; place a call to hire someone to pull off the birthday party.

A simpler, slower pace to life pays many dividends, not the least of which is a newfound ability to use creativity to solve our problems instead of money. "We try to come up with a creative solution," explains Elaine St. James, "rather than a buying solution."[8]

Rx 8 *Stay Off the Treadmill*

Harvard economist Juliet Schor explains how, instead of an earn-and-save cycle, most Americans have adopted a work-and-spend cycle. This involves a nonstop and accelerating treadmill of working more, wanting more, buying more, owing more, and then working more again.

If we buy expensive houses and automobiles, obviously these purchases need to be paid for. Things are paid for in dollars; dollars are earned by working; working consumes time; and time is what we are trying to gain. Therefore, *fewer things = less work = more time.*

Rx 9 *Counter the Culture with Like-minded Friends*

Culture is not a passive agent in our possession problem but instead a powerful force that demands we buy its wares and live by its rules. Acquiescing to such demands inevitably leads to overload and margin erosion. Many of these cultural expectations wither under the scrutiny of Scripture, yet we willingly subject ourselves to their control.

When Linda and I made our dramatic lifestyle change, we asked God to redesign our lives according to that which was spiritually authentic. Because God's opinion is always the healthy option, our redesigned life indeed turned out to be healthier and more satisfying than the life we were leading under the tutelage of culture.

God tells us we cannot be conformed to the world and be free at the same time. "Do not conform any longer to the pattern of this world," the apostle Paul declares, "but be transformed by the renewing of your mind."[9] In other words, Christians who desire freedom must become a "contrast-society." This does not mean we drop out but simply that we refuse societal servitude.

Willingly and knowingly we wrestle control from culture and set our orientation in the opposite direction. It is wonderful if a community of believers can support one another in making such countercultural decisions. The more different we are from the ambient culture, the more we need to be surrounded by like-minded friends who will support our value structure.

Rx 10 *Pass It Around*

The idea of owning some things in common is both practical and biblical. Why should each family own its own canoe, Rototiller, chain saw, and food dehydrator? When we share graciously the things God has given us, the blessing flows to others. It helps contain the clutter, ease the debt burden, and build community.

Rx 11 *Redefine Happiness*

"Grandma, I just found out what happiness is. It's that feeling you have just after you buy something." Vicki Robin, coauthor of *Your Money or Your Life,* relates overhearing this from a four-year-old. And yet how many of our children—at least superficially—believe in the same creed? Indeed, how many of us often share the same feelings?

Happiness comes from being loved and knowing truth. To convince our children of this reality—to say nothing of a watching world—will require more than preaching. It will require a lifestyle consistent with our definition.

Rx 12 *Change Your Value System*

In the context of possessions, there are three important rules about values. The first is that people are more important than things. The second is that people are more important than things. And the third is that people are more important than things.

In my study is a calligraphy that Linda commissioned, containing a passage from Dickens' *Bleak House*. It is the testimony of an unusually virtuous woman who, in the end, marries the tender-hearted physician. "We are not rich in the bank, but we have always prospered and have quite enough," Esther says contentedly. "I never walk out with my husband, but I hear the people bless him. I never go into a house of any degree, but I hear his praises, or see them in grateful eyes. I never lie down at night, but I know that in the course of the day he has alleviated pain, and soothed some fellow-creature in the time of need. I know that from the beds of those who were past recovery, thanks have often, often gone up, in the last hour, for his patient ministration. Is not this to be rich?"[10]

Simple words from a simple life. But, indeed, who could wish for more? If we but valued what Esther valued, she would lead us away from a life of worry, envy, and clutter into a life of freedom, joy, and service.

Rx 13 *Forget the Joneses*

Life in America has become essentially a comparative experience. We are not content or discontent in accordance with what we have—we are content or discontent in accordance with what our neighbor has. Stop looking at the Joneses—they are partly responsible for getting us into this mess. As an act of intention, let's turn our eyes away from our neighbors. "If you get into the comparison game," warns Tim Kimmel, "the world will *eat your lunch*."

Rx 14 *Change Your Lifestyle*

Some people are so exhausted, stressed, breathless, and indebted that they appropriately decide to work less and slow down. The only problem is—they forget to change their lifestyle.

If we are serious about making changes to address overload, there must be commensurate lifestyle change. Largely, it seems to me, such a lifestyle change will require a change in the way we use and value possessions. Instead of a life defined by the cultivation of things, it will be a life given over to deeper, more transcendent issues of the spirit.

Rx 15 *Decide Your Possession End-Point*

In America, says Russ Crosson, "We tend to measure success with a *thingometer*." But how many possessions are enough? Seldom do we address this important issue in specific, objectively measurable ways. "The concept of satiation has very little standing in economics," explains John Kenneth Galbraith. "The more wants that are satisfied the more new ones are born."[11] While these statements are clearly true in culture at large, they should never be true in our individual lives, for this is the picture of chronic discontent.

Think specifically about satiety and contentment. How much money do we need to make? Write it down. What kind of car will we be satisfied with? Write it down. How many suits do we need? How much will we spend on shoes? How often do we need expensive cuts of meat? Write it down.

Let's not write down the answers for our neighborhoods. This is a private issue between us and God.

Rx 16 *Make Room*

In Tolstoy's *War And Peace*, Napoleon is marching on Moscow in 1812. Within a few days, the city is doomed to fall, so all the people are busy packing their possessions to evacuate.

One wealthy count has more than thirty carts loaded with furniture and valuables in the courtyard of his mansion. But also in the courtyard and lining the streets of the city are wounded soldiers, waiting inevitable death at the hands of Napoleon's advancing army. Suddenly, the count's daughter sees it: possessions on the carts to be rescued; wounded people on the ground left to die. With tears in her eyes, she runs to her father, pleading to put the wounded on the carts. The count, who has a tender heart as well, sees the shame of it. Weeping, he hugs his daughter: "The eggs are teaching the chickens."

The count quickly tells the servants to take the possessions off and put the wounded on. The servants, who one minute before were doing "the only thing there was to do" — loading the possessions — were now doing the "only thing that could be done" — taking possessions off the carts and putting people on.[12]

What is on our carts? Possessions? Things that consume both our time and money? Things that are temporal, perishable, here today and gone tomorrow? May we have the grace to unclutter our carts to make room for that which matters most.

CHAPTER 13

■■■■■■■■

Work

■ Work expands to fill the time available.—PARKINSON'S LAW

■ All junior executives should know that if they work hard ten hours a day, every day, they could be promoted to senior executives so that they can work hard for fourteen hours a day.—JOHN CAPOZZI .

■ Leslie works part-time. That way, she has plenty of time left over to be busy.—TIM KIMMEL

■ We are frequently asked if it is possible to "have it all"—a full satisfying personal life and a full and satisfying, hard-working professional one. Our answer is: NO. . . . Excellence is a high cost item.—TOM PETERS

The turn of the millennium is witnessing an unprecedented era of high job creation and low unemployment. Since 1980, even though the U.S. economy has *lost* more than forty million jobs, at least seventy million new jobs have been *created*. Currently, we have a record 122 million jobs in the U.S. The economy's updrafts have created not only new jobs, but also new products, new services, new industries, new global markets, new millionaires, and new stock market records.

Yet, during this same stretch, the economy experienced down drafts as well. For many workers, hours are long, wages are low, benefits are fading, pace is fast, stress is unmanageable, morale is down, and security is threatened. One in six workers admits that he or she thinks about quitting on a weekly basis.[1] At one high-tech company, an executive was given a cynical standing ovation when he announced long-expected layoffs with severance packages. For these frustrated employees, Dilbert was no joke.

Work is obviously God-ordained. A life without meaningful

169

work is a tragic life. Each person is healthier—as the entire society is healthier—if we have appropriate, fulfilling work that can be done with pride and integrity. "As our ancestors have known," explains British economist E. F. Schumacher, "there can be no joy of life without joy of work."[2] But work overload is a different matter entirely. It is, like all other overloads, destructive.

OVERWORKING

The Japanese have a death-by-overwork syndrome called *karoshi* where otherwise healthy men simply drop dead at their desks. Yet a recent international study reveals that the Japanese do not lead the world in work hours—the U.S. does.

NUMBER OF HOURS WORKED ANNUALLY, 1995[3]

Country	Number of working hours
USA	1,896
Switzerland	1,838
Japan	1,832
Spain	1,772
United Kingdom	1,762
France	1,755
Italy	1,720
Netherlands	1,717
Eastern Germany	1,705
Western Germany	1,602

Harvard economist Juliet Schor, whose book *The Overworked American* sparked a national discussion, explains that in the last twenty years, the average U.S. worker has added the equivalent of one month to the work-year. Berkeley sociologist and work trends author Arlie Hochschild notes that today women are working, on average, 41.7 hours per week, while men are logging 48.8 hours.[4] With two-thirds of married women working outside the home, this means the median husband-wife unit is putting in ninety hours a week on the job. And that's before you count the hours of domestic labor on the home front.

Such expanding work is surprising, even shocking. The reasonable prediction of the 1960s claimed that, by 1990, people would be working only twenty hours a week. Productivity gains through technology would increase wages, thereby decreasing work hours accordingly. As a result, one wage earner per family—working only four hours a day—would be sufficient to buy a house, purchase health care, put braces on the children's teeth, pay for college, marry off the daughters, and save for retirement. Even though this prediction seemed reliable at the time, it didn't happen. The prediction was leisure, but the reality is overwork.

A brief history of work shows that, throughout the nineteenth century, the workweek averaged roughly sixty hours. According to the University of Iowa's Benjamin Hunnicutt, these hours gradually declined until, in the 1920s, the forty-hour workweek firmly established itself.

Indeed, once the workweek lowered to forty hours, some companies dropped it even further. Kellogg's, for example, instituted the popular six-hour day in 1930 which lasted in some form until 1985. But mostly, the forty-hour week held. In 1980, however, contrary to predictions, work hours began to *increase,* not decrease. The slope of the increase since 1980 roughly mirrors the slope of the decrease prior to 1920.

REASONS FOR OVERWORKING

There are many reasons why work hours began to unexpectedly increase.

Economic necessity, whether real or perceived, is the most obvious reason. Many workers, trapped in low-paying, dead-end jobs, found it necessary to log longer hours just to stay even. Many others who worked middle-class jobs all their lives found wages not even keeping up with inflation. Still others were caught in the cascading circumstances of societal change: college graduates with huge educational debts; recently divorced women starting over; single mothers with mouths to feed, medicine to buy, and child care to pay.

Corporate downsizing is another contributor to the overwork syndrome. In a deregulated and increasingly competitive market, many companies have found it "necessary" to cut jobs. These companies discovered it was cheaper to pay remaining workers overtime than to pay longtime employees high salary and benefit packages. This might have enhanced corporate bottom lines, but it shredded employee creativity, morale, and any sense of company loyalty.

Increasing job insecurity is another contributor to high work hours. Those companies who ruthlessly—and visibly—put thousands of employees on the street instilled fear in the remaining work force. Such employee fear also contributes to stagnant wages, even in the face of a robust economy. Threatened workers, it seems, are wary of pressuring management for raises. This fear not only freezes wages but also causes worker hesitancy to say no when overtime is demanded of them. "Willingness to accommodate work often involves giving up weekend and vacation plans," explains work researcher Leslie A. Perlow. "You can only say no so many times."[5]

Consumptive lifestyles are yet another prominent reason for work-hour inflation. According to economist Schor, all of our productivity gains since World War II have gone toward producing and consuming more goods and services rather than more leisure. In so doing, people habituated themselves to a lifestyle of high consumption, one they now find difficult reversing. Trapped in exhausting work schedules by lifestyle excess, they also have high levels of consumer debt. This then completes the loop, as personal indebtedness is currently *the* major factor determining people's willingness to reduce hours.

An overdeveloped work ethic is yet another reason. While work is clearly important, nowhere in Scripture is it treated as the highest form of human endeavor. Yet today, according to Hunnicutt, work has become a modern religion, and the *mythology of work* causes people to ignore all other kinds of responsibilities. "The job resembles a secular religion," he writes, "promising personal identity, salvation, purpose and direction, community, and a way for those who believe truly and simply in 'hard work' to make sense out of the confusion of life."[6] Even though such revering of work causes significant personal, family, and spiritual problems, it is highly rewarded by our societal structure.

Viewing the workplace as home is perhaps the most disturbing reason for high work hours. In a recently observed trend, both men and women are looking for an escape from the increasingly chaotic home front, and they find it in their work. Sure, work is sometimes stressful—but anything is better than home. "We know from previous research that many men have found a haven at work," explains Hochschild, in her book *The Time Bind: When Work Becomes Home and Home Becomes Work.* "This isn't news. The news of this book is that growing numbers of working women are leery of spending more time at home, as well. They feel torn, guilty, and stressed out by their long hours at work; but they are ambivalent about cutting back on those hours."[7]

WORK OVERLOAD AND OUR FRAGILE SOCIAL CONTRACT

The enormous job creation and sustained economic growth of the past decade have handsomely rewarded movers and shakers, CEOs and CFOs, investors and stock holders. But what about the average guy in the trenches who shows up day in and day out, the gal on the line who works through her Carpal Tunnel Syndrome and wakes up every night in pain? What about that mom and dad who put in a combined ninety-hour work week while little Susie and Johnny sit in day care? In a large—and still growing—number of cases, this family is falling further behind. When they can't even afford dental care, how are they going to afford college tuition? This is the kind of frustration that worker backlash is made of, and management knows it. So do both political parties.

Since the end of World War II there has been an implicit social contract in the U.S. between labor and management that workers would get a share of the wealth they helped create. Today, it isn't happening; the opposite is. Wage inequality has returned to the level of 1940, the end of the Depression. America has the most unequal distribution of income among advanced industrialized countries. Thirty years ago the ratio of CEO salary and the lowest worker was 35 to 1. Today it is about 200 to 1.[8]

"By all odds, this should be a season of economic celebration in America. . . . But there is a gaping hole in this success story," explains *U.S. News & World Report*'s David Gergen, "and that's why there is no celebration. . . . What about average American workers? Their tale is deeply troubling." Gergen goes on to point out that, compared to previous economic expansions, payrolls are growing much more slowly.[9] Perhaps wage stagnation was justified in days when productivity was flat. But lately, that has not been the case. Says Lawrence Perlman, chairman and CEO of Ceridian Corp., "There has been an extraordinary decoupling between productivity growth and compensation growth."[10]

The point is, the average family is clocking an unprecedented number of hours on the job, even to the detriment of family well-being. But they are not seeing the benefit of all their hard work and extra hours. As long as wages stay flat or decline while prices increase—which is the case for the majority of Americans—people will feel the need to put in *even more* hours. Wrong direction. My suggestion: Pay the same wage scale Jesus would pay if He owned the company.

EFFECTS OF OVERWORK

Even as employers continue to insist on "more," many workers are beginning to say "enough is enough." Something has to give. Signs and symptoms of overwork are readily visible and should not be ignored.

Productivity

Studies have shown that somewhere between fifty and sixty hours of work per week, productivity and efficiency begin to reverse. One study in England revealed that, at sixty hours a week, performance declined twenty-five percent. When workers are stretched too thin, fatigue and resentment surface. Yet some managers never stop pushing the limits—speeding up the line, electronically recording keystrokes, cutting down on breaks, even monitoring bathroom trips.

Illness

Overuse syndromes such as *Repetitive Strain Injury* and *Cumulative Trauma Disorder* are being called "the industrial diseases of the

Information Age." Carpal Tunnel Syndrome is one such condition reported with increasing frequency.

Sleep Disorders

With the advent of electricity and the incandescent bulb, artificial lighting stretched the day into night, thus contributing to our epidemic nationwide sleep gap. According to a survey sponsored by the National Sleep Foundation in Washington, D.C., "A staggering forty-seven percent of workers in the United States said they have trouble sleeping, two-thirds of whom think insomnia has a negative impact on their job performance, including their ability to handle job-related stress, make decisions, and solve problems."

The total annual cost of insomnia to U.S. businesses, including absenteeism, medical costs, and decreased productivity, is an estimated $100 billion. "Clearly, the high-pressure business environment of the 1990s, with its downsized work force and increased competition, is having a profound impact on the American workplace," warns Louis W. Sullivan, M.D., former U.S. Secretary of Health and Human Services.[11]

Family

The family issues are, for me, the most pressing. I am a pro-work person, and this chapter should not be taken as an anti-work treatise. But, simply stated, work must assume its rightful place, leaving at least *some* time for the family. Hunnicutt is appropriately concerned about the "hemorrhage of time" *away* from the critically important institutions of the family and church, and *toward* the institution of work.

"This is a selfish world," says ninety-eight-year-old pediatrician Leila Denmark, who still works four days a week treating children. "Parents are working their brains out to buy nice homes and cars. If we're ever going to make America better, we've got to tell [parents]— no matter how educated, how poor or how rich—to take care of [their children]. When I worked in the slums in 1918, that's where all the bad kids were because their parents didn't take care of them. Today, you find them in the suburban homes of the finest doctors and lawyers; their kids have gone bad because they have no time for them."[12]

Women

Many women feel trapped in what has been called "the stalled revolution." Decades ago they began pouring into the workplace for reasons of both personal ambition and economic necessity. Yet now, to their dismay, they are doing the math: Time spent on their outside-the-home jobs combined with time spent on their domestic work often exceeds eighty hours per week. The exhaustion is not imaginary. Many feel they have accommodated all they can accommodate. *Something* needs to be done. Families and churches should honestly confront all the issues involved and then assist in making whatever adjustments need to be made.

Men

Let me simply quote a turn-of-the-century Yiddish poem that appeared in—of all places—*The Wall Street Journal*.

> I have a son, a little son,
> A boy completely fine.
> When I see him it seems to me
> That all the world is mine.
> But seldom, seldom do I see
> My child awake and bright;
> I only see him when he sleeps;
> I'm only home at night.
> It's early when I leave for work;
> When I return it's late.
> Unknown to me is my own flesh,
> Unknown is my child's face.
> When I come home so wearily
> In the darkness after day,
> My pale wife exclaims to me:
> "You should have seen our child play."
> I stand beside his little bed,
> I look and try to hear.
> In his dream he moves his lips:
> "Why isn't Papa here?"[13]

FOUR EXAMPLES

Air Force

On a number of occasions, the Pentagon has asked me to talk about margin. As these high-performing military employees are pre-selected for stoicism, their interest in margin surprised me. But they are human and have limits just as everybody else. Take, for example, their current crisis in pilot retention.

Each pilot has undergone five million dollars worth of training. It is obviously a good thing if they reenlist when their term is finished. But currently, pilots are leaving in record numbers to take jobs in the commercial sector. Why? It is not simply that the commercial sector pays better (although it does). Workload considerations also play a role. Since the Gulf War the workload has quadrupled, while the number of pilots has been cut in half—an astounding eightfold increase in job responsibilities. Congress is attempting to address this by increasing the bonus for re-upping from $60,000 to $110,000. Yet despite this added incentive, it is predicted that until something is done about workload issues, pilots will vote with their feet and not their wings.

Engineers

The recent book *Finding Time: How Corporations, Individuals, and Families Can Benefit from New Work Practices* describes work stress among software engineers, thus highlighting issues important throughout many occupations. "Knowledge workers, like senior executives, experience immense pressure to . . . put work above all else,"[14] observes University of Michigan business professor Leslie A. Perlow, who studied a Fortune 500 company to write the book. "Engineers believe that they must be perceived as always willing to 'accommodate the demands of the work.' . . . They should be willing to do whatever is asked, not just in terms of producing output but also in terms of working whatever hours are deemed necessary to get the job done."[15] As long as nobody's getting hurt, what's the big deal? The big deal is—somebody's getting hurt.

A case in point: the Apple Computer staff designing the Newton. "The pressure to finish, exhilarating at first, eventually overwhelmed some of the young designers," explains a *New York Times* article. "After eighteen-hour days, some engineers went home and cried. Some quit. One had a breakdown and ended up in jail. One took a pistol and killed himself."[16]

Medicine

Medicine has a long, proud history of overwork. Today, however, something is different. To be sure, doctors are still putting in long hours — but the difference is, we are not bearing up very well under new pressures. The enormous changes in medicine have rocked physicians, and most are trying to regain some semblance of personal and professional equilibrium. On top of all the unprecedented structural changes, the societal reimbursement for being a doctor is lower than in times past, thus not sufficiently blunting the work stress. A medical disability company observes that many — if not most — practitioners now applying for disability "involve some impairment that the doctors could ignore as long as they were professionally motivated."[17]

This professional overwork ethic begins in medical school and intensifies in residency training. Enormous time commitments are simply expected. One week during residency I worked 128 hours — and, quite frankly, besides falling asleep in the middle of my spaghetti, I didn't think much about it. But studies reveal such overloaded schedules do indeed cause detrimental changes in medical trainees, replacing the altruistic motivation of patient service with the more primitive motive of shift survival. "For many residents, fatigue cultivates anger, resentment, and bitterness rather than kindness, compassion, or empathy," observes Michael Green, M.D., in a provocative *Annals of Internal Medicine* article.[18]

Ministry

I am deeply concerned about the stressful changes in the pastorate over the past few decades. According to one report, only one in three pastors "finishes well." Clergy burnout is so common that

Focus on the Family's H. B. London, Jr., has called the pastor "an endangered species." Denominational executive Dr. David Rambo reported that ninety percent of pastors say they are inadequately trained to cope with ministry demands, eighty percent say their ministries have had a negative effect on their families, and seventy percent have a lower self-image now than when they started in the ministry.[19] Ministry hours are long, while expectations are often conflicting—and sometimes impossible. These pressures inevitably wear on pastors, who frequently feel no permission to reveal their distress. At least twenty-two organizations exist for the sole purpose of pre- or post-burnout counseling for pastors.

In addition, the overwork associated with ministry "success" and rapid church growth can bring problems. In one instance, church attendance was swelling dramatically and the facility was bursting at the seams. Every day lives were transformed and the course of eternity changed. God was working in extraordinary ways, and the more God worked, the harder the staff worked. *If we worked seventy hours a week and touched this many lives,* they reasoned, *what would happen if we worked eighty hours, or ninety?*

There was no real structure for accountability. The staff was burning out and the core was splitting. As the pace became over-whelming, cracks began to appear in the foundation—fatigue, relational carelessness, sin. In this instance, some of the leadership got a second chance and the church went on to experience phenomenal growth. Still, the lesson is clear: Just because their field is spiritual, pastors are not immune from the stressors of work overload.

PRESCRIPTIONS FOR AVERTING WORK DREAD

If pressures at work seem to mount faster than your motivation and energy, the following prescriptions might bring balance and a new perspective.

Rx 1 *Ask the "How Much Work Is Enough" Question*

Work is so dominant in our value structure that many will not— or cannot—even bring themselves to ask the question. It seems heretical, similar to "How much education is enough?" But it is spiritually essential that we ask these questions about every aspect of our lives. Our inability to even *think* about such issues is all the evidence we need that such thought is essential. Idolatry is often marked by subtle and unchallengeable presuppositions.

Rx 2 *Rethink the Work Ethic*

The work ethic is an important puritan remnant and part of what developed our national greatness. It is an essential component of maturity. It contributes to integrity on the job. It often results in the fundamentally important ability to pay our bills along life's way. As parents, we are pleased to see it evolve in our children. But emphasizing the importance of a work ethic should not be taken as a defense of workaholism. A work ethic is laudatory; workaholism is, by definition, intemperate. "Work is an obligation, not an obsession," explains burnout author Charles Perry, Jr.[20]

Let's rethink work for a minute. What are we really exalting? Is it work as *God* defines it, or work as *we* define it? Is it *work,* or is it *success?* The success ethic is not the same as the work ethic, and is often opposed to godliness.

A biblically authentic work ethic does not mean that work is all-important, that our ability to earn money defines our worth, that other important relationships and spiritual obligations take second place, or that people should be layered according to their professional level. And it does not mean that working seventy hours a week is more virtuous than working forty hours a week.

Rx 3 *Avoid the Extremes*

I commonly see two extremes regarding work: work avoidance and workaholism. Both are unbalanced and deviant from God's intention. I would rather a person work too much than not at all—but it's close. While not working at all can be devastating, working too hard can be likewise devastating, only in a subtler—and more socially acceptable—way. The best approach, it seems to me, is to stay in the sanctified middle. Have a solid work ethic that honors God, but be equally obedient in each of the non-work areas that God is so closely watching.

Rx 4 *Define Yourself in Terms Other Than Work*

A nearly universal psychological truth in American society, and one that has mainstream acceptance, is to obtain our identity and esteem by our work. While granting that work is a signifi-cant *part* of our lives, it is not the *essence* of our lives. This distinction is important because if we achieve our esteem through our work (defined as "gainful employment"), when we want more esteem we work more hours. But if we are already putting in fifty hours a week and feeling empty, increasing to sixty hours a week is a hollow answer. You cannot correct a wrong by doubling it.

Ultimately our identity comes from God and is not contingent on our job description or how many hours we work. At the deepest level of our spirit, life always flows smoother if we agree with God's definitions.

Rx 5 *Take Personal Responsibility*

Many people feel trapped in their work circumstances. But it is important to realize that we live in lives of our own choosing. Rather than blaming all our problems on external forces and circumstances, it is good to shine a light on our own motives. "Highly-stressed people tend to seek a place to lay blame," explained family researcher Dolores Curran. "My schedule was brutal, and I found myself complaining to whoever would listen. Finally, one good friend said gently, 'But you scheduled yourself.'"[21]

Perhaps the majority of overworked, overstressed workers today have contributed to the situation by personal expectations and lifestyle choices. No one will fix these problems for us. Often we will find options to consider if we are bold enough, creative enough, or countercultural enough. It is our life, and it is ultimately our responsibility.

Rx 6 *Be Cautious of Promotions*

Promotions are a sign of affirmation and respect, a reward for a job well done. But there can be hidden costs to these promotions: more stress, longer hours, and more travel. It is wise to gauge the consequences carefully. Write down the positives versus negatives. Discuss them with your spouse, close friend, pastor, or accountability group. Pray. Delay the decision to allow impulsivity to wane. If the promotion seems spiritually and relationally sound, pursue it with enthusiasm. If you have significant doubts, wait.

Consider building your career more slowly than you otherwise would, leaving sufficient time to invest in family when the children are young. It is usually too late to invest in children when they are no longer children.

Rx 7 *Defend Boundaries*

It goes without saying that workers must give good work for their pay. But it also goes without saying that employers must allow workers a private life away from work. There is an important border that exists in this relationship, but one which modern technology is rapidly blurring.

Beware, for example, of the "electronic leash." When your employer offers you a pager and cell phone, think twice about the advisability of accepting such technology. "Are wireless communicators instruments of liberation, freeing people to be more mobile with their lives—or are they more like electronic leashes keeping people more plugged in to their work . . . than is necessary and healthy?" asks author David Shenk.[22] While such equipment might at times make good business sense (and usually a status symbol as well), there are other times when "unrestrained reachability" has worrisome consequences.

Rx 8 *Get Real*

A friend works for the U.S. government in a high-level job. The workforce in his department has been steadily cut, even as job demands have relentlessly increased. The office was continually asked to do more and more with less and less, a common mantra in today's environment. Finally, the top executive in this office told headquarters, "No, we will not do more and more with less and less. We will do *less and less* with *less and less*."

I don't know how this was received. But when work demands have been pushed to the breaking point, such resistance becomes a marker of sanity.

Rx 9 *Balance Life with Work*
When bringing up the topic of balance in the workplace, be prepared
for possible ballistics. One junior level manager, who himself put in
seventy-hour workweeks, was reporting in a division meeting on a
workplace climate survey: "I said that the people I worked with
wanted a better balance between work and family. I got it right
between the eyes . . . : 'Don't *ever* bring up "balance" again! I don't
want to hear about it! Period! Everyone in this company has to work
hard. We work hard. *They* have to work hard. That's the way it is.' "[23]

Despite this level of often predictable cultural resistance,
attempts at balance are important if only because God says they are.
An unexamined life will drift toward imbalance. Yet an unbalanced
life will not be kind to us in the area neglected. And if God has told
us to perform in a certain area—even at the "decent minimum"
level—then we will not thrive if we disobey.

Listen to God's advice. Take control of the affairs of your life in
each area where God has given explicit instructions and bring them
into alignment with God's Word. You will discover that the Father
always provides whatever time and resources we need to accomplish
His will.

Rx 10 *Develop Interests Outside of Work*
When the sole meaning of our existence is found in our work, the
tendency is to escalate hours on the job. But then if we are laid off
or fired or disabled or retired, our whole life seems crushed. Instead,
when the workday . . . or workweek . . . or work career is ended,
there should be another level of meaning waiting to absorb our
efforts. Develop a diversity of interests and involvements. Take up
a hobby. Give yourself in service to those less fortunate. Volunteer
to teach Sunday School. Befriend an international student.

Strive to make work interesting and enjoyable. But more than
that—strive to make *life* interesting and enjoyable. Work is a
smaller circle within the larger circle of life.

Rx 11 *Place Priority on the Family*
On one occasion I was giving a talk on parenting at a medical conference. The physician speaking before me, in a stunning display of

self-disclosure, revealed how forty years earlier, her five-year-old son came up to her and said, "Mommy, who do you think I would rather have die—you or Sparky?" This child, for no precipitating reason, said he would rather his mommy die than his dog. It was a hard story for me to follow, particularly because I know the physician who shared her heart is a genuinely compassionate person. But it certainly underscored the importance of my call to invest in our families.

"As I think back on my own life, my biggest regret is not spending more time with my kids," explains Chuck Colson. "Making family your top priority means standing against a culture where materialism and workaholism are rampant. It means realizing that you may not advance as fast in your career as some of your colleagues—at least for a few years. It means being willing to accept a lower standard of living . . . knowing you're doing the right thing for your children, giving them the emotional security they'll draw on for the rest of their lives."[24]

The way our society and our work environments are currently structured, strangely, we give the least time to those we value most. If we are wise, we will understand that success as defined by the world, isn't success. Success in God's eyes is measured by love. One day, He will push the delete button, wiping out all the time clocks, bank statements, productivity sheets, and 401K plans. All that will be left is love. And what has been true all along will suddenly be made clear.

Rx 12 *Keep Work Work and Home Home*

Arlie Hochschild has touched off a national debate with her provocative subtitle *When Work Becomes Home and Home Becomes Work*. With expanding workplace hours, home life often is neglected. As a result, the home front becomes more and more chaotic. Rather than honestly addressing this increasing level of domestic disorder, people volunteer for even *more* hours at work. They realize, of course, this will not solve their family chaos. But they are no longer interested in "solving" family problems, just escaping them.

Now that the syndrome has been explained, watch for the symptoms. Don't avoid the chaos at home—fix it.

Rx 13 *Value Mom*

Many women leave their stay-at-home job for the marketplace, not for economic reasons, but for self-esteem reasons. Whereas once outside-the-home work for women was stigmatized, now stay-at-home work is stigmatized. This has clearly compounded the work overload problem for those women who feel they are not worthwhile if they don't hold down paying jobs—but are stressed and exhausted if they do.

All people need recognition and affirmation, and studies reveal that if high value is assigned to the domestic work of motherhood, the entire family is happier. Let's remove the stigma and return the appropriate value to mom—all those NFL players can't be wrong. As the saying goes, *Every mother is a working mother.*

Rx 14 *Consider Working Fewer Hours*

"The executive who works from 7:00 A.M. to 7:00 P.M. every day," quips John Capozzi, "will be both very successful and fondly remembered by his widow's next husband."[25] By what criteria do we decide how many hours should be in our workweek? This question obviously has major implications for our time budget. Discover the optimal number of hours to assure you do not lose your passion for the work God has given you and to assure that your family can remain healthy.

If this entails fewer hours, be aware of the possible consequences of cutting back. You might experience decreased esteem from colleagues. Your production numbers will decrease, along with your income. You might discover that you are no longer playing "by the rules of the profession." But, on the other hand, in this era of flextime, job-sharing, home offices, and telecommuting, you might also find more openness to experimenting with creative job configurations than ever before.

Rx 15 *Consider a Job Change*

If conditions at work are overly stressful and the hours are unreasonably long, consider a job change. But make any such changes carefully and prayerfully. Even though some work settings are glorious compared to others, overall it is helpful to remember that the world is a stressful place these days. The grass is not necessarily greener on the other side of the fence.

So look before you leap. Do your homework. It is also helpful to know that quitting a stressful, overloaded job is usually not a good idea until you have a replacement lined up. Otherwise you will find that the stress of accumulating debt exceeds the stress of high work hours.

Rx 16 *Cut Down the Commute*

The average commute is forty-five minutes a day, but for many it is more accurately measured in hours. Predictions indicate commuting pressure will only increase. For example, every ten seconds, a new stop sign goes up, and every thirty seconds, a new traffic light is installed.

Long, stressful commutes contribute significantly to work overload. Commuters who drive to work often show up too tired or too irritated to function effectively. If this is a problem in your work, consider going in early or late to avoid traffic. Or perhaps telecommute part of the week or even full-time. Another solution might be taking a job closer to home, or even moving closer to work.

Rx 17 *Open a Home Office*

Thirty-five million households today have a home office. This increasingly utilized strategy has much to commend it. It eliminates commuting time and obviates the need for extra vehicles, office clothes, and even childcare. Especially if you only work part-time, it can be an excellent solution. But it is not for everyone. We shouldn't be naive about how hard it is to be home and yet "unavailable" to children, spouses, and a myriad other distractions. One word of caution: For workaholics, a home office can be lethal.

Rx 18 *Job Share*

There are many more flexibility structures available today for those willing to be creative—or for those willing to ask the boss. Increasingly, two people (often women, but not exclusively) get together and work out the details of a sharing arrangement. Such job sharing allows flexibility for time off, vacation, and personal emergencies. If, for example, you suddenly need to take off three days for a funeral, the other worker might be able to fill the gap. I even know of a husband and wife, both physicians, who job share one full-time clinic position.

Rx 19 *Increase Work Flexibility Through Simplicity*

Many people overwork for one simple reason — they overspend. Overliving our income puts inordinate pressure on work hours. As long as we consume one hundred and ten percent of what we make, we will have little choice in cutting back work hours or changing to a less stressful job. Simplicity, on the other hand, brings flexibility to our work options. In this sense, consumption constrains us and simplicity frees us. Leave a margin.

Rx 20 *Bring the Kingdom of God to Bear*

Any job — even people-centered work — can become routine, automatic, and similar to an "assembly line." When this happens, the spiritual and relational dimension of work tends to disappear, replaced instead by pure productivity. When speed and overload are factored in, the assembly line-productivity-efficiency model dwarfs all other considerations.

Medicine, for example, can easily be an assembly-line profession. The recent changes in the health care field all flow in that direction. "There will be a relentless set of cost pressures for at least the next twenty years, which means those warm and fuzzy generalists will be told to see a patient every ten minutes," predicts Steven A. Schroeder, M.D., president of the Robert Wood Johnson Foundation. "They may find it's hard to be warm and fuzzy and maintain the income they'd like."[26] Such rhetoric throws down the gauntlet in compassion's face.

Long ago I decided assembly-line medicine was an unsatisfactory way to practice. Jesus' standard was to bring the kingdom of God to bear in every human interaction — and I wanted no less with every patient interaction. Of course, no physician can be super-doctor every time, and such was not my intention. But I could at least care. I could resist the modern temptation — often subtle — to dehumanize the patients. I could look into their eyes and attempt to touch their need. I could take on their burden for a minute or fifteen, listen intently, and try to lift their load.

This is what I mean by bringing the kingdom of God to bear. Everyone reading this book, no matter what your station in life or chosen career, can do the same. Whenever we come into contact with another human being—in the setting of work, or in the general setting of life—we have two choices: to relate in the kingdom of love, or to relate consistent with the commercial affairs of the world.

Don't let work overload drain the vitality of the kingdom. We are God's representatives. Let's represent His interests lovingly.

■ ■ ■ ■ ■ ■ ■ ■ ■

Focusing on Love

■ I don't know where we're going or how we'll get there, but when we get there we'll be there—and that's something, even if it's nothing.—J. PERELMAN

■ Martha, Martha, you are worried and upset about many things, but only one thing is needed. Mary has chosen what is better, and it will not be taken away from her. —JESUS, LUKE 10:41-42

One Friday evening during high school, our son Adam went to stay overnight at a friend's house on the lake. Their plan—quite ambitious for two teenage boys on a Saturday morning—was to get up at 4:30 A.M. and go fishing. I was initially skeptical they would be able to pull this off. Yet, because Adam was an early riser who loved fishing, it seemed that perhaps they had a chance.

Late Saturday afternoon, Adam drove up the driveway. "Did you guys get up at 4:30?" I asked.

"Not exactly," he replied. "We got up at 9:00."

"Oh," I chuckled. "You slept through the alarm, huh?"

"Not exactly," he said. "Ryan hit the snooze alarm forty-two times."

THE NEW HUMAN CONDITION

Such a Tom Sawyer-Huck Finn response to the alarm is humorous and benign. But, interestingly, we see ourselves in this mirror as well. When the overload alarms go off in our lives, we hit the snooze button. The issues are too big, the challenges too great. And besides, we're too tired. So we roll over and go back to sleep. "Hopefully," we mutter, "when it goes off next time, these problems will be gone."

But overload is not going away. Thanks to progress, it is the new human condition. And it is unavoidable.

Progress rules the Western world. It is, by now, autonomous. It has a strength and speed all its own. Our economy depends on progress, so there is no political will to shut it down. Nor, in one sense, should there be. Progress is not misbehaving. It is not evil. We are not talking about a conspiracy here. Progress is, after all, only doing what we asked it to do. We just did not realize the downside would feel quite like this.

As we have seen, progress works by always giving us *more*. Of *everything. Faster and faster.* Often at exponential rates.

Because progress isn't going to change, we have to change. Simply put, we have to learn how to live under these new conditions. We have to learn about the reality of human limits. We have to discover where our threshold lines are. We have to learn to *accept* our limits—no easy task when we have been so strongly programmed for growth and expansion. The rules of life are different on this side of overload, and we need to understand the practical implications for living, for working, for relationships, for faith.

Passivity is not a valid response. We must become active agents, forging the kind of response that is spiritually and relationally authentic. We need to intentionally cultivate a margin to buffer ourselves against the onslaught of overload. Many people, however, are too busy surviving each day to think deeply about it. Others are too frightened to make substantive changes. Still others have the interest and the resolve to change, but just don't know what to do.

This book has presented over 175 prescriptions for possible change in response to overload. These are suggestions, not laws. Because each person is different—different personalities, different families, different work, different expectations—each will make different choices from among these prescriptions.

But no matter who we are, there is no exemption to overload.

If we all are finite, that means we all have limits. And if we all have limits, that means we all have thresholds. And if we all have thresholds, that means it is just a matter of time before progress finds these thresholds and exceeds them. There are no exceptions to this sequence—only pretended exceptions.

CHOOSING APPROPRIATE CHANGE

Given that we all are different and have so many possible prescriptions to choose from, how do we know which options to select? If overload requires us to adjust our thinking, how do we decide which changes are most important?

There are three broad categories of change for us to consider:

those things we *cannot* change;
those things we *might wish* to change; and
those things we *must* change.

Those Things We Cannot Change

Many things in life will not budge, even when we get mad—for example, progress. Just because it overloads us does not mean that it will consider changing its behavior. If your boat sinks in the middle of the Pacific Ocean, just because you get mad at the saltwater does not mean it will dry up to accommodate you. Progress and the Pacific have that in common: Neither is going away.

We can't stop progress. We can't change the fact that progress rules the day. We don't have a veto. Quite honestly, I don't even think *progress* can stop progress. The adjustment to a non-progress world would be so profound that it is virtually impossible to consider. About the only thing that would stop progress is a major economic depression or World War III. But just because we can't stop it does not take away from us the option of making individual changes to deal selectively with the untoward effects of progress.

Concerning progress, perhaps the best response is a wary coexistence. There have been thousands of benefits that progress has gifted us with, from anesthesia to abundant crops to sanitation. If we are careful, we can sort out the good from the bad. In a fallen world, it should come as no surprise that progress contains much of both.

Those Things We Might Wish to Change

Despite the things we cannot change, still we have thousands of possible options before us. Many of these options have been temporarily hidden by the strong pressures to conform to cultural expectations and live in culturally prescribed lifestyles. But even though they have been temporarily obscured does not mean they have been permanently excluded from us. If our resolve is steady enough, we can take these options back and individually become as countercultural as we wish. It helps if we are willing to be two standard deviations off the mean. And it also helps immensely if we are surrounded by like-minded people who will support our value structure.

We might, for example, wish to move to a smaller house or drive an older car. We might wish to live a somewhat simpler life, or going further, to live a radically simpler life. We might wish to have only one wage-earner in our family. We might wish to throw out fifty percent of the clutter in our homes. We might wish to wear the same pair of pants to the office for two weeks. We might wish to declare a moratorium on shopping for a month. Our choices are limited only by our imagination and our willingness to be different if sanity and godliness require it.

Most of the prescriptions offered fall into this second category—things we *might wish* to change. Let's not become legalistic about them. They are merely suggestions that will help some individuals more than others. Replacing overload with legalism is not improvement. We need equal freedom from both.

Those Things We Must Change

God still has opinions about things. Some powerful people who have opinions tend to be pushy with their opinions. In a way, so is God—not in the sense of being authoritarian, but in the sense of being right. He will let us choose whatever we want. But He is always right, which means if we choose contrary to His opinion we end up being wrong. This does not stop us from selecting that option, and often it doesn't even seem to slow us down. But being wrong carries a penalty. It is far better being right.

Those things we *must change* go beyond the realm of preference and enter the realm of Truth. When God says something that pertains to Truth, it is best if we listen. Even if we don't feel like it, we ought to pay attention and act on His advice. Even if the entire culture endorses the polar opposite, still we should listen to God. Even if it costs us everything, we should do it. God's advice always turns out to be the healthy option—even when it doesn't seem so at first. This is part of the narrow road of faith.

It is important to follow God because He really is the only One who knows where He is going. He has given us instructions and expects us to follow them. "Why do you call me Lord, Lord," asked Jesus, "and do not do what I say?"[1] If we wish to demonstrate our love for God, explained Jesus, we should do it through our obedience. If we do not obey, apparently, we do not love.[2] It is a reliable marker.

What are the things we must do? We must forgive. We must be content. We must not judge, but instead grant grace, the kind that God has granted us. We must gently tell others the reason for the hope within us (many people forget the gently part).[3]

But most of all, we must love. Not money, not things, but people. We must invest ourselves in those relationships God has blessed us with. Overload tends to block such an investment. Overload tends to obstruct the flow of love. This is why the problem of overload deserves high attention on our spiritual agenda.

OVERLOAD AND LOVE

We were put here for love. There isn't any theological dispute about it—love is the goal of the Christian life. Scripture teaches us that God is love. It teaches us that the greatest commandment is to love. It teaches us that all the commandments are summed up in the one commandment to love. It teaches us that without love, we are nothing.[4]

On that day when everything is forced through the fire of judgment, love is the only thing that will exit out the other side. It will stand alone, vindicated. It will finally and clearly be seen for the dominant, unbeatable, infinite, glorified force it has always been, just obscured for millennia by layers of fallen clutter.

We were put here to love and serve people every day of our lives. Success is nothing more than that. Anyone who says that success is more than that is not basing it on the Truth.

What does this have to do with overload? Overload sabotages love. Notice, there is no chapter on *love overload*. It isn't possible. Love is the one thing we want to see increasing at exponential rates. But the overload syndrome will not allow it.

FOCUS

The terrain outside my bus window had been baked by the desert heat. I watched with fascination as the timeless Bedouins sat guarding their sheep under the same burning, relentless sun that had parched the face of Abraham. As far as the eye could see, nothing but barrenness. I was straining to locate Mt. Nebo, where Moses was taken by God, when the Jordanian guide shattered my reverie. "All of the great religions of the world," he said, "were founded in the desert." Only one sentence, then he lapsed again into silence.

I am not sure about the historical accuracy of his statement, but there was enough provocation in it to set me back in my seat. At first, I bristled. *All you need is a sun-baked desert and a half-baked guru, and presto, a new truth is born. That's the last thing the world needs right now is another crackpot who claims to have discovered the Final Word—available now in this four-cassette volume for only $29.95.*

But God pressed down upon me, taking the oxygen away from my resistance. As I continued to look out at the desert, I went beyond offense to interest. Might it be true that the spiritual quest is intensified in the desert? Surely if you don't count sun and sand, here is no overload. One has nothing to do . . . nothing to do but think. Day after day, no change. Day after day, no distractions. Day after day, focus. Is it possible that one's thoughts might eventually climb to matters of the divine in such a setting? Abraham, Moses, David, Elijah, John the Baptist, Jesus, Paul—all spent time in the desert. Is this more than just a geographic coincidence?

If true, what is it about this desolate environment which facilitates spirituality? Is it dryness? heat? sun? barrenness? And where
today can one find such a desert? In our frenzied, overloaded existence, how is it possible to focus on *anything,* let alone on God? Intel
chip makers, in defending their quest for speed, report that human
attention begins to wander after *one-half second!*

After years of reflection, I believe the guide's remark contains a
lesson for us. The desert is waiting, poised to teach us. But
Americans do not know about deserts, and furthermore, we are not
interested in experiencing them. We do not know what it is like to
be alone for weeks on end, clothed only with sandals and burlap,
supplied with a small sack of bread and dried fish. Instead we know
cities and highways, noise and lights, activities and entertainment.
We know overload. We specialize in overload.

Most of us would find such a desert experience unbearable.
One month and we would wilt. Our skin would shrivel and our
lips would blister. We would probably hallucinate from the boredom.
Despite such indisputable dreariness, the experience might yield
surprising benefits.

Out of the boredom, the suffering, the barrenness, and the
silence would grow a vine called *focus*. Our thoughts would begin
to modulate more in the direction of a few central themes. We
would stop thinking about where we left the hairspray, what time
the Superbowl starts, or whether we have enough Parmesan cheese
for spaghetti. We would start thinking more and more about Truth,
about life and death, about existence, and about God.

THE INSUFFERABLENESS OF SUPERFICIALITY

Without focus, little of significance is accomplished. Unfortunately
such is the status of our lives. The *significant* has been forced to
wrestle with the *superficial*. From the start, it is a conflict *significance*
should have been spared. Yet never before have so many minutes of
every day gone into activities and choices which have so little to do
with what it means to be alive. If we spend our overloaded work-
days filling out forms in triplicate, fighting with copy machines,
and fending off solicitors, we will have little chance to change the

course of history. In the average lifetime, we will each spend eight months opening junk mail, one year looking for misplaced objects, and two years calling people who aren't in. What does this have to do with love?

Trivialities have always existed. But life has never held such a high percentage of superficialities as it does today. Shopping for "high-flying" basketball shoes, scanning a dozen television programs to find something good to watch, deciding between deodorant roll-on versus spray, giving the poodle a haircut, shuffling through three hundred pages of the Sunday paper, moussing hairdos, putting racing stripes on bicycles. Doesn't life have a purpose? How can we accomplish this purpose when more and more of what we do means less and less? The answer is to concentrate on the purpose, to return to it continuously.

DILUTION AND DISTRACTION

Contemporary overloading opposes focusing in at least two ways: dilution and distraction. *Dilution* occurs when too much comes too fast. A diamond on the beach is valuable until the waves crash over it. Then the diamond is nothing, sucked up by a trillion trillion tons of ocean. The gem itself is unchanged, but its value is unrecoverable because volume has displaced value.

Relationship is particularly vulnerable to dilution. We try to focus on our spouse, a child, or a friend but find that a dozen activities intervene. Soon the spouse leaves for a meeting, the child goes to soccer practice, and the friend goes to a class across town. These activities have merit, but in profusion they dilute. Relationship is replaced by experience, and even experience is watered down.

If dilution is an overload phenomenon, *distraction* is an interruption phenomenon. Interruptions are so much a part of daily living that we often do not recognize them as pathogens. Focusing requires momentum, but distraction breaks momentum's back. Focusing has to do with meditation, with contemplation. When an issue is important, we have to live with it, to dwell on it, to lock in on it. Sometimes this takes days, sometimes years. Sometimes it takes a lifetime.

Whatever the topic and whatever the duration, interruptions distract us from the important. Distractions include such noise-makers as telephones and beepers, televisions and boom boxes. Additionally, distractions are found among the many "advantages" of progress, from fashion to traffic to technology.

It may be that one task requiring our focus is parenting. But the distraction is the new car we bought which resulted in more debt and more work. Or it may be that the task is saying, "I'm sorry." Yet just when I start to speak, the pager goes off. Mr. Jones's hemorrhoids are bleeding again, and I'm needed in the E.R.

Focused or distracted: I have ridden the pendulum to both extremes (and continue to). At times focus has been sustained—although always with effort. At other times the pace of my life could best be described as furious. Perhaps this is why our family so values our time in developing countries. Life there is quite simple. While I admit that sometimes the simplicity becomes tedious, other times it is wonderfully focused. The important has time to be important without competition from the superficial.

Revisiting the desert for a moment, we now notice that essential to spiritual thinking is the ability to focus. *This* is what the desert allows. Life simplified to its basics minus dilution minus distraction. Under these conditions, momentum has a chance.

Jesus was exceptionally focused. His intent was the glory of the Father, and nothing could distract Him from it. This does not mean He did not rest. It does not mean He never enjoyed Himself. It simply means He could not be distracted.

FOLLOWING THE MAP

Although in our traveling we routinely focus on a destination, too few of us do the same in our living. Yesterday passes and tomorrow arrives, while our randomness builds only a house upon the sand. Doesn't it make sense to set our compass on the Son, to travel in His direction?

Choosing the kingdom road, we are warned, is not easy. The gate is small and the way is narrow. "Only a few find it."[5] These words ought to stir our vigilance and sharpen our focus. One would think we might tremble with fear, panicked lest Christ be correct and we fall off that narrow way. But no, Jesus always seems to be talking more to our neighbor.

Because we would be incapable of guessing in which direction Truth lies, God has agreed to help us. His Word is our manual, and without it we would have no hope. It was given not to punish us, but to free us and guide us back to Him. With its help we can rediscover what the appropriate content of our focusing ought to be—love.

GOAL-FOCUSED, GOD-FOCUSED

With this background, we are ready to consider a few final suggestions and principles which might assist us in our focusing task against the backdrop of increasing overload.

Commit to Focusing

If we do not commit, our lives will become diluted and distracted, for such is the nature of modern overload. We first must decide what it is we wish to aim for and then concentrate on it. "Run in such a way as to get the prize."[6] Each morning ask, "What is it I wish to do with this day?" Then ask, "One hundred years from now, what is it I would wish I had done with this day?" Do the latter.

Accept Responsibility

If we do not focus, life will "just happen" to us, and quickly at that. It is our own responsibility to do something about it and no one else's. "It's become clearer and clearer to me," states Mary Pipher, "that if families just let the culture happen to them, they end up fat, addicted, broke, with a house full of junk and no time."[7]

Do Not Focus on the Faults of Others

I am the problem—not my neighbor. "Let everyone sweep in front of his own door, and the whole world will be clean," observed Goethe.

Study the Scriptures

They are our only accurate Guide. Stop guessing about what the Lord has said, and let God tell you Himself. Rout out opinions and replace them with Truth.

Above All, Focus on the Glory of God and the Love of His People
These are the noblest of all endeavors, the highest of all privileges, and the sum of all existence.

Is our randomized righteousness enough to please Him? Never. But this is not bad news. If focusing is our duty, it is also our joy. If holding to the narrow road is our obedience, it is also our deliverance. Walking toward the Son is the best thing to do when you live in a storm.

ON OUR DEATHBED

Imminent death has a way of focusing our attention as nothing else. Priorities are straightened out with a jerk. Our relational failures and successes are suddenly magnified, and we wonder how all the distractions of busyness could have obscured what has now become so obvious.

While still in my training, I was called to the Intensive Care Unit bed of a dying man. He was perhaps sixty-five years old and bleeding from the neck. My job, at midnight, was to stop the hemorrhage. I talked with the nurse and glanced quickly at the chart. He was terminal, a neck tumor having eroded his carotid artery.

The scene was extraordinary. Surrounding this remarkable patriarch was his family—wife, children, and their spouses. Despite the blood, there was no hysteria. The patient was calm and alert. An oxygen mask in place, his eyes glanced lovingly from person to person around the bed. The family was gathered close, holding his hand, sober but not crying. Their eyes glistened; their mouths wore sad, affectionate smiles. They knew he was going to die and that it would probably be soon.

I put pressure on the neck wound. Not surprisingly, this caused stroke-like symptoms which seemed to reverse within a short time after I relaxed the pressure. Eventually, the bleeding slowed. I was in the room for about an hour, and then left knowing I would be back.

Later that night, they paged me STAT. The scene was similar. The patient, waning yet alert; the family still in a tender vigil. But this time, the hemorrhage couldn't be stopped. His blood pressure dropped. He looked again lovingly at his family and died.

There was something unforgettable and deeply moving about this experience. It was, of course, medically dramatic. But beyond that, I felt an awesome privilege to be in attendance as this man said good-bye. I knew few details of his life, yet it was apparent he had lived without relational regrets.

When I lie on my deathbed, I don't want to hide behind the excuse of overload. I want to be able to look my family in the eye, each one, and say, "I love you." And I want the experience of my life to confirm those words.

Overload distracts us from the true meaning of life. Overload distracts us from love. And in the end, excuses don't hold up. The choice, it turns out, has always been ours.

We want comfortable excuses. Instead, God gives us the Choice. It is in the hardest of life's choices that love is most clearly revealed. "The distresses of choice," said Auden, "are our chance to be blessed."

Notes

Introduction — *Time to Rest, Space to Heal*
1. Peggy Noonan, "You'd Cry Too If It Happened to You," *Forbes 75th Anniversary Issue*, 14 September 1992, p. 64.
2. Henri Nouwen, "Moving from Solitude to Community to Ministry," *Leadership*, Spring 1995, p. 81.

Chapter 1 — *Overload and the Reality of Human Limits*
1. Leo Tolstoy, translated by Ronald Wilks, *How Much Land Does a Man Need? and Other Stories* (New York, NY: Penguin Books, 1993).
2. 2 Corinthians 4:7.
3. Elaine N. Aron, *The Highly Sensitive Person: How to Thrive When the World Overwhelms You* (Secaucus, NJ: Birch Lane Press, 1996).

Chapter 2 — *Blame Progress*
1. Richard A. Swenson, M.D., *Margin: Restoring Emotional, Physical, Financial, and Time Reserves to Overloaded Lives* (Colorado Springs, CO: NavPress, 1992). See Part One and the Appendix: Graphs.

Chapter 3 — *Accessibility*
1. Advertisement of Digital Alliance for Enterprise Computing, *The Wall Street Journal*, 26 April 1996, p. B7.
2. Advertisement of Lucent Technologies, *The Wall Street Journal*, 17 March 1997, p. A9.
3. James M. Cerletty, M.D., "I'm Dying of Easy Accessibility," *The Journal of Family Practice*, 42 No. 4, April 1996, p. 335.
4. Lance Morrow, "Hoy! Hoy! Mushi-Mushi! Allo!," *Time*, 29 January 1990, p. 84.
5. O'Ann Steere, "E-mail Cautions: Just Because You Can E-mail a Missionary, It Doesn't Mean You Should," *Computing Today*, September/October 1997, p. 25.

6. Cerletty, p. 335.

7. Joshua Quittner, "Invasion of Privacy," *Time*, 25 August 1997, p. 30.

8. "How You're Spied On: Everyday Events That Can Make Your Life a Little Less Private," *Time*, 25 August 1997, pp. 32-33.

9. Quittner, pp. 32-33.

10. Janna Malamud Smith, *Private Matters: In Defense of the Personal Life* (Reading, MA: Addison-Wesley, 1997), p. 38.

11. Dallas Willard, *The Spirit of the Disciplines: Understanding How God Changes Lives* (New York, NY: HarperSanFrancisco, 1988), p. 101.

12. Dallas Willard, "Spiritual Disciplines," Focus on the Family 1997 Attorneys Conference, May 1997.

Chapter 4—*Activity and Commitment*

1. John Charles Cooper, *The Joy of the Plain Life* (Nashville, TN: Impact Books, 1981), p. 28.

2. David and Becky Waugh, "The Urge to Serve Beyond Our Means," *Leadership*, Winter Quarter 1984, pp. 101-105.

3. Gordon MacDonald, *Ordering Your Private World* (Nashville: Oliver-Nelson, 1985), p. 36.

4. Mildred Tengbom, "Harried Lives: If You're a Frenzied Mess, It's Time to Decide What's Really Important to You," *Focus on the Family*, October 1985, pp. 10-12.

5. Brian J. Walsh and J. Richard Middleton, quoting Augustine, *The Transforming Vision: Shaping a Christian World View* (Downers Grove, IL: InterVarsity Press, 1984), p. 99.

6. Ted W. Engstrom and R. Alec Mackenzie, quoting Charles Shedd, *Managing Your Time: Practical Guidelines on the Effective Use of Time* (Grand Rapids, MI: Zondervan, 1967), pp. 30-31.

7. Thomas R. Kelly, *A Testament of Devotion* (New York, NY: Harper & Brothers Publishers, 1941), pp. 115-116.

8. J. Grant Howard, *Balancing Life's Demands: A New Perspective on Priorities* (Portland, OR: Multnomah Press, 1983), p. 144.

9. Anne Morrow Lindbergh, *Gift from the Sea* (New York, NY: Pantheon, 1955), p. 115.

10. Jean Fleming, *Between Walden and the Whirlwind: Living the*

Christ-Centered Life (Colorado Springs, CO: NavPress, 1985), p. 40.

11. Robert Banks, *The Tyranny of Time: When 24 Hours Is Not Enough* (Downers Grove, IL: InterVarsity Press, 1983), p. 247.

12. Roy McCloughry, "Basic Stott: Candid Comments on Justice, Gender, and Judgment," *Christianity Today,* 8 January 1996, p. 25.

Chapter 5—*Change and Stress*

1. Alvin Toffler, *Future Shock* (New York, NY: Bantam Books, 1971), pp. 1-2.

2. "Longer Lives, Less Cash," *U.S. News & World Report,* 12 August 1996, p. 14.

3. Rodger Doyle, "House to House," *The Atlantic Monthly,* March 1993, p. 95.

4. James Dobson, "Americans on the Move," *Focus on the Family Bulletin,* July 1995, p. 1.

5. William Manchester, "A World Lit Only by Change," *U.S. News & World Report,* 25 October 1993, p. 6.

6. Frederic Flach, M.D., *Resilience: Discovering a New Strength at Times of Stress* (New York: NY: Fawcett Columbine, 1988), p. xv.

7. Walt Schafer, *Stress, Distress, and Growth* (Davis, CA: Responsible Action, 1978), p. 114.

8. Matthew 11:28.

9. L. D. Kubzansky, I. Kawachi, A. Spiro, III, et al., "Don't Worry: It's Bad for Your Heart," *Circulation,* 18 February 1997, pp. 818-824.

10. Matthew 6:34.

11. Corrie ten Boom, *Don't Wrestle, Just Nestle* (Old Tappan, NJ: Revell, 1971), p. 37.

12. John 16:33 (KJV).

Chapter 6—*Choice and Decision*

1. Alvin Toffler, *Future Shock* (New York, NY: Bantam Books, 1971), pp. 264 and 269.

2. Robert Kanigel, "Too Much of a Good Thing?" *The Washington Post National Weekly Edition,* 12 January 1998, p. 25.

3. Calvin Trillin, "Pride of the Pudgy," *Time,* 24 March 1997, p. 42.

4. S. D. Gaede, *Belonging: Our Need for Community in Church and Family* (Grand Rapids, MI: Zondervan, 1985), p. 101.

5. George Barna and William Paul McKay, *Vital Signs: Emerging Social Trends and the Future of American Christianity* (Westchester, IL: Crossway Books, 1984), p. 97.

6. Leonard Laster, "Analytical Overload: An Emerging Syndrome," *Hospital Practice,* 15 May 1997, p. 49.

7. Kanigel, p. 25.

8. Mimi Wilson and Mary Beth Lagerborg, *Table Talk* (Colorado Springs, CO: Focus on the Family Publishing, 1994), p. 55.

9. Gaede, pp. 90 and 148.

10. Edward Wenk, Jr., *Tradeoffs: Imperatives of Choice in a High-Tech World* (Baltimore, MD: The Johns Hopkins University Press, 1986), p. 211.

11. Larry Crabb, *Understanding People: Deep Longings for Relationship* (Grand Rapids, MI: Zondervan, 1987), p. 163.

12. "If any of you lacks wisdom, he should ask God, who gives generously to all without finding fault, and it will be given to him. But when he asks, he must believe and not doubt" (James 1:5-6).

13. "You do not have, because you do not ask God" (James 4:2).

14. Deuteronomy 30:19-20.

15. Joshua 24:15.

Chapter 7—Debt

1. Paul E. Billheimer, *Destined for the Throne: A New Look at the Bride of Christ* (Fort Washington, PA: Christian Literature Crusade, 1975), p. 53.

2. "Harper's Index," *Harper's Magazine,* March 1997, p. 13.

3. "Harper's Index," *Harper's Magazine,* June 1996, p. 13.

4. Fred Vogelstein, "Giving Credit Where Credit Is Undue," *U.S. News & World Report,* 31 March 1997, p. 52.

5. Karen Gullo and Vivian Marino, "Debt Threatens Families,

Economy," *Cedar Rapids Gazette,* 10 March 1996, p. 2F.

6. Fred R. Bleakley, quoting Maury Harris, "A 125% Solution to Card Debt Stirs Worry," *The Wall Street Journal,* 17 November 1997, p. A2.

7. Bleakley, p. A2.

8. John Capozzi, *If You Want the Rainbow . . . You Gotta Put Up with the Rain* (Fairfield, CT: JMC Industries, 1997), #66.

9. Damon Darlin, "The Newest American Entitlement," *Forbes,* 8 September 1997, p. 113.

10. Darlin, quoting Lawrence Chimerine, p. 116.

11. John deGraff, producer, *Affluenza*—Public Television Special, first aired September 1997.

12. Russ Crosson, *A Life Well Spent: The Eternal Rewards of Investing Yourself and Your Money in Your Family* (Nashville, TN: Thomas Nelson Publishers, 1994), p. 93.

13. "Do not conform any longer to the pattern of this world, but be transformed by the renewing of your mind" (Romans 12:2, NIV). "No soldier in active service entangles himself in the affairs of everyday life, so that he may please the one who enlisted him as a soldier" (2 Timothy 2:4, NASB).

14. Paul Borthwick, *101 Ways to Simplify Your Life: Practical Steps for Restoring Sanity to Your World* (Wheaton, IL: Victor Books, 1992), pp. 42-43.

15. Borthwick, pp. 73-82.

16. J. Avorn, quoting R. Fein, "Benefit and Cost Analysis in Geriatric Care," *The New England Journal of Medicine,* 310, 1984, pp. 1294-1301.

17. Russ Crosson, "Your Changing Finances in a Changing World," Focus on the Family 1997 Physicians Conference, November 1997.

Chapter 8—*Expectation*

1. Peggy Noonan, "You'd Cry Too If It Happened to You," *Forbes 75th Anniversary Issue,* 14 September 1992, p. 60.

2. Doug Trouten, "All Dressed Up," *Minnesota Christian Chronicle,* 3 April 1997, p. 2.

3. David Elkind, *The Hurried Child: Growing Up Too Fast Too*

Soon (Reading, MA: Addison-Wesley, 1981), p. 3.

4. *All-Consuming Passion: Waking Up from the American Dream*, Pamphlet by New Road Map Foundation, Seattle, WA, 1993, p. 6.

5. Gregory Beals and Leslie Kaufman, quoting David Wolfe, "The Kids Know Cool," *Newsweek*, 31 March 1997, p. 48.

6. "Perspectives," quoting Alex Molnar, *Newsweek*, 12 May 1997, p. 29.

7. Kenneth A. Myers, "Is There Really a Generation Gap?" Quoted in *Currents: Comments on Beliefs and Values in Today's Society*, July/August 1997, p. 20.

8. Randall Rothenberg, quoting Joseph Turow, "How Powerful Is Advertising?" *The Atlantic Monthly*, June 1997, p. 114.

9. John Leo, "Decadence, The Corporate Way," *U.S. News & World Report*, 28 August–4 September 1995, p. 31.

10. Chief Justice Warren Burger, "Current Quotes," *U.S. News & World Report*, 2 September 1985, p. 12.

11. George Pattison, "A Profile of Physicians in Sport: George Sheehan, M.D.," *The Main Event*, 1 No. 11, November 1986, p. 10.

12. David A. Sorensen, "Because I Can!" *Decision*, March 1996, p. 32.

13. Henri J. M. Nouwen, *Out of Solitude: Three Meditations on the Christian Life* (Notre Dame, IN: Ave Maria Press, 1974), pp. 18-19.

14. Gilbert Brim, "Losing and Winning," *Psychology Today*, September 1988, p. 52.

15. Charles Colson, "A Nation That Has Forgotten God," *Jubilee*, Summer 1996, p. 19.

16. Barbara DeGrote-Sorensen and David Allen Sorensen, *'Tis a Gift to Be Simple: Embracing the Freedom of Living with Less* (Minneapolis, MN: Augsburg, 1992), p. 19.

17. C. S. Lewis, *Mere Christianity* (Glasgow: Collins, 1952), pp. 160-161.

18. Louis McBurney, M.D., and David McCasland, "The Danger of Aiming Too High," *Leadership*, Summer Quarter 1984, pp. 30-35.

19. Tim Kimmel, *Little House on the Freeway: Help for the Hurried Home* (Portland, OR: Multnomah, 1987), pp. 159-160.
20. Lewis, p. 90.
21. Arlie Russell Hochschild, *The Time Bind: When Work Becomes Home and Home Becomes Work* (New York: Henry Holt and Company, 1997), p. 217.
22. Philippians 4:11-12; 1 Timothy 6:6-19; Hebrews 13:5.
23. A. W. Tozer, *The Pursuit of God* (Harrisburg, PA: Christian Publications, Inc., 1948), p. 112.
24. Matthew 16:24.

Chapter 9—*Hurry and Fatigue*

1. Mortimer B. Zuckerman, "America's Silent Revolution," *U.S. News & World Report,* 18 July 1994, p. 90.
2. Peg Zaemisch, "Relishing Life Is Harder on the Run," *Dunn County News,* 26 November 1995, p. 4A.
3. Bob Benson, *"See You at the House." The Very Best of the Stories He Used to Tell* (Nashville, TN: Generoux Nelson, 1989), pp. 147-148.
4. Jacques Ellul, *The Presence of the Kingdom* (Colorado Springs, CO: Helmers & Howard, 1989), p. 56.
5. David Sharp, "So Many Lists, So Little Time," *USA Weekend,* 15-17 March 1996, p. 4.
6. Elizabeth Berg, "What's Your Hurry?" *Women's Day,* 5 February 1991, p. 54.
7. Chuck Swindoll quoted in David Kraft, "Isaiah Versus Tums," *Closer Walk-The Navigators,* July 1992, p. 37.
8. Psalm 23:2.
9. Jeremy Rifkin, *Time Wars: The Primary Conflict in Human History* (New York, NY: Simon & Schuster, 1987), pp. 223-224.
10. Mayo D. Gilson, "Redeeming the Time," *News and Reports-CMS,* March/April 1988, p. 81.
11. John Ortberg, *The Life You've Always Wanted: Spiritual Disciplines for Ordinary People* (Grand Rapids, MI: Zondervan, 1997), p. 81.
12. John M. Capozzi, *If You Want the Rainbow . . . You Gotta Put*

Up with the Rain (Fairfield, CT: JMC Industries, Inc., 1997), #8, #14, #39, and #48.

13. H. Arthur Dunn, "Biblical Concepts of Time: Helping Individuals and Families Live More Meaningfully," Doctoral Dissertation for the Talbot School of Theology, Biola University, March 1993, p. 78.

14. H. Arthur Dunn, quoting Ben Patterson, *The Grand Essentials* (Waco, TX: Word, 1987), p. 123.

15. Dolores Curran, quoting Buck Sterling, *Stress and the Healthy Family: How Healthy Families Handle the Ten Most Common Stresses* (San Francisco, CA: Harper & Row, 1987), p. 118.

16. Benson, p. 165.

17. F. W. Boreham, "The Mistress of the Margin," in *Mushrooms on the Moor* (New York, NY: Abingdon, 1915), p. 259.

18. Robert Banks, *The Tyranny of Time: When 24 Hours Is Not Enough* (Downers Grove, IL: InterVarsity Press, 1983), pp. 213-214.

19. Isaiah 40:31 (KJV).

20. H. B. London, Jr., quoting Henry Blackaby, "So Writes Dr. Luke . . . About This and That," Focus on the Family 1997 Physicians Conference, November 1997.

21. Psalm 37:7 (KJV).

Chapter 10 — *Information and Education*

1. W. Auckerman, "Editor's Page," http://cjmag.co.jp/magazine/issues/1996/dec96/edlet.html

2. "Poll: Info Overload Can Hit Efficiency, Cause 'Information Fatigue Syndrome,'"quoting Dr. David Lewis, Reuter News-London, *CNN Financial Network*, 15 October 1996.

3. Richard Saul Wurman, quoting Peter Large, *Information Anxiety: What to Do When Information Doesn't Tell You What You Need to Know* (New York, NY: Bantam Books, 1990), p. 35.

4. Marc Ringel, M.D., quoting Alfred North Whitehead, *Accessing Medical Information from a Desert Island with Telephone Service* (Greeley, CO: Desert Island Press, 1996), p. vi.

5. Paul J. Fink, M.D., "Response to the Presidential Address: Is 'Biopsychosocial' the Psychiatric Shibboleth?" *American*

Journal of Psychiatry, September 1988, p. 1063.

6. David Shenk, *Data Smog: Surviving the Information Glut* (New York, NY: HarperEdge, 1997), pp. 30-31.

7. Walter Isaacson, "Man of the Year . . . Driven by the Passion of Intel's Andrew Grove," *Time*, 29 December 1997-5 January 1998, pp. 48 and 50.

8. Thomas Becker, "Thinking Small," *Newsweek*, 12 January 1998, p. 8.

9. Sam Vincent Meddis, On the Web, "Regarding Information Overload: Swings and Stars," *USA Today*, 20 August 1997.

10. 2 Timothy 3:7.

11. Elizabeth Shaw, "Is This What Life's About?" *Newsweek*, 5 May 1997, p. 22.

12. Julia King, quoting Mike Rusk, "Info Overload: A Hazard to Career," *@Computerworld*, 21 October 1996.

13. Kenneth S. Warren, M.D., quoting Lewis Branscomb, "The Evolution of Selective Biomedical Libraries and Their Use in the Developing World," *The Journal of the American Medical Association*, 257 No. 19, 15 May 1987, p. 2628.

14. Wurman, pp. 14 and 140.

15. Jeremy Campbell, *Grammatical Man: Information, Entropy, Language, and Life* (New York, NY: Simon & Schuster, 1982), pp. 222-223.

16. Wurman, pp. 53-54.

17. Ringel, p. 7.

18. L. Harold DeWolf, *A Theology of the Living Church* (New York, NY: Harper & Brothers, 1953), p. 45.

19. John 17:17.

20. 1 Corinthians 3:18-19.

Chapter 11 — *Media Overload*

1. Anne R. Carey and Suzy Parker, "Matinee Idles," *USA Today*, 10 October 1997, p. 10.

2. Ted Baehr, "Miracle on Main Street?" *Focus on the Family*, April 1995, p. 2.

3. Johnnie L. Roberts, "Hit the Eject Button," *Newsweek*, 11 August 1997, p. 46.

4. Most parents are blissfully unaware of the lyrics that sell millions each year, making these performers not only wealthy but also cultural icons to an alienated generation. Although to read such lyrics can be distressing, we will not solve the problems inherent in this ghastly phenomenon until the trend is fully understood and adopted on our national agenda. Words and themes in this genre of music include such "classics" as:

- Ice-T: cop-killing, a killer stalking President Bush, sodomizing Tipper Gore's nieces
- Geto Boys: slitting women's throats and cutting off their breasts
- Nine Inch Nails: self-loathing, sexual obsession, torture, suicide, and dismemberment
- Dr. Dre: "rat-a-tat and a tat like that / Never hesitate to put a nigga on his back"
- Marilyn Manson: nightmarish, X-rated scenarios of the occult, suicide, torture, greed
- Prince: "My sister never made love to anyone else but me . . . incest is everything it's said to be!"
- 2 Live Crew: "Nasty As They Wanna Be" album uses the "F" word 226 times, "bitch" 163 times, explicit genitalia reference 117 times, oral sex 87 times
- Judas Priest: forced oral sex at gunpoint
- Slayer: sex with the dead (necrophilia) and satanism

5. Gerald Early in *The Hungry Mind Review,* Winter 1996-1997, quoted in "Reflections," *Christianity Today,* 2 March 1998, p. 62.
6. Bob DeMoss, Workshop Presenter, *Current Thoughts and Trends* Conference, March 1997, Colorado Springs, CO.
7. Dan McGraw, "All Technology Is Local," *U.S. News & World Report,* 28 July 1997, p. 44.
8. George Gilder, "Happy Birthday Wired: It's Been a Weird Five Years," *Wired,* January 1998, p. 40.
9. Nicholas Negroponte, "The Third Shall Be First," *Wired,* January 1998, p. 96.

10. Susan Cornwell, "Dataholics," *Reuters@* (London), 9 December 1997.

11. John Leo, quoting Bill Maher, "Now Don't Interrupt!" *U.S. News & World Report,* 13 January 1997, p. 16.

12. Al Menconi, "Our Collective Soul Is Dying," *Minnesota Christian Chronicle,* 16 February 1995, p. 6.

13. Ben J. Wattenberg, *The Good News Is the Bad News Is Wrong* (New York, NY: Simon & Schuster, 1984), pp. 112 and 378.

14. Michael Medved, "Hollywood's Excuses for Sex and Violence," *Current Thoughts and Trends,* December 1995, p. 27.

15. Victor C. Strasburger, "Tuning in to Teenagers," *Newsweek,* 19 May 1997, p. 18.

16. Edward Cornish, *The Cyber Future: 92 Ways Our Lives Will Change by the Year 2025* (Bethesda, MD: World Future Society, 1996), p. 12.

17. Edna Hong, *The Nostalgic Almanac* (Minneapolis, MN: Augsburg, 1980), p. 106.

18. E. F. Schumacher, quoting James Coleman, *Good Work* (New York, NY: Harper & Row, 1979), p. 166.

19. Bob DeMoss, "Do You Know What Your Kids Are Watching?" *Focus on the Family,* August 1994, p. 3.

20. Allan Bloom, *The Closing of the American Mind: How Higher Education Has Failed Democracy and Impoverished the Souls of Today's Students* (New York, NY: Simon & Schuster, 1987), pp. 58-59.

21. Romans 12:9.

22. Craig Lambert, quoting Carrie Becker, "Literacy in High Gear: Lust for Books," *Harvard Magazine,* November/December 1997, p. 11.

Chapter 12—*Possession*
1. "Shopping Mania," quoting Thomas O'Guinn, *Signs of the Times,* March 1988, p. 6.

2. Brigid Schulte, "Living Large," *Saint Paul Pioneer Press,* 19 October 1997, p. 4A.

3. John Kenneth Galbraith, *The Affluent Society* (New York, NY: Mentor Books, 1958), p. 117.

4. Galbraith, p. 120.
5. Elaine St. James, *Simplify Your Life* (New York, NY: Hyperion, 1994), p. 11.
6. Anne H. Soukhanov, "Word Watch," *The Atlantic Monthly,* February 1993, p. 120.
7. Cynthia Crossen, quoting Liz Perle McKenna, "Americans Have It All (But All Isn't Enough)," *The Wall Street Journal,* 20 September 1996, pp. R1 and R4.
8. St. James, p. 105.
9. Romans 12:2.
10. Charles Dickens, *Bleak House* (Boston, MA: Houghton Mifflin, first published in 1853), p. 665.
11. Galbraith, pp. 117 and 125.
12. Leo Tolstoy, *War and Peace* (New York, NY: Washington Square Press, first published in 1869), pp. 430-431.

Chapter 13—*Work*
1. Cindy Hall and Julie Stacey, "Quitting Time," *USA Today,* 10 February 1997, p. 1B.
2. E. F. Schumacher, quoting Thomas Aquinas, *Good Work* (New York, NY: Harper & Row, 1979), p. 118.
3. Hans J. Heine, International Editor, Institut der Deutschen Wirtschaft, *Industrie Anzeiger,* 1996, p. 7.
4. Arlie Hochschild, author of *The Time Bind,* interviewed on "The News Hour with Jim Lehrer," 15 July 1997.
5. Leslie A. Perlow, *Finding Time: How Corporations, Individuals, and Families Can Benefit from New Work Practices* (Ithaca, NY: Cornell University Press, 1997), p. 36.
6. Benjamin Kline Hunnicutt, *Kellogg's Six-Hour Day* (Philadelphia, PA: Temple University Press, 1996), p. 12.
7. Arlie Russell Hochschild, *The Time Bind: When Work Becomes Home and Home Becomes Work* (New York, NY: Henry Holt and Company, 1997), p. 246.
8. Lester Thoreau, author of *The Future of Capitalism,* interviewed on "The News Hour with Jim Lehrer," 2 September 1996.

9. David Gergen, "Squeezing American Workers," *U.S. News & World Report,* 22 January 1996, p. 68.

10. Don L. Boroughs, quoting Lawrence Perlman, "Winter of Discontent," *U.S. News & World Report,* 22 January 1996, p. 52.

11. "Insomnia and Related Problems Show Alarmingly High Rates," quoting Louis W. Sullivan, *Medical Tribune,* 17 April 1997, p. 6.

12. "Wise Woman," quoting Leila Denmark, *Physician,* September/October 1996, p. 22.

13. Rabbi Jeffrey K. Salkin, "Smash the False Gods of Careerism," *The Wall Street Journal,* 29 December 1994, p. A8.

14. Perlow, p. 3.

15. Perlow, p. 35.

16. Perlow, pp. 91-92.

17. Barbara Carton, quoting Margaret Ryan Downing, "What's Up, Doc? Stress and Counseling," *The Wall Street Journal,* 6 January 1995, p. B1.

18. Michael J. Green, M.D., "What (If Anything) Is Wrong with Residency Overwork?" *Annals of Internal Medicine,* 1 October 1995, 123 No. 7, p. 515.

19. David L. Rambo, "Come Apart Before You Fall Apart," *Briefing by the President on Matters of Interest to Colleagues in Ministry,* March 1993, p. 1.

20. Charles E. Perry, Jr., *Why Christians Burn Out* (Nashville, TN: Nelson, 1982), p. 139.

21. Dolores Curran, *Stress and the Healthy Family: How Healthy Families Handle the Ten Most Common Stresses* (San Francisco, CA: Harper & Row, 1987), p. 162.

22. David Shenk, *Data Smog: Surviving the Information Glut* (New York, NY: HarperEdge, 1997), p. 187.

23. Hochschild, pp. 70-71.

24. Charles Colson, *A Dangerous Grace* (Dallas, TX; Word, 1994), p. 198.

25. John M. Cappozi, *Why Climb the Corporate Ladder When You Can Take the Elevator?* (New York, NY: Villard Books, 1994), #374.

26. L. Tye, quoting Steven A. Schroeder, M.D., "New Doctors Become GPs," *Boston Globe*, 10 March 1997, pp. A1 and A7.

Conclusion—*Focusing on Love*
  1. Luke 6:46.
  2. John 14:15,21,23-24.
  3. Matthew 6:15; Colossians 3:13; Hebrews 13:5; 1 Timothy 6:6-8; Matthew 7:1-5; 1 Peter 3:15.
  4. 1 John 4:8; Matthew 22:36-39; Galatians 5:14; 1 Corinthians 13:2.
  5. Matthew 7:14.
  6. 1 Corinthians 9:24.
  7. Mary Pipher in Family Therapy Networker, "The Day We Live In," *Current Thoughts and Trends*, July 1997, p. 14.

Author

RICHARD A. SWENSON, M.D., is a physician and futurist with a B.S. in physics Phi Beta Kappa from Denison University. After having taught at the University of Wisconsin Medical School for fifteen years, he currently conducts research and writes full-time about the intersection of culture, health, faith, and the future. Dr. Swenson and his wife, Linda, live in Menomonie, Wisconsin, with their sons, Adam and Matthew.

Pain and the absence of margin are related. This is a brand new disease of the 90's. It is the pain of progress.

Pg. 21 - Comparison of 1800's and today shows we have what they lacked yet despair accompanies our prosperity. People are in anguish but progress doesn't care.

Marginless - insidious - more dangerous than seems evident

Last 40 years more of everything.

Today, we hurt more than we use to. Our relationships are being starved to death by our speed. Doesn't God lead anyone beside still water any more?

By putting progress in the hands of our fallenness, we have magnified nearly every human flaw.

Break the addiction of progress.

Micah 6:8 * Pg. 34 Walking humbly with God or living in anguish.

Progress's biggest failure has been its inability to nurture and protect right relationships.

Pg. 36 - Scripture teaches us...

Pg. 42 - Unprecedented era - characters

Changes today are exponential

Pg. 42 - Illustration to show exponential changes.

Graphs - Appendix - Pg. 247

A train with 500 cars = "good or bad"

If the negatives are sufficiently dangerous, they cannot be offset by the positives no matter how beneficial the positives are. List of negatives - Pg 53

Evil today has more power at its disposal then ever before.

Scripturely prescribed relational life have suffered major set backs over the last three decades.

When we have no margin and our limits have been exceeded, then problems take on a different dimension.

Analogy of our live as a raft and the changes of a river. Pg 38

Stress is not the circumstance, it is our response to the circumstance.

We only have so much adaptive energy, so reserve it for occassions where the issues are significant and not waste it on trivial conflicts.

We have always had stress but stress today is different in quantity and quality

Reasons for exponential stress today- Pg. 62

Affirming relationships are best protector of stress damage.

Physical hard work is not a stressor

Mental frustration, etc. can be catastropic

Mental stress leaves no attention left over for spiritual things.

What strains some does not bother others

Overload - a new problem for today.

Margin is the amount allowed for unanticipated situations.

When the reserves of physical energy are down, the body cannot effectively resist stress

Sleep, exercise, nutrition.

1865 - Wrist-watch

1967 - Time prediction (Pg. 148)

Page 149 - In a lifetime the average person will

How loss of time effects families – Pg. 154

Pg. 168 – Finances – problems.

Immanuel Kant "Give a man everything he wants, and at that moment everything will not be everything."

Page 191 = Progress and discontent (air conditioning)

Allowing history to happen to us is unforgiveably foolish – Pg. 235

Jesus' human side knew limits.

Page 21 – Tolstoy's story of limits and greed, health expectations, Too much.

The driven notion that we must relentlessly pursue activity every waking minute is fatally flawed – both practically and theologically.

Margin Illustration – 80% 100% 120%
Page 44

Accessability overload – the absence of hiding places

E-mails, cellphones, etc. Page 52 -

Advertisements + media are forcing
a breakdown in social cohesion

More knowledge → more insecurity

Ch. 10 - information overload facts

There is an urgency of wants.

Everything we own, owns us.

Because progress isn't going to change,
we have to change.

We need to intentionally cultivate
a margin.

Jesus could not be distracted.